Aspen's Fund Raising Series for the 21st Century
Edited by James P. Gelatt, PhD, CFRE

Corporate and Foundation Fund Raising

A Complete Guide from the Inside

Aspen's Fund Raising Series for the 21st Century
Edited by James P. Gelatt, PhD, CFRE

Fund Raising Basics: A Complete Guide
Barbara Kushner Ciconte, CFRE, and Jeanne G. Jacob, CFRE

Planned Giving Essentials: A Step by Step Guide to Success
Richard D. Barrett and Molly E. Ware

Strategic Fund Development: Building Profitable Relationships That Last
Simone P. Joyaux, ACFRE

Capital Campaigns: Strategies That Work
Andrea Kihlstedt and Catherine P. Schwartz

Successful Special Events: Planning, Hosting, and Evaluating
Barbara R. Levy, ACFRE, and Barbara H. Marion, CFRE

Corporate and Foundation Fund Raising: A Complete Guide from the Inside
Eugene A. Scanlan, PhD, CFRE

Donor Focused Strategies for Annual Giving
Karla A. Williams, ACFRE

Aspen's Fund Raising Series for the 21st Century
Edited by James P. Gelatt, PhD, CFRE

Corporate and Foundation Fund Raising

A Complete Guide from the Inside

Eugene A. Scanlan, PhD, CFRE
Senior Vice President
The Alford Group Inc.
Washington, DC

With a chapter by
Helmer Ekstrom
former President
American Association of Fund-Raising Counsel
New York, New York

AN ASPEN PUBLICATION®
Aspen Publishers, Inc.
Gaithersburg, Maryland
1997

Library of Congress Cataloging-in-Publication Data

Scanlan, Eugene A.
Corporate and foundation fund raising: a complete guide from the inside / Eugene A. Scanlan.
p. cm.—(Aspen's fund raising series for the 21st century)
Includes bibliographical references and index.
ISBN 0-8342-0936-5 (pbk.)
1. Fund raising. I. Title. II. Series.
HG177.S29 1997
361.7'068'1—dc21
97-9837
CIP

Orders: (800) 638-8437
Customer Service: (800) 234-1660

About Aspen Publishers • For more than 35 years, Aspen has been a leading professional publisher in a variety of disciplines. Aspen's vast information resources are available in both print and electronic formats. We are committed to providing the highest quality information available in the most appropriate format for our customers. Visit Aspen's Internet site for more information resources, directories, articles, and a searchable version of Aspen's full catalog, including the most recent publications:
http://www.aspenpub.com
Aspen Publishers, Inc. • The hallmark of quality in publishing
Member of the worldwide Wolters Kluwer group.

Editorial Resources: Brian MacDonald
Library of Congress Catalog Card Number: 97-9837
ISBN: 0-8342-0936-5

Printed in the United States of America

2 3 4 5

This book, and especially many of the ideas and approaches in it, is dedicated to my wife and life partner Joanne. Her own experiences as a staff member of two major foundations as well as her experiences and insights gained as a senior staff member of the Council on Foundations helped give me a reference point to ensure there is a sense of reality to all that follows.

When I made the commitment to write the book, she also made a commitment to spend many weekends and evenings listening to me clatter away on the computer. As an avid reader, she used this time well, probably finishing one or two books for every fifteen to twenty pages I wrote. And, of course, without her encouragement and subtle reminders, this book would still be an idea floating around in my head.

Table of Contents

Preface

Question: How many people survived Custer's Last Stand?
Usual Answer: None
Actual Answer: Thousands—the Sioux and the Cheyennes
It all depends on your point of view.

(Welch and Stekler 1994)

As the above example shows, your point of view determines much of how you respond to situations. If your point of view about raising funds from corporations and foundations is that you get grants by sending proposals, you may well be following in Custer's footsteps.

Corporate and Foundation Fund Raising: A Complete Guide from the Inside is intended to give you a point of view that will enable you to succeed in getting grants. It is both a "how to" manual and a way for you to get at least a glimpse inside the world of organized philanthropy by hearing the thoughts and ideas of grant makers. In addition to the general discussions and specific examples used to illustrate particular points, you will find Strategy Tips throughout the book. You will also find at the end of the book an annotated list of recommended additional readings.

Many publications on grant making and proposal development speak with the voices of those who have never been on the inside of the grant-making process—there is a point of view expressed, but it is not the whole story. The contributors and I have been "on the other side of the table." My four-plus years of experience reviewing proposals and making grant recommendations to a foundation board, as well as my continuing contacts with the foundation world, have given me a different perspective on the process of seeking and getting grants, and hopefully these experiences and those of professional grant makers will give you a new point of view.

Some books on grant seeking treat foundations and corporations as if they each were a single, often unknowable entity. But, like all organizations, they involve people. This book attempts, within the broad range of generalities that must be made, to move away from the view that each foundation or corporation is an "it" and toward the view that each is better described as a "they." The book will go into some of the dynamics of grant maker boards and staffs, how they interact, and how decisions can get made. Like every other aspect of fund raising, it is a very human process—one that cannot easily be measured and put into formulas. Like fund raising, grant making is still very much an art, not a science. While there are guidelines, procedures, requirements, etc., you can never be sure of the outcome until your organization receives and deposits the grant check, or, hopefully not as frequently, receives the dreaded decline letter. This book will give you a better understanding of the human part of grant seeking and grant making.

The above may sound as if you have little or no control over the grant process. But the whole point of the book is that there are many things you should know and can do to help increase the

> This book attempts to move away from the view that each foundation or corporation is an "it" and toward the view that each is better described as a "they."

odds in your favor. There cannot be guarantees, only good—and better—strategies. Each experience with a foundation or corporation should be seen as a time to learn something new, to test strategies, and to evaluate what worked and what didn't work. Sometimes I think many of the better fund raisers have developed the habit of persistence above all else. Are you willing to go back to a foundation three or four times after your organization has been turned down but when you believe you are on the right track? Or does the first decline letter mean the end of your contact with that foundation? As we shall see, even a turn down can be an opportunity to develop a more creative approach to a particular funding source.

The book is intended for everyone from novice fund raisers to seasoned professionals, as well as other staff and even board members and other volunteer leadership. Those not directly responsible for fund raising often see the corporate and foundation fund-raising process as sending in proposals or letters asking for support. I once worked at an organization where the president announced to the development staff on a Friday that she wanted "45 proposals to go out of here by Monday." Despite our protests, she insisted and, indeed, 45 proposals were out by that Monday. We did not receive enough grant money to cover even the cost of the postage. This book can be used to educate your leadership on how to achieve grant-seeking success and how to avoid the trap of "send out more proposals." Much of the key information in the book, especially the data on giving and getting and the basic vocabulary used by many foundations and corporations, should be known by your organization's senior staff and board members. The information and ideas presented here should also be the basis of not only understanding organized philanthropy but also forming overall organizational plans and strategies for seeking support from these sources.

> **This book can be used to educate your leadership on how to achieve grant-seeking success and how to avoid the trap of "send out more proposals."**

This book is also intended to give an overview of trends and issues within organized philanthropy as well as some of the bigger societal issues that are affecting grant making. Much is changing in the nonprofit sector and the next few years will see dramatic shifts in sources of funding, funding priorities, and organizations themselves as they seek to respond to these pressures. Organizations that are prepared to develop more strategic approaches to fund raising, whatever the sources of support, will survive and even prosper. Other organizations will fall by the wayside. Those that survive will see the challenges as opportunities, and will have a point of view, plans, and action steps that will ensure their success.

Fund raising, like many other areas, often uses words and phrases borrowed from warfare. "Strategy" is usually used in terms of the overall picture—the big plans for the entire war. "Tactics" usually refer to the plans and operations for a particular battle. It was only recently in my hobby reading that I learned there is a third category, which is neither strategy nor tactics, but is in between: what military analysts call the "operational art" (Tanner, 1996). In military language "operational art" refers to the combination of battles, maneuvers, uses of the terrain, and even avoidance of battles to support, but not necessarily achieve, strategic ends. Thus in the Civil War some Confederate forces deliberately moved away from their Union foes or fought small battles to draw off fighting units that otherwise would be more concentrated against other Confederate forces.

Fund raising, including grant seeking, should be very strategic. There needs to be an overall plan tied to a larger organizational strategic plan. And fund raising should, when particular prospects are approached, be very tactical. The specific steps and plans that will help increase the likelihood for success should be spelled out for each prospect in detail and agreed to by all concerned. But in between these is the operational art that is the focus of this book. There are other sources that can explain how to develop strategic fund-raising plans, and the diversity of the foundation and corporate funding worlds is so great that only minimal time can be spent explaining tactics (as applied to a particular foundation or corporation) in this volume. But the operational art concept as applied to fund raising can have immense value. In between your overall fund-raising plan and the tactics you will develop for each appropriate source, there is the need to concentrate on choosing your "battles" carefully, picking specific objectives to go after, knowing the "terrain" of organized philanthropy, and even avoiding some possible funding sources until you are ready to take them on and have a higher probability of success. The "operational art" approach is well worth remembering.

Finally, despite the military analogy above, this book is intended to be fun. Many of the fund-raising books I pick up are more serious than funerals. I will try to intersperse the "how to" with some "war stories," and other material to lighten things up a bit, while still making key points. As a friend of mine once said, "we should keep the 'fun' in fund raising." But I'll let you be the judge of that.

References

Tanner, R. 1996. *Stonewall in the Valley*. Mechanicsburg, PA: Stackpole Books.

Welch, J. with P. Stekler. 1994. *Killing Custer*. New York: W.W. Norton & Company.

Acknowledgments

The author wishes to acknowledge the following people and organizations who helped make this book possible: Jim Gelatt, Ph.D., President of Prentice Associates, who recruited me to author this book for Aspen Publishers, Inc.; Kathleen E. McGuire, Developmental Editorial Assistant at Aspen Publishers, who showed enormous patience and, as I asked, prodded me at the right times to meet the next "drop dead" deadline; all of my colleagues at my employer, The Alford Group Inc., several of whom only smiled when I kept saying "I've got to finish THE BOOK"; and the other contributors, including Helmer Ekstrom, Dr. John E. Hopkins of the Kalamazoo Foundation, Rayna Aylward of the Mitsubishi Electric America Foundation, and Bill Somerville of the Philanthropic Ventures Foundation.

A special note of thanks is also due to all of my colleagues at The Chicago Community Trust, where I learned my foundation craft and started to develop many of the ideas that became part of this book. And, finally, this book is dedicated to my wife Joanne, whom I met at The Trust, and who since has become my foundation.

Chapter 1
Overview

I was involved with a board of directors that was discussing the board's role in raising funds. The discussion had been somewhat forced, as the board members generally had never actively raised money for the organization. After some harrumphing, one board member passionately expressed his view: "I could never ask anyone for money. Why . . . that's . . . that's begging!" It was a long evening.

The Investment Approach and Key Questions

Corporations are often very successful at raising funds. They sell stocks, make profits on their products, and use other vehicles to generate money to meet their needs. The basic idea is that they offer something (a product, stock, a service) and people pay money for it; the company uses the money generated to pay for the costs of developing and making the product, operating the company, marketing, and other expenses. But many corporate executives who sit on nonprofit boards of trustees or boards of directors do not seem to be able to apply the same principles to the nonprofit world.

Nonprofit organizations, like for-profit organizations, generate capital by providing things to people. The "things" may be services, which generate fees; products, which generate revenues; or, in the case of fund raising, what? Raising dollars, at first glance, appears to be a one-sided transaction with the recipient organization getting the benefits and the donor getting little except possibly a tax deduction. But donors are, in reality, investors in your organization. If you take this approach to all of your donor prospects, whether they are individuals, foundations, or corporations, the nature of the transaction becomes clearer.

Investors always are looking for a return on their investments. Each investor may have different objectives—short-term gains, long-term security, etc. Donors and donor prospects also have different "investment" objectives. For some, the return on their investment may be the feeling or belief they are helping others—those your organization serves. By contributing to your organization, another person may be fed for another day, a child may be saved from disease, a dance company will

> Donors are, in reality, investors in your organization.

continue to perform, or a college will continue to provide a quality education. The dividends on their investments are the feelings associated with benevolence or a desire to thank the agency for benefits given to the donor.

For other investors, the return on their investments may be more focused on themselves. There may be substantial tax benefits that help motivate them to give, or there may be other factors. Some donors, for example, have an "edifice complex"—the desire to see their names on buildings. Other donors want to show they can help change society in some way, or even demonstrate to their peers that they, too, have the charitable spirit. Some want to memorialize their family, or even themselves. This is not to be critical of the latter motivations for people to invest in nonprofit organizations, only to recognize that there are "things" people get in return for their investments. The dividends in giving are just less tangible than in many other kinds of investing, and may be unique for each person.

What are the implications of the "investment" approach to fund raising? I often teach a brief seminar on strategies to approach foundations and corporations for gifts. I start each session with the following: "I'm really here to sell you stock in a company. Do you have any questions or are you ready to buy the stock?" At each session, the participants almost always come up with the same set of questions:

- What does the company make or do?

- What is its history?

- What are its plans for the future?

- Who is the competition?

- What are the finances and budget of the company?

- Who runs it?

- What have been the past dividends (return on investment) and what are the dividend projections?

- Who else owns the stock?

- How is the performance of the company measured?

- Why should I invest in this company versus other places I could put my money?

These are the basic questions any potential investor might ask. They are also *exactly* the same questions a foundation, corporation, or individual will probably ask—or at least will expect answered, even if the questions aren't asked directly. Different places and people may focus more on some of these questions than on others. For example, foundations are more generally concerned about an organization's future plans rather than its history. As one person said about stock investing, "Pan American Airways had a great history—would you buy stock in it or in Intel?" Corporations are increasingly concerned about the bottom-line return to them on their nonprofit investments. For many corporate giving programs, the questions revolve around the direct return to the companies—increased sales due to their ties to the nonprofits, or greater recognition that they are, indeed, good corporate citizens and are returning something to the communities that house them. The bottom-line approach is one reason organizations such as the United States Olympic Committee can successfully sell corporate sponsorships for $40 to $50 million. And individuals may not directly ask many of the questions, but will probably have them in mind when they are asked to give. Their return on investment may focus on helping others, personal recognition, or returning something to an organization that has helped them.

The best approaches to foundations and corporations (and individuals) always seek to answer all of the investment questions, even when they are not asked directly. The best letters of inquiry, proposals, meetings with corporate and foundation staffs, and other approaches to organized funding

> **The best approaches to foundations and corporations always seek to answer all of the investment questions.**

sources always focus on these questions and how the needs of the potential funder, as well as the needs of the organization seeking support, can be met.

When I was a program officer, I directly asked many of these questions. I also reviewed submitted materials (such as audits), called other agencies, researched other information, etc., to get the answers to the other questions. For example, I usually asked social and human service agencies what other agencies in their area were doing similar work or serving similar people. All too frequently, the agency representatives I was meeting with did not know, even when I knew there was a similar agency a few blocks away from them. The point was not to trip them up, but to see if they knew who their competition was and what was different or unique about their agency as opposed to the other agency. One of the returns we were seeking on our investments (grants) was maximizing the use and impact of the foundation's funds in the most efficient and effective ways possible. When we sat in our board meetings and defended our grant recommendation, we needed to be sure that we could explain what made the agency or its program unique, or how the program was not duplicating existing efforts, or was enhancing much-needed services to a segment of the population. We needed to be ready to answer the almost inevitable questions from board members:

- How is agency X different from agency Y?

- Will this grant help the agency meet real needs in the community, or are there other, more important needs that we should fund?

- Will this grant enable the agency to do something that will not duplicate existing programs or services provided elsewhere?

- Will this grant enable the agency to reach new populations that are not now being served or that need service?

Assumptions of the Book

All of the advice, suggestions, and strategies in this book are based upon the investment model of

contributing and the basic need for your organization to answer the critical questions, even when they are not asked directly. Later sections will focus more specifically on the different returns on investment expected by various funding sources, but I urge you to keep the importance of this concept in mind.

The book is also based upon the concept of raising money, regardless of the source, as a strategic process. You don't get grants by sending proposals. If that is all you do, your proposal will rest among many others representing the same approach. If you are to be successful in raising money from foundations and corporations, there are many things that must be done before a proposal ever goes out the door, and there are many things that must be done after it is in the hands of the potential funder. Proposals are only one relatively small part of a strategic process that can involve much time, energy, and hard work on your part and on the part of your organization (if only some boards and CEOs understood this). But the potential payoffs and long-term benefits to your organization are great.

In these days of word processing and more than enough boiler plate approaches to documents, it's easy to send out 45, 50, or 100 proposals. One major organization I have been consulting with reported proudly that its foundation fund-raising operation " . . . last year sent out 1,200 proposals and will send out 1,400 this year." I made the mistake of asking what the return (in terms of grant dollars) was on that effort. The volume of your proposals may speak louder than words, at least about your strategic approach to fund raising.

The Grant-Seeking Process

I like to see the grant-seeking process as a straight line (see Figure 1–1). Only a small segment of this line—somewhere around the middle—is the actual creation and submission of the proposal. The rest of the line represents all of the steps you should try to take before actually doing the proposal and

> **Proposals are only one relatively small part of a strategic process.**

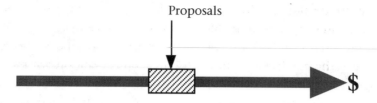

Proposals

$

Figure 1–1 The Grant-Seeking Process

all of the steps you need to take after the proposal is submitted. This same diagram also describes how you need to spend your time and energy; it should not be concentrated on the proposal, but spread across the entire process, which will be described in detail later. The important point is that the process of raising funds from foundations and corporations takes time, energy, and strategies. Your success will reflect all of these factors.

Strategy Tip: Develop a problem-solving approach to your work. I believe many of the best development professionals and fund raisers are problem solvers. Identify "problems" (I'm using this term in the broadest sense to include everything from the specific needs of your organization for which you are seeking support to real organizational problems and concerns) and create solutions. Effective and creative solutions in themselves can have strong appeals to potential funders. This book will often discuss creative ways in which fund raisers have partnered with funders to solve problems and meet needs both within the organization and outside of it.

Example: A small organization, which was primarily supported by United Way funding and which had few other resources, was about to celebrate the 100-year anniversary of its founding. The organization had never produced an annual report and the board and staff believed the attempt should

be made to have a centennial anniversary annual report. The report would be useful for public relations efforts underway as well as for the planned major capital campaign. But the limited resources almost made this impossible unless special outside funding or contributed services and support could be obtained. The problem was clear. The outside consultant (there was no fund-raising staff) heard the problem and asked a number of questions: Who prepared the organization's yearly audit? The executive director cited the major local accounting firm. The consultant recognized that the head of the accounting firm was also the chair of the board of the local community foundation, so strategically approaching the accounting firm could also have later implications for the upcoming capital campaign. The consultant, executive director, and board chair together developed a strategy to seek the support, either through a gift or through in-kind services, of the accounting firm in covering the costs of the design and production of the annual report. In return, the name of the accounting firm would be prominently displayed on and featured in the report.

The third assumption underlying this book is ethics. Unfortunately these days the ethics—or the lack of ethics—of fund raising are often in the news. Most fund raisers have a strong sense of the ethics of the profession. They believe in open and honest relations with donors and prospects, using gifts for the purposes for which they were intended, and giving prospects and donors accurate information on the organization. A few fund raisers do not follow even the most basic ethical principles; thus we are all somewhat cursed by the actions of a few—

witness the continuing effects of the United Way scandal. The increasing pressure by senior staff and board members on fund raisers to produce also is causing some to step over the line into unethical behavior. The attitude is sometimes "If I can get the gift, maybe it won't matter." But it does, and chances are, sooner or later, it will catch up to you.

You might call the following "A Bad War Story—Dishonesty Doesn't Pay." A new development officer accompanied the president of the organization on a series of visits to major foundations around the country. At one foundation the president outlined the current and planned programs for which support was being sought. The foundation program officer did not express much interest in these. The president then proceeded to outline another program. The new development officer, even though she had only been on staff for about two months, believed she was fairly familiar with all of the current and planned programs of the organization, but did not recognize the program being described. The program officer seemed fairly interested and the president went into more detail.

After the meeting, the development officer said, "I thought I knew all of our programs, but that was a new one on me." The president said, "Of course it was, I just made it up. I thought the foundation would like it, and they did, since he asked us for a proposal." When the president and the development officer arrived back at the office, an emergency staff meeting was called. The program staff were told, among many puzzled looks, to come up with the total program design and budget within a few days so that the proposal could be gotten out within the week it had been promised to the foundation.

The proposal was assembled and sent out. The end result was nothing. It is very likely the foundation saw through the whole process and also saw that the program did not fit clearly within the organization's mission and plans. The wasted time and energy of the staff, and the anger caused by the "drop everything and do this now" approach probably wouldn't even have been covered by the grant if it had been received. So much for honesty.

Now here's "A Good War Story—Honesty Pays." The foundation I was at received a request from an organization for a fairly substantial grant. I was assigned to review the request and develop the recommendation to our board. A short time after I started to review the request, I got a call. The voice on the other end seemed hesitant. The conversation went something like this:

"Hello, I'm Mr. Smith. I've just started as the new executive director of the XYZ Agency. I believe you have a grant request from us; it was submitted by the previous director."

"Yes. I have your proposal. Is there a problem?"

"Well, yes. I've only been here a few weeks, but as far as I can tell, the previous director seemed to have thrown away any bills he got when the agency didn't have the money to pay them. So I don't have any idea how much we owe, or even to whom we owe money."

Something in my head clicked and said "Problem!"

I said: "I think we will stop consideration of your proposal—and you and I better meet."

We did meet shortly after this conversation. At that meeting I returned the proposal to him and asked him if he had any more information on the extent of the problem. He said he was trying to find out more, but between running the agency and everything else, it was a slow and difficult process. Our foundation had recently established a small grant program (up to $2,500) to help support the "technical assistance needs" of agencies; it required only a brief form and the sign-off of our executive director. Because the agency's director seemed to be open and honest in his concern and desire to resolve the problem, I suggested he apply for a technical assistance grant to hire a professional to do the follow-up on the bill problem, which he did. This grant was approved.

As it turned out, the bill problem was a major problem—the person doing the follow-up found out there were over $300,000 in unpaid bills. Once the amounts and payees were identified, the new executive director came back to me with a one-year plan to pay off the creditors. He proceeded to keep me informed on their progress and happily reported about a year later that all outstanding bills were paid and the agency had put in place detailed fiscal controls to ensure nothing like this could happen again. Soon thereafter, I received an updated version of the original grant request, which was approved.

Yes, the agency had a problem. But the director openly shared it with the foundation staff. Once the extent of the problem was identified, he came back with a plan to resolve it and he kept us informed of his progress. Honesty paid off.

In all of your relations with current and potential funders, whether they be individuals, foundations, or corporations, you should always be honest and upfront with them. If there is a problem after you've submitted a proposal or after you've received a grant, let them know. But also come prepared with a solution to the problem. Your plan should be realistic and include a time frame as well as the steps you will take to resolve it and how you will prevent it from recurring again.

All agencies from time to time face problems or difficult issues. Sometimes these seem to happen when you least want them, such as when you're getting a massive new program up and running or when a major fund-raising campaign is starting up. Sometimes the plans that you outlined so carefully in your proposal and that help win you a critical grant suddenly go awry. Everything may have gone on hold, or even seemingly fallen to pieces. If this happens, let the funder know and explain your plan to solve it. Your honesty and openness, as in the case above, may win you a new friend and help ensure future support.

One other point on taking the high road on ethical issues: although a lot of people don't seem to realize it, foundation staffs talk to each other. As a program staff member, part of my job was to call other foundation funders of organizations that were applying to us to find out what the grantee's track record was. If there were questions or doubts raised by these other foundation staff members about the honesty and ethics of the applying organization, my checking process would get a lot more detailed.

> In all of your relations with current and potential funders, you should always be honest and upfront with them.

And the final assumption: fund raising and development work are still very much an art, not a science. There are some who feel fund raising can be reduced to a step-by-step process that even the novice can follow and be successful. Yes, there are some basic principles to successful fund raising. But every organization is unique; its needs may, on the surface, sound like those of another organization. But go a little deeper and the uniqueness of the organization will come through and many of the step-by-step approaches will have to go out the window. Uniqueness will come in many forms: volunteer leaders and their understandings of their roles; staff leadership; mission, goals, and objectives; programs and services; constituencies; investors and the "returns on investment"; sources of support; and so on. All of these factors and the organization's unique mix make it different—and special.

The art of fund raising can, like any of the arts, be learned in part by example. But each individual must also combine the examples, principles, and other information with his or her creativity and his or her own unique situation. The paints, canvas, brushes, and subject can be supplied; the painting is a result of these plus the creativity of the artist. That is why there is a difference between "paint by numbers" and a da Vinci masterpiece. That is also why there is a difference between fund raising and FUND RAISING!

Statistical Evidence

> Thou shalt not sit
> With statisticians nor commit
> A social science.
>
> W. H. Auden

Despite the above quote and my lifelong aversion to "sadistics," as it was known in graduate school, some statistics can help give a clearer view of the big picture and how foundation and corporate giving fit into the overall pattern of giving nationally. The best single source of statistics on charitable giving in this country is *Giving USA*, published annually by the AAFRC Trust for Philanthropy. The Trust was founded in 1985 by The American Association of Fund-Raising Counsel, an association of national consulting firms. *Giving USA* is an excellent review of the current state of charitable giving, including where the money comes from and where it goes. I often recommend fund raisers and development staff use *Giving USA* with their own senior staff and their boards to ensure a better understanding of the scope of philanthropy nationally and how their organizations fit into the big picture.

How much money was given nationally to the nonprofit sector in 1995? Most people who guess come up with numbers much lower than the actual number. In 1995, according to *Giving USA 1996,* $143.85 billion was given to nonprofits by foundations, corporations, individuals, and through bequests (estates, wills, etc., or "individuals once removed," as I call them). Look at the "Fortune 500" companies and see how many even come close to this value. Giving, as compared to the 1994 figures, increased overall by 10.78 percent (7.75 percent, when adjusted for inflation) (Kaplan 1996).

If you ask people what the effect of the economy is on yearly giving, the usual answer is that giving goes up when the economy is doing well and goes down when the economy is not doing well. On the surface, this makes sense. In reality, it's not the case. Every year since records were kept, the actual dollar amount of charitable giving has gone up. In 1993, $125.27 billion was given. In 1990 $111.88 billion was given, and in 1965 $14.67 billion was given (all figures are in actual dollars, not adjusted for inflation) (Kaplan 1995, 15).

Despite the actual yearly increases, adjustments for inflation mean that some years the change was downward, as compared to the previous year (see Figure 1–2 below) .

The next important piece of information, and one that often surprises people as much as the information on how much was given, is where the philanthropic money comes from. Many people assume a large portion of the dollars comes from foundations and corporations. A common answer I've heard is "Oh yes, it's places like The Ford Foundation and the MacArthur Foundation that give a lot of the money, isn't it?" No, it isn't. The *Giving*

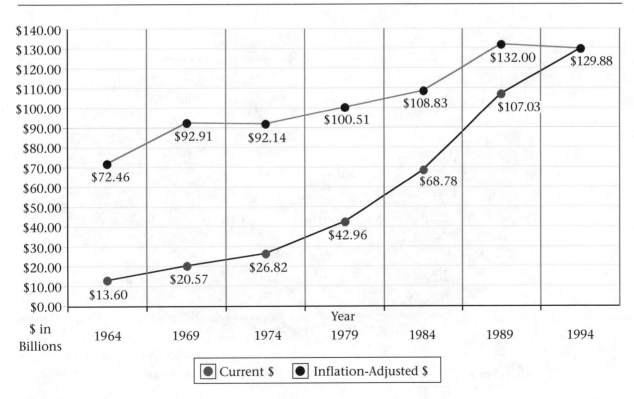

Figure 1–2 Total Giving, 1964–1994. *Source:* Reprinted with permission from A.E. Kaplan, *Giving USA 1995*, p. 14, © 1995, AAFRC Trust for Philanthropy.

USA 1996 chart clearly shows where the money given to nonprofits comes from (see Figure 1–3).

Individuals gave 80.8 percent of all money given in 1995. And, if you add in the gifts from "individuals once removed" (bequests), the total from these two sources was 87.6 percent or $126 billion of the $143.85 billion given. Foundations represented only 7.3 percent of all dollars given and corporations represented only 5.1 percent of the total.

There is a strong message here, which many people and organizations seem to miss. The best source for the philanthropic dollar over the long term is the individual. Foundation money and corporate money have their places. They can be useful to supplement other sources of funds, for starting up new programs and services, or for meeting special needs. But, as will be discussed in detail later,

corporate and foundation funds are often limited in their purposes and in their duration. A single foundation source may only provide a grant to an organization over a period of two or three years. And, increasingly, the corporate philanthropic dollar is difficult to get.

Speaking of the corporate philanthropic dollar, the trend in corporate giving is not encouraging. *Giving USA 1995* figures show corporate giving, adjusted for inflation, has generally been declining since 1987 (Kaplan 1995, 76). In 1987, corporate dollars peaked at $7.49 billion, adjusted for inflation. In 1994, corporate giving was $6.11 billion, adjusted for inflation. The 1995 figures show corporate giving up to $7.4 billion, an increase of 4.56 percent over 1994 when adjusted for inflation. What is happening with corporate giving? Corporate mergers and takeovers have elimi-

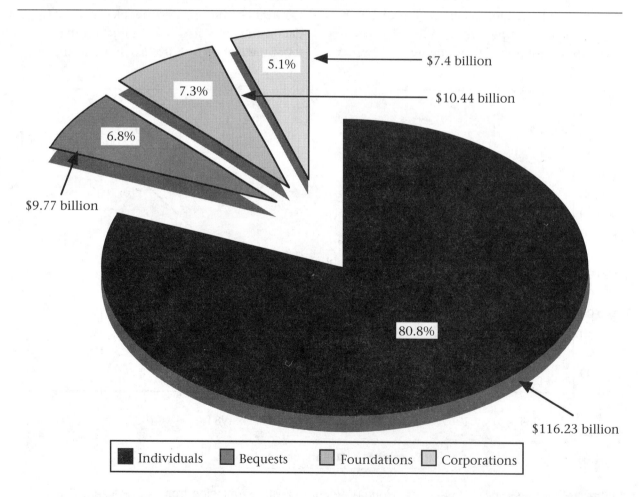

Figure 1–3 Giving 1995: $143.85 Billion. Sources of Contributions. *Source:* Adapted with permission from A.E. Kaplan, Initial Press Release, *Giving USA 1996*, © 1996, AAFRC Trust for Philanthropy.

nated or greatly reduced many corporate giving programs. Companies are increasingly pressed by competitors and their stockholders to be "lean and mean"; the corporate philanthropic program, and often the staff, is one of the easier parts of the company to remove. Companies themselves increasingly must show the impact on their bottom lines—their overall financial situation—of any of their activities. It is more difficult to show the impact of giving away philanthropic dollars than it is to justify many of the other activities of the typical corporation, so it is correspondingly easier to justify elimination or cutting back of the company's philanthropic operations. The rise of "cause-related marketing" whereby a company ties itself to a nonprofit in a way that both benefit (for example, the American Express contribution of $1 to the campaign for the renovation of the Statue of Liberty for using your American Express Card) also demonstrates corporations' interest in giving when there is a direct return to them.

And what about foundation giving? Foundation giving, unlike corporate giving, has been on the increase. In 1995 foundation giving was $10.44 billion. This represented a 5.10 percent increase

over 1994 foundation giving. But in 1993 foundation giving increased 6.45 percent as compared to the previous year; 1993 represented the second highest increase since 1988 (Kaplan 1995, 62).

According to the fifth edition of *Foundation Giving*, in 1993 there were 37,571 grant-making foundations, with approximately 1,800 foundations formed recently (The Foundation Center, 1995, 12). The report goes on to point out that the major funders raised their 1993 giving by almost 11 percent and community foundations increased their giving by almost 13 percent (see later sections for a more detailed explanation of these foundation types). *Giving USA 1995* points out that there are only 457 foundations with assets of $50 million or more, but "they control 66.2 percent of the assets and award 48 percent of . . . the grants" (Kaplan 1995, 65).

Where did the philanthropic dollar go? Figure 1–4 from *Giving USA 1996* depicts where the $143.85 billion went in 1995.

Religion continues to receive the bulk (44.1 percent) of philanthropic money, with Education second (12.5 percent), Health third (8.8 percent), Human Services fourth (8.1 percent), and Arts,

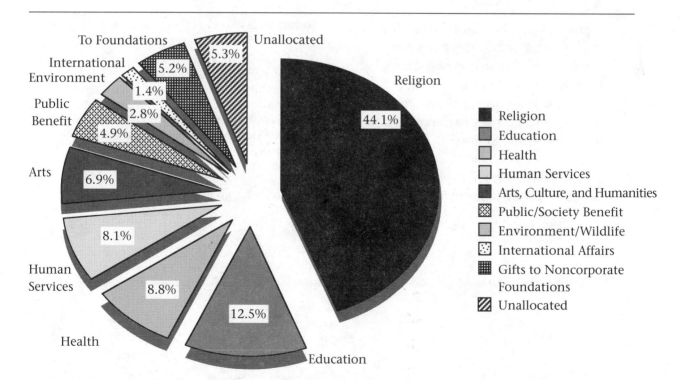

Figure 1–4 Giving USA 1995: $143.85 Billion. Uses of Contributions. *Source:* Adapted with permission from A.E. Kaplan, Initial Press Release, *Giving USA 1996*, © 1996, AAFRC Trust for Philanthropy.

Culture, and Humanities fifth (6.9 percent). Taking the longer-term view and comparing 1995 figures to 1994, adjusted for inflation, *Giving USA 1996* points out that giving to Human Services and International Affairs declined (–2.88 percent and –9.14 percent respectively) while all other categories received increased funding, even when adjusted for inflation (Kaplan 1996). The most dramatic increase in giving was to the public/society benefit category (which includes civil rights organizations, scientific research institutes, public affairs and public policy groups, and consumer rights organizations), which showed a 14.14 percent increase over 1994. One important figure in *Giving USA 1995*, in terms of this book, is gifts to noncorporate foundations, which were $7.43 billion in 1995, up from $6.34 billion in 1994.

Finally, do you know the size of the nonprofit sector in this country? *Giving USA 1995* states there were 1,118,131 organizations classified as exempt by the Internal Revenue Service. Of these, 575,690 are classed as 501(c)(3) "charities" (Kaplan 1995, 30). It is probable that there are hundreds of new 501(c)(3) organizations formed every year. You are not alone!

Strategy Tip Know the numbers! The above information is all too often not part of strategic fund-raising planning at many organizations. Yet the numbers can give considerable perspective on the proverbial "big picture" as well as alert you and your organization to major trends and issues related to fund raising. Most people, including most boards and senior staff, are not aware of the national picture. Make it a point to get this information out to your board and other staff; if possible, present it to a board meeting and have some time for discussion of what it all means, including what it can mean for your organization. Make sure everyone in your organization who is even remotely related to any fund-raising efforts knows the numbers. And, always be sure to relate your organization's specific plans and strategies to the bigger picture.

Note: If you want to explore extensive information on changing attitudes, perceptions, and reactions to recent media attention to the nonprofit sector, you should read *Giving & Volunteering in the United States: Findings from a National Survey* (Independent Sector, 1994). This two-volume set provides extensive data and information on trends related to giving, the relationship of volunteering to giving, public attitudes about charitable organizations, motivational factors related to giving, and other information.

References

The Foundation Center. 1995. *Highlights of the Foundation Center's Foundation Giving, 1995 Edition.* New York: The Foundation Center.

Independent Sector. 1994. *Giving and Volunteering in the United States: Findings from a National Survey.* Washington DC: Independent Sector.

Kaplan, A., ed. 1995. *Giving USA 1995.* New York: AAFRC Trust for Philanthropy.

Kaplan, A., ed. 1996. *Giving USA 1996.* New York: AAFRC Trust for Philanthropy, press release.

Chapter 2

Foundations, Corporate Foundations, Corporate Giving Programs: What You Need to Know

Common Characteristics of Foundations

I am often surprised by how little staff, including some development staff, know about foundations and giving programs. But then before I got into the field myself, I remember I knew even less than most people. When I first heard about my future employer, The Chicago Community Trust (at the time holding assets over $100 million and one of the largest foundations in the country), I thought it was a bank!

When I teach my class on foundations, I often ask a question at the start of each session: "What are the common characteristics of all grant-making foundations?" Here are some of the usual answers (remember the Custer example?) and my usual responses:

> **What are the common characteristics of all grant-making foundations?**

- Answer: "They make grants."

  Comment: "Some foundations don't make grants. Even some that have money for grants may not do so, because they are over-committed on previous grants, or they are reviewing their policies and procedures, or they have special permission from the Internal Revenue Service not to make grants for a period of time."

- Answer: "They all have money to give away."

  Comment: "There are foundations that do not have money. They, like your organization, may actually be trying to raise money and thus could be competing with you. Also, there are foundations that are paper foundations—they exist on paper but have not received their assets yet."

- Answer: "They have 'foundation' in their names."

  Comment: "There are many organizations with 'foundation' in their names that are not grant-making foundations; and there are many grant-making organizations that do not have 'foundation' in their names. Here are some grant-making foundations: The Chicago Community Trust, the Dillard Fund, the Downs Perpetual Charitable Trust, the Female Association of Philadelphia, Firestone No. 1 Fund, the Ford Memorial Institute, C.I.O.S., Fall River

Women's Union, the Institute for Aegean Prehistory. You get the idea."

- Answer: "They have staff."

Comment: "Most foundations do not have staff. One estimate is that, out of 37,571 foundations known to exist in 1993, about 1,200 have staff members; many foundations that have staff use part-timers or people with other assignments beyond their foundation roles. A general rule of thumb, but a rule with many exceptions, is that the larger the permanent assets of the funder, the more likely it will have some staff, even part time."

- Answer: "They have purposes or guidelines for giving."

Comment: "There are foundations, especially those in the early stages of formation, that may not yet have defined their purposes or guidelines."

- Answer: "They're listed in one of the foundation directories."

Comment: "Tried to trick me! Well, yes, the foundations listed in the foundation directories are usually grant-making foundations, at least in theory. But, because of the large number of foundations, each directory has criteria established as to what foundations it will include. The criteria may be based on the size of the assets held by foundations, and/or the total dollar value of grants made in a given year. So, many grant-making foundations are not listed in the directories. They may be 'too small' to meet the criteria established by a specific directory, or they may be too new to be included, as much of the directory information is often two to three years old." More on that point later.

- Answer: "They publish information on the foundation."

Comment: "Although encouraged to do so by many sources, most foundations have no published information available. In some cases their published information, if anything, may even be a postcard, as I've seen from one funder. There is one source of information common to all foundations: their IRS forms, which are available at offices of the Foundation Center and in the Center's cooperating collections."

- Answer: "They have a board of directors or trustees."

Comment: "Correct! A foundation may not have 'foundation' in its name, it may not have assets, or make grants, or have a staff, but it almost always has a board. The board can be 3 people or it can be 100 people. A board is required by IRS regulations."

- Answer: "They fall into one of the Internal Revenue Service's classifications for grant-making foundations and have filed the appropriate forms with IRS."

Comment: "Correct. In fact, the only two common characteristics of all grant-making foundations are the existence of a board and the meeting of IRS requirements to be classed as a grant-making foundation."

As Kermit the Frog might have said if he were seeking grants, "It's not easy finding green."

The So-Called Average Foundation

What are the characteristics of a typical, or average, grant-making foundation? Of the 37,571 plus foundations in the country, the so-called average foundation would probably look like this (The Foundation Center 1995, 1–2):

- Assets: +/– $4.3 million

- Grants: +/– $267,800

- Grant recipients: local agencies and organizations, primarily

- Board: 3 people, probably all family members

- Staff: none

- Publications: none

Categories of Foundations

The problem with the "average" foundation is it fails to reflect the great diversity of the foundation world. "Typical," in terms of foundations, is almost nonexistent. As described in detail in Chapter 3, there are many types of foundations and even more ways to classify them. As a preview, here are *some* of the basic ways I usually categorize them:

- Community foundation

- Corporate giving program

- Corporate foundation, without assets

- Corporate foundation, with assets

- General purpose foundation

- Special purpose foundation

- Family foundation

- Operating foundation

But let's make things a little more complicated. There are other factors or variables that can also be used to further describe these basic types of foundations (and even the basic descriptions I use are not the same used elsewhere). Some of these factors include staffed versus unstaffed; large versus small staff; program-specific staff versus generalist staff; newly established versus older, established; closely held (run by the donor and/or members of the immediate family) versus not so closely held (run by others); paper (established but without assets) versus funded (holding assets); local-serving (grants to local agencies and organizations) versus regional or national-serving; broad purposes versus narrow purposes (in terms of guidelines); traditional interests (those of the foundation's founder or major donor and/or his or her immediate family) versus narrow focus versus broad focus (all in terms of actual grant making); conservative versus liberal; pattern grants (generally to the same types of agencies and organizations for the same purposes) versus creative grants (grants to new and innovative programs and causes); proactive (reaches out to organizations and the area it serves, helps bring together groups to address emerging issues and needs, may take a leadership role in the area it serves) versus reactive (acts based upon proposals received); quiet (not well known) versus public (seeks to promote its work and image); and so on.

Given all of the above possible ways to describe foundations, you might end up describing a particular foundation as ". . . a medium-sized, family-run, part-time staffed, generalist-staffed, regional-serving, broad-purpose, narrow focus, conservative, pattern grant, reactive, quiet foundation."

Why is all of this important? Why not just focus on getting a grant instead of spending time classifying and subclassifying foundations and corporate funders into types and categories? Remember the line diagram in Figure 1–1? The more time you spend carefully analyzing prospective funders and understanding each one you have initially targeted, the better will be your chances of developing strategies for successfully approaching them for grants. Each piece of information you collect about a given prospect helps you form a picture of that particular prospect. I like to think of the information as "snapshots" taken while walking around the outside of a building. The snapshots will give you some ideas about the building before you enter it—and maybe help you decide whether or not you even want to enter it. The snapshots may tell you some things about what happens inside the building, but they will not be able to tell you all that happens inside.

Foundation information, no matter what the source, is only a series of snapshots, none of which is the complete picture. Some of the gaps in one snapshot can be filled in by another snapshot that overlaps it, but there will always be things you cannot find out about a particular foundation, no matter how much research you do. And remem-

> "Typical," in terms of foundations, is almost nonexistent.

ber, each source of information on a foundation has its own biases and limitations. This directory lists examples of recent grants while that one does not. That directory gives some information on board members' other activities while not including information on grants made. The foundation annual report lists assets and grants made, but does not include information on the staff. Somewhere in all of this you will find yourself guessing, but it should always be an educated guess—"reading between the lines," as I call it—based on good information and analysis.

Following are two examples of what you can, and cannot, know about your foundation prospects (both based on my own experiences).

The "medium-sized, family-run, part-time staffed, generalist-staffed, regional-serving, broad-purpose, narrow focus, conservative, pattern grant, reactive, quiet foundation" description above is a fairly accurate description of a foundation I once visited in California. Based on my research and review of their published materials and directory information, I noticed some important pieces of information. The foundation at the time had about $180 million in assets, which placed it in the medium-sized classification. Most of its grant making was in California. It had broad purposes, according to its annual report, and made many grants every year. But it had one staff person, who devoted only part of her time to the family's foundation activities; the rest of her time was spent on other business-related interests of the family that had established the foundation. I concluded that the staff person probably was overwhelmed with proposals and felt overworked.

When I arrived in her office, I noticed two large piles of what were obviously proposals on the floor near her desk. One pile was approximately four feet high, while the second pile was about one foot high. I asked her, "What's the difference between those two piles of proposals?" She sighed and said, "The small pile is all the proposals where I recognize

the name of the organization." So much for the weeks of time and energy put into those poor proposals in the larger pile—in most cases, they probably wouldn't be read. My conclusion was correct. My strategy, if we were to pursue funding from that foundation, was to get better known by the staff person (minimally) and to develop linkages to the family members who ran the foundation.

My second example shows that no matter how much you think you know about a foundation and how it operates, there are things you may never know (sometimes even when you are foundation staff!) that can influence its grant-making decisions. The foundation I worked at received a joint proposal from four organizations to develop a common project. One of the agencies had been selected by the participants as the fiscal agent for the project and therefore would be the grant recipient. The staff person handling it, after a complete review, recommended a grant in her write-up to our board.

At the board meeting there was the usual complete discussion of the proposal and the recommendation for a grant by board members. As I watched the board members during the discussion, I noticed the board chair, who had not yet commented on the request, gradually getting red in the face (I knew from past experience this was a strong sign of his impending anger). The discussion seemed generally in favor of the grant recommendation. Finally, when the discussion had seemingly run its course, and amid several nods of agreement about the grant recommendation, a board member turned to the chair and said, "And what do you think about this?" The chair slammed his fist on the table several times and exploded. "In 1939 this group organized a strike against my company and two people were killed! As long as I sit on this board I will not approve a grant to this group!" The staff member who had reviewed the grant, now hunched low in her chair, turned to me with a pained look on her face and said "I wasn't even born in 1939. How was I supposed to know that?"

Whatever the facts of the case, the foundation director quickly realized the board would not act against the wishes of the chair and the proposal was withdrawn for re-evaluation. Later, the project did receive a grant, having passed with minimum comments from the board when it was resubmitted. Same project, same four organizations. Why did it pass the second time? The agent submitting the proposal was a different organization. The chair could accept a grant to the other organization. Grant made, case closed.

Remember that building you were walking around? You may never see what goes on in some of its rooms, even if you have the best possible set of snapshots. And sometimes you may not want to know what goes on in those rooms!

Reference

The Foundation Center. 1995. *Highlights of the Foundation Center's Foundation Giving, 1995 Edition*. New York: The Foundation Center.

Chapter 3

Corporate Foundations and Corporate Giving Programs: What You Need to Know

Whereas Chapter 2 was designed to give an overview of many factors that should be part of your exploration of foundations and corporations, this chapter will explore corporate foundations and corporate giving programs in more detail. Chapters 4 and 5 will examine private foundations and community foundations. Each of these chapters will also present what many see as the major trends and issues affecting the three basic types of organized philanthropy. The generalizations are to help guide your thinking, but there are always many exceptions to every generalization.

The Corporate Giving Program

Corporate giving is structured in several ways ranging from very informal to highly organized. The three *most* basic models of corporate philanthropy and some of the characteristics of each are presented below.

Figure 3–1 illustrates a basic corporate giving program.

Basic Concept: Each year the company takes some of its pre-tax profits and gives these funds to nonprofit organizations.

Managed By: Staff person and/or senior corporate management assigned this responsibility. The corporate giving program may be one of several responsibilities of the person assigned to this role. Staff titles for the person responsible for corporate giving might be: Director or Vice-President for Community Relations; Director or Vice-President of Corporate Giving; Director or Vice-President of Public Affairs; Corporate Giving Officer.

Decisions Made By: Usually a small committee of senior management. However, in some companies the board of directors may make final gift decisions, while in others the staff assigned the responsibility may be able to make decisions on all requests or on gifts up to a certain amount. In some cases a committee of employees is selected each year

> Corporate giving is structured in several ways ranging from very informal to highly organized.

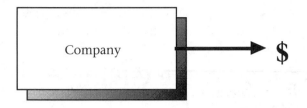

Figure 3–1 Model One: Corporate Giving Program

to review requests and to make decisions or recommendations to the decision-making group.

Other Characteristics: Gifts and the ability to make gifts are closely tied to the company's profitability each year, so there is less likelihood of a corporate giving program making multiple-year grants (grants with payments spread out over a period of more than one fiscal or calendar year). Gift decisions are usually oriented toward established organizations, such as the United Way, United Way agencies, educational institutions, traditional human service agencies, and major cultural arts institutions. Some companies are particularly interested in the number of their own employees that actually use an organization's services or programs, or at least the potential for their employees to get assistance or benefit from a nonprofit organization. Newer agencies or organizations, controversial causes, and organizations having a very narrow focus are not as favored by corporate donors, unless they tie in closely with the company's bottom-line interests. Gifts are frequently focused in the areas of company operations (plant and/or the headquarters location). For family-owned or closely held companies, grants will probably parallel the family's particular philanthropic interests. Some companies' gift interests may, in part, focus on gaining access or recognition with key community, area, or national political leadership, or even with other corporate leaders. For example, a gift approach on behalf of a particular nonprofit to a company's senior management by the CEO of a company that is a major purchaser of their products can considerably increase the likelihood of success.

The company may have a matching gift program for its employees. A matching gift program allows the company to match its employees' gifts to nonprofit organizations, usually in a ratio of 1:1 (one dollar from the company for each dollar given by the employee to a nonprofit organization, usually with a specified limit on the maximum size of the matching gift). However, some companies give 2:1 or even 3:1 matches. Some companies specify the types of agencies or institutions that are eligible to receive matching gifts (i.e., private colleges and universities) and/or the geographic area where agencies and institutions must be located in order to be eligible for matching gifts. It is always a good idea to learn about a company's matching gift program, if they have one, and to find out if your agency or organization is eligible to receive matching gifts. Many organizations encourage donors to check with their employers about matching gifts programs. Donor response materials often include a brief statement, such as "Please check with your employer about how your gift may be increased through a matching gift program."

Increasingly, as with all corporate giving, a corporate giving program and specific corporate gifts are reviewed in terms of their direct benefits to the donor company (see also later section on trends and issues in corporate giving). The company's owners (stockholders), top-level management, and the staff responsible for corporate giving are all concerned that gifts can be justified, with the goal being improving the corporate bottom line. The bottom line may include such areas as increased sales and profits, greater market penetration for the company and its products, enhanced public awareness and/or awareness of key potential customers of the company, an improved corporate image in its community or nationally, linking the company to a cause that is valued by the general public and/or the company's customers or potential customers, or free/low-cost publicity and advertising. Some companies take what might be called a "hard bottom line" approach, with strong emphasis on showing the direct (even measurable) benefits to the company's profitability. Others take a "soft bottom line" approach, with emphasis on some of the more intangible benefits to the company, such as increased goodwill or a more positive image in the community, being seen as good neighbors, and sometimes even making gifts that appear to neu-

> **Some companies take what might be called a "hard bottom line" approach, while others take a "soft bottom line" approach.**

tralize a possible or real negative image. Examples include tobacco companies funding cultural events and public television, and major chemical companies funding environmental advocacy organizations.

The overall process of the corporate giving program can be very structured, with application procedures and guidelines, corporate giving committee meeting dates where decisions are made, and so on, or it can be loosely structured, with corporate grant decisions as one item on regular or yearly management meeting agendas. As with any potential funder, it is always a good idea to ask about how the decision-making process works and also about how frequently decisions are made, if it is not clearly spelled out in the company's own materials. Approaching a corporation for support through its corporate giving program may require your organization to plan your request considerably in advance of when the funds will actually be needed, especially if the decision process only occurs one or two times per year. Also, as companies with direct corporate giving programs approach the end of their fiscal year, they may have a much better idea of their profitability, and therefore a better idea of how much will be available for grants. Be sure to check on the fiscal-year period (which often does not parallel a calendar year) when reviewing corporate materials or meeting with company representatives.

To briefly summarize, corporate giving is usually very directly tied to corporate profitability and the bottom-line interests of the company. Giving is often directed to established organizations and causes.

The Corporate Foundation with Yearly Funding

This foundation is illustrated in Figure 3–2.

Basic Concept: At some point the company established a separately incorporated company foundation with its own board of directors. However, it is important to note that the membership of the board of directors may include all or some of the company's own board members and/or its senior management. For family-owned or closely held companies the corporate foundation board may include, or consist entirely of, family members or the owners. Each year the company transfers some of its pre-tax profits to the company foundation, which, in turn, makes grants to nonprofit organizations.

Managed By: The person responsible for directing the corporate foundation may have this role as his or her full-time responsibility or may have this as a part-time responsibility along with other roles at the company. The corporate foundation may also have additional professional or support staff assigned to it in either full-time or part-time arrangements with other corporate responsibilities. Titles of corporate foundation management might reflect their dual roles, such as Vice-President for Corporate Affairs or Vice-President for Community Affairs (corporate roles) and President of the XYZ Company Foundation (foundation role).

Decisions Made By: Usually the foundation's board of directors makes the decisions; however, as with the corporate giving program, the staff may

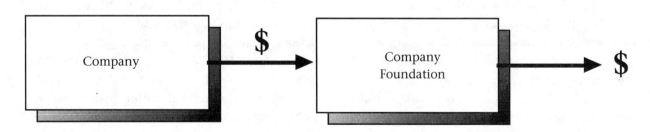

Figure 3–2 Model Two: Corporate Foundation with Yearly Funding

be assigned the responsibility to make decisions on all requests or on gifts up to a certain amount.

Other Characteristics: Grants and the ability to make grants are also closely tied to the company's profitability each year, so there is the same impact on grant making that was discussed earlier in the corporate giving program. However, the corporate foundation may also have its own limited permanent assets, such as stocks of its parent company, from which it can distribute income (and therefore represents more of a hybrid of this model and the third model discussed below). Or the corporate foundation may have ungranted funds left over at the end of the fiscal year, which can be used for grants the next year.

Corporate foundations with few or no assets tend to have many of the same characteristics as corporate giving programs, including the direct connection between corporate yearly profitability and the ability to make grants, grant making focused on "hard" or "soft" bottom-line issues for the foundation's parent company, and, usually, a strong tendency to support more traditional and established organizations and causes. However, if the foundation board includes people who may not have overlapping corporate management responsibilities, or if it includes family members of corporate owners or others not closely tied to the company, the corporate foundation grants program may show more flexibility and responsiveness to new and different organizations and causes. But keep in mind that there still will probably be an underlying interest in the corporate bottom line and in funding agencies and organizations in areas where the company does business or that meet its particular needs.

Whereas later sections of this book will specifically discuss research approaches to funding sources, it should be pointed out here that corporate foundations with few or no permanent assets can often be identified in foundation directories by examining the assets and total of grants made sections of the description for a particular corporate foundation. If the figure for assets is less than the figure for total grants made, this is a clear indication the corporate foundation is funded from yearly pre-tax profits of the parent company. Also, examining the list of corporate foundation board members and the board list and senior management list of the parent company can indicate how closely held the foundation is by its parent. If all or most corporate foundation board members are corporate board members and/or senior management, the foundation will probably be very closely tied to the corporate interests. If the foundation board does not closely parallel the corporate leadership, or if the foundation board includes several family members who are not employed by the company, it may operate somewhat independently of the corporation's bottom-line interests. In some cases the corporate foundation may even operate much like a family foundation (see the next chapter for a more detailed discussion of family foundations).

The Corporate Foundation with Permanent Assets

This kind of foundation is illustrated in Figure 3–3.

Basic Concept: At some point in the past the corporation established a separately incorporated grant-making foundation. Also, at some point in time or possibly over a period of time the company gave the corporate foundation permanent assets (usually stock of the company). The earnings on these assets become the funds used for making grants and provide the operating costs of the foundation.

Managed By: Part- or full-time professional and support staff. The chief operating officer of the corporate foundation may also have a corporate title (such as President of the XYZ Corporate Foundation and Vice-President for Corporate and Community Affairs) indicating both dual responsibilities and a close tie between the company and the corporate foundation. Or the chief operating officer of the corporate foundation may only have a title (President or Chief Executive Officer) reflecting his or her full-time responsibilities in the foundation. There may be other management staff at the vice-president or assistant/associate director level, as well as staff assigned to review proposals and make recommendations for grants (usually called program staff or program officers, although they may also carry assistant/associate director titles). Support staff may be also employed by the

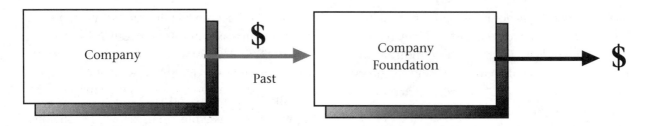

Figure 3–3 Model Three: Corporate Foundation with Permanent Assets

corporate foundation. In some cases, other staff may also be assigned to the corporate foundation on a part-time basis with other responsibilities within the company.

Decisions Made By: Usually the board of directors of the corporate foundation makes final grant decisions. However, as with other types of foundations, staff may have the ability, through board authorization, to make grant decisions up to a certain specified dollar level.

The corporate foundation board may have some overlap with the corporate board or staff leadership or may include family members from those owning or operating the company. Or it may reflect a desire by the corporate foundation to include community leadership. It is always valuable to review the background information on the foundation's board members, in part to understand how closely it is or is not tied to the corporate management.

Other Characteristics: Corporate foundations having permanent assets usually operate more like private foundations (see Chapter 4), but still reflect to some extent broad corporate interests. There is generally somewhat less direct concern with the specific interests of senior corporate management and stockholders. Because the corporate foundation is less dependent on the ups and downs of corporate profits (especially those corporate foundations with large permanent asset bases), and be-

cause they are not as directly tied to the company by virtue of both their board and staff management, they can often make multiple-year grant commitments and are more willing to take risks with grants to new and different organizations. Their focus tends to be on the soft bottom line, with funding often going to such areas as community improvement and enhancement of community services, as well as to United Ways and United Way agencies and other organizations.

Sometimes a corporation can have an established corporate foundation with its own asset base and grant program and maintain a separate corporate giving program, as presented in the corporate giving program model. In at least one case I have seen what I called a "triple hit," with gifts totaling about $350,000 coming from the corporate foundation of a company, the same company's corporate giving program, and a family foundation. Why did this happen? The CEO of the company chaired the company's gift committee (its corporate giving program following the first model above), served as board chair for the separately incorporated company foundation, which holds its own assets, and also chaired the board of his family foundation, which he had established from his personal funds. And it so happened that he has a very direct personal interest in the agency because one of his family members was using its services. It was surely a case of 1 + 1 = $350,000!

Other Models

The three models above are somewhat generic but can be applied to most corporate giving programs, although there are many hybrids of these models. For example, a closely held or family-

> **Corporate foundations having permanent assets usually operate more like private foundations.**

owned business may not have a corporate foundation or corporate giving program but may have an associated family foundation. Funding from this foundation may be directed to family members' interests, which may not be closely related to corporate products or the corporate bottom line. Another hybrid is a corporate foundation with some permanent assets, but which also receives some of the pre-tax profits from the company each year.

Other Paths to Enlightenment . . . and Support

The emphasis above has been on providing a basic understanding of how corporate philanthropy is organized. But there are other ways your organization can receive funding and support from corporations; overlooking these alternative paths means you may well miss opportunities to achieve your objectives. These other paths fall into two broad categories: nonphilanthropic cash support and noncash support.

According to *Giving USA 1995* (Kaplan 1995):

It is important to note that corporate foundations are not the source of most corporate contributions. The Foundation Center reported that corporate foundations paid $1.5 billion in grants circa 1993. According to the Council for Aid to Education, total corporate giving that year was about $6.1 billion. So, $4.6 billion was contributed directly to nonprofits from companies (79).

Giving USA 1995 also notes:

[Corporate-assistance expenditures] . . . include disbursements of cash, property, and products to charity that are not reported as charitable contributions, loans of company personnel, use of corporate facilities or services, and loans at below market rates. The median amount of a sample of companies reported spending for these functions increased by 18% between 1992 and 1993. Median cash disbursement amounts increased by 52%,

and median product and property donations increased by 74% between 1992 and 1993—when total corporate charitable giving of these did not grow (77).

Although trends and issues in corporate giving will be discussed in detail below, it is obvious from the above information that corporate noncharitable support of the nonprofit sector is growing rapidly, while its traditional philanthropic grant making is not.

Nonphilanthropic Corporate Cash Support

What is nonphilanthropic cash support? As discussed above, many companies have various forms of organized philanthropy: foundations, corporate giving programs, etc. But companies also have other significant resources that, if they see a good match between their corporate interests and your organization, can be of direct benefit to meeting the nonprofit's need for support. Remember in Chapter 1 the discussion of key questions potential funders will ask? An example was given of the United States Olympic Committee "selling" corporate sponsorships for over $40 million each. These funds do not come from corporate philanthropic dollars but rather come from corporate budget areas such as marketing, advertising, and product promotion. Why is a company willing to pay so much to have its product or name listed as "the official (airline, soft drink, etc.) of the United States Olympic Committee"? For the companies it's once again a fairly simple bottom-line decision. Linking their names with the Olympics enables them to reach a vast audience, adds to the prestige of the companies and their products, and ties them to a highly visible and recognized organization; all of these can increase their market penetration and sales. Thus the $40 million paid out is seen as a good business decision with an expected return on

> **Companies also have other significant resources that can be of direct benefit to meeting the nonprofit's need for support.**

their investment considerably in excess of what was paid. For these and other reasons the sponsorship fees come directly out of marketing budgets or other defined budget areas within the company.

Partnerships with the Corporate Sector

Corporations can also link up in other ways with nonprofits. A nonprofit agency may provide particular services or other "products" that could benefit the corporation and its employees. Many companies see this pairing of themselves and their objectives and needs with nonprofit organizations as a partnership that extends considerably beyond the usual relationship created by corporate philanthropic support. For them and for the nonprofit it can be a "win-win" situation.

Your organization may not be seen by the corporate sector as worthy of a $40 million investment. But there may well be particular aspects of your organization that would appeal to the corporate sector and to their investment of nonphilanthropic dollars in what you are doing. Some of the key questions you should ask in your review of the possibilities of a partnership with the corporate sector include:

- What do you have to offer a company that would benefit their corporate goals and objectives as well as your organization's goals and objectives?

- How could a partnership with your organization enable a company to reach new markets, sell more products, improve its image, or enhance in other ways what it does?

- Are there specific services and programs that your organization has which can be used by the company for its benefit and the benefit of its employees, especially on a fee-for-service or contractual basis?

- And, a very important consideration, how much is your organization willing to do—and, sometimes even give up—to build a connection with a corporation?

What Nonprofits Can Offer a Corporation

What are some of the specific things nonprofits can offer to a corporation? A very basic list might include:

- Pairing up with a cause that is widely recognized as important and usually is not seen as controversial, especially when there is a logical connection between the company, its products, and the cause or organization. Example: A walk to raise money for a particular cause obtains corporate sponsorship from a company that makes jogging and recreational footwear.

- Enabling the company to reach new or critical markets more directly and in a way that increases the company's recognition and positive image. Example: An organization obtains research scholarship funds from corporations that make products used by its members. Each company giving over a specified amount to the endowment of this fund is allowed to name its fund and also to present the scholarship awards in front of the membership at the organization's annual conference. Major donor companies are featured in the organization's publications and also use articles about their participation in their own corporate newsletters and annual reports.

- Helping the company reverse a negative image or negative publicity. Example: A company is seen as "anti-environment" by the public. Several environmental groups develop partnerships with the company to specifically help it take a more "environmentally friendly" approach to its work while, in turn, the company helps support the environmental programs of the nonprofit organizations.

- Providing direct advice and expertise to a company. Example: A nonprofit think tank concerned with how technology can better be used by the nonprofit sector periodically meets with senior staff of some major technology manufacturing companies to discuss their findings, analysis of technology use, and needs of nonprofits.

- Providing direct services on a fee-for-service or contractual basis to employees of a company. Example: An agency that provides family counseling services contracts with a large company to provide its employees with these services at its main facility. Employees receive family counseling services as a benefit of employment with the company at little or no cost to themselves; the company has happier and more productive employees at minimal cost to itself, with the services delivered in a way that is efficient and effective.

- Providing direct support to the company's manufacturing or service operations. Example: A nonprofit sheltered workshop for people with disabilities provides product packaging services under contract to a company.

- Enabling the company to have access to key political or other leadership. Example: Every year a nonprofit organization honors a key national political leader with an award recognizing his or her legislative and policy contributions to its area of interest. Companies are offered sponsorship opportunities for the awards dinner and those providing significant sponsorships are prominently featured in the program, by signage, and in the announcements at the awards dinner. They also are invited to a small "select" reception prior to the dinner for the awardee.

Limits to Partnerships

These are all examples of ways nonprofits and companies can work together for mutual benefit, while generating nonphilanthropic cash support for the nonprofits. In every case it will be important to realize that your organization will have to be willing to carefully analyze what it has to offer the corporate sector that might attract companies into a partnership. But it is equally important to clearly and carefully think through how much your organization is willing to give up to create corporate partnerships. Corporations can, because of their power and financial resources, easily overwhelm a nonprofit agency and, at times, even change or re-

shape the nonprofit's own goals and objectives. Sometimes money doesn't just talk—it screams. It is easy for a nonprofit to be seduced by a possible association with a company and the resulting cash and other benefits. It is equally easy to create a program or service just because an organization believes it will be appealing to a company (or any funder), even if the program or service is not directly in keeping with the organization's own purpose.

Here's one example of a company's potential to take over a program of a nonprofit. A small local nonprofit organization put together a Saturday afternoon entertainment program for children living in its immediate neighborhood; many of the children came from families with marginal incomes and working parents or a single parent. Saturdays would otherwise be a time to just hang out, with not too many other options in the area for recreation. The program proved very popular and attracted some limited local grant funds. It also attracted the attention of a major national company, which targeted much of its advertising and product promotion to children. The company made an initial modest grant from its charitable giving arm to help support the program. After a while, the company asked the nonprofit if it could pass out coupons for purchasing its products at the weekly entertainment sessions. This seemed like a reasonable request, and, when agreed to, the company provided some additional funds for the program (probably from its marketing budget). The company next asked if its corporate "character" could be present at the sessions to pass out the coupons; again, the nonprofit agreed, and additional funding was provided.

Sometime later some of the company's senior staff met with the nonprofit and proposed that the nonprofit develop a "package" of their program, which the company would take on the road to cities around the country. A substantial fee for doing

> Corporations can easily overwhelm a nonprofit agency and even change the nonprofit's own goals and objectives.

this would be paid to the nonprofit; however, the "package" would be the property of the company and would be used for its own purposes. Almost all connection between the nonprofit and the program would be lost. It was at this point the nonprofit agency said "no"; it would have essentially given up any involvement and control of the program, which would have become a purely promotional vehicle for the company.

So it is important to plan carefully and determine your organization's limits before you start to develop your organization's corporate partnerships. And know where the line is that, when crossed, means your organization has sold its soul.

Noncash Corporate Support

What is noncash corporate support and what should you know about it? Noncash corporate support is a rapidly growing method companies use to help nonprofits without making direct grants of money. Companies and nonprofits, often working together, have developed creative ways that nonprofit organizations' needs can be met through corporate assistance of many types.

A Case Study

A small nonprofit with a limited budget would like to develop a videotape that will present its story and make an appeal to viewers for contributions. The plan calls for the video, once created, to be used by board members and other key supporters as part of presentations they will host in their homes for small groups of friends and business contacts. It will cost the organization approximately $20,000 to shoot, edit, and finalize the video as well as make the necessary copies for distribution. The organization has no money in its budget to cover these costs. One approach the organization could take would be to try to obtain a grant from a foundation or other funding source to pay for the video. The development staff research possible local funders, but none are interested in making a grant for the video. One of the board members has a friend who is a senior manager of a large company headquartered in the same city. As part of its

facilities, she remembers, the company has a large staff training operation, which brings in corporate employees from around the country to upgrade their management and sales skills. The training operation has an extensive in-house video production facility to produce the tapes used in these programs.

She and the organization's executive director meet to discuss possible strategies and approaches to the company. They decide that they will approach her contact at the company to ask for his advice and help on making a request that the video production facility shoot and produce the tape at no cost to the organization. In return, they will offer the company the opportunity for recognition at the end of the video reflecting the company's contribution.

The organization's board member and the executive director meet with the board member's corporate contact in his office. They present him with a one-page outline of the proposed videotape, including contents, how it will be used, projected costs, the results of their research on possible funding sources, and a brief overview of the organization and who it serves. They also offer to give the company full recognition, if it is willing to take on this project, by both listing the company as the producer of the video and as an in-kind contributor. They ask if he can suggest who in the company should be asked for this help and how to best approach the company. He is already somewhat familiar with the organization through his friend on the board and offers to set up a meeting with the company's CEO, the organization's board member and executive director, and himself.

Prior to this meeting, the company senior manager and his friend on the organization's board are taken on a tour of the organization's facilities and are given an orientation to its programs and services. He is also given a brief overview of how the video will fit into the overall fund-raising plans of the organization and how it will specifically be used to help generate much needed support.

At the meeting with the company CEO, the senior corporate manager strongly advocates for the importance of the organization and the needs it serves and also explains, with the assistance of the organizations' board member and executive director, how the video will be used as part of major fund-raising presentations to key prospects in the community. He points out that the video will be seen by many people who represent a cross section of the city's civic and corporate leadership. The company CEO sees that his senior manager is very impressed with the organization and appears to have a good understanding of its importance and the needs it meets. The CEO says that he would like the company to shoot and produce the tape, but he would first like to see the organization for himself and learn more about it before he makes a final decision.

In the next few weeks he is taken on a complete tour of the organization. He meets some of those it serves, meets key staff members, and reviews the services, programs, financial support base, and fund-raising plans of the organization. He also meets a few board members, who escort him around the organization and explain why they are committed to being a part of it.

After his visit, he again meets with the CEO and the board member plus his senior manager. He offers to have the company shoot and produce the video; he also would like to take a few minutes in the video to explain why he believes the organization is meeting critical needs in the community and why he personally wanted his company to do the video. He also recommends that the organization consider his senior manager for a board position when the next nominating process starts.

What can we learn from this brief case study? One obvious point is that the organization got its video created at no cost to itself. But there are several other lessons in the case. A major point is that the organization, although it may not have planned to do so at first, ended up using the somewhat simple objective of developing a video into a more strategic approach of involving potential new leadership and a possible major supporter in the organization. They created the basis for building a strong and potentially long-lasting relationship with the company; this relationship, if properly cultivated over time, could have ongoing major benefits for the organization. The organization also took the time and the trouble to educate both the senior manager and the CEO about what it does

and who it serves, including providing an on-site look. Key volunteer leaders were involved in these visits; ideally, they were peers of the CEO or his senior manager. The organization carefully spelled out, prior to any contact with the company, how it would use the video as well as the benefits of having the video to the organization and its fund-raising program. But the organization also was willing to give ground in terms of what and how the company would get credit; while the organization did not originally plan to have the CEO himself on the tape, it was willing to do so. Involving the senior staff person as a board member, if he is willing and if it is appropriate, will help build strong ties to the company. Possibly, at some future time, the current senior manager may move into the CEO position. Often organizations try to involve only corporate heads; here, there is a chance to build an even longer relationship than with the CEO. The next task for the organization is to maintain and develop the relationship with the company over time. Possibly the company and CEO might be asked to host a premiere of the video at a reception for current major donors. Further down the road, the organization might turn to the company for other forms of assistance. It also might plan to recognize the company's contribution of the video production services at the organization's annual recognition dinner for major contributors. It does periodically keep the CEO informed, without overwhelming him with information, of how successful the video has been in the fund-raising program.

What Corporations Can Provide

Corporations can provide many resources and assistance to the nonprofit sector, of which the above case is only one example. It is important to realize the broad range of noncash corporate support that is possible as well as to think creatively about your organization's needs and how these could be met through a corporate partnership. It is equally important to define your organization's limits of what it will and will not do for a potential corporate partner. At the same time, the organization should define what points it is willing to negotiate and what points it will not negotiate. There

> **It is important to realize the broad range of noncash corporate support that is possible as well as to think creatively about your organization's needs and how these can be met through a corporate partnership.**

is always some need for flexibility, as the case above points out.

What are some examples of noncash corporate support? An excellent resource, even though it was published several years ago, is *Resource Raising: The Role of Non-Cash Assistance in Corporate Philanthropy* by Alex J. Plinio and Joanne B. Scanlan, Ph.D. While other publications have included sections on noncash corporate support, this publication continues to be notable for the many actual examples of ways the corporate sector can assist nonprofits. Some of the examples given are:

- provision of services and facilities, such as computer and technology services, mailing services, transportation, rental space at no cost, land, dining and meeting facilities, and art collections

- public relations services, such as printing and duplication, audio-visual and graphics arts services, special events/meeting planning, "piggyback" and public service advertising

- loaned talent, such as strategic planning assistance, dispute resolution and negotiation services, energy conservation audits, real estate assistance, special consulting, legal and tax services, market research help, personnel policy services, etc.

- volunteers from the company workforce to carry out a project, fix up a facility, conduct a phonathon, etc.

- products, supplies, and equipment, such as office equipment, food, and other items

- program-related investments (Plinio and Scanlan 1986, 31–44)

Program-related investments are generally ways that nonprofits and corporations can develop partnerships focused on mutual goals and designed to create a tangible return to the for-profit as well as a new income source for the nonprofit. Program-related investments have frequently been used to bring together the corporate, nonprofit, and sometimes the public sectors around issues such as neighborhood redevelopment, with each partner having a particular role to play in the partnership. For example, the company might provide funds to match public funds for new housing for lower income people. Other examples cited in the publication include low interest or even no interest loans, either combined with or separate from grant dollars or public moneys; and corporate funds being used as start-up moneys for nonprofit-run businesses.

Needed—Creative Approaches

Companies, like nonprofit organizations, have needs. Corporate funding, in the form of traditional grants of funds, is increasingly difficult to obtain because of growing emphasis on the corporate bottom line and decreasing emphasis on what some companies used to view as their traditional charitable roles in the communities they called home. This certainly does not mean the corporate sector has or ever will give up its charitable giving entirely. It does mean that fewer and fewer companies can justify their charitable support strictly on the basis of benevolence. It also means that companies are developing increasingly creative ways to assist the nonprofit sector without resorting to direct charitable contributions.

Nonprofits must recognize and respond to the needs of and pressures on the corporate sector in new and creative ways. Emphasis should be on developing partnerships with a more strategic approach rather than simply "getting the grant." Partnerships should be negotiated with the company

> **Nonprofits must recognize and respond to the needs of and pressures on the corporate sector in new and creative ways.**

in ways that will ensure both the company and the nonprofit retain their integrity and have a clear understanding of the return on investment for each, while providing the company with clear opportunities for involvement and recognition. The initial approach should not be to give a company the plan, whatever it may be, but rather to work with the company and involve its key staff in development of the partnership so the organization and the company will both receive maximum benefit from the arrangements.

The keys to a successful corporate-nonprofit relationship will include: a clear understanding of each other's needs and the benefits to each; understanding of the different motivations each has for coming together; defining the limits on each party (how much each is willing to give up to have the relationship); providing the company with recognition appropriate to its needs; and giving the relationship the time and energy needed to make it successful.

But even beyond that, it is important for the organization seeking corporate involvement to develop creative approaches to the potential relationship. These approaches should be based upon as complete as possible an understanding of the company, including its history, plans, products, competition, priorities, management, locations, workforce, attitudes toward its community, financial state, structure, ownership, and other factors. Ideally, the corporate involvement should help provide leverage for meeting the broader needs of the nonprofit organization; again, this is the more strategic approach but also the approach that may be more appealing to the corporation.

Example: A nonprofit organization is relatively new and has not yet had a full year-end financial audit. As it begins to explore possible foundation funders, it finds out that most require a copy of the organization's audit be submitted with any grant application. The organization takes this information along with its fund-raising plan to a local accounting firm. The organization points out that a one-time contribution of services for its first audit will qualify it to apply to many potential funding sources that it could not otherwise consider. The audit firm agrees to a one-time-only contribution of services for the audit.

Example: A small nonprofit organization decides to conduct a golf tournament to raise funds, but realizes that its limited staff and volunteers cannot provide the people resources to run the tournament. A board member of the organization is an employee of a large local firm. He and the executive director of the organization approach a vice-president of the firm and ask if some of the employees would be willing to provide the needed volunteer support for the tournament. The company agrees to publicize the need for volunteers by placing announcements in its employees' newsletter, placing a large banner in the cafeteria, and posting a sign-up sheet on the main bulletin board. Once the company has agreed and it becomes clear that many employees have volunteered to help with the tournament, the organization meets with the CEO to tell her how successful the recruitment program was and to thank her. She offers to help and, when asked, accepts the role of master of ceremonies for the tournament. The company also donates several products for prizes, and receives special recognition in all of the tournament publicity. The organization continues to keep the company involved in its activities.

Example: A nonprofit human service agency has opened a new office in an area of town where it has never operated before. It is soon apparent that most people in the area, especially those needing its services, aren't aware of the new office. The agency has limited funds for publicity, but would like to get information out to people in the area. The major public utility in the area recently had a substantial rate increase approved accompanied by considerable negative publicity. The agency meets with officials of the utility and presents a proposal that flyers about the new office location be placed in the billings sent to people in the area. The utility officials, mindful of the recent negative publicity, offer to do this and to create a coupon arrangement that will enable those visiting the agency and using its services for the first time to receive a $5 discount on their next month's utility bill.

Trends and Issues in Corporate Support of Nonprofits

The corporate world is changing rapidly and it is expected that the rate of change will increase substantially over the next several years. Competition, changing world markets, and newly emerging industries, especially in such areas as technology, are driving the sharpening corporate focus on survival and success. Some companies, for example, have drastically shifted their product lines and major interests, abandoning what had been their bread and butter and moving on to different things. One of many recent examples of this trend is Glenayre Technologies, Inc., which until 1992 had, as its primary business, oil and gas pipeline construction and real estate. The company moved into wireless telecommunications and has seen its sales for the most recent year increase by 87 percent and net income increase by 128 percent; it now holds 80 percent of the market share for paging switches and a 65 percent share of the market for paging transmitters.

Other companies are being taken over, are merging, or are setting up alliances with companies that are complementary to, rather than competitive with, their interests. Frequently when a company with a strong corporate philanthropic program is taken over or merges with another firm, the philanthropic program is one of the first areas examined and all too commonly is eliminated or scaled down considerably. Staff involved with corporate giving may be cut back or eliminated as the new entity seeks to become lean and mean. Major operations may be closed down or downsized, headquarters offices may move, and key staff may be let go. Again, it is the emphasis on the corporate bottom line that often drives these decisions.

One result of these trends is the growing concern of those company staff, who are involved with the corporate giving program either in a part-time or full-time capacity, that they can justify their roles and the specific impacts—on both the recipient organizations and the company—of their support of nonprofit organizations. They also may more narrowly define what they will and won't fund, staying away from groups that might be considered controversial or gifts that might generate negative publicity. More and more they emphasize the return to the company in their review of requests; this emphasis is also reflected in the decision-making process. In some firms it is likely that corporate

gift decisions, which may have previously been the responsibility of a less-senior officer, are moved to a higher level in order to ensure the decisions are appropriate to the major interests and objectives of the company.

The company may shift away from many gifts and nonprofit support with a broad focus to a few gifts where there will be maximum impact for both the company and the nonprofit organization. Bigger corporate gifts to a few organizations can also be seen as increasing the critical mass needed for positive publicity for the company and for projection of a corporate good neighbor image. Corporate giving may also shift from cash gifts to support through other means (donations of equipment, supplies, etc., where there is a tax advantage to the company or donations of people and services).

The competitive and financial pressures on many companies may also mean there are simply fewer dollars to give. Funds may be directed to research or more intensive marketing of the products or services of the company. Other money may be directed toward increasing stockholder dividends or redefining the corporate image through a new publicity campaign. At times, funds may be needed to fend off lawsuits or for other specialized purposes. All of this means that limited philanthropic efforts by the company, whether through direct gifts or other measures supportive of the nonprofit sector, may become even more restricted.

Perhaps the best way to get some flavor of the current issues and trends in corporate philanthropy is to sit in on a recent discussion of trends and issues in corporate support of nonprofits (AAFRC Trust for Philanthropy 1995, 1–5). The AAFRC Trust for Philanthropy is the educational and philanthropic arm of the American Association of Fund Raising Counsel and the publisher of *Giving USA*. The Trust also sponsors the Gurin Forum every year, which provides a focused discussion and debate on key topics related to philanthropy and support of nonprofit organizations. The complete transcript with conclusions of the May 1995 Forum is reprinted with permission below because it brings into focus the key trends, issues, concerns, and even controversies related to corporate support of the nonprofit sector.

Charlayne Hunter-Gault, moderator for the Gurin Forum, stated:

Given the revolutionary changes taking place in the American political arena today, depending on your political perspective, it remains to be seen if we are in for the best of times or the worst of times. . . . As today's forum topic indicates, we are most assuredly in the midst of changing times. Today we are going to look at the impact of these changing times on corporate philanthropy and, more specifically, on the role of corporate leadership.

In the philanthropic arena, as Martin Grenzebach, the chair of the American Association of Fund-Raising Counsel's Trust for Philanthropy, and J. Patrick Ryan, chair of the American Association of Fund-Raising Counsel, have written in *Giving USA 1995,* during the past year there was much public debate about the practices of both nonprofits and fundraising professionals in this country while simultaneously we've been in the midst of a virtual explosion of . . . new voluntary associations all over the globe.

Some students of the field have observed that corporate social responsibility has indeed changed with the times, and not for the best. They cite the fact that corporations gave less than five percent of the total of all philanthropic contributions and that growth has remained flat for the past few years. The new face of corporate giving, they assert, is not the face of a philanthropic staff and executive officers driven solely by a mandate to do good but rather, increasingly, the face of market researchers and public relations departments with a strategic plan aimed at the bottom line. Such a trend suggests that corporate philanthropy as we have known it is dying. Others argue that this is a complete misreading of current trends and that companies today spend more on nonprofits than ever before. . . . We are going to examine the current trends and their impact on the nonprofit world; we will look at the values of a new generation of corporate leaders whose instincts have been honed in the world of millisecond changes. We will look at such questions as:

- How different is the way our new leaders make decisions and balance demands with the corporate structure they are accountable to?
- How different is their sense of community and their understanding of the social contract?
- Is there a point where good business and corporate social responsibility meet?
- How do we ensure where ever that line is, the new generation of corporate leaders steps up to it in ways that ensure that corporations remain a dynamic force in enhancing the daily lives of our citizens as they together construct the architecture of the future?

Gurin Forum Report

Two of the philanthropic community's most hotly debated topics—changes in corporations' approach to philanthropic giving and the nonprofit community's most effective response to those changes—were the focus of the AAFRC Trust for Philanthropy's Maurice C. Gurin Forum, held in May 1995, New York City.

More than 200 nonprofit managers, fund raisers, and corporate leaders listened as the Gurin Forum's five panelists, representing a wide range of perspectives, examined the values of and de-

Source: Reprinted with permission from New Times, Tight Money: How Corporate Leaders Respond, *Giving USA Special Report: Trends in Corporate Philanthropy,* pp. 1–5, © 1995, AAFRC Trust for Philanthropy.

mands on the new generation of corporate leadership and the impact that changes in corporate philanthropy will have on the nonprofit community.

The five panelists were Myra Alperson, senior research associate at The Conference Board; Betty Stanley Beene, president and chief executive officer of the United Way of Tri-State; Fred Krupp, executive director of the Environmental Defense Fund; Westina Matthews, vice-president of philanthropic programs at Merrill Lynch; and Charles McCabe, Jr., executive vice-president of corporate marketing and communications for Chemical Bank.

Forum moderator Charlayne Hunter-Gault opened the two-hour session, noting that the broad general agreement that corporate social philanthropy has changed has not translated into agreement on the character, explanation, or merits of the change.

The public debate on corporate philanthropy has two sides, Hunter-Gault said. "There are those who believe the new face of corporate leadership is increasingly the face of market researchers and public relations departments with a strategic plan aimed at the bottom line. [Those who espouse this point of view believe] such a trend suggests that corporate philanthropy as we have known it is dying. Others argue that this is a complete misreading of current trends and that companies today spend more on nonprofits than ever before."

Luis Rudin, co-chair of Rudin Management Company and one of New York City's most energetic advocates, devoted his keynote speech to the principle of "giving back." He spoke of his own family's commitment to New York's philanthropic needs: "To us, philanthropy is a little bit of self interest. It's a paying back to the city of New York what it gave to us. If we can get that mentality across to a lot of other people we can win the battle." Observing that he doesn't see as much corporate philanthropy in New York as he hoped for, he urged corporate leaders to "replant in this town and country the seeds of a better life and a better world."

The panelists agreed that the new generation of corporate leaders, pressed to maximize the returns on every dollar, often sees charitable gifts as charitable investments that, like every other investment, must show a return. Further, they agreed that corporate philanthropic programs invest in good

causes strategically, looking for positive exposure to the press and consumers, goodwill and loyalty among employees and the community, and the opportunity to make a difference.

But, the experts agreed, creative nonprofit organizations that adapt their fund-raising strategies to reflect business concerns can continue to generate support from the corporate community.

"The newest trend in corporate giving strategies is to bring the giving process closer to business goals," according to Ms. Alperson. Preliminary findings of a survey she conducted for The Conference Board of those strategies reveal that companies envision significant bottom-line results from revamped, more strategic contributions programs: enhanced public image, increased employee involvement and loyalty, and stronger customer ties.

"As I conducted interviews, I came to feel that the word 'philanthropy' does not apply to the types of corporate donations programs in place at many companies," she said. "'Corporate social investment,' the term used by the insurance industry, is a more straightforward term that reflects a more business-like attitude which means that a company does expect some sort of return for its donation."

Betty Beene agreed in part. "We see corporate giving changing too, but in direction, not in intensity. We have seen a growing number of companies which have interests in directing a portion of their gift, either to a specific geographic area or a particular project. We believe that those decisions are increasingly linked to the company's strategic business interests."

She cites as examples some of the largest pharmaceutical companies, which have expressed interest in affecting services to the ill, and some food product manufacturers' interest in feeding programs. Ms. Beene said, "Corporations aren't doing their job if they don't look at the issue of corporate contributions and ask what is the return on that."

Westina Matthews added that economic concerns are partially driving the strategic approach: "The declining economy has impacted on our budget. We do more strategic planning, and we must justify our budget. The 'tyranny of the lists' no longer exists," she continued, referring to lists of major corporate donors that nonprofits would use to entice other corporations to make donations to their causes. According to Ms. Matthews, her supervisors now respond to the lists by saying, "so what. . . . How does adding our name to a long list distinguish us in any way?"

From the marketing perspective of Chemical Bank's Charles McCabe, Ms. Alperson's survey and Ms. Beene's observations reinforce the importance of finding a good match between a corporation's interest and a nonprofit's needs. He said, "My role as a marketer is to put our limited marketing dollars in causes that will get us the biggest bang for our buck. As a marketer, what catches my attention is great press. What we're looking for is good exposure, good positioning, and good contacts, and you're looking for the funding. There's nothing wrong with having a class nonprofit and a class corporation joining hands in a victory celebration. It's image enhancement for both of us, and it makes an everlasting impression on the corporation."

Although Ms. Alperson's survey found that structured strategic plans drive only a relatively narrow percentage of corporate contribution programs, more and more companies are seeking a synergy between giving strategies and marketing to build a customer base. "The rationale for such an approach is clear," she said. "You can't operate a successful corporate giving program if you don't have a successful business."

Despite the increased focus on matching strategic business needs to philanthropic opportunities, panelists agreed that the corporate leaders of the new era, like their forebears, seem to have a strong sense of community and responsibility. Betty Beene said that the pressure on corporations to link corporate giving to strategic corporate interests does not translate into a transformation in "the content of the character" of corporate leaders.

"Corporate leaders still care deeply about their community and about individuals," Ms. Beene said. "What has changed is the environment in which they must operate and the demands on their time. Without question, there is more competition for a share of mind of every CEO and every top executive."

According to Fred Krupp, of the Environmental Defense Fund, his experience has been "this new generation of corporate leadership cares deeply about the environment. The burden is on non-

profits not to sit around and wonder why their board members aren't active but to listen and think of creative ways to engage board members."

Ms. Beene added, "Like everybody else, corporate leaders are working harder and longer, and the stress is tremendous. It is incumbent upon all of us in the nonprofit arena to structure our requests for their time and guidance in such a way that increases the likelihood they can give it to us."

Giving back to the communities which support them continues to be the major focus of corporate philanthropy, and for many organizations there are an increasing number of those communities around the world. According to Charles McCabe, "The major goal of our social policy unit, which dispensed more than $518 million in gifts last year, is to improve the communities where we do business. We help minority businesses, provide education and job support, college scholarships. Our employees participate in blood drives and volunteer at nonprofits as part of their 'after school' activities."

It is also true that corporations' definition of "community" is evolving. According to Ms. Matthews, globalization of Merrill Lynch's corporate resources translates into globalization of competition for its philanthropic resources. "Our revenues increasingly come from non-domestic [locations], and our employees live outside the U.S. In addition, other U.S. cities besides New York are important to us," Ms. Matthews noted. "The pie has not gotten larger which means we have to cut it differently."

Decisions about dividing up the pie are also increasingly being driven by a desire to be effective philanthropists. According to Ms. Beene, corporate leaders are increasingly interested in making a measurable difference in one or two areas. "They are interested in moving the needle on one problem in some measurable way because of their giving." Ms. Matthews seconded that notion when she noted that Merrill Lynch "looks for creative ways to give and make an impact."

"There is more focus to our giving," added Ms. Matthews. She referred to a recent Merrill Lynch decision to no longer give money for international disaster relief because "that's not who we are." To define its priorities, Merrill Lynch grounds its philanthropic programs and giving in a larger set of principles. "Our giving is grounded in a larger vision: five principles, one of which is responsible citizenship," reported Ms. Matthews. According to Ms. Matthews, Merrill Lynch's Philanthropic Program unit must show what it has done to contribute to the organization's overarching principles. "As part of the evaluation for my department and myself, we are asked what has your department done for responsible citizenship. Giving away the money is not enough."

Fred Krupp and Betty Beene referred to another set of pressures corporate leaders now face: the new political mood in Washington. "What will the role of corporate America be as we see the huge cutbacks happening nationally and locally?" asked Ms. Beene. "We all know that need will be defined very differently a year from now than it is today. I do know that it is unreasonable to expect corporate America to step up and do everything that government once did."

Mr. Krupp discussed what he fears may be a new trend in politics to stigmatize corporate philanthropy to certain types of organizations. This latest political bias, expressed recently by House of Representative's Majority Leader Richard Armey (Texas), who criticized corporations that contribute to groups he referred to as "left-wing," singling out Ducks Unlimited and The Nature Conservancy, may turn simple matching gift decisions into small acts of courage. "Those of you who have corporate giving and matching gifts programs are going to enter a time when it falls on you to define what America is all about. There will be pressures to narrow what corporate giving means, and those pressures will be very real," said Mr. Krupp. He added that the new political mood will require corporate leaders to step forward, "exercise their leadership to speak out against bad public policy."

Restraints on corporate philanthropy increasingly frustrate nonprofits that are trying to do more as government proposes to do less. The disparity between resources and need raises serious questions for nonprofit organizations about the most effective approach to corporate giving. Panelists urged nonprofit managers and fund raisers to identify ways to exploit new and alternative forms of corporate support by thinking strategically and creatively about values and interests that a nonprofit and a corporation may share.

"With changes, there are opportunities," said Ms. Matthews. "Direct giving is not as easy to get. But there are, if you plan and are strategic, and thinking of in-kind opportunities, ways we can respond."

Beene suggested three adjustments nonprofits must undertake to win corporate support for their activities. First, prove your organization's effectiveness and efficiency so corporations will know you're a good investment. Second, devise and propose creative matches between your organization's activities and a corporation's strategic interest. Third, understand the time pressures on corporate leadership and ask for specific commitments rather than for broad support.

Mr. Krupp cautioned nonprofits particularly those like EDF, which are policy and advocacy organizations, to think carefully about corporate partnerships. Krupp noted that while EDF has had a highly successful partnership with McDonald's, focusing on cooperatively developing less-polluting ways of doing business, EDF also has a very restrictive corporate contribution policy. "Our credibility and our good name are our most important assets," Krupp asserted. "I wouldn't want anyone to think we pulled our punches or let a company or industry off easy because we were the recipients of their largesse."

Increased volunteerism by corporate employees is an increasingly important, less traditional source of indirect corporate support for nonprofit managers to consider, panelists agreed. Ms. Matthews, Ms. Beene, and Ms. Alperson noted that corporations are increasingly supportive of employee involvement in contributions programs. Employee philanthropic activity can take the form of volunteering, matching grants, participating on contributions committees, blood drives, walk-a-thons and more. "Employee involvement is an integral part of many contributions programs," reported Ms. Alperson. Volunteering plays a role at nearly 90% of the surveyed companies and is seen as a way to leverage donations through the contribution of time and expertise."

"Volunteering is increasingly important to us," noted Ms. Matthews. "Not in the traditional way of 'loaned' executives. But we are seeing more group efforts, which is encouraged at Merrill Lynch because teamwork as a strategic value is important at our company. We look for opportunities for employees to team together in the community."

Ms. Beene urged nonprofit managers to take advantage of what she termed the "democratization" of corporate leadership. As more and more corporate senior staff are ready and willing to assist with philanthropic efforts, nonprofits should seek them out but be prepared to ask for help with specific tasks. "We are increasingly populated with top corporate leaders who are giving us strong quality time. This happens because they understand that they effect change when they come to the table."

"All of us in the nonprofit sector have essentially thought the greatest ideas come out of the corner office with the thickest carpet," Ms. Beene said. "I think the reality today is that when we can get the time of both the CEOs and their other leaders in that corporation to work with us at varied levels we are better. I want our finance committee populated not with CEOs but with the chief financial officers, the auditors and the treasurers of corporations who know the right kind of questions to ask."

According to Westina Matthews, the fact that CEOs today generally are less interested in serving on five to ten nonprofit boards where they are just a name and prefer to serve on one or two boards at nonprofits that meet the company's strategic interests results in an increased corporate commitment in terms of support by senior staff. "We're only interested in serving on one or two boards. Understand, with that commitment comes staff. . . . The quality of the leadership you're getting from the CEOs for the not-for-profit is going to be much better and stronger."

The panelists encouraged nonprofit managers to look beyond the company's traditional philanthropic programs. Mr. McCabe reiterated the value of seeking corporate support from divisions such as marketing rather than relying solely on the traditional support from a corporation's foundation or philanthropic unit. The synergy between a corporation's marketing goals and its giving program opens the door to new sources of corporate support, according to Mr. McCabe.

"While our social policy unit distributed $18 million in contributions in 1994, none of the marketing division's philanthropic activities show up in that number," said Mr. McCabe. "The marketing division is a new source of funding." According to Mr. McCabe, the marketing division is the driving force behind Chemical Bank support for the Achilles Track Club, a club for handicapped runners, and for support of the Radio City Music Hall Christmas Show, which translates into tickets for thousands of disadvantaged children.

"With creativity, you can approach marketing departments for support. Let us know what's in it for us. Let us know how your constituency meets our needs," Mr. McCabe said. "Check your demographics. Each of you has series of publics; your donors, neighbors, board members, workers. They might be of interest to us. They might be our prospects. How can you deliver them to us? That then starts getting our interest up."

He continued, "Put a creative package together that will help the firm you're approaching achieve its sales and image goals. Delivery of an idea like that to a corporation guarantees you a sit-down (meeting). But remember, your idea has to meet a marketing department's three criteria: it must have strong public relations potential, be cost effective and hit the target markets."

For both nonprofit organizations and corporations, in-kind contributions are an increasingly attractive source of corporate support. "We're seeing a real push in that direction," said Ms. Beene. "It just makes good business sense."

Ms. Matthews concurred. "In-kind giving is more and more important to us," she said. "When we have excess furniture or computers we look for opportunities to make these kinds of gifts."

The new United Way Tri-state offices are a prime example of the new opportunities posed by increased interest in in-kind contributions. According to Ms. Beene, their new downtown office space is donated by Chemical Bank, the partitions in the offices come from Merrill Lynch, the fax machines are from Pitney-Bowes, the computers are from IBM, and the telephones are from AT&T.

It is increasingly clear that nonprofit organizations will have to be more strategic in their approach to corporations. The Gurin Forum panelists urged nonprofits to accept the trends in corporate support and to revise their corporate outreach accordingly. As Ms. Beene said, "The key for the future is optimization."

"We in the nonprofit sector must respond to these trends. It requires a new set of skills to work in partnership," said Beene. "The truth is, it will be survival of the fittest. Those who can do tasks most efficiently and effectively, in partnership with corporations, will be able to deliver the maximum amount of services to people who need them."

Ms. Matthews noted that corporations are looking for innovative and creative opportunities to give to charities while satisfying the budgetary and strategic demands of the business. "People want to share," she said. "It may not be dollars, but people are willing to share their personal resources. Our challenge as corporations and nonprofits is to find ways to make the matches to share what we have."

"I think we have reason to be hopeful," concluded Fred Krupp of EDF. "I see deeper and clearer values on the leadership levels. Corporations can play a useful and important role in constructing the society we desire."

There can be no doubt that nonprofit managers and fund raisers are watching the corporate philanthropic world transform itself. Corporate leaders, spurred on by the need to maximize and prioritize the financial and human resources of their organizations, are redefining their philanthropic goals and restructuring giving programs to achieve both social and institutional objectives. Increasingly, corporate involvement with nonprofits must advance some strategic objective of the business: improving community relations, reaching out to a target market, generating positive press, or cementing employee relations.

The challenge to the nonprofit and fundraising community is to understand the changes, develop creative ways to adapt to them, and continue to provide the services their organizations promise. Fund-raisers and nonprofit managers who understand this shift and begin to think strategically about creative connections and alliances between their organization and a corporation have the greatest chance of surviving and adapting to the very real changes now taking place.

Charlayne Hunter-Gault's Wrap-up advice for nonprofit and corporate leaders:

Reality check • Creativity • Change • Hope • Challenge • Care

"It's been a real reality check and also a challenge. I think that we've heard the gauntlet handed down to both the corporate side as well as the nonprofit side. You've got a lot of work ahead of you but I think you've just heard encouraging words. There's a reason for hope, that the work that you put into it will be profitable to both sides."

Lessons for Nonprofit Leaders

- Charitable gifts are really charitable investments; they must show a return.

- Companies envision significant bottom-line results from: enhanced public image, positive press, increased employee involvement and loyalty, and stronger customer ties.

- Find a good match between a corporation's interest and a nonprofit's need.

- Structure requests for time and guidance from CEOs or managers in such a way that increases the likelihood they can give it.

- Listen and think of creative ways to engage volunteer talent and board members.

- Reinvent volunteer opportunities to match the constraints of the busy corporate leader.

- Identify ways to exploit new and alternative forms of corporate support by thinking strategically and creatively about shared interests.

- Prove your organization's effectiveness and efficiency.

- Ask for specific commitments rather than broad support.

- Utilize middle manager corporate volunteers effectively; the greatest ideas do not only come out of the office with the thickest carpet.

- Seek corporate support from divisions such as marketing.

- Show the corporations how your constituency meets their needs.

- Accept the changing trends in corporate support and revise your "ask."

- Think strategically about creative partnerships.

- Be known as a good investment.

Lessons for Corporate Leaders

- Corporate giving strategies need to be brought closer to the business goals.

- Giving strategies can be linked to a specific geographic, business, or program focus.

- Invest in projects that have good exposure, good contacts, and good positioning.

- Demand a "synergy" between giving strategies and marketing to build a customer base.

- Identify your corporation's definition of "community."

- Make a measurable difference in one or two major areas.

- Improve the communities where you do business.

- Volunteerism by corporate employees benefits the employer and employee.

- A well-thought-out corporate giving strategy is the best response to narrow-minded, politically motivated criticism.

- Return on investment should include quality-of-life enhancements for employees, customers, and future labor pool.

- Challenge nonprofits to think of creative ways to engage your resources.

- Align your company with a first-class nonprofit.

- Be creative with giving opportunities: dollars, employee expertise, in-kind.

What's Happening Here?

Trends and Issues Facing Foundations

Given the complexities of the world of organized philanthropy it seems appropriate to discuss the major trends and issues affecting foundations. In the earlier section on corporate philanthropy there was discussion of the "revolutionary changes" taking place in American politics in the last few years and the impact of these changes on corporate philanthropy. All indications are that these same changes are having a major impact on other types of foundations. Nonprofits, especially those relying heavily on public (city, county, state, and/or federal dollars), are more frequently seeking support elsewhere, especially from private and community foundations and the corporate sector. Pressures to supplement or replace public dollars are increasing, in part out of a sense of panic, and also out of the realization that the flow of public dollars is being or will be decreased and, in some areas, eliminated. For some organizations, foundations and corporate support are unfortunately seen as a possible "quick fix" for actual or anticipated shortfalls due to public support cutbacks. So the rush is on to get foundation and corporate support.

Even without this pressure, many nonprofits are becoming more sophisticated in seeking funds from foundations. Possibly one of the biggest changes that has increased the ability of nonprofits to generate proposals is the widespread availability of computers and word-processing. Even 15 years ago this was not the case; generally, only the larger nonprofits could afford computers. At one point I knew a foundation officer in Chicago who flatly

> **For some organizations, foundations and corporate support are unfortunately seen as a possible "quick fix" for actual or anticipated shortfalls.**

stated he would never accept a word-processed proposal! Now, all but the very smallest agencies have computers and, if necessary, can rapidly generate proposals and other documents.

Another trend is the greater professionalization of the fund-raising/development function. As more and more people enter the profession, and as those in the profession become more skilled at what they do, foundation research and proposal development are becoming specialties with growing levels of sophistication. The ability of nonprofits to hire people with these special skills is, in part, directly related to the size of their operating budgets. But even some smaller agencies are seeing the hiring of skilled and experienced professional development staff, including those with foundation and grant-seeking skills, as a good investment. There are still many organizations without any staff specifically responsible for fund raising and development, and there are still nonprofits that believe an unskilled beginner can be as successful at raising the needed funds as the experienced professional. Indeed, some organizations still believe the first place to cut, when budget cuts are necessary, is the fund-raising/development area. There are also still persistent rumors that General Custer dismissed some of his best scouts because he knew "where the Indians are."

A third trend directly impacting the ability of nonprofit organizations to seek support from foundations and corporations is the growing number and sophistication of the available sources of information (see also Chapter 8). For many years The Foundation Center's directories were, aside from the publications put out by a limited number of foundations, the only major source of information. Now other companies, such as The Taft Group, are publishing foundation and corporate giving directories. Also, local and regional organizations are issuing their own directories of foundations and corporations in their areas. Finally, there is the rapidly expanding number of computer-accessible electronic information resources on organized philanthropies. These tools include:

- Computer databases (published on disks or CD-ROMs) on foundations and corporate donors,

and on grants made, such as those published by *The Chronicle of Philanthropy*, Orca Systems, The Foundation Center, and The Taft Group

- Related computer databases, such as Taft's Boardlink™, which gives information and crosslinks information on over 130,000 corporate and foundation board members

- Internet-accessible information on foundations and corporations, including World Wide Web home pages for some foundations and other resources, such as the Council on Foundations and The Foundation Center's home pages (see below)

- Prospecting and research services, including those provided by The Foundation Center, Taft, some consulting firms, and other resources

These tools, some of which are still relatively costly, can greatly aid the preliminary search process when an organization is seeking potential support from organized philanthropy. While Chapter 9 will go into considerably more detail on using these resources, it is important to point out that each of the resources has certain limitations. None of the resources mentioned above are comprehensive; all have (usually specified) criteria for inclusion—or exclusion—of the sources listed, such as the dollar amount of grants made in a given year (one source only includes foundations that have made grants in excess of $2 million for the year for which information is reported), or other criteria. Also, the information presented in many of these resources can be two, three, or even four years out of date. This usually reflects the time necessary for the foundation to release or publish its information, the time necessary to prepare the directory or database, and other factors, such as the fiscal year of the foundation. All of these factors may well mean the information you are reading is at least two years old and may not accurately reflect the current interests and giving of the foundation.

Internet resources are evolving so rapidly anything said at this point will probably be out of date by the time this book is published. However, some of the larger foundations are posting their current guidelines and other information on their World Wide Web home pages (somewhat like an electronically accessible encyclopedia without much organization). The Foundation Center home page (at http://www.fdncenter.org) and the Council on Foundations home page (at http://www.cof.org) enable the user to navigate to many foundations' home pages. At least one foundation directory is online: Access.Point Fundraising System (at http://www.acesspt.com). Other nonprofit organizations are going on line, using the World Wide Web, and many more organizations already have e-mail (electronic mail, using the Internet) addresses (see also Chapter 9 for a more detailed listing of Web sites useful for research). It is probable that some foundations may soon accept e-mail proposals, as well as messages and other inquiries.

Foundation Responses

All of these trends mean that foundations are increasingly being targeted and are receiving a growing volume of proposals. Their responses to these pressures are reflected in several trends on the other side of the philanthropic table, including the following:

- Many foundations are examining their grant guidelines—their statements about what they will and won't fund—and are more carefully defining their specific interests and areas they will support; for many the list of areas or types of grants they will not make is growing longer and the list of what they will support is shrinking. For example: fewer funders are willing to provide operating dollars or deficit reduction dollars; there is more interest in funding defined types of programs or projects (often those with time limitations on them); there is less willingness to provide start-up funds or to fund new organizations and needs; there is more emphasis on promoting collaborative efforts among nonprofits and avoiding duplication; there is more funding targeted to specific concerns including basic human needs; there is growing emphasis on evaluation of the impact of grants made—including having the applicant better define the evaluation method in

the proposal; and, generally, there is less interest in providing what the foundation views as "high-risk" grants—grants that may not show the desired return on investment for the foundation, or that may even result in unwanted publicity or worse.

- Beyond refinement of grant guidelines, there appears to be an increasing number of foundations that are specifying they want to receive a "letter of inquiry" (see Chapter 11 on approaches to foundations), a brief description of the organization and the program and activity for which support is being sought, rather than a full proposal. If the foundation believes the request is appropriate to its criteria and priorities (some of which may be stated and some of which may not be stated), it may then invite a full proposal.

- Some foundations are also increasingly resorting to "RFPs," Requests for Proposals, which are sent to selected organizations that the foundation believes have the capability of creating the defined program or service the foundation is interested in supporting.

- Other foundations have resorted to not accepting unsolicited proposals or requests for support and will only fund predefined organizations.

- Some foundations are encouraging collaborative and cooperative efforts within the nonprofit sector, in part to create greater efficiencies and prevent overlapping and duplication, and also to more effectively utilize their own funding resources.

Beyond these more obvious trends, there are also less obvious but equally important factors at work within foundations, especially those with staffs. As the volume of proposals increases, staff must resort to various techniques to keep their workloads under control. One way is to become more exacting in their proposal review process with emphasis on getting proposals out of the review process, whenever possible and appropriate. Thus some foundation staff may, as in the example cited earlier, give a complete review only to proposals from organizations they already know or recognize. Other staff may only need to see that the submitter has not done his or her homework—for example, by asking for a grant of $100,000 from a foundation that has never made a grant exceeding $25,000—in order to remove the proposal from the review process. Meetings may only be held with applicants when there is serious interest on the part of the foundation and the foundation staff in the organization and its work. Other reflections of the increasing volume of proposals and contacts can include phone calls not being returned, letters and other inquiries not being acknowledged, and standardized forms and application procedures being used; all of these are intended to better control the workload. In some foundations, the board may give staff members more power to turn down or return proposals that don't exactly match the foundation's interests. Some staffed foundations are also developing more structured systems to manage the influx of proposals. An example might be the hiring or designation of a "proposal coordinator" or person with a similar title and responsibilities to manage the initial processing of incoming requests to ensure that all required materials are included. This person may also be responsible for conducting a preliminary review of the proposal to ensure that it meets basic foundation guidelines and criteria.

Another approach taken by staffed foundations to help manage the workflow might include the foundation's board giving staff authority to make grants up to a specific level, thus taking some of the decision-making workload off the board's agendas. Another option might be to have board committees established and empowered to act on requests or approve grants up to a specified level, with the full board acting on requests or grants above the specified level. This process enables foundation boards to keep their agendas somewhat streamlined without resorting to more frequent meetings.

> As the volume of proposals increases, staff must resort to various techniques to keep their workloads under control.

Unstaffed foundations face similar challenges, but often on an even greater scale because the board members or individual(s) they designate must directly deal with the inflow of proposals and other correspondence while still carrying out their other jobs and activities. Unstaffed foundations, like their staffed counterparts, will probably be increasingly specific about what they will and won't fund and will become more closed to unsolicited requests for support. Inquiry letters will be a more accepted method to control workflow. Some, including a growing number of the smaller foundations, may find refuge from the flood of proposals in the "RFP" or "no unsolicited requests" techniques mentioned above. Others may even find unlisted phone numbers and post office boxes as effective ways to stay out of fund raisers' spotlights.

Societal Trends

The bigger societal trends are also affecting the foundation world. While on one hand cutbacks—real and possible—in public funding are driving more nonprofits to seek support from organized philanthropy and other sources, these same cutbacks, coupled with changes in the economy away from a long-standing industrial/manufacturing base, mean there are growing needs that are not being fully met. One of the great traditions of American society continues to be the growth of the voluntary sector to meet special and unmet needs. Remember these numbers? There are, according to *Giving USA 1995*, 1,118,131 organizations classified as exempt by the Internal Revenue Service. Of these, 575,690 are classed as 501(c)(3) "charities" (Kaplan 1995, 30). Many of these organizations have been created to respond to new or growing needs in society. For example, 15 years ago there were no organizations for people with AIDS; now there are many. Organizations serving the homeless, those assisting victims of family violence, special interest advocacy organizations, and other groups are only the tip of the nonprofit iceberg. Beyond these are the growing numbers of association foundations, policy research centers, environmental groups, etc. If there is a cause, a concern, an issue, or a need, there is probably—or will probably soon be—a nonprofit organization created to focus attention on it, serve those in need, or help resolve it.

Somewhat counter to the dynamics of the nonprofit sector is the fact that foundations are often not great risk-takers when they are considering investing their philanthropic dollars in the sector. They may be slow to change their funding priorities in response to new and emerging needs; they may not want to risk investing in the new organizations that are created in response to changing and growing needs. At times, they may even feel that their grants, even though seemingly large to many outsiders, can have little or no impact on an issue, need, or concern. A few may admit that their grants, focused on a particular area or need, have had little impact or have created only minimal change. Others may declare "victory" over a cause or issue and then move on to change or refocus their funding priorities. Still others may attempt to continue to fund the same or similar organizations; these organizations themselves may be changing in response to emerging or new needs.

The foundation world is, like many other sectors of society, facing new and growing pressures. And, also like other parts of society, the thousands of foundations that make up organized philanthropy are responding to these pressures in varied ways. Some foundations are—and probably will continue to be—innovators and activists. They will seek to do more than simply make grants in response to requests. They may convene organizations focused on particular needs and issues to better coordinate their efforts, projects, and programs. They may convene experts and publish reports on new and emerging trends in society. They may resort to the RFP process to help stimulate new approaches to growing needs or changes. They may bring together the public and private sectors, including nonprofits and businesses, to develop common solutions to major problems, or even just to improve communication. They may create and spin

> **Foundations are often not great risk-takers when investing their philanthropic dollars in the sector.**

off new organizations to meet new needs. They may meet with other foundations with common concerns to develop more systematic approaches to their funding of specific areas. All of these are things that foundations have actually done over many years, and will continue to do. Some foundations have learned that they can effectively play a variety of roles: community leader, catalyst, analyst, convener, advocate for change, and builder of public awareness. While these and other roles are often seen as the sole preserve of the larger foundations with the clout of sometimes massive amounts of funds, even some of the smaller foundations have realized they can take a more activist role.

But many foundations will continue to play more traditional roles as primarily funders of the nonprofit sector. This, too, is appropriate because the foundation world is almost as varied as the rest of our society, and it is this variety that gives philanthropy its rich and changing texture. Philanthropy will continue to thrive and grow only with diversity and change. Yes, there have been abuses in the foundation world, as there have been in almost all areas of life. And yes, some regulation of this sector is needed. But laws should also encourage the growth of foundations and permit the great variety of foundation types and models. We need "liberal" and "conservative" foundations; we need "activist" and more passive foundations; we need large and small foundations; we need foundations that are organized and operated according to a number of different models; and, as even the most conservative of politicians have observed, we need more foundations.

There are still other trends that will probably have impacts on the foundation world, but in what ways remain to be seen. One of these trends is the growing diversification of American society and culture. It is almost universally recognized that over the next 10 to 20 years in many areas of the country minorities will become majorities. Different ethnic and cultural traditions have different views of how society should—or even if it should—respond to specific needs and different concepts of philanthropy. As diversity continues to increase and impact all segments of society, what will be the effects of these differing views on the nonprofit sector and on organized philanthropy? Will some needs currently seen as critical be seen as less important than other needs? For example, in some cultural traditions, people with mental or physical disabilities may be more likely to be cared for in the home than in the present predominant U.S. culture. Philanthropy is also viewed differently in different cultures. Some traditions, for example, include family-based philanthropy directed first toward members of the extended family who may be in need or who may require assistance with a business or other venture. On the other hand, Charles Dickens in *Bleak House* had a character, Mrs. Jellyby, who practiced "telescopic philanthropy": she pursued philanthropy in the furthest reaches of the world, while at the same time neglecting her own family. How will these traditions affect the foundation world? Traditions of the nonprofit sector and organized philanthropy may be adopted and adapted by those from other cultures. But will this be the case, or will the sector and the foundation world be changed into some new and very different variation? Will the emphasis shift to less formal, less organized approaches to meeting and supporting needs and concerns?

There is also another societal trend that many are saying will have a major impact on philanthropy and the nonprofit sector: baby boomers. Baby boomers are usually defined as those born between 1946 and 1960 who represent a substantial bulge in the population stream due to their numbers. According to *The 1996 World Almanac and Book of Facts,* a 1993 analysis shows that people between the ages of 35 and 54 (this includes some people born immediately prior to the baby boom period) constitute 27.1 percent of the total U.S. population, by far the single largest group in terms of numbers (391). As the entire population ages, the median age increased from 30 to 34 between 1960 and 1994; the number of people aged 65 or older ". . . rose from 17 million, or one in 11 . . . in 1960 to 33 million, or 1 in 8, in 1994" (382). People 65 years of age and older represented 12.1 percent of the population in 1993 (391). These older adults to a large extent represent the parents of the baby boom generation.

So what does this information have to do with the philanthropic world and the nonprofit sector? As older Americans pass on, they will be leaving their savings, investments, other property, etc., to their children. A recent article in the *Washington Post* cited a study done three years ago by Cornell University economists Robert Avery and Michael Rendall, which estimated that the "World War II generation" (people reaching maturity during the immediate pre-War and World War II period) have an estimated $10 trillion in assets. Other studies cited in the article put the figure at $7 trillion (Thompson 1996). The fact remains that there is starting to be an enormous "transfer of wealth" to the baby boom generation, which may substantially impact all aspects of philanthropy and the nonprofit sector over the next 10 to 20 years.

The *Washington Post* article cited another directly related trend as well: the investment of assets by members of the World War II generation in organized philanthropy. Through careful and conservative approaches to their finances, and through the appreciation of the value of their homes, investments, and other assets, many members of this generation have substantial net worths. Frequently, they may not even realize the value of everything they hold; the house they purchased in the late 1940s or early 1950s for $10,000 or $20,000 may now be worth $200,000 or $300,000—and the mortgage may have been paid off many years ago. The stocks they acquired through their company's stock purchase option plan (often used by companies instead of a retirement plan) for a modest payroll deduction may now be worth many hundreds of thousands of dollars. Thus the total net worth of these individuals, most of whom have been characterized as "middle class," may exceed $1 million!

But what of the younger generation who will inherit this wealth? There is conflicting information about the extent of their charitable interests versus their self-interests. Will the baby boomers and their immediate descendants be as generous and concerned for others as those in previous generations who have founded and maintained organized philanthropy? Or will the funds be directed to the establishment of personal wealth and family security, especially with the growing uncertainties about the economic future? For example, growing concerns over the viability of health care and social security systems may encourage people to retain their inherited or acquired wealth as personal insurance against an uncertain future.

Despite the considerable uncertainty about what will happen as the transfer of wealth accelerates, there is little denying that nonprofits and organized philanthropy both have their collective eyes on this prize. Foundations—especially community foundations (see Chapter 5 for a discussion of community foundations)—are focusing more attention on getting people of the World War II generation to understand the benefits of organized philanthropy. Nonprofits are promoting the advantages of planned giving to members of this generation, many of whom are already generous and long-time donors to a variety of causes. Efforts are also underway at many levels to build a sense of community service and philanthropy into the education of younger generations in the hope that they, too, will become the volunteers, leaders, and donors of the future. In part, these efforts are based on the concern that the growth of working families and single parents, as opposed to the traditional and now obsolete breadwinner-model family, will continue to decrease the potential for volunteer involvement in the nonprofit sector. But there is also a distinct fear that recent scandals and negative press in the nonprofit sector are turning people away from their traditional charitable inclinations.

Public Policy and Its Impact

Finally, or maybe not finally, there is the impact of politics on organized philanthropy and the nonprofit sector. Actual or proposed government cutbacks in funding of nonprofits have already been discussed in terms of shifting the fund-raising focus to private sector support. Politics has entered into the equation as claims are made that private sector contributions and volunteerism can make up for the cutbacks in public funding. Both sides, in making their arguments for or against this possibility, often sight the same figures on the growth of charitable giving in the United States. The side claiming that the private sector can make up for the cutbacks says that much public funding is wasted on large administrative bureaucracies, es-

pecially for federal programs, and that this waste, coupled with greater private giving and use of volunteers, can accommodate the changes. The cry is "We need to end the welfare state."

The other side claims that the numbers just don't add up, and the changes being sought are not just fiscal but are systemic. This side states that many of the services and most of the cash payments to those with the most basic needs are funded by public monies, and that these could not be sustained with private support, even if there were enormous growth. The cry is "We need to keep the safety net."

In mid-1996 the Twentieth Century Fund issued a report entitled "What Charity Can and Cannot Do," written by Julian Wolpert. The press release accompanying the release of the report stated:

> The conclusion seems inescapable. Charitable nonprofit organizations lack the resources to sustain the nation's poorest residents even at minimal safety-net levels. They do not transfer substantial cash payments to low-income people except purely for maintenance needs during local emergencies. Nor can they carry out such large-scale services as sustaining mentally and physically handicapped people. The type of direct bonding with the needy and the handicapped envisioned in the conservative agenda is probably not feasible in the short run even if its virtues could be established. The intensity of personal attention required would be too costly if provided by nonprofit professional staffs, whereas voluntary activity is certainly not at a level, nor could it be beefed up enough in the short run, to cope even with current needs.

The report, drawing from other sources, including the *Nonprofit Almanac, 1992–1993: Dimensions of the Independent Sector* (1992), and Virginia A. Hodgkinson et al., *The Impact of Federal Budget Proposals upon the Activities of Charitable Organizations and the People They Serve* (1995), goes on to give some significant information on the size and support of the nonprofit sector:

Charitable organizations now account for about 7% of national income and about 6% of total U.S. employment. Their revenues and expenditures are considerable ($350 billion a year), equivalent to about one-seventh of the combined spending of federal, state, and local government. As recently as the mid-1950s, charitable organizations raised 70 percent of their income from private donations. Now, only about 9 percent of their revenue comes from individual, corporate, and foundation gifts and donations. Thirty-seven percent comes from government grants and contracts and 54 percent from dues, fees, and other charges. Significantly, then, they get more than half of their revenue from paying clients. Government funding as a share of total revenues accounts for 36 percent in health services, 17 percent in education, 42 percent in social and legal services, and 11 percent in the arts (Wolpert 1996, 9).

What will happen with all of this is anybody's guess. But there are strong indications that, as one side claims, the numbers just don't add up: even massive increases in charitable giving and volunteerism cannot make up for the needs created by the actual and proposed federal cutbacks and other shifts in the business of charity, planned or underway. As the report also points out, discussions of flat tax systems would, if implemented, also impact charitable giving by eliminating many of the current tax advantages that currently exist for contributions.

Overall, organized philanthropy is in a state of rapid change that reflects the greater society. Changes in the foundation and corporate philanthropy worlds will result from the internal dynamics of the sector, but also from the broader trends and issues in society. Beyond these, there will be the impact of perceptions of organized philanthropy and its responsiveness to the needs of society by those who define public policy. Scandals, actual or perceived, misuse of philanthropic dol-

> **Overall, organized philanthropy is in a state of rapid change that reflects the greater society.**

lars, perceived unresponsiveness to needs and change, and so on, may result in new laws that directly regulate organized philanthropy or that directly affect it through changes in tax legislation or other legislation at the federal, state, and local levels. The tax advantages of forming private or community foundations may not always be there; will people continue to form foundations if this is the case? But legislation and tax law may also become more favorable to organized philanthropy and the nonprofit sector if the trend toward less government involvement in direct service delivery and support continues. Public officials may want to free up the sector to better carry out its business and to grow.

So there is obviously much uncertainty and the next few years will be exciting and challenging times for the world of organized philanthropy and the nonprofit sector. The key word will be change—the one constant—and the success of individual nonprofits and foundations will, to a considerable extent, depend upon their abilities to change and adapt.

References

AAFRC Trust for Philanthropy. 1995. *Giving USA Special Report: Trends in Corporate Philanthropy*. New York: AAFRC Trust for Philanthropy.

Kaplan. A., ed. 1995. *Giving USA 1995*. New York: AAFRC Trust for Philanthropy.

The 1996 World Almanac and Book of Facts. F. Famighetti, ed. 1995. Mahwah, NJ: World Almanac Books.

Plinio, A. and J. Scanlan. 1986. *Resource Raising: The Role of Non-Cash Assistance in Corporate Philanthropy*. Washington, DC: Independent Sector.

Thompson, T. "The Changing Face of Philanthropy." *The Washington Post*, 31 March 1996, sec. A–1, A–17.

Wolpert, J. 1996. "What Charity Can and Cannot Do." New York: The Twentieth Century Fund.

Chapter 4

Private Foundations: What You Need to Know

Facts and Figures

Most foundations are private foundations. And most private foundations are small and unstaffed. In fact, if you had to pinpoint the "typical" foundation, it would probably have assets of less than $1 million, have a board consisting of family members of the donor or founder, have no staff, and make grants to local agencies that were supported by the donor in his or her lifetime. Based upon an approximately 5 percent payout, yearly grants would probably total about $50,000. According to the fifth edition of *Foundation Giving,* some key facts to know about the depth and breadth of the foundation world are:

- Of the known foundations, only about 25 percent (10,000 or less) have assets of more than $1 million.

- The foundations with more than $1 million in assets in 1994 accounted for 97 percent of all assets and 87 percent of total foundation giving.

- In 1994 there were approximately 2,290 foundations with staff; if there are approximately 40,000 foundations, only about 6% have any staff at all, and this includes foundations with part-time staffs.

- The total number of foundation staff members in the United States, including full-time and part-time staff, is estimated to be about 10,000–12,000 people.

- The assets of foundations have continued to grow, with actual growth of about 115 percent in constant dollars since 1980. Some foundations have grown more rapidly than others, with some doubling their assets over the past four to five years (The Foundation Center 1995, 1–2).

Diversity of Foundations

Private foundations share one common characteristic (in addition to meeting the Internal Revenue Service requirements to be classed as a foundation and having a board of directors or a board of trustees): they are diverse! It is very difficult to define "typical" foundations in terms of how they function and what they do beyond the mostly statistical description provided above (which discusses what may be more accurately called the "average" foundation). People often tend to describe private foundations as "big" or "small" based upon the assets they hold or possibly the size of grants actually made. Other times foundations are described as "liberal" or "conservative;" this is usually based upon the types of organizations and causes the foundations will or won't fund. Some foundations have been called "open" while others are called "closed," depending upon their willingness to do such things as meet, accept proposals from previously unsupported organizations, or change their guidelines in response to new and emerging needs. Other terms I have heard used to describe foundations include: "friendly" and "unfriendly," "structured" and "loose," "easy" and "difficult" (or even "impossible"), or "helpful" and "unhelpful."

The categories given above tend only to reflect the responses of people to the foundations' treatment of them and their organization and thus are usually subjective. In fact, conservative foundations have funded liberal organizations. Small foundations can make large grants by limiting the number of grants or resorting to multiple-year payments of their grants. Some foundations are open when there are clear mutual interests between the foundation's purposes and an organization, but more closed to organizations where this is not the case. One person's friendly foundation is another person's unfriendly foundation (it may depend on the foundation staff person met with, the amount of homework done by the organization prior to meeting with the foundation, or other factors).

Because these types of classifications tend to be subjective, I prefer to use three broad categories when thinking about private foundations. Even these are not mutually exclusive, but I find them helpful classifications that are based upon something more specific than how the staff treat people or whether or not a grant was received. These categories are also somewhat more objective in that they are based upon each foundation's purposes, actual grant making, and/or governing structure.

I. General Purpose Foundations

General purpose foundations are those foundations that, in both their purposes (areas of interest or guidelines) *and* their actual grant making fund a broad variety of organizations, needs, and causes. This clearly does not mean they will fund everything and anything. General purpose foundations, like many other foundations, usually have clear guidelines or statements about their funding priorities; the difference is their priorities are usually

> General purpose foundations are those that fund a broad variety of organizations, needs, and causes.

very broad, especially when compared to "special purpose foundations" (see below). General purpose foundations may be able to have a wide focus because of a substantial base of assets, but this is not always the case. Those that do have a large asset base can "do whatever they want"—they have considerable flexibility in their grant making due to the amount of money they have for grants each year. Some general purpose foundations may not have substantial assets but reflect the broad interests of their board members or their staffs. Again, the key to whether or not a given foundation is "general purpose" is *both* their areas of interest and what they actually do with their money (also see Chapter 8 for a further discussion of these two areas). I once ran across a small New York foundation that had as its purposes "To promote world peace, nuclear disarmament, and international cooperation," but all of their grants went to several small local human service and youth organizations, usually for operating support.

Among the largest foundations, The Ford Foundation is an example of what I class as a general purpose foundation. Ford has defined very broad interest categories and funds within those categories. It also undertakes new areas of funding in response to changing needs and priorities. And, at times, it will fund areas and organizations that are new or don't quite fit its broad categories. Other foundations also can fit into this general purpose category.

II. Special Purpose Foundations

Special purpose foundations are those foundations that have defined or selected a few primary areas of interest for their focus and actual grant making. A special purpose foundation might indicate its only or primary interest is in supporting cancer research, or, somewhat more broadly, agencies serving children and youth. Special purpose foundations might also have defined three or four major "program areas" toward which they will direct their grant making, such as: "prevention of violence against women and children, homeless families, medical care for the otherwise underserved, and the juvenile court system." The overall concept is that the focus of the foundation and its grant making is more narrow than that of the general purpose foundation. Many foundations already fall into this category; given the trends cited above, it is likely more and more foundations will move into this category as they attempt to more carefully define what they will—and won't—fund.

III. Family Foundations

A family foundation is defined as a foundation primarily directed by members of the family of the individual(s) who established the foundation or whose assets became the basis for the foundation. The usual way to identify a family foundation in your research is to look at the board of directors or board of trustees. If the board list reads something like this: "Sally Smith, James Smith, Barbara Smith, Byron Smith, and Anne Smith-Jones," it is, most probably, a family foundation. But other configurations might include the family attorney, a business partner of the founder, etc., in addition to family members. Most family foundations are derived from a single source of wealth, the assets (stocks, the family business, property, etc.) of the original donor(s).

It is important to remember that this category is not entirely separate from the general purpose and special purpose foundation categories listed above. A family foundation can also be a general purpose foundation, or, more likely, a special purpose foundation. This category is generally based upon the governance structure of the foundation rather than the purposes and grant making. However, it is a very useful category because it can give important clues about the interests and operations of the family foundation.

Family foundations, especially when they are newly established, often focus their purposes and grant making on the traditional interests of the donor(s) and the family. Thus if the founder and the founder's spouse were primarily interested in

and supported the arts through their personal contributions, the foundation established would probably direct much of its grant making to the arts. If the founder(s) or original donors had interests in national organizations or international issues, the foundation's interests would probably follow these patterns. Guidelines, at least initially, will be defined that reflect these traditional interests. To some extent, the process for the establishment of the original family foundation guidelines is often backward, as compared to the process for establishment of the mission and guidelines at other foundations; for family foundations the guidelines are frequently derived from giving patterns rather than the reverse. At times, the original donor may have clearly indicated to the family verbally or in writing that he or she wanted to establish a foundation, or may have even drawn up the basic documents and actually established the foundation. Sometimes the original donor also had in mind, or clearly specified, the purposes of the foundation. But other times these are steps the board must take after the donor has passed away.

As the statistics above show, most foundations are family foundations. And almost all foundations, except community foundations, started out as family foundations. Even many of the largest private foundations in the country were established by and, in their early years, run by, an individual donor and his or her family. The Ford Foundation no longer has a member of the Ford family on the board of directors, but for most of its history there was at least one Ford on the board.

Family foundations, as the statistics also demonstrate, are not usually staffed. A board member, the family attorney, an employee of the company owned by the family, or a trust officer of a bank may be given the task of sorting through the proposals, handling correspondence, and the other day-to-day tasks of the foundation. If there is a staff person, he or she may be employed by the family or its company and may have a portion of the work time allocated to the foundation and a portion of his or her salary paid by the foundation. But, again, most family foundations are not staffed.

One of the interesting observations about family foundations is that they can evolve and change over time. As the years pass, the board may have fewer and fewer family members on it; they may have been replaced by friends and other business associates, community leaders, and others who no longer have the close ties to the original donor(s) and founders. Or the board may now include several third and fourth generation members of the original family. In both cases the ties to the original founders and donor(s) and their philanthropic interests will not be as strong. The foundation board may begin to consider funding other needs and causes rather than the traditional interests of the donor(s) and founders. New needs may have arisen since the establishment of the foundation, and these board members may believe they should be more responsive to these emerging needs and concerns. One result may be a review and redefinition of the foundation's mission and guidelines, with the revised versions allowing for the new needs and broader interests of the board members. Grant making may expand beyond the traditional areas or may be focused in an entirely new direction.

Another way family foundations can change is to more narrowly focus their guidelines and grant making. Sometimes the original donor(s) or founders had very broad philanthropic interests and the foundation attempts to parallel these in its grant making. Over the years there may be a growing recognition by the board that the resources of the foundation are being spread very thin and may not be making much of a difference in the funded organizations. At this stage the board of the family foundation may decide to focus their funding on certain selected needs, causes, or even organizations. In this sense the family foundations are moving from being general purpose to special purpose foundations, or are moving from special purpose foundations to "very special purpose" foundations.

Another factor that might cause a family foundation to evolve is asset growth. The foundation, when established, might have had a very small asset base; this would limit its grant-making ability, since grants are usually made based upon the earnings on the assets held by the foundation. The most logical and easiest thing to do in terms of grant making is to fund the traditional interests and organizations supported by the donor(s) and found-

ers. But over the years the assets may have grown through diversification of the holdings (usually stocks and bonds with some cash instruments), wise investing, corporate buy-outs, and other reasons. The family foundation may find it can continue to support the traditional causes and needs, but it can also do other things. Again the board may decide to change the mission and guidelines; in these cases the family foundation may move from a special purpose foundation toward becoming a general purpose foundation, or at least a "broader special purpose" foundation.

Another factor that can influence the grant making and purposes of a family foundation is the hiring of staff, especially when the foundation was previously unstaffed. Whereas board members may have previously primarily acted as processors of incoming proposals and may have seen their role as measuring whether or not a particular proposal met the traditional grant-making interests of the donor(s), the arrival of staff can significantly change the dynamics of the foundation. Board members may now be somewhat more free to examine the overall policies and direction of the foundation. They also may see the staff person as a resource who can more readily tell them "what is going on out there" in the community they serve. Meetings with potential grantees may now become part of the proposal review process, and the staff member of the foundation may become an advocate for new or emerging groups in the community that need support. Of course, the staff person may be only part time or may be seen by the board of the family foundation as merely a processor of the paperwork. But a staff member can also be a much more active player and change agent in the life of the foundation.

Private foundations, to repeat a point made earlier, exhibit great diversity in many areas, including:

- geographic area served (very local to international)

- board composition (family members to national and international leaders from many fields)

- staffing (unstaffed, in most cases, but some with staffs of over 200 people)

- assets held (several thousand dollars to billions of dollars)

- grant size (grants ranging from a few dollars to millions of dollars)

- grant-making interests (a few specified organizations to almost any type of organization)

- procedures (highly informal to very formal and structured)

- published information available (none, in the majority of cases, but very detailed in some cases)

- permanency, with most private foundations primarily making grants out of assets that are intended to be held forever ("in perpetuity"), but some seeking to "go out of business" by dispersing all of their assets as grants, often within a specific time frame

These are the more factual differences among private foundations. The more intangible descriptive factors are based upon individual experiences, but may include characteristics such as openness, liberal versus conservative, etc., as listed above. Both the diversity of foundations and the very fact that individual foundations do change who they are and what they do are clear indicators that approaches to foundations must be highly individualized, thoroughly researched, and designed to match the interest and needs of the grant-seeking organization with the mission and purposes of the grant-making foundation. It is fatal to assume that all foundations are alike, operate in the same manner, make their decisions solely based on their guidelines, or will fund your organization "because it is deserving."

Reference

The Foundation Center. 1995. *Highlights of the Foundation Center's Foundation Giving, 1995 Edition.* New York: The Foundation Center.

Chapter 5

Community Foundations: What You Need to Know

A Brief History

In the early 1900s there was already a growing concern on the part of some civic leaders that the existing patterns of giving through trusts and estates, and possibly the newly emerging concept of a private foundation, was flawed (the first U.S. charitable foundation was the Carnegie Corporation, founded in 1911 by Andrew Carnegie). An 1880 British publication *The Dead Hand* by Sir Arthur Hobhouse stated the problem: large amounts of charitable money were being directed by the wishes of deceased persons, despite the rapidly changing needs of society (Nielsen 1985, 243–245). A few saw the need for a new form of organized philanthropy that would be more responsive to the changing needs of society as well as bring together many individual funds in a way that would better benefit communities.

The leader of the community trust movement, as it subsequently became known, was Frederick Goff, a Cleveland banker (242–264). (See Nielsen for a more complete discussion of the evolution and development of community foundations). Goff's idea, first implemented in Cleveland in 1914, was to bring together the banking and civic leadership of communities in a partnership to establish and manage many charitable trusts. The banks would manage the funds and a committee or board of civic leaders would make the grant decisions and oversee the operation of the foundation. Donors would have the purposes and intents of their gifts honored as long as it was practical, but the foundation's board or committee could change the purposes and use of these funds in response to changing community needs. These organizations became known as community trusts or community foundations.

Common Characteristics

Community foundations share some common characteristics. These include:

- They serve a specific geographic area. The area can be a city, a metropolitan area or county, a state, or even a region. There have been some attempts to establish national community foundations. Sometimes, depending upon the wishes of the donor, grants may be made outside the specified area or the community foundation may have some subsidiary or associated community foundations that serve other areas, but generally there is a specific area served.

- They have broad philanthropic purposes. Almost all community foundations have the potential to fund almost any type of 501(c)(3) nonprofit organization within their area. Thus the community foundation can potentially fund social service/human service agencies, cultural institutions, health care agencies, educational institutions, environmental groups, public policy centers, and other organizations in the geographic area it serves. However, there may be restrictions on the ability of the foundation to actually fund these organizations depending upon both the availability of funds for the community foundation and the specific types of funds it holds (see below).

- The assets (permanent funds or funds held by the foundation "forever") and the other financial holdings of the community foundation are made up of a number of funds, primarily given by individuals through estates, trusts, direct transfers, or other means.

Community foundations, from the inception of the Cleveland Foundation, have played a much more activist role than traditional private foundations in the areas they serve. Soon after it was founded, the Cleveland Foundation created panels of leading experts who undertook studies of Cleveland's social welfare and school systems and made recommendations for major reforms. This highly public effort as well as the involvement of the community and financial institution leadership soon attracted major donors to the Cleveland Foundation, and the community foundation movement has not looked back since.

Goff became the Johnny Appleseed of community foundations, tirelessly spreading the idea to other major cities. By 1920 there were 19 community foundations; by the 75th anniversary of the

---

Community foundations have played a much more activist role than traditional private foundations in the areas they serve.

---

founding of the first community foundation there were an estimated 300, with 62 being founded during the decade of the 1980s (Scanlan 1989, 3). By 1995 there were an estimated 420 community foundations (personal conversation with Council on Foundations staff, January 14, 1996). Some community foundations are now among this country's largest foundations, regardless of type, in terms of their asset bases. Others are among the smallest of foundations and may even exist only on paper with no actual funds. Many, regardless of size, are actively promoting themselves to potential donors and, in some of their fund-raising efforts, may even be directly competitive with other nonprofits in the geographic area they serve.

The Basic Model and Variations

What is it that has made community foundations the fastest-growing type of organized philanthropy? There are some specific tax advantages to giving to a community foundation, as opposed to setting up a private foundation, but it is probable that other unique features have drawn donors to community foundations. One distinct advantage to a potential donor is the ability of the community foundation to provide management and administration of the donor's funds; if the donor were to establish a private foundation rather than elect to give to the community foundation, he or she would be responsible for ensuring all forms, registrations, etc., were taken care of, and he or she (plus the board) would be responsible for processing proposals, handling grant payments, and other activities normally carried out by a foundation. Sooner or later staff might have to be hired, an office found, equipment purchased, and so on. Especially for those who are philanthropically minded but who have somewhat limited funds (as compared to those held by large private foundations), the community foundation enables a person to have his or her own "foundation" without many of the headaches associated with the establishment of a private foundation.

Community foundations consist of an assortment of individual funds. Funds are left to or given to the community foundation primarily by individual donors through estates, trusts, direct gifts of cash or other assets, or other means. At the time the funds are turned over to the community foundation, the donor (or his or her estate or through other documentation) specifies how the funds are to be used by the foundation (see below for a more detailed explanation of types of funds held by community foundations). The donor or the instruments of transfer usually specify the name of the fund, which becomes part of the "corpus" or permanent assets of the community foundation. A community foundation can hold hundreds of funds under its umbrella. The donor may also specify which financial institution is to maintain the funds. The earnings on these assets become the source for the grants made by the community foundation, much like the operation of a private foundation or corporate foundation with its own assets. The community foundation usually assesses a fee on each fund it maintains; in the larger foundations this fee helps pay all or a portion of the operating costs of the community foundation. Some community foundations also have special "administrative funds," which are part of their permanent assets and the total income is used for the operating costs of the foundations.

There are several variations on this basic model. For example, some community foundations have "pass through" funds that they administer but which the donor has specified are to be totally distributed to one or more organizations rather than held as part of the permanent assets of the community foundation. Some community foundations may hold and maintain the permanent endowment funds for other agencies; the advantage to the agencies is the administrative responsibilities are with the foundation, but the agencies still receive the income on their funds. Some community foundations have funds that may serve a variety of purposes, but are "time limited" and must be totally distributed at the end of some number of years; these fall somewhat in between "pass through" funds and permanent funds.

Types of Funds

Generally, all funds held by community foundations fall into one of four major categories based upon how the earnings are to be distributed.

Designated Funds: These are funds for which the donor or donors have specified the earnings are to be distributed to a specific list of agencies each year. Usually, the instruments establishing designated funds specify that "X percent of the yearly earnings are to be distributed to the A Agency, Y percent to the B and C agencies, and Z percent to the D, E, and F agencies" or similar language. Some designated funds may specify dollar amounts (such as "$5,000 of the yearly income or earnings is to be distributed to each of the following agencies") rather than percents; or a combination of dollar amounts and percents may be used. The obvious concern when only dollar amounts are specified is what happens with the excess earnings on the funds, if no other purpose is given. In some designated funds the excess may be used at the discretion of the foundation, thus meaning the particular fund is both designated and restricted or unrestricted.

For the community foundation, designated funds are usually an administrative matter, with no need for the recipient agencies to submit proposals (unless the instrument establishing the fund so specifies). However, if one or more of the specified agencies closes its doors permanently, the community foundation may redesignate the income to other agencies that serve similar purposes or needs. Sometimes the original document establishing the fund at the community foundation includes language enabling the foundation to do this; at other times the foundation may have to go to court to undertake the change. There also have been court cases by agencies against community foundations based upon the agency's belief that the essential focus of their services has not changed, while the community foundation believes the focus has changed enough to redirect the income from the designated funds to other agencies.

Restricted Funds: Restricted funds are those funds held by the foundation for which the donor or donors have specified some purpose but have not specified particular agencies to receive the earnings on the funds. The statement of purpose might be something like: "Income from the Alan B. Smith Fund is to be used toward agencies and programs that assist disabled children" or "Income from the Jane B. Jones Fund is to be used toward cancer research." The fund's purpose is restricted in some way to particular types of agencies or particular needs or causes, but it is up to the community foundation to determine which agencies or organizations actually receive the grants. The foundation must also be careful to ensure, as much as possible, that the intentions of the donor or donors are honored.

Sometimes, especially with older restricted funds, the restrictions themselves may become obsolete. For example, the foundation where I worked had a very old restricted fund that was for the purpose of "promoting the humane slaughter of packing house animals . . ." in Chicago. With the closing of the stockyards, the original purposes of this fund could no longer be met. Income from the fund is now used for organizations concerned with finding homes for stray and abandoned animals in the city, such as the Humane Society.

At other times the wording of the restriction itself can become a concern to the community foundation. I was once reviewing the restrictions on one fund and found it was worded something like this: "The income from this fund is to be used toward support of agencies that serve blind, emotionally disturbed, and orphaned children." When I reread this restriction a few times, I decided to call our attorney to see if the children served by the agencies had to fit all three categories at the same time, or if, for example, we could still meet the restriction by making grants to an agency that served only blind children, but not ". . . blind, emotionally disturbed, orphaned children." After some checking by the attorney, I was assured that the use of commas in the original document establishing the fund allowed us to fund agencies serving one or another of the three categories. At first glance this may seem a silly concern; however, community foundations have to be very careful and our attorney assured me, after some research, this was a legitimate issue!

Knowing if a community foundation has restricted funds can be a key part of your organization's strategy for approaching the foundation. It is frequently a good idea to ask a community foundation staff member when meeting or speaking to him or her by phone if the foundation has any restricted funds for which your agency might

be eligible. At times, some community foundations have difficulty finding agencies or organizations that might be eligible to receive the restricted funds, especially if the restrictions are fairly narrow. So, always be sure to ask about restricted funds, especially if the foundation's materials are not very clear about the purposes of the restricted funds.

Unrestricted Funds: Unrestricted funds are those funds which the donor or donors have stated in the instrument establishing the fund may be used in accordance with the general purposes of the community foundation. That is, grants may be made from the earnings on these funds as long as the grants are consistent with the mission and, usually, the geographic area served by the community foundation. These are the favorites of all the fund types held by community foundations because they give the most flexibility to meet changing and emerging community needs. For example, 20 years ago AIDS was not an issue anywhere in the U.S., but now many community foundations are funding AIDS-related organizations, in part because they have the flexibility with their unrestricted funds to do so. However, it is possible that some restricted funds might also be used for these purposes, depending upon the specific wording of the fund and how broadly or narrowly it can be interpreted.

Advised Funds: Advised funds are those for which the donor has created an advisory process for recommending distribution of the grants. Advised funds can have formal committees, which actually review proposals and submit their recommendations as to whether or not to fund particular requests to the decision-making body of the community foundation. Or the fund's advisors might be several family members who meet periodically with the board or staff of the community foundation to give the foundation a general sense of how they would like the earnings on the fund used. Advisors sometimes include the donor or donors, family members, friends, experts in the areas the donor or donors wish to support, the family attorney, and/or others. The advising process, therefore, can be very formal or very informal.

The key word to remember about advised funds is "advised." The advisors to the fund can only recommend or suggest. The community foundation legally has the right to either follow or not follow the suggestions and advice as to specific grants; the final decision making rests with the community foundation, not the advisors. Unless there are some special provisions, the fund is part and parcel of the foundation's permanent assets and cannot be taken back by the donor(s) or advisors if they do not like how the earnings are being used by the foundation.

Most community foundations have a mix of fund types. How much—or how little—flexibility each community foundation has in its grant making is, to a large extent, determined by both the size (dollar value of the assets) of each fund and by its particular type as well as the overall mix of funds. Thus a community foundation with total assets of $10 million on first observation might have the capability to make roughly $600,000 to $900,000 in grants every year. But if 90 percent of the funds it holds are designated to go to specific agencies, its actual grant-making ability (in terms of restricted, unrestricted, and advised funds) might only be in the range of $60,000–$90,000. After removing income from restricted funds that can't apply to your agency and income from advised funds where the foundation will usually attempt to follow the advice of those selected to provide it, the flexibility of the community foundation may be even more limited. So it is important to examine the information provided by the community foundation and to ask questions of the staff or board about the mix of funds and the flexibility of the foundation to make grants to agencies or organizations such as yours.

Overall, though, community foundations are an excellent potential funding resource for a variety of types of organizations. Even some regional and national organizations may be eligible for funding if they conduct programs or services within the service area of a particular community foundation. The largest community foundations (Cleveland, New York, Chicago, San Francisco, Boston, and others), because of their enormous base of assets and mix of fund types, have considerable flexibility to address, through their funding and other activities, new issues and needs, emerging organizations, and new programs as well as community crises and emergencies. These foundations even can create and spin off new organizations to meet specific needs and concerns. They can also undertake studies of community problems and issues, much as the Cleveland Foundation did at its inception, convene meetings of agencies and organizations to better coordinate services and programs, and carry out a number of proactive functions.

But, while the largest community foundations can use their staffs and dollar resources (which often give them enormous "clout") to do a variety of things, many of the smallest community foundations may be primarily focused on building their asset bases to a point where they can become viable. Achieving the necessary "critical mass" of assets and funds is often the central issue for these smaller foundations that must, of necessity, be on the front lines of fund-raising efforts in their communities.

One More Type of Foundation

In addition to community foundations, corporate foundations and giving programs, and private foundations, there is a fourth type of foundation that should be mentioned. This is a strange beast: the operating foundation. The operating foundation is, in its most basic form, set up to make grants to itself—to its own programs, projects, and services. Its grants may also be directed to individuals in the form of scholarships and fellowships, research grants, etc. The operating foundation is thus inward-focused, unlike the other types that, at least in principle, are outward-focused. The operating foundation probably has a narrow purpose, such as cancer research or medical education. It holds permanent assets, which produce income for its operations and its specific programs and projects. Some operating foundations also can and will make grants to other organizations, but only if these groups parallel the specific purpose of the foundation. If, in your research, you come across an operating foundation, check carefully to see if, in fact, it also makes grants to other organizations and whether your organization is eligible.

Factors Causing Change in Foundations

Overall, it is clear that the foundation world has two major characteristics: diversity and change. Foundations can range from the small family foundation, which is unstaffed and consistently gives to the same organizations the donors supported during their lifetimes, to the "mega-foundations" with large staffs, broad interests, and funding of groups and organizations all over the world. Even the major categories used in the past few chapters do not do full justice to the 40,000 plus foundations that now exist. For every example used, there are probably several exceptions, different models, and new ways of organizing and operating foundations.

In addition to diversity, the foundation world is characterized by change. Change applies to both the foundation world as a whole and to individual foundations, which themselves change over time. As of this writing, many foundations are currently experiencing rapid growth in their assets due to the unprecedented growth of the stock market. This growth can greatly increase the grant-making ability of the foundations and can enable them to expand beyond their traditional grant-making patterns into funding of new areas and concerns. But will this last? Or, by the time this book is published, will the entire picture be different and will the foundations need to contract their grant making due to shrinking assets?

Another area impacting change in the foundation world is tax law and legislation. Tax law and legislation can have substantial impacts on private, community, and corporate foundations and corporate giving programs. Tax laws can provide favorable or unfavorable benefits to those interested in establishing foundations; a law that decreases

> **Overall, it is clear that the foundation world has two major characteristics: diversity and change.**

the tax advantages of having a private foundation, for example, may encourage those looking at the possibility of establishing a smaller foundation to seek alternate arrangements, such as giving the funds to a community foundation or establishing a trust fund. Pending legislation, a scandal involving a foundation, and other factors can sometimes also discourage people from establishing foundations. In the corporate sector increased competition and bottom-line pressures can also lower corporate priorities related to giving programs and corporate foundations. In 1969 tax legislation specifically spelled out many previously unstated provisions applying to community foundations. These regulations required, in many cases, substantial alterations of fund agreements, control of funds, and accounting procedures, and changed the way most community foundations operated.

Accounting standards and procedures applicable to nonprofits generally, and to foundations in particular, can also cause major changes in the way foundations operate. Currently, there is considerable controversy about new accounting standards that are to be applied to all nonprofit organizations. Whereas it is not the intent of this book to discuss these changes, I will point out there was a similar controversy when I served on the staff of a community foundation. The controversy raged over the accounting industry's proposed change in the wording of the statement accompanying audits of nonprofit organizations, including foundations. The proposed wording was to become something like: "This audit was not conducted in accordance with generally accepted auditing standards." The intent of the accounting profession was to state that nonprofits did not generally meet the same standards applied to the business world. However, to the nonprofit world the statement was a red flag to current and potential donors, implying that there was some problem in the records and accounting of the organization. After considerable controversy, the proposed wording was dropped.

A final area that can have a major impact on the foundation world, especially community foundations, is general public perceptions of the nonprofit sector. This is especially true for community foundations because of their reliance on contributions from many sources. If the public sees and reads media coverage of misuse of funds by nonprofits, abuse of foundations' tax-exempt status, or other so-called scandals, there is generally less inclination to support foundations and their work. These perceptions usually change over time, but can affect the field.

References

Nielsen, W. 1985. *The Golden Donors*. New York: Truman Books.

Scanlan, E. ed. 1989. *Community Foundations at 75: A Report on the Status of Community Foundations*. Washington, DC: The Council on Foundations.

Chapter 6

Foundation Boards and Staffs: What They Do, How They Decide, and the ROI Factor

While there has been some earlier discussion of foundation boards, staff members, and internal operations, this chapter will go into much greater detail on the internal workings of foundations as well as some overall concepts that can help you better define your strategies. Again, it is important to remember that any time general principles and concepts are presented in this book, you need to test them out for each foundation you are interested in approaching. The great diversity of foundations can mean that the particular concept may have considerable, some, or no relevance to any particular foundation.

The Return on Investment Concept Revisited

At the very beginning of this book we discussed the Return on Investment (ROI) concept as it applied generally to donors. It is worth repeating some of the key points of that earlier discussion:

- Investors always are looking for a return on their investments. Each investor may have different objectives—short-term gains, long-term security, etc. Donors and donor prospects also have different "investment" objectives. For some, the return on their investment may be the feeling or belief they are helping others—those your organization serves. By contributing to your organization, another person may be fed for another day, a child may be saved from disease, a dance company will continue to perform, or a college will continue to provide a quality education. The dividends on their investments are the feelings associated with benevolence or a desire to thank the agency for benefits given to the donor.

- For other investors, the return on their investment may be more focused on themselves. There may be substantial tax benefits that help motivate them to give, or there may be other factors. Some donors, for example, have an "edifice complex"—the desire to see their names on buildings. Other donors want to show they can help change society in some way, or even demonstrate to their peers that they, too, have the charitable spirit. Some want to memorialize their families, or even themselves. This is not to be critical of the latter motivations for people to invest in nonprofit organizations, only to recognize that there are "things" people get in return for their investments. The dividends in giving are just less tangible than in many other kinds of investing and may be unique for each person.

Foundations and corporate giving programs generally expect different types of returns on their "investments" (gifts and grants) in nonprofit organizations, depending on several factors. The corporate "bottom line" emphasis was presented briefly in the section on corporate foundations and corporate giving programs, but will be repeated here with some further discussion. The basic approach below is to tie the particular types of foundations and giving programs to their specific ROIs.

The Corporate Foundation and Corporate Giving Program—Expected Returns

We have already discussed the rapidly growing emphasis of the corporate sector on bottom-line returns. The business climate here and worldwide is characterized by:

- very high levels of competition (some say "cutthroat competition")

- mergers, acquisitions, and take-overs

- rapidly changing markets and products

> Foundations and corporate giving programs generally expect different types of returns on their investments.

- increasing use of and reliance on technology at all levels

- greater public scrutiny and accountability, including greater media coverage

- high degrees of corporate insecurity and decreasing complacency about a company's place in the corporate world

- downsizing and cutbacks

- a changing regulatory climate

- greater emphasis on fiscal management and tight controls on expenses

- growing emphasis on defining more carefully the mission, strategic plans, and focus of each company

In short, companies are learning that they simply cannot continue to operate in the "same old way" that they always have. The upstart company, the small company with a better product, a better idea, or sometimes just better marketing, can quickly upset the larger company and even drive it into oblivion. Each company wants to maintain and improve its market advantage and enhance its rank in its particular area of products or services. Companies are still in business to make money for their owners, despite all that has been said about serving the greater public good. They can, through their corporate giving programs, foundations, non-cash contributions, and other means, still benefit the larger public. But, they must ask themselves more and more frequently, to what end?

The answer given in a growing number of cases, of course, is to benefit their own ends. Or, to put it another way, companies have moved from asking "How can we help them?" to "How can we help them and, in so doing, improve our bottom line?" Overall, corporate philanthropy in the last 10 or 15 years (at least in my view) has changed from a focus on benevolence that was separated from corporate profit motives to a focus on an ROI of directly improving profits. Corporate philanthropy has thus become one more means of building corporate profitability, rather than a separate "goodwill" function of the company.

Of course, this statement covers a multitude of good works and even some sins. Some companies still see their philanthropy as separate from the corporate bottom line. Funded corporate foundations, in many cases, still are primarily focused on the philanthropic motive rather than the profit motive. But the pressures on the corporate world are great and growing. It seems nearly inevitable that philanthropy and the bottom line will become more closely tied over the next decade.

This is not a criticism of the corporate world; it is merely a statement of the obvious. The challenge to the nonprofit sector is to recognize the pressures on the corporate world and the resulting pressures on corporate philanthropy and corporate views of their ROIs. It is the clever and creative nonprofits that will develop new ways to achieve "win-win" results in their approaches to companies for support. These nonprofits seek to create corporate partnerships where there is a clearly identified ROI to both parties. No longer is the nonprofit merely seeking funding for its own ends; it recognizes the corporate partner must also receive something from the transaction, and it has to be something more than "feeling good" or "helping others." In a strong sense the profits of the transaction, if well designed, accrue to both parties.

The Community Foundation—Expected Returns

Community foundations generally tend to be much more driven by their missions and the needs of the specific geographic area they serve than most other types of foundations. Board members and staff both play key roles in interpreting the mission and community needs as they carry out their respective functions. Overall, the community foundation's ROI is outward-focused in the sense that, by fulfilling its mission, the foundation will improve the lives of those in the community it serves. Community foundation boards and staffs generally seek to make their "investments" where they believe there is the most need and where there will be the greatest potential return to the community.

At the same time, to continue the investment analogy, they try to keep some sense of balance in their portfolio of investments, generally recognizing that funding, as much as possible, should be put into all of the areas that are part of the community: human service agencies, cultural organizations, educational institutions, health care agencies, etc. Religious agencies usually may be funded only for programs that provide services to people, regardless of their religious affiliations.

But how are the community's needs determined? Community foundations can do this in a number of ways. At one end of the spectrum is the formal needs-assessment process, such as that which was initiated by the very first community foundation, The Cleveland Foundation, at its inception. The community foundation may undertake this process itself or use outside resources, such as a local university, to carry out the process. The assessment is usually not focused on total needs of the community, but on one particular area, such as education, services for children, capital needs of area nonprofits, etc. The findings of the assessment process may result in the development of a special multiple-year grants program or grants initiative by the community foundation as well as other activities focused on addressing the problems and needs in that area. For example, if a study of services provided to poverty income level children determines there is considerable duplication of services and little coordination among agencies, the community foundation may bring together representatives of many of the agencies so that they can begin to work together on these issues. The community foundation "carrot" to help ensure the success of this process is its grants.

But the needs-assessment process is usually not as formal, except where the community foundation has both the staff and the resources to carry out a detailed assessment and/or sees a pattern in proposals it receives that indicates something more is going on in the community that needs to be looked at carefully. Often the process may consist

> It seems nearly inevitable that philanthropy and the bottom line for corporate giving will become more closely tied over the next decade.

of bringing together representatives from several agencies to discuss the needs they perceive in the community related to their services and programs. The community foundation may then seek to create a special grants program or focus, or may take other steps to help ensure needs are better met. Again, the "carrot" is the community foundation's potential grants.

Probably the most frequent way that community foundations determine needs is through an informal process based on actual proposals received and observations leading to a general sense of what is happening in the community. Boards and staffs of community foundations both can play important roles in this process, although there are great differences among community foundations as to how this occurs. Some boards rely on the staff to keep in touch with the needs of the community and to let them know when the staff see emerging needs or new areas for support. A staff person may perceive some emerging trends based upon his or her discussions with organizations or on proposals being sent to the community foundation. Other boards take a more proactive role and may direct the staff to explore specific areas or needs. Overall, the process is usually informal and not very structured, but the board and staff still come to some understanding of some areas the foundation needs to look at more closely and/or fund more extensively.

An example of how this more informal process can work and how a community foundation can respond follows:

During the late 1970s fuel prices began to increase, the gas crisis hit, and "energy conservation" became a watchword. At the time I was working at a community foundation. We soon noticed a number of agencies were applying for grants to repair outdated and inefficient heating equipment, better insulate their facilities, or save on energy costs in other ways. The foundation's director came up with the idea of a special "Energy Conservation Fund" to address these problems. The board was asked to allocate a grant from the unrestricted funds to establish the Energy Conservation Fund and approved the grant. The fund was established to provide grants and low-interest or no-interest loans for energy conservation measures by area non-

profits that owned their own facilities. The underlying principle was that the energy savings and resulting cost reductions would easily offset the loan payments. The community foundation staff hosted a meeting with staffs of several area private foundations to ask each to make grants to our foundation for the Energy Conservation Fund; several did so within the next few months. The staff of the community foundation also decided outside expertise was needed to carry out energy audits of those organizations that applied for grants so that the energy savings of the planned measures could be calculated as well as other energy conservation measures recommended. The local senior executive service corps was contacted and they located several retired individuals with engineering backgrounds and direct experience in energy systems and conservation; this group developed the energy audit system and provided the service to the nonprofits. Overall, the program was a great success and helped meet a major need in the geographic area served by the foundation.

But community foundations can also operate with a much more board-centered concept of their return on investment. That is, the specific likes and dislikes of the board or its individual members can drive the expected returns to the foundation. When community foundations operate in this manner, they are functioning much more like a family foundation (see below) as to the returns expected on their grants. Earlier in the book you read an example of where an irate board member almost single-handedly had a request for support turned down, primarily because of his personal beliefs about the applying organization. Community foundation board members individually or sometimes as a group can act from their own political (small "p") or personal self-interest rather than in accordance with the mission of the foundation or the needs of the community. This may happen in the case of a particular grant request or it may happen at some or even most board meetings. In such cases, which are probably rarer in community foundations than in other foundations, the return on investment might be the self-interest of a board member or some of the members. Again, this is not usually the case in community foundations but it does happen.

One way community foundations and other foundations can deal with such issues is through "conflict of interest" policies and statements. Many foundations with a sense of responsibility have each board member file or report on his or her other involvements, particularly with the nonprofit sector. For example, each year all board members may be asked to complete a form listing their board and committee relationships with other for-profit organizations and not-for-profit agencies. At one foundation I am familiar with, the policy was that should a grant request come before the board for discussion, any board member associated with that organization was to state he or she was so associated and to explain how he or she was involved. The individual was also disqualified from voting on the grant request. However, the board member could participate in the discussion. In one case a board member announced he was the chair of the capital campaign for a hospital that had submitted a request to the foundation for support of the building campaign. He then proceeded to present a monologue on the value of the organization to the community and the need for the facility. At the end of his statement he said "Of course, I can't vote on this one." It probably would have been hard for the board to turn down this request, even if it did not have considerable merit.

In summary, community foundations generally have an outward-focused set of expectations of their returns on the investments of their grant dollars. However, the degree to which this is true may be influenced by a number of factors, including the nature of the board, the relationship between the board and staff, available funds to carry out needs assessments and other related activities, and other factors. A personal observation is that, of all the types of foundations, it is the community foundations that have the most benevolent concept of ROI.

The Large General Purpose Foundation—Expected Returns

First, it is important to remember that a foundation can be large in terms of its asset base, and thus its grant-making ability, or large in terms of its staff size, or large in both respects. Much of the ROI for the large foundation will depend on its sense of its own mission and focus. A large foundation such as the Ford Foundation (both asset-rich and staff-large) can, by virtue of its resources, have a very broad program focus. The board may set the overall sense of direction, usually very general, for the foundation, but leave it up to the staff to define how the various individual program areas will be defined and implemented. In some cases boards allocate specific dollar amounts for grants to each of the foundation's program areas. Program area directors can become their own fiefdoms, vying for attention for internal resources and grant dollars. The ROIs in such cases can be meeting the program officer's definition of the important needs in his or her area and his or her assumptions about what makes for a program or organization worth funding. But staff members have to also be careful not to stray too far off base from the general mission of the foundation or to get involved in funding organizations that might cause problems for the board or bring negative attention (primarily through the media) to the foundation.

Some larger foundations conduct strategic planning sessions with boards and staffs participating to explore past and current funding efforts and to examine different possible approaches to their grant making. The results of these sessions might be a longer-term (2–5 years) plan for funding as well as other changes, such as new program areas, revised staff structures, or redefined roles for board and staff in the grant process.

However, there are large foundations with smaller staffs (see below for a discussion of staff-driven versus board-driven foundations). In these foundations it is more likely that the ROIs are directly related to the interests of the board and are tied to the foundation's stated or unstated mission and beliefs about its philanthropic role. For example, a foundation may see its philanthropic role as supporting conservative interests, causes, and organizations in the nonprofit sector. The ROI to

> **Much of the ROI for the large foundation will depend on its sense of its own mission and focus.**

such a foundation might be the advancement of those causes and organizations that are most closely aligned with the beliefs of its board members. This is not to say such an approach is wrong (of course, there are "liberal" foundations that function the same way), but only that it exists. In some cases the foundation's particular ROI may not be very obvious to the outsider; it may only be determined through careful research.

The Special-Purpose Foundation—Expected Returns

Because these foundations have more narrowly defined their purposes, as compared to the large general purpose foundation, it is usually easier to define the expected ROI. For example, a foundation that states its primary purpose is to fund medical education at selected medical schools and research on new methods of medical education is clearly interested in advancing medical education. Its return would be the support of medical students at the schools it has selected and development of improved ways to teach in medical schools. Of course, not every special-purpose foundation is as clear about its ROI. A foundation that states it funds only cancer research may have an expected ROI of supporting research at only selected (but unspecified) institutions or supporting research only on certain types of cancer.

The Family Foundation—Expected Returns

The ROI for most family foundations (and therefore most foundations) is meeting the specific philanthropic interests of the donor or donors, even if they are "no longer with us." These interests may get reinterpreted or even changed dramatically over time as fewer family members serve on the board, as the original intent and interests of the donor are no longer relevant, or as additional grant funds

> **The ROI for most family foundations is meeting the specific philanthropic interests of the donors.**

become available through the growth of assets. But the initial philanthropic ROI of many family foundations is to continue supporting the giving interests of the donor or donors.

How can the ROI for a family foundation change over time? Supposing Mr. I. M. Wealthy and his wife contributed to the local art museum, where Mr. Wealthy has been the board chair for many years, during their lifetimes. They also give some smaller gifts to Mr. Wealthy's college and a few other local arts-related agencies. Mr. Wealthy passes away, leaving his estate to his wife but with a provision that, upon her death, part of the assets of the estate will be used to establish a private family foundation operated by the Wealthys' children. Mrs. Wealthy continues to fund the local art museum and Mr. Wealthy's college, and she gives continuing small gifts to a few other arts agencies the family has traditionally supported. The ROI for the Wealthy family is their feeling of supporting agencies that they have always enjoyed and been a part of through their participation and volunteer involvement.

After several years, Mrs. Wealthy also passes away and the Wealthy Family Foundation is established, with I. M. "Buck" Wealthy, Jr., as chair. At the first meeting of the board, which consists of I. M. Wealthy's brothers and sisters, a few of their spouses, and the family attorney, Buck speaks movingly of his parents and their dedication to the local art museum and his father's college. He concludes by saying "If Mom and Pop were still here, I'm sure they would want us to continue to give to these fine institutions." The college and the art museum are notified of the Wealthy Family Foundation's interests (surely these fine institutions had been cultivating the Wealthy family all along) and soon there is the Wealthy Wing of the art museum and Wealthy Hall at the college.

It is years later. The board of the Wealthy Foundation has changed somewhat and now includes a few family members, some local business leaders with a long association with the family, and a few relatives who are not as close as the immediate family. At the annual meeting the board chair announces that all long-term grant commitments have been paid off (mainly the obligations on multiple-year pledges to the art museum and the college), the foundation's assets have been growing due to good investment practices, and there is now considerably more money for grants. Buck Wealthy, the chair emeritus, summarizes the history of the foundation. He recommends that the Foundation continue to fund arts-related organizations, including the new art school the museum has created. Sally Wealthy Smith makes a moving statement about the growing needs of the homeless (she is also a board member of the Area Agency for Homeless Services) and recommends grants also be provided to agencies meeting basic human needs. She concludes by saying "When Mom and Pop were alive, we didn't see these problems. But if they were here now, they would want to jump right in and help." Other board members endorse these needs. The Wealthy Foundation Annual Report announces it will now consider grant requests for support of the arts, arts education, and for programs meeting basic human needs.

Notice how the Wealthy Foundation has evolved from an ROI of meeting the traditional giving interests of the donors to something else. The foundation now has a broader ROI, which includes both an expanded version of the traditional giving interests (from art museum to cultural arts support to cultural arts and arts education) and meeting some area basic human needs. The original foundation's interests and some of the changes reflect the personal interests of the family but also reflect the changing needs of the community. Yet the changes have occurred while the family members have been able to maintain the belief that "this is what our parents would want." In future years the Wealthy Family Foundation may find itself supporting a broad range of arts, education, and human service organizations; the ROI may have thus moved from one of maintaining the traditional family philanthropic interests to meeting the broader needs in the community.

The Alternative Foundation—Expected Returns

"Wait a minute," you say. "You didn't mention anything about alternative foundations!" Alternative foundations, in my view, are not really a class of foundation so much as an expression of an opin-ion about how foundations "should" do business and what they "should" fund. If a foundation doesn't meet the traditional "should" definition in one or both of these areas, some call it an "alternative" foundation. Some foundations are called "alternative" because they tend to fund organizations pursuing what is seen as a liberal or radical social agenda. Others are called "alternative" because their boards or donors may come from segments of society other than those usually associated with foundations.

To some, the one common characteristic of alternative foundations seems to be their ROI of advancing certain causes that are not considered to be in the mainstream of American life. However, this is probably an oversimplification and could result in some foundations that fund very conservative causes also being classed as "alternative," although they would never describe themselves this way. Alternative foundations, at least in the conventional sense of this description, have supported women's rights organizations, abortion rights, gay and lesbian organizations, AIDS programs, free-speech-related issues, environmental groups, prison and government reform, education, the arts, human services, health care, international programs, etc. As this list shows, alternative foundations actually fund in the same areas other foundations fund, and they frequently fund the same organizations. The list also shows that what might be considered a liberal or radical or even conservative cause or issue at one point in time may become more widely accepted later. It is probably because the ROI of alternative foundations is seen as so outward-focused that they fall into this classification. And often, a close examination of their grant-making patterns shows the "alternative foundation" label may not be entirely appropriate.

I consulted with an organization that provided educational programs to judges around the country. Now, as you may guess, sitting judges are not usually seen as "wild and crazy people" with radical agendas. In fact, the educational programs were, of necessity, required to provide balanced perspectives rather than advocate a point of view. We approached a New York-based foundation that, by most standards, would fall into the alternative foundation classification, based upon the politics of its founder and the usual grants it made. We were able to obtain a grant from the foundation because, I believe, we were able to show that the educational programs provided were effectively broadening the judges' perspectives on some key legal issues. Again, it is important to stress the organization and its educational programs were not promoting a particular point of view; the foundation funding, therefore, was not endorsing a particular item on the social agenda or a cause, except the cause of having better-educated judges making legal decisions.

In summary, the ROI—what the foundation is looking for as a return when it makes grants—can be a very important factor in determining which foundations you approach and what your strategies are for approaching them. But how do you determine the actual ROI of a particular foundation? Later chapters will discuss researching foundations and developing particular strategies for approaching them, but at this point suffice it to say that the ROI for a given foundation may be able to be determined by the type of foundation (this will give you some general assumptions to test as you carry out further exploration), its stated purposes or mission and guidelines, and a close comparison of these to its actual grants and grant patterns. Also helpful will be some understanding of who makes up the board of the foundation, whether it is staffed or not, asset size, and many other factors, which will be presented in more detail below.

The Board and Staff Factors

ROI is a very important concept to consider in developing your strategies for approaching foundations. But it is also very important to have some understanding of foundation boards and staffs and their interrelationships. Other guides to raising money from foundations and corporations rarely speak of the internal workings of the potential funder. In this section we will explore several key points you should know as you develop your approaches to foundations and corporations. These points can cut across all types of foundations, so keep in mind that the descriptions below can apply to each of the foundation types covered earlier.

Also, refer back to the discussion of various types of corporate foundations and corporate giving programs above for more specific information related to these sources.

The Board-Only Foundation

As has been mentioned, most foundations do not have staff. So the descriptions given here cover most foundations, especially the "typical" family foundation. When there is not a staff, proposals, inquiries, information requests, etc., usually are directed to one of several possible people:

- the foundation's board president or chair

- another member of the board (frequently the board secretary) who has been designated to be the chief contact person

- an administrative or support staff person at the board president or chair's employer or company or at the company of one of the other board members

- an attorney who has been designated to handle the affairs of the foundation

- a person not falling into any of these categories, such as the spouse of a board member, a family friend, a bank officer or staff member, or someone else

It should also be pointed out that some foundations without staffs use the services of a firm or individual that specializes in managing foundations. These organizations or people are usually hired on a contractual basis and may function much like staff of a foundation. However, the foundation is still technically without staff.

Supposing you are the board chair of a family foundation that has no staff and that is located in a moderate-sized city. The foundation's brief brochure lists you as the contact person; you are currently employed full time as a partner in a law firm. Because the foundation has broad purposes, every day you receive:

- calls asking for more information from agencies interested in applying for funding

- letters asking for information

- calls from people asking to meet with you

- unsolicited proposals

- occasional visits by people who are "just dropping by" to meet you

As you attempt to fulfill your regular job obligations and your foundation role (which also includes various reporting requirements, tax forms, etc.), what is your reaction going to be? In terms of your own priorities, especially during the work day, the foundation will probably not be at the top of your list. A first reaction might be to delegate some of the responsibility to one of your support staff members. Of course, for him or her, it may not be a priority either. Calls may not be returned right away, brochures are sent "when I get the chance," and most requests for meetings are turned down, unless you give the OK.

But the flood still continues. At a board meeting you express your frustrations about dealing with the foundation and your job. One board member suggests narrowing the guidelines and being more specific about what the foundation will and won't fund. Another member suggests adding some wording to the brochure stating "no unsolicited proposals will be accepted by the foundation." A third member suggests the foundation pick a list of agencies it will fund every year and only fund these. All of the suggestions seem to have advantages, and the latter two will definitely cut your workload. So, to the outsider, the foundation is deciding to essentially close its doors and limit communication, no matter which option is chosen. But in the view of the foundation board members, they are helping to limit the burden on the chair and his or her staff.

If there is any trend in the world of unstaffed foundations, the above example is a summary of what it will be. Unstaffed foundations will continue to take steps to limit the burdens on those desig-

> **Unstaffed foundations will continue to take steps to limit the burdens on those designated as the contacts with potential grantees, and on the board members themselves.**

nated as the contacts with potential grantees, and on the board members themselves. These steps may include, as presented in the case above:

- Redefinition of grant guidelines to give the foundation a more narrow and more clearly stated focus. In one sense, some family foundations may return to their roots and the whole process of the evolution of a family foundation described earlier may reverse itself, somewhat like the universe collapsing back to its core. The guideline list of areas, programs, and types of agencies not eligible for funding will grow larger, and the corresponding list of areas, programs, and types of agencies eligible for consideration for funding will grow smaller. But at least things may be clearer for those searching for support.

- A change to a Request for Proposal (RFP) approach in which the foundation will accept only requests from organizations that it has asked to apply. From the foundation perspective this helps limit the workload even more than the refocused guidelines approach, but the downside is the need to identify in some systematic (and justifiable, if called into question) way the agencies that will be invited to apply for funds. This consideration may lead to the next approach.

- Defining or designating the specific agencies that will receive grants from the foundation. This is somewhat of a last resort in that it removes almost any interaction with other potential grantees, new agencies, or changing community needs. But, again from the foundation's standpoint, it does effectively cut the burden of responding to requests, calls, and visits.

• There is another option that foundations sometimes include at their formation and other times consider after operating for a while: actually closing the doors and going out of business. Some foundations decide at their inception or further down the road to completely disperse their assets and end their existence. At times, the documents establishing them also specify that all assets will be dispersed within a given time period, such as 25 years. Other times, this happens after some experience has been gained in running the foundation. But it is always an option.

Unstaffed foundations are not alone in facing growing problems of effectively dealing with the workload. But, without staff, their options are limited and their reactions may fall into one of the possibilities mentioned above. Some also seek another way out—they add full- or part-time staff, and thus move into another category for our discussion. Some also decide to turn their foundation over to a community foundation; there, the private foundation can become one of the named funds of the community foundation, and the former board members, family members, or others may act as advisors to the fund, if they so choose.

The Part-Time Staffed Foundation

Of the foundations that are staffed, many probably have one or possibly two part-time staff members. A somewhat typical pattern is the family foundation that has realized it no longer can function with only an all-volunteer board. A next logical step in its evolution would be to add a part-time staff member, possibly someone already employed by the family-run business, an employee of one of the board members, a spouse or someone else wanting only a part-time position, or even a member of the immediate family. The addition of a staff member adds a new set of dynamics to the foundation. One obvious change is that now things can be delegated by the board to the staff person. But, even if the board members had not thought of them when the decision was made to hire a staff person, other issues will arise. Questions to be answered may be:

• What are the specific responsibilities of the staff person versus the responsibilities of the board?

• Should all proposals come to the staff person or can board members still accept proposals?

• How should the board relate to the staff person? One-on-one, only through the board chair, or how?

• Should the staff person be the only one who meets with and speaks with potential grantees or should the board continue to do this—and how should meetings and other contacts be coordinated?

• Should the staff person attend board meetings and, if so, what should his or her role(s) be?

• What should the staff member's proposal review process be?

• What should be prepared by the staff member for each board meeting—just the proposals as they have been submitted, summaries of the proposals, or summaries and recommendations as to whether or not each agency should receive a grant and how much?

• Should the staff person be able to turn down requests, or send them back only if they don't meet the foundation's guidelines?

• Should the staff person be allowed to approve small grants up to a given amount? (Also see later section on this topic.)

Sometimes, when they examine these questions, foundation board members realize they have traded one set of problems for another. Also, prior to having any staff the foundation board may have divided up the proposals for review by the various board members with each being assigned some to review and present at the meeting. Now all the proposals may be channeled to a single person who may again be faced with problems of allocation of work time between foundation business and his or her other responsibilities.

How large of a problem can this be and what can be the effect on the processing of your proposals? Toward the beginning of this book I gave an example of a part-time staff member who would only review proposals if she recognized the name of the organization. The part-time staff member shares a common and important characteristic with his or her full-time foundation staff members and even with the board members: the desire to minimize the flow or flood of inquiries, calls, letters, and proposals. Above, we gave examples of how board members can seek to minimize contacts with the foundation; these will also obviously help the staff, whether it is one part-time person or a large staff. Here are some examples of ways staff members can better control contacts:

- Strictly interpret guidelines. For example, if the foundation guidelines state it will not fund religious organizations, the staff member may elect to not accept proposals from social service agencies that may have a religious connection (but in fact are open to all and may only serve a small number of people of that denomination).

- Only review proposals from agencies known to the staff and/or the board (see the earlier example).

- Not fund new or start-up agencies, especially if they are in the "gray" area of the guidelines. For example, if the foundation will not fund drug treatment programs, it may not consider proposals from drug education programs.

- Not consider a proposal if, in any way, it indicates the applying agency has not completely done its homework in reviewing the foundation materials and information available on the foundation. For example, a foundation may never have made a grant over $25,000. An organization may ask for a grant of $35,000. While the limit may not even be clearly stated in the foundation materials, the staff person may see this as sufficient reason to disqualify the proposal. Or possibly the foundation states it funds "in the New York metropolitan area," but is not more specific. The staff person may

decide not to consider northern New Jersey as part of the metropolitan area, and thus disqualify any proposal from organizations located there.

- Only meet with organizations after proposals have been submitted and reviewed by the staff.

- Only meet with a few selected organizations, especially if they are known to the foundation, or not meeting at all with most applicants.

- Not return most calls or telling callers that they must send a letter requesting information or a letter of inquiry (see Chapter 11) or a full proposal.

- Develop other and possibly unstated criteria for screening proposals.

From the outside the perception of foundations using these and other work control techniques and screening criteria is that they are closed, inaccessible, "unfriendly," or worse. From the inside the perception of foundation staff and board is that they are trying to keep the work flow under control.

Part-time foundation staff may well be faced with the most pressures of any foundation staff. They cannot share the workload, must usually be the primary or only contact point with the foundation, can be caught between the applicants and the board, and are held solely responsible by the board for the day-to-day management of the foundation. At times, they can also be seen by the board as the point person in protecting the board from direct contacts by prospective grant seekers.

This and what follows is not intended to defend or attack how foundation staffs function. It is only intended to give some necessary insights into the process and pressures on foundation boards and staffs, so you can more effectively develop strategies for successfully approaching foundations and working with their leadership and staffs.

The Small Staffed Foundation

First, "small" in this context does not refer to the size of the foundation's assets or its capacity to make grants, but rather to the size of its staff. For the purposes of the following discussion, a "small" staff will be considered to be a minimum of one full-time person and, somewhat arbitrarily, up to a total of five to six full- and part-time people.

The dynamics of the small staffed foundation, especially one with more than one full-time staff member, are quite different from those of the unstaffed, part-time staff, and large staffed foundation. There is still a central contact person, usually with the title of "President" or "Executive Director," or possibly "Program Director." He or she will probably be the primary person to interface with the board; in some cases, he or she may actually be a member of the board. The chief staff person, because he or she is full time, is clearly responsible only for the work of the foundation; there is no longer the problem of divided attention and time. Now there also can be some delegation of workloads and differentiation of responsibilities with different levels of staff. But the executive director or president also now must become an administrator and supervisor as well as a processor of proposals and inquiries. Some, or even all, of the proposal review function may be delegated to a person who may have the title "Assistant Executive Director," "Vice-President," or "Program Officer." This person may also be responsible for handling inquiries from organizations and other external contacts—or the responsibilities may be divided between or among the senior staff members.

Having one or more senior staff probably means someone will serve in a support staff role. This person or these people may act as receptionist, secretary, administrative assistant, or in other ways. One individual in a support role may be responsible for responding to inquiries for information and/or preliminary screening of incoming proposals to see if all required information has been submitted. A staff member may also have these functions and may also assist with preparation of all materials for the board meetings, handling administrative paperwork and correspondence, or other functions.

One important point to make about small foundation staffs is that staff, whether two or six, usually have different and defined functions, and there is now a point person—the executive director or the president—between the board of the foundation and the staff. There is also a staff between the executive director or president and the people and organizations seeking support or information. So the layers that you have to deal with are somewhat thicker, and it becomes more important to know where the different responsibilities lie in terms of what you need. For example, calling the executive director or president directly if you only need the guidelines or other published information is probably not appropriate.

Another thing that happens when there is one full-time staff member at a foundation—or especially when there is more than one—is that systems and procedures usually become more formalized. Instead of merely piling proposals up as they come in, proposals may be checked in and acknowledged as being received. If more than one person is responsible for reviewing proposals, the review process itself and the materials presented to the board for consideration may also become more formalized so the board gets consistent information from the reviewers. Staff, because they are not merely responding to the influx of inquiries and proposals, may also have the luxury of taking a more proactive approach to the work of the foundation. They may:

- meet occasionally with other foundation staff members to discuss common issues or concerns

- join a local, regional, or national group of grant makers to discuss issues and learn about new ways to carry out their jobs

- develop policy or action plans and recommendations for the board

> The dynamics of the small staffed foundation, especially one with more than one full-time staff member, are quite different from those of the unstaffed, part-time staff, and large staffed foundation.

- develop recommendations related to new areas for consideration for funding, changes in the guidelines, or other new approaches for the work of the foundation

- lead or participate in strategic planning sessions with the board

They may also spend some time evaluating the impact of the foundation's grant making or looking at the larger trends and issues in the areas (geographic and program) served by the foundation. Overall, the staff of a smaller staffed foundation can begin to move away from merely being a processor and manager of the work flow. They will probably develop more formalized systems and structures, possibly become more proactive in their approach, and hopefully help open the foundation's board up to new approaches and ways to do its philanthropic business.

But foundation staffs, especially when there is more than one professional staff member, can also fulfill another important role: they can begin to become advocates to the board for the causes, needs, and issues that they see in the community served by the foundation. It is difficult for a single staff member to advocate changes or new funding areas to the board of a foundation; the board members, especially in family foundations, are usually not his or her peers (unless the staff member is also a member of the family). But with two or more staff members, especially with two senior staff members, there can at least be some corroboration of what is being recommended, and the feeling that this is a team approach, not just one person's opinion.

This important concept was explained very clearly to me when I first started working at a foundation. A staff member who had been there for awhile was talking to me about the roles of staff versus those of the board of the foundation. He said: "You know, one of the major roles we on the staff can play is to function as advocates for the organizations and causes that come to us for support. We have to be the intermediaries who translate what we see and hear out there in the community to our board so we can convince them to respond." This view of the roles of foundation staff clearly moves them beyond people who merely process the paperwork of the foundation; foundation staff can become key players in helping you and your agency through their process and in opening up the foundation board to new ideas and new ways of doing business.

But once again keep in mind these are generalizations, which are meant to help guide your thinking and strategy development. A foundation with a large staff can be just as effective as a foundation with one part-time person at cutting you off from interaction with the board or limiting your contact. Some staff members of foundations may see their roles not as advocates or helpers, but as blockers and people whose job it is to "run interference" to protect the board from all of the hordes seeking to "get money" from the foundation. So staff size may not reflect staff attitudes about their jobs and roles. Nor does a larger staff necessarily mean more systematic approaches to the work of the foundation. Large foundations can be extremely unsystematic in their application processes and grant making. And, sometimes, even small foundations with limited staffs or no staffs can be very systematic in their approaches and very open to meetings, new funding initiatives, etc. One unstaffed family foundation I am familiar with has the husband or wife (the founders of the foundation and both board members) meet with representatives from each organization that submits a proposal for consideration.

The Larger Staffed Foundation

As foundations develop larger staffs, all of the trends that we see in the smaller staffed foundation continue and there are also some new wrinkles to take into account. Procedures and structures usually become more formalized. Staff roles and responsibilities may become even more differentiated. A professional staff member may become responsible for carrying out an initial review of all incoming proposals to ensure they meet foundation guidelines and include all required materials. This person or the executive director or president may assign proposals to particular staff members, based upon each person's current workload, expertise, or other factors. A business office may be created to oversee grant payments as well as other administrative matters of the foundation (personnel policies, salaries and benefits, internal operations, bank and investment relations, etc.). Records and filing systems may become more structured because there are more records to keep and because more staff are using them.

However, the change that can most affect you and your organization has to do with what are now probably called the "program" staff, the people whose sole or primary function is to review proposals and prepare recommendations to the board as to funding or not funding requests. As foundations acquire larger staffs, they can move in one of two ways as to the roles and responsibilities of program staff. One approach is to have all program staff function as "generalists." Foundation guidelines will usually specify one or more program areas the foundation is interested in supporting, such as the arts, health care, children and youth, etc. When generalists are on staff, a given program staff member may be reviewing proposals from an arts organization, a health care agency, and a youth service agency. He or she is given proposals to review, regardless of the type of organization. The distribution of proposals to staff is usually based upon workload, timelines, and other factors. Smaller staffed foundations and even foundations with moderate-sized staffs frequently use the generalist approach. When approaching such a foundation, you will not be able to pinpoint, in advance of sending your proposal, the staff person who will be reviewing it. Usually, only after the proposal has arrived at the foundation and been assigned to a staff member will you be able to find out who is handling the proposal. It is important to recognize that the initiative for finding out who on the foundation staff is reviewing your proposal will usually rest with you and your organization, unless the foundation program officer chooses to contact you directly. Some foundations are very closed about their review processes and may not be willing even to share information about who is carrying out the review, especially if the staff are usually not inclined to meet with applicants.

The second model that foundations with larger staffs frequently use is the "specialist" model. In this model program officers are divided into specialty areas, which usually parallel the program areas the foundation supports. For example, one specialist may review only proposals from youth service agencies while another specialist will handle all proposals from health care organizations. It is more likely that foundations using the specialist model will hire program staff with some expertise and experience in the area they will be serving; foundations hiring generalists will probably seek people with a variety of backgrounds to serve as their program staffs.

In larger foundations with a number of specialists serving as program staff, there may well be a formal division of the program areas. Program staff members may carry such titles as "Program Director, Health" or "Director, Children and Youth Program," or "Program Coordinator, Arts and Culture." In the largest foundations these individuals may have other professional program staff reporting to them; the effect is much like departments in a corporation with department heads or directors. Some of the largest foundations have several program area directors and several staff reporting to each of the directors. The foundation's board and staff may develop projections of the foundation's income available for grants for the next fiscal year and may assign each of the program areas a set amount for grants in that area. Usually some grant funds are set aside for "out of program area" grants or for special grants; in part, such funds also provide some protection against projections that are not realized because of lower performance on investments or other factors.

Some of the largest foundations may also have staff members who are assigned to specific projects or "special grant initiatives" the foundation is undertaking. These staff members oversee a program that may not neatly fit the usual program interests of the foundation or that may have a more narrow focus than the usual program areas. It is common for some of the larger foundations to focus their resources and grant dollars on particular areas of concern to the foundation, emerging issues in the geographic areas they serve, or new needs, such as the Energy Conservation Program at the community foundation. Another example might be a private foundation that has funded children and youth-related agencies for a number of years. The foundation program staff responsible for this area notice they are receiving increasing numbers of proposals and inquiries for support of child abuse programs. In discussions with other foundations' program staffs they learn that these foundations are also receiving growing numbers of such inquiries and proposals. The foundation staff meet together and develop a three-year child abuse initiative, which may include:

1. collecting data on the magnitude of the problem in the community by two professors at the local university's sociology department

2. hiring by the foundation of a professional expert in the area of child abuse to oversee the project

3. creating (and funding of meeting costs) a community task force to review the data and to develop recommendations to better coordinate agencies and services for abused children

4. creating a matching grant incentive program for agencies to add child abuse services or expand existing child abuse services

5. contracting with an outside firm to develop an evaluation of the entire program and its effectiveness at the end of the three-year period. After board approval, the program is implemented.

What does all of this mean for your organization? A foundation that takes the "specialist" approach makes your approach strategy development somewhat easier because there is an identifiable person or identifiable people at the foundation who are specifically responsible for the general area, service, or program that you would like funded (assuming, of course, the foundation has included your area in its funding priorities). In the case of a special project or grants initiative, the foundation has probably made its priorities and staff responsibilities even clearer. So, if you are fortunate enough to have an organization or a program or project that matches up with the foundation's initiative, your

chances of receiving support may increase considerably.

There is one complication to all of this. Some of the larger foundations, especially some of the largest in terms of staffing, can become somewhat like mazes with staff titles and possibly even responsibilities that seem to overlap each other or duplicate or cut across the specific area for which you may be seeking support. For example, supposing your organization is planning to develop a program for female substance abusers. Your research shows that the XYZ Foundation has a program area on substance abuse and another area for women's programs. If you want to or are able to approach a specific staff person, which area do you choose? Fortunately, there are only a few foundations where you will face this issue, but you should be aware of it.

Strategy Tip: If you are uncertain about which program person to speak with or where to direct a specific proposal or inquiry, it is best to pick out the person responsible for the area you think is most likely the appropriate one, call him or her, and get some clarification of how and to whom your approach should be made.

This strategy also gives you the chance to begin to open the door and to start developing a relationship with the foundation.

Strategy Tip: When your project or program appears to fit into more than one of a larger foundation's program areas, approach the second area if you are not comfortable with the results of your approach to the first area. For example, a small national organization developed a program focused on issues related to women and certain methods of birth control. The organization's approach to the person responsible for women's programs at a large national foundation was not very successful. The organization re-approached the program officer in charge of the population program area of the foundation and received a much more supportive and helpful hearing. Although a grant was not received, the staff member of the organization felt the second person would be much more useful when the organization wished to develop new programs in this area.

Overall, staffing patterns and staff size are useful pieces of information to know as you develop your strategies. The above discussion can help you consider what possible approaches will work best with the different foundations. And, the more you know about each of your foundation and corporate prospects, the more successful you will be when seeking funding.

Staff Roles in the Review Process

In the discussion of part-time staffed foundations several possible issues were raised about staff roles and responsibilities versus those of the board. Foundations with staffs vary considerably in what staff members do and how much responsibility they have. Much of what the staff can or can't do is determined by the board of the foundation. In some cases staff are primarily information processors, and, to some extent, "protectors" of the board. The other extreme is staff members who are permitted to turn down or even approve grants (see following discussion on "staff discretionary grant-making ability"). In a few cases the foundation board's main function may be only to ratify the actions taken by the staff of the foundation or to broadly approve the program areas and possibly the fund allocations for each. In larger staffed foundations, there probably will be considerable differentiation of roles of professional staff with many levels of responsibility and position. In smaller staffed foundations professional staff will have roles that are more alike and may even overlap. Thus a program officer's roles might fall into one of the following sets of responsibilities (none of which should be seen as mutually exclusive or fixed forever, and all of which are merely examples of the possibilities):

- Review incoming requests for information and respond by phone or by sending materials. Review proposals to ensure all required materials are included. Prepare a summary of each proposal for the board meeting. Prepare all other materials for the board meeting (accounting reports, investment reports, etc.). Ensure that all applicants are notified of decisions and that for grantees appropriate forms are filled out, payments sent, and final reports filed with the foundation.

- Meet with applicants after proposals are received or before they are sent. Review proposals and prepare a summary of each for the board meeting. Prepare a recommendation to the board as to whether or not the proposal should be funded and, if it is to be funded, the amount and time period (1 year, 2 years, etc.) of the grant as well as any special conditions (challenge or matching grant, etc.). Meet with the board to review each request and the recommendations, answer questions about the organization and why a grant was recommended or not recommended as well as the amount of the grant. Ensure that all applicants are notified of decisions and that for grantees appropriate forms are filled out, payments sent, and final reports filed with the foundation.

- Meet with applicants after proposals are received or before they are sent. Review proposals and approve grants or have the executive director or president of the foundation approve grants up to the amount authorized by the board. Turn down other requests. Prepare summaries and recommendations for other proposals for the board meeting. Meet with the board to review each request and the recom-

> **Foundations with staffs vary considerably in what staff members do and how much responsibility they have.**

mendations, answer questions about the organization and why a grant was recommended or not recommended as well as the amount of the grant. Ensure that all applicants are notified of decisions and that for grantees appropriate forms are filled out, payments sent, and final reports filed with the foundation.

- Initiate foundation outreach activities to the area or community it serves, including meeting with agencies and organizations falling within the staff person's area of responsibility. Develop funding priorities appropriate to community needs. Implement the grant program (including meetings, proposal solicitations and review, grant approvals within budget limitations, grant follow-up, etc.). Evaluate the success of the grant program and report to the board at its annual meeting.

As should be clear, the major differences among these options are the amount of initiative given to the foundation staff and their authority to make funding decisions. Like the foundations themselves, staff roles and responsibilities can change over time. As board members become more comfortable with staff and with the division of responsibilities, the board may give the staff more authority to make some decisions in the review and grant process. At some point staff may be authorized to approve small grants (usually up to a specified dollar limit) without going to the board for its approval. These may require the approval of the executive director or the ratification of the board, or the board may simply allocate an amount of money that the staff can use for such grants. Further down the road the board may give the staff even more grant-making authority; in some cases the board may move into a more passive role as staff become the key decision makers.

Sometimes this evolutionary process is driven by the board, but other times it is driven by the

---

Staff roles and responsibilities can change over time.

---

staff. However, most often it is the board members who must decide how far they are willing to go and how much power they are willing to give up to the staff. Workload pressures on the staff can help drive the process of change at the foundation; staff can press the board to make changes in procedures, tighten up guidelines, or use the other methods discussed earlier. At staffed foundations, remember, boards are usually cut off from the day-to-day workflow and have to rely on staff to give them some indication of how the foundation is responding to the flow of proposals and inquiries. But, one way or another, the day-to-day workload will also be reflected in the board meetings of the foundation. If the board was able to review and make decisions on 50 proposals in its quarterly three-hour meeting, how will it be able to handle 100 proposals in the same three-hour time period? When foundation boards see these problems arising, they, like their staffs, begin to develop methods to keep the decision process manageable.

The above concepts and ideas are very important to your understanding of how foundations operate and, to some extent, why they operate the way that they do. As an outsider to the foundation, you may see the foundation as something like the classic "black box;" you know what you put into it and you know you will get something out of it, but you don't know what happens inside. The above discussion is intended to give you some indication of what may happen inside and why it may happen in a particular way. But also again keep reminding yourself that every foundation is unique in some way and in any specific case the generalities may not apply.

Board- versus Staff-Driven Foundations

There is a very important concept that can be derived from the above discussion of board versus staff roles at foundations—the concept of board- versus staff-driven foundations. This concept can help you understand where the primary authority and decision-making process are located within a foundation. Think of a straight line (see Figure 6–1). On the left end of the line is "staff" and on the right end of the line is "board." This line describes the continuum of authority and decision making within a foundation. In most foundations an "X" designating the primary focus of decision making and authority would be at the board end of the continuum. These are board-driven foundations. In these foundations grant decisions, policies and procedures, guidelines, etc., are all decided at the board level, although there may be some input from staff.

Figure 6–1 A Board-Driven Foundation

But in other foundations the board has turned over some of the power to staff. In these foundations the "X" designating the primary focus of authority and decision making will be moved somewhat toward the staff end of the continuum, indicating the foundation is moderately staff-driven (see Figure 6–2).

X
Staff ━━━━━━━━━━ Board

Figure 6–2 A Moderately Staff-Driven Foundation

The third example is a highly staff-driven foundation. In this type of foundation the "X" designating the location of power is much closer to the staff end of the continuum. In these foundations staff may be able to make major grants, set guidelines and procedures for their program areas, and generally define how the day-to-day process at the foundation works. Boards of such foundations may primarily carry out an oversight role and may need only to ratify or approve grants over a certain level (see Figure 6–3).

Why is knowing about staff- versus board-driven foundations important? In a board-driven

Figure 6–3 A Highly Staff-Driven Foundation

foundation, especially when the "X" is at the board end of the continuum, when you meet or speak with a staff member you are, in a sense, dealing with an intermediary. That person may be able to decide if your proposal or your organization and its programs fit the basic guidelines of the foundation, but can only convey your request, possibly along with the staff member's recommendation, to the real decision makers, the board. Your job is essentially to "sell" your request to the entire foundation by working through someone who may be an advocate for your request, or who may not support it. In board-driven foundations it may be difficult to get a clear understanding of what the decision will be and what the rationale is behind it. But in a staff-driven foundation, especially one where staff have considerable authority and decision-making ability, you may actually be dealing with the decision maker, especially if your request falls within that person's limitations (see staff discretionary grant-making ability section below).

Also keep in mind that there are many variations on the board-staff continuum. Here are just a few:

- Some foundations have established board or board-staff committees, which are authorized by the board to make decisions on grants up to a certain level. For example, the ABC Foundation may have a board committee of five to six people who review all proposals and staff recommendations for grants up to $50,000; the full board is required to approve any request where the staff has recommended a grant over $50,000.

- Other foundation boards may have authorized the executive director or president (chief staff officer) to approve grants up to a certain dollar level; above that level the full board must approve any grant. For example, the executive director of the DDD Foundation is permitted to approve grants of up to $5,000 without having to get full board approval. At each board meeting the board ratifies these decisions.

- At some foundations, the level of grants that can be approved is tied to the level of staff. For example, at the EEE Foundation, program officers can approve grants of up to $1,000; program directors can approve grants up to $5,000; and the executive director can approve grants up to $10,000. Any grant above $10,000 requires the full approval of the board of directors.

- At some foundations, project or program grants up to a certain level may be able to be approved by the program officer responsible for that area. Other types of grants, such as operating grants, capital grants, etc., up to a certain level may require approval by the executive director or by staff consensus (see example below in the staff discretionary grant-making ability section).

Strategy Tip: Always review foundation publications and materials with an eye to where the decision-making authority is within the foundation. A few foundations clearly spell out their review procedures, which will tell you much about where the decision making occurs, but most do not. You may have to interpret information or "read between the lines" but the information can be very valuable.

Strategy Tip: If you are speaking with a foundation program officer or director, always ask him or her how the foundation's decision-making process works, if it is not spelled out clearly in the foundation's materials or elsewhere.

Staff Discretionary Grant-Making Ability

When staff of a foundation are allowed to make grants directly, they are said to have "staff discretionary grant-making ability." From the above points you can probably see how knowing whether or not a staff member at a particular foundation has this ability can benefit your approach strategies. If you have done your homework on the foundation and speak with a staff member who has discretionary grant-making ability, you may only have to win over one person to get a grant. Sometimes the grant can be fairly substantial. A few of the largest foundations permit staff to make grants of $25,000, $50,000 or even $100,000!

Here is a real example of how the process can happen. A small national organization approached a large foundation for an operating grant. Prior to submitting a proposal, a meeting was held with a program officer of the foundation. The foundation staff person informed the executive director of the organization that the process for approval of an operating grant at this level ($25,000) required staff consensus and final approval by the foundation's chief staff person, the president. He suggested that a proposal be submitted for the operating grant, which was done. About two months later a letter was received from the foundation stating the operating grant request had not been approved.

The executive director of the organization called the program officer, who explained that, while the foundation made some operating grants, they were difficult to get approved. The executive director thanked the staff member, but next asked him if he would be interested in considering a request for support of a new project of the organization. He said yes, and, when he heard a brief description of the project, said it was within his program area. The executive director asked if he needed a full proposal and he said no; a brief letter describing the project would be all that was necessary. The director asked him if it was OK to request $25,000 for the project (the total cost was about $45,000) and the program officer said that would be fine. The letter was subsequently sent off and about three weeks later a grant check of $25,000 was received.

What happened here? First, the foundation generally appears to fall in the "staff driven" category in that staff could make grant decisions up to a certain level (based on other experience, probably about $50,000). The foundation also had a different set of procedures, depending on the nature of the grant request. If a request was for operating support (the first request), the approval process apparently included consensus by the program officers from the different areas and a final approval from the president. But if a grant request was within one of the program areas (the second request), and if it was under the maximum level for staff-approved grants, the program officer could approve the grant with no further action required. This two-tiered process also explains why, in the case of the first request, the decision took two months and in the case of the second request, the decision only took three weeks.

Strategy Tip: Always think of alternate ways you can approach a foundation, especially if your request is turned down. But also realize that some foundations may not allow you to reapply for a period of time after you have been turned down.

Strategy Tip: If you are meeting or speaking with a foundation program officer, always ask if he or she has staff discretionary grant-making ability. If the staff member says yes, you should next ask what the maximum level allowed is. Also ask if there are other approvals required and what the approximate turnaround time for a decision is.

Strategy Tip: If the maximum level for a staff discretionary grant is below what

your organization actually needs, but you believe there is some chance that you can obtain other grants, you should consider seeking a level of support appropriate to both the real needs and the range of grants program staff are allowed to approve. While you may not get all that you need, you will probably be able to use the grant from this source to leverage other grants. Also, especially if you have never received a grant from this particular foundation, adding it to your list of supporters will also benefit your future fund-raising efforts.

Knowing about staff discretionary grant-making ability can both help define your strategies with particular foundations and help win another advocate for your organization and its needs. Always keep this possibility in mind when approaching potential foundation and corporate foundation sources.

This chapter has covered a lot of territory: ROIs, foundation boards and staffs, internal operations, board-driven versus staff-driven foundations, and staff discretionary grant-making ability. At first glance, you may not be too sure what many of these points have to do with seeking grants. Knowing as much as possible about each foundation source—even beyond the basic descriptive information it may provide—can give you definite advantages as you develop and execute your strategies. It is increasingly important to understand as much as possible about how a given foundation operates, why it operates that particular way, what the internal dynamics might be, where decision making is located, what the staff can and can't do, the uniqueness of each foundation, the similarities to

---

Knowing about staff discretionary grant-making ability can both help define your strategies with particular foundations and help win another advocate for your organization.

---

other foundations, and the other factors that can affect both your strategies and the eventual outcome of your request. You should be moving away from the "black box" approach to foundations and corporate foundations and toward a view that includes understanding of the many factors you need to take into account to successfully seek grants.

Chapter 7

Where to Start: Know Your Organization

Key Questions and Examples

When I teach a seminar on seeking support from foundations and corporations, I usually ask a simple question: When you are getting ready to raise money from these sources, where do you start?

Most of the answers focus on getting foundation materials and/or doing research on the potential funding sources. Almost never has anyone said to start at home base—to look at your own organization carefully before even thinking of beginning research. Why is this the place to start? The biggest single problem I saw while serving as a program officer was that the representatives of the organizations that approached our foundation all too often did not know some of the most basic information that we wanted to discuss with them. Remember, we had already received each organization's proposal and supporting materials. By the time we met with each organization, we had usually done a complete review of their proposals and materials and may have already begun preliminary research on such issues as:

- What other similar organizations are there in our community and in the area the applicant agency serves?

- What is the previous proposal and grant history of the organization with our foundation?

- Where else has the organization received grant funding recently?

- Does it have the proposal to us pending at another foundation or is it currently receiving funding from other foundations for this or other projects?

- Are board members active in other organizations and what are their professional roles/positions?

- If the organization is a United Way agency or received funds from other federated groups, what are the experiences of these funders with the organization?

- What are the primary and secondary funding sources of the organization?

- Is most of its funding from one source or a variety of sources?

- How does the organization raise money?

- If the organization has a strategic plan, is it following the plan and how does it measure progress on the plan?

- If the organization is proposing a new program or project, has it done its research to determine others' experiences with similar programs or projects?

- Is the evaluation plan realistic?

Unfortunately, all too often our applicants had not done their homework. Those we met with or spoke with on the phone—including board chairs and members, senior staff, project and program staff, and development staff—were frequently not able to answer what we considered critical basic questions. Yet most of the information we were asking about was, or at least should have been, in the proposal and supporting materials. Here are some real-life examples:

- Should the board chair know the basic purpose of the organization? One board chair didn't; he thought the agency was a day care program when in fact it provided medical therapies to physically disabled children.

- Should the board chair know about a proposed major new program for which several hundred thousand dollars in foundation support was being asked? I called the board chair of a particular organization when I noticed he had not co-signed the proposal cover letter (more on this later), and he professed surprise about both the request to us and the plans for the program.

- Should the chief executive officer know what are the primary sources of support for the agency's operations? Some did not or had to defer to another staff member or to the agency's own materials.

- Should the chief executive officer know about similar agencies in the area? Many did not or at least were not able to describe what these other agencies did and how the applicant agency was different.

- Should the chief development officer know about all fund-raising efforts by the organization? Some did not and could discuss only what they did, not the total fund-raising program.

- Should the chief development officer or the chief executive officer know where else the organization had applied for support of the program or project for which they were seeking support from our foundation? Some did not.

These are only a few examples of problems some applicants for support experienced when I asked them what I considered basic questions. I had, or at least I had tried, to do my homework. But it was often too obvious that these leaders did not truly know their own organizations.

But there is another reason to start with your own organization before you begin to explore potential funding sources. Knowing your organization can help guide and simplify your research efforts and can enable you to pinpoint potential funding sources much more quickly. This is especially true if you take a more analytical approach to understanding your organization and what it does or is planning to do.

It is especially important that development officers who are new to the staff of a particular organization undertake an exploration of the history, current programs and needs, and plans of the organization before beginning approaches to potential funders. But it is equally important that all who are or who might be involved in the approach process have as complete as possible an understanding of the organization. This includes the board chair and other board members, campaign volunteer leadership, senior staff, development staff, and often the program staff who will manage the program or project for which support is being sought.

What follows are discussions of each of the key areas that anyone who is or who might be involved in the proposal process should review carefully prior to any direct contact with a potential funding source.

Needs

What are the needs "out there" in the world that your organization seeks to serve? Why are these needs important, as opposed to other needs? Can the needs your organization is trying to meet be quantified? (If the organization is serving people with AIDS, for example, what is some of the basic information on the prevalence and growth of AIDS in this country?) If the organization is new, what "out there" brought about its creation? How are needs evaluated and how is this information disseminated and used? If your organization is not in the business of meeting the most basic human needs (food, shelter, etc.) why are your services, program, and even mission still relevant and important? How does your organization network with other similar organizations?

Is there really a need for an organization like yours or is it continuing to function and serve needs that no longer exist or have changed? What is happening beyond your organization that is affecting the organization and how, in turn, is it responding to these outside forces? The needs area is often critical to potential funders, many of which have fairly clear views, as often expressed through their guidelines, of what their priority concerns and areas of interest are. Is the organization filling a unique niche or is it one of many meeting particular needs? Being one of many organizations meeting particular needs is not necessarily a bad thing, if it can be demonstrated that the scope of the problem or needs is substantial and/or the organization has some unique approach to meeting the needs.

For some organizations the issue of needs being met is not as clear-cut as for others. A social service or human service agency can usually make a good case that it is truly serving those with particular needs. But what about an elite and heavily endowed private college? Or a scientific institution that specializes in basic research? Each is also serving particular needs, which can probably be defined. Organizations should not be seen as single purpose entities or only of a single type (such as educational) when they probably have a variety of programs and services to meet many needs.

Example: An internationally recognized scientific research institution, which specializes in complex basic research in areas such as physics, biology and genetics, and astronomy, was seeking to expand its funding support. Most of those who knew the organization recognized it for its scientific leadership. Few also knew that the institution was also providing extensive training for public school teachers on how to better teach mathematics and the sciences. Even fewer knew that the institution also carried out its own science education program for inner-city children. The institution was meeting both the needs for basic scientific research and the equally important but very different needs for quality science education in the public schools where it is headquartered.

Mission

What is the mission of the organization? Is the mission of the organization still appropriate and relevant to what it does and what it plans to do and the real needs "out there"? It is also important to know how and how frequently the organization reviews its mission and when this was last done. Be sure board members and staff can articulate the mission in a clear and consistent way and that each person knows not only what the mission says, but what it means. Another key question related to mission the foundations and corporations may want to look at is how does the proposed program or project fit into the organizational mission? If it does not clearly fit, the potential funder may assume your organization is "running after the money." That is, it is trying to be successful in getting a grant by creating something the organization thinks the foundation or company will fund rather than creating a program or project appropriate to the needs of the organization and its mission. For example, a social service agency creates an arts program that is not focused on the usual clients of the agency nor does it fit with the normal services of the agency. It applies for a grant from a foundation that is primarily focused on funding of arts organizations but does not generally fund social service agencies. Is the agency "running after the money" or is there a legitimate reason—and a real need—for the arts program? When receiving such requests, many foundations would want to examine the proposed program in relation to the mission of the agency, its usual pattern of services, those it serves, and the real needs of the community.

History

It is important to have a good understanding of the history of the organization. Why was it founded and how has it changed over time? Has the organization only changed in response to outside circumstances and pressures or has it changed according to plans and strategies? What in the history of the organization makes it unique or special? What are some of the stories from the organization's history that show its impact and its effectiveness? Who was the leadership of the organization in the past? How have the needs it seeks to serve changed during the organization's history? What were some of the major services provided in the past that are no longer provided and what caused these changes? Some organizations are very good at keeping their histories while others are not. Of course, newer organizations have somewhat less difficulty developing their histories than older organizations that have not kept records.

Strategy Tip: A significant anniversary, such as the 10th anniversary, 25th anniversary, etc., may be a good time to prepare a brief historical overview of your organization that can be used with members, those served, current donors, potential donors, and others. A historical overview can also be used in strategic planning processes as well as help pro-

vide a benchmark for future looks at the organization's history.

Present Services and Programs

What are your organization's present services and programs? What other organizations have similar services and programs? What makes those of your agency unique or outstanding? Knowing the present services and programs is relatively easy in smaller organizations, but in larger organizations with complex arrays of services this can be difficult. There is also a frequent and unfortunate tendency in some organizations to keep the fund raising/development and program functions separate, which can make it very difficult for the fund-raising arm of the organization to know exactly what the program areas are and are doing. At one organization where I served as director of development it was necessary for me to insist that I be included in meetings of the program area staff, especially when new programs were being developed.

Strategy Tip: Get involved in your organization's planning function as much as possible. Frequently the input of the fund-raising or development person during the early stages of planning a new program or project can help structure the program or project in ways that may make it more appealing to potential funders. Participation in these planning sessions gives the development staff member the information he or she needs in order to create appropriate funding strategies.

An in-depth understanding of your organization's present services and programs is only a first step. You also need to have a complete understanding of who the organization serves and how it fits into the community's network of services and needs. Further, you need to know how present services are staffed and directed as well as how their effectiveness is evaluated. Are your staff members who deliver services trained and qualified in ways appropriate for what they do? Evaluation can be both internal and external. For example, many organizations have established systematic internal evaluations; knowing how these work and how frequently they occur is very important as more and more potential funders are seeing the evaluation component as a critical part of any funding request. But many organizations also have their services and programs, or possibly the entire organization, evaluated by external groups. These can include accrediting agencies, other funding organizations, or consultants hired to conduct evaluation studies. It is very important to have a good understanding of how these processes work, when they occur, and who carries them out. Accreditation is becoming one of the factors many potential funders examine for organizations that have accrediting agencies in their fields. Having accreditation or certification gives the potential funder an indication that there are some external, somewhat objective measures of the organization, its resources, and its effectiveness.

Even beyond these factors, you need to know how new programs and services are created (see earlier discussion of involvement in the planning function). Is the creation process "top-down"—starting at the board or senior staff level? Or is it based on analysis of the needs of those the organization serves? Or does the creation process involve many different parts of the organization? Many funders like to see that there is a systematic process for the creation of new programs and projects, just as there should be a systematic process for evaluation. Often, organizations are cursed with what I call the "brilliant idea syndrome." This occurs when one person, usually a senior staff member, gets a "brilliant idea" and, without much further thought or review, the "brilliant idea" is suddenly a new program or project. This is not to say that staff at all levels should be discouraged from coming up with new or better ways to do things. But there needs to be a process in place to ensure that there are opportunities for maximum input and evaluation before any "brilliant idea" is turned into a concrete program or project.

Example: Here is an illustration of how a "brilliant idea" can go wrong. An organization's executive director came into a program staff meeting and announced she wanted the organization to undertake creation of a major symposium series in connection with an upcoming exhibit at a local museum. The symposium was beyond the usual functions of the organization, which was primarily concerned with advocacy and legislative action. Staff, already busy with their normal functions, were told to "drop everything" and come up with the specific plans for the symposium series. The development director was told to "immediately" raise the $45,000 estimated as the cost of the "brilliant idea." The results for the organization were: three months of chaos during which much of the regular and important work of the organization was put on hold; staff became angry and frustrated; 45 proposals sent shotgun-style to foundations were turned down (see earlier discussion); no available funding for the "brilliant idea;" and, in the end, no symposium. Further, the "brilliant idea" resulted in a long-term impact on the work of the organization as there was a major loss of momentum, as well as a list of potential funders who probably didn't care to see another proposal from the organization in the near future.

Structure, Board, and Staffing

What is your organizational structure? Does your structure make sense in terms of your mission, budget, and programs? Are board and staff roles clearly defined and understood? Are necessary functions covered by the structure and staffing arrangements? Is there duplication of effort, overlapping functions, unclear lines of authority and responsibility? Or is the structure designed for efficiency and effectiveness in delivering the services and programs to those receiving them? Are some functions that should be critical to the organization, such as development and fund raising, relegated to lower levels in terms of the organizational structure or are they given appropriate importance? Is the board of the organization actively involved, as shown by board committees and clear lines of authority, or is the board primarily a rubber stamp for staff actions? Are staff qualified for the roles and responsibilities that they have, or have they been put into their roles for other reasons (friends of the board chair, relatives, etc.)? Are staff burdened with multiple roles, some of which may not be appropriate given their other responsibilities? Are there clear methods and processes for staff evaluation, promotion, and upgrading? Are salaries, within the resources available, appropriate for the levels of responsibility and rank, or are some people clearly overpaid while others are underpaid? Are board members selected according to specific criteria in order to meet real needs of the organization, or are they picked because they know other board members? Do board members have to earn their way onto the board by first serving on committees, or can almost anyone get on the board, regardless of his or her previous experience with the organization?

A clear and correct organizational chart can help answer some of these questions, as can position descriptions for all staff. The best position statements also include references to the staff evaluation system and criteria for evaluation. But, beyond these, there are other areas related to the board and staff that may require more extensive work. Leadership and staffing are critical to many potential funders. A board that is itself not clearly "invested" (at least in terms of its commitment) in the organization, a board that meets infrequently and with only minimal attendance, can be a warning sign of potential trouble and a red flag to potential funders. Board members who say "put me on the stationery, but don't bother me" (as I once heard) signal to a potential funder that a better investment could likely be made elsewhere.

Example: Do your board and staff know who is responsible for what, in terms of planning and fund raising? The following table illustrates one view of how responsibilities might be assigned (see Table 7–1).

Obviously, some of my biases come through with these questions. But I have repeatedly seen organizations with great causes serving real needs that, at their core, lacked the board and staff leadership to move them forward. If the basic commitments do not exist at the board and/or senior staff levels, why should an outside funder invest in the organization? Moving back to our investment analogy, would you buy stock in a company if the leadership didn't really seem to care too much about the company or what it did?

Example: I received a proposal from a neighborhood development organization for a grant toward one of their major programs. The organization was meeting a real need in a neighborhood with very critical housing and service needs. I noticed that the proposal, which requested a substantial level of funding, was only signed by the executive director. Given the high level of the request, I called the board chair. She was obviously not familiar with the proposal, but, after my opening comments, proceeded to angrily inform me that the board was suing the executive director. She almost shouted a long litany of problems and charges, most of which I clearly heard as I held the phone as far from my ear as possible. After the monologue was finished, I thanked her for her comments and called the executive director who confirmed, from his view, what the issues were and that there was a major gulf between him and the board chair. Needless to say, I could not recommend a grant, at least until the internal situation was resolved. But everything else about the request, including its direct appeal to the foundation's priorities, would have put the organization on track for funding. We just didn't believe we should invest in a ship where the admiral and the captain were wrestling for control of the wheel in the middle of a pack of icebergs!

Strategy Tip: Does your organization have internal or organizational politics or problems? Of course, the reality is that most do to some extent, and most potential funders recognize that fact. The two keys for the potential funders are 1) how serious are the problems, especially as related to their overall impact on the organization and to the particular project or program they might support, and 2) how does the organization deal with and resolve these problems? If you are in a fund-raising/development position and you see that internal politics or problems

Table 7–1 Resource Development Responsibilities

Board	Chief Executive Officer	Development Officer
	Policy/Planning	
Oversight of Agency Strategic Planning	Implementation and Integration of Agency Strategic Planning	Resource Development Strategic Planning
Policy Determination	Policy Formulation	Policy Formulation and Implementation
	Monitoring/Supervision	
Functional Oversight of Policy Implementation through Resource Development Committee	Supervision of Development Officer	Staff the Resource Development Committee
Ensure Comprehensive Planning, Training, Involvement, and Support through Resource Development Committee	Ensure Institutional Staff Support and Resource To Carry Out Policies and Plans	Coordination of All Resource Development Activities
		Supervise and Evaluate Development Staff

Source: Courtesy of The Alford Group Inc., Skokie, Illinois.

may interfere with approaches to potential funders, you should make senior staff aware of your perception of the potential danger these problems can cause to favorable funding decisions. While money doesn't always talk, the chance that needed or desired funds will not be acquired can help bring about a resolution or at least a start toward resolution of the internal problems. Your honesty and openness can result in successful funding approaches.

Operating Budget and Sources of Support

How large is your organization's operating budget? What are the primary sources of support (contributions, fees for service, sales income, public funds, etc.) for the organization? How consis-

tent have these sources been over the past few years? How does the organization help ensure that each part of the mix of support continues and, if possible, is enhanced? What is or will be the impact of changes in funding sources upon the organization and how does it plan to make up the difference if one or more sources decreases?

I was surprised at how often organizational representatives, meeting with me at the foundation, had little idea of how to answer these questions. At times, board members did not know the size of the operating budget or the primary sources of support. Some board members and senior staff were not aware of how funds were raised and where they came from (individuals, foundations, corporations, etc.). At some organizations it soon became obvious that board members were not involved in the budget development process but merely signed off on what was presented to them.

Other organizations would bring or send program staff to meetings with the foundation, but these staff members seemed to have little information on the budget, especially the general budget of the organization. Sometimes organizations came in that were faced with an actual or possible budget crisis, such as the cutting of public funds or a decrease in United Way allocations. When asked what their plans were to make up for these differences, all too often the answer was "we don't know" or "I guess we'll have to come up with something." Budget planning and development, like program planning and development, often lacked a systematic approach within many organizations, or the process was carried out by one or two individuals rather than involving key parts of the organization. The overall impression was that one of the most important factors to the organization's continued existence—funds—was often kept separate from its day-to-day functioning and was assigned to one or two individuals.

In my view, every development officer and every person, board and staff, who is or might be involved in the grant-seeking process needs to be able to answer the key questions discussed above and to know the basic budget facts of the organization. It is also helpful to have a three- to five-year budget history of the organization as well as some sense of what will happen in terms of funding and support over the next three to five years. If there is or may be an upcoming budget problem or funding crisis, it is always a good idea to have a plan in mind that will address the problem or crisis.

Strategy Tip: One way to look at and present budget information is to give the size of the current or most recent budget in dollars and to show sources of support with percents. For example, for an operating budget of $5.5 million, sources of support for the most recent fiscal year included fees for service (35 percent), direct mail fund raising (25

---

percent), membership dues (20 percent), contributions (10 percent), foundations (5 percent), and corporations (5 percent).

Organizational Needs

What are the basic program, project, resource, and staff needs of the organization over the next three to five years? How does the program or project for which you are seeking support fit into these needs? What is the specific justification for the proposed program or project? Again, it is important that those in leadership roles in your organization have an overview of the total needs as well as the specifics of the proposed program or project for which support is being sought. Many organizations wrestle with a constantly changing list of priority programs, projects, and other needs. It is hard, for example, for an organization with a limited budget to decide which is more important, replacing a leaky roof or using the money to support an existing program or project when public funds supporting it are decreased. But some sense of the organization's major priorities and a common understanding of these priorities among board and staff can help keep focus on what is truly important versus what can wait or be taken care of later.

Some organizations, when they are examining their needs, put together a "wish list," which can include everything they've ever needed or wanted to do. While the exercise of creating a wish list can be a creative process, all too often the list that comes out of the process is not grounded in the realities of organizational mission, capabilities, and available or even potential resources. This can become all too apparent when price tags (cost estimates) are attached to a wish list and the total dollars needed end up exceeding the even most optimistic estimate of what the organization could raise or get in support from other sources. If a wish list is developed, it is often appropriate to rank priorities and to focus on what should be the top five or six needs of the organization for the next few years.

But there is also another category of need that may arise: the "crisis need." A crisis need can arise

---

Every development officer and every person who is involved in the grant-seeking process needs to know the basic budget facts of the organization.

---

as the result of a natural disaster that directly affects the organization and/or the need for the services it delivers. It can be an externally imposed fiscal crisis caused by such things as a sudden cutback or delay in public funding, or it can be an internal fiscal crisis, such as an unanticipated deficit, a law suit decided against the organization, etc. Or it could be a crisis related to the physical facilities the organization occupies, leadership, or something else unexpected. Many organizations face such crises from time to time. In knowing your organization it is important to know how it manages crises and if it has contingency plans to deal with possible future crises—or if it merely waits for things to happen. Potential funders may want to have some idea of contingency plans of the organization, especially in areas affected by public support cutbacks.

Strategy Tip: Many organized funders (corporations and foundations) tend to be reluctant to fund crisis needs of organizations, especially those related to internal and organizational factors. This is even more true if they see a pattern of continuing crises in a particular organization, such as recurring financial deficits, high staff turnover, problems resulting from a lack of planning and forethought, failures caused by a lack of board involvement and oversight, etc. More and more frequently foundations and corporate donor guidelines specify they will not fund operating deficits for organizations. They also like to avoid "problem" organizations—organizations that seem to have a continuing series of crises or that always seek financial help to get them through situations. When you are approaching foundations and corporations for support, it is always best to be honest and upfront about any organizational problems. But it is equally important that the organization demonstrate it has plans or solutions for dealing with a particular crisis. In a sense, the organization needs to show it is making

every effort to control its own destiny and that the volunteer leadership and the staff are part of this effort. So, if your organization has a real problem or crisis, especially one related to the purposes for which you are seeking support, be sure you can present the plan or solution to the crisis or problem when you meet with potential funders.

Organizational Plans

Some foundations and corporate funders now require that organizations submit three- to five-year strategic plans as part of the proposal application materials. Even beyond your organization's basic needs for the next few years, it should have a firm sense of direction and the resources necessary to get where it wants to go. Does it want to continue to grow and expand? Or do the plans include downsizing or streamlining operations and programs? Does the organization want to stabilize and build on existing operations or move into entirely new areas?

Remembering our investment approach, would you want to book a cabin on a ship if you had little or no idea where it was going? Unfortunately, all too many organizations seek support based on their history or even their current programs and services, not on where they are going. Someone once said, when discussing foundation and corporate support, "People look at the past and present, but buy the future." Another person has said "Your organization may have been around for a hundred years, but the important thing is where it will be in five years."

The planning function, then, is critically important both to the future of the organization and to fund-raising success. Effective planning should involve almost every level of the organization including the board, staff, other volunteers, donors, and even community leadership. Many organizations go through a strategic planning process, only to create an impressive document that is shelved and forgotten, unless someone asks, "Do you have a strategic plan?" The plan is removed from the shelf, the dust is blown off, and it is proudly presented with the comment "Yes, we do—and here it is!" An effective strategic plan is a living, changing document that includes the goals, the steps to achieve these goals, the timelines, the roles and responsibilities of board, staff, and possibly others, and specific ways to evaluate progress toward the goals. The plan is integral to the organization, even at the level of day-to-day operations, and it is subject to change as new needs arise or as the flow of events inside and outside the organization necessitate. An effective strategic plan becomes the guide for budget and program planning, additions or expansions of services and staff, new initiatives, fund raising, and evaluation of the impact of these areas on the organization, its mission, and those it serves. A major part of the plan should include not only the goals and objectives but what resources (people and money) will be necessary to achieve these goals and objectives. The resource development/fund-raising component of a strategic plan must, of necessity, be one of its strongest parts because if the needed resources are not available, the goals and objectives cannot be achieved. Overall, strategic planning is a frequently espoused concept in the nonprofit world, but it is all too frequently poorly implemented and not taken very seriously by those who should value it most. While the objective here is not to get into the specifics of the strategic planning process, the importance of having a strategic plan and knowing what it is—and using it—cannot be stressed too strongly.

Past History with Funders

Do you know your organization's past history, especially for the last several years, with funders and potential funders? What have been the primary foundations and corporations that have supported your organization in the recent past? In what other ways, if any, have they been involved with your organization? When people review past funding and support information, they frequently look only for outright grants and gifts rather than exploring the full range of foundation and corporate involvement. It is very important to look not only at grants received, but past event participants (sponsors, underwriters, donors of noncash items, providers of volunteer support, etc.), past board giving, annual appeal contributors, and others.

It is even appropriate to know where requests were turned down and, if possible, the reasons for the turn downs.

Examples: I had just started working with a new client in my consulting role. As part of the initial meetings I was collecting information on past and present funding. I asked the development director if there had been any major corporate support or involvement and she said, "No, we've hardly ever received any corporate grants." I later learned that the corporate sector was very heavily involved through sponsorships, underwriting, product donations, and volunteer support in the annual golf tournament benefiting the organization. At another organization I was once told that corporate sponsorships of an event did not count as corporate support!

Knowing this information about your organization can help you develop the necessary groundwork for a planned and more strategic fund-raising approach, if it is not already in place. It becomes more critical to go through the exploration process if you are new to the organization. Find out as much as you can about past relationships with corporate and foundation funders and potential funders. Determine, as best you can, how the past contacts were established and maintained, who was the primary contact (development staff, executive director, board member, etc.) at your organization, what were the purposes of the "asks," and what happened. Find out if past programs supported by corporation and foundation funding were successful and what their impacts were. If copies of final reports to foundation and corporate grant makers are available, review them carefully. Talk to other staff or board members who may have been involved in past funding approaches. At times, it may even be appropriate or even necessary to interview past development staff of the organization (espe-

> Even beyond your organization's basic needs for the next few years, it should have a firm sense of direction and the resources necessary to get where it wants to go.

cially when files and contact notes are not well maintained).

The overall objective of your exploration should be to construct a three- to five-year historical overview of past and current support and involvement by the corporate and foundation sectors in your organization. But don't forget to also include foundations and corporations that turned down your organization in the past. The turn downs may have occurred for a number of possible reasons, some of which might have changed over time. Examples include:

- guidelines of the foundation or corporation might now be more inclusive or more directed toward the programs and services of agencies like yours

- the leadership or staff of the foundation or corporation might have changed and might be taking a different approach to funding

- the foundation or corporation might have more funds available to make grants than in the past

- your agency might have changed its focus or programs and services

- the specific reasons your request was turned down might not apply to your new request

- the needs in the community may have changed

- the research on the potential funding sources was not as complete as it should have been

- the strategies developed for approaching the funding source were not well designed or effectively implemented

Why is developing a historical overview of past funding—and turn downs—so important? Because

> **Find out as much as you can about past relationships with corporate and foundation funders and potential funders.**

your best corporate and foundation prospects are the past funders and supporters of your organization. And your next best set of prospects *may* well be those foundations and corporations that have turned you down in the past; this latter point assumes, of course, that the "homework" (research and cultivation) done was on target. But also, as will be explained later, these past funders and even the potential sources that turned down previous requests can be the basis for developing new potential sources of support.

Strategy Tip: If you are new to an organization and can find out which foundations and corporations funded or supported the organization within the last three to five years but are not now funding it, you should make every effort to contact them and introduce yourself as the new person responsible for corporate and foundation fund raising; of course, you should also do this with any current corporate or foundation funder. The contact should be either by letter or, preferably, in person. If you are setting a meeting date, explain who you are and your role and offer to come in and update the funder on the organization as well as hear about the foundation's or corporation's current funding guidelines and interests.

When you contact or correspond with past funders, indicate your position and role, thank them for their past support and, if possible, explain the impact their past support has had on the organization and those it serves. Update them on current programs and services, sources of support, other changes that have occurred since the last support was received, planned programs and projects (especially those that might be of interest to the foundation or corporation), other needs, and any other key points about the organization.

The overall objective of your letter or meeting should be to begin to develop a long-term relationship with each foundation or corporation and with staff (or board) at each potential source. Meetings and correspondence should be kept upbeat and positive and should speak directly to the difference that past funding from each source made in the organization.

Strong Points and Weak Points

We've looked at the past, the present, and the future. What could possibly be left to know about your organization? More and more frequently funders are interested in evaluation—how does the organization measure its *overall* effectiveness in carrying out its mission? This is quite different from program evaluation, which is centered on the effectiveness and efficiency of a single program in meeting its specific objectives. Some types of organizations can provide immediate answers to the question of having an overall evaluation. These are the organizations that are accredited by an outside body or organization (colleges and universities, hospitals, and rehabilitation facilities are examples). Every few years they are visited by representatives of the accrediting agency, who conduct a complete review of many aspects of the organization related to what it is and what it does. The results and the awarding or re-affirming of the accreditation give the organization a "seal of approval" that is valuable to a greater or lesser extent, depending on the type of organization and the area of services it provides.

For other organizations the question of overall evaluation is often not as clear. Some organizations do self-evaluations as part of a strategic planning process. Others may hire outside consultants or other specialists to carry out an organizational evaluation from time to time or in response to a particular situation. Sometimes an evaluation is part of a campaign feasibility study. Other times evaluation is only applied to the program area, but not to such areas as business operations, general administration, or fund raising (although in some ways the latter may, on the surface, be the "easiest" to evaluate). Many organizations tend to drift along without too much total organizational evaluation, unless some outside force, such as a funder or potential funder, wants the type of information

provided by an evaluation process. It is somewhat like stepping back and evaluating yourself. You may do this in one or two areas, such as your appearance. But when was the last time you did a complete evaluation of yourself—your life—and came up with some conclusions about major strong points and areas needing improvement?

Yet, many times in job interviews I have been asked, "What are your strong points?" (easy to answer), followed by, "What are your weak points?" (whoops!). The honest organization keeps looking at itself in some formal or informal way and asking these questions. The information can be very helpful for everything from improving operations to building a strategic plan. In the realm of fund raising it can be essential. Most organizations, like people, can easily describe their strong points. But, funders may ask, directly or indirectly, "What are the organization's weak points or areas where it acknowledges it needs improvement?" And, even beyond this, what are the organization's specific plans to address these weak areas? As was the case in our discussion of organizational problems, funders like to know that there are specific plans and strategies to address areas that need improvement. From the funder's view, it is better to invest in an organization that has a realistic view of itself than to put money into a great, shining ship called—the *Titanic*.

But there is another reason to know your organization's strong points and the areas it needs to improve. The areas needing improvement and particularly the specific solutions your organization develops to address these areas can become means to raise funds when there are costs connected to the solutions.

Example: Your organization has an old but still used paper system for tracking work with its clients. Staff members relate a number of problems they feel are tied to the record system. The program staff conduct a survey of clients and find out that there are many real problems associated with the record system, and these problems are result-

> **Funders may ask, directly or indirectly,**
> **"What are the organization's weak points?"**

ing in more administrative work, fewer clients being served, wasted appointment time, unhappy clients, and often uncollected third-party payments due. The business office explores several options and finds a computer-based system that can replace the manual records system for minimal cost. Based upon their projections of costs and benefits, the new system, which includes training for every staff member who would use it, should pay for itself within 10 months. However, the costs were not in the yearly budget. This is an opportunity for fund raising and, given your organization's approach both to the problem (including finding out if it is a real problem) and to its solution, the organization is well positioned to seek outside support.

The other side of not dealing with organizational strengths and weaknesses is that potential funding prospects may find them out in other ways. So know what the weaknesses are and deal with them openly and honestly. And be sure, as much as you can, that your organization takes the same attitude.

The Program/Service Grid: One Way to Know Your Organization

You are the development director of a social service agency. What does your agency do? Your first answer might be along the lines of "we provide social and human services, such as family counseling, counseling services for children and teens, and other social service programs to people in the community." When looking for corporate or foundation support, this approach can be very limiting. If you are researching potential funding sources, your tendency, based on the answer above, would be to look solely at foundations and corporations that fund only social service/human service organizations and programs. But organizations, and especially the programs, projects, and services of organizations, are not that simple.

Below I have outlined a process that can be carried out either in a fairly simple way or in a more complex manner but that will possibly help open up new ways of understanding your organization as well as new funding prospects. Going through this exercise will also help you to begin to think

more strategically about your organization and its funding potential, not only with foundations and corporations, but also with individuals and other possible sources. The idea behind the program/service grid is to match your organization's programs and services with the major categories of funding from foundations and corporations; by so doing, you will better be able to identify and research a wider variety of potential funding sources.

Example: Before working with the grid, it might be appropriate to explore how a particular program or service should be examined. You have just arrived as the new director of development at a social service agency that provides a number of direct services to clients, such as family counseling, counseling for emotionally disturbed children, substance abuse counseling for teenagers, etc. As you look at the primary programs of the agency, you realize some contain other components. The substance abuse counseling program also includes a series of lectures and discussions at the local high school on ways to prevent involvement with drugs and alcohol. The family counseling program has developed a series of training sessions on peacefully settling family disputes before they turn into violent episodes; these are carried out in conjunction with the local community college. The staff of the program for emotionally disturbed children are working with actors from a local theater company to create acting opportunities and performance experiences for some of the emotionally disturbed children.

Your review is showing you that the social service agency has programs and services that can be classed in more than one category of corporate and foundation giving and that therefore might enable you to tap new sources of support. The acting/drama project, because it is still in the planning stages, will require new funding as there are currently no available resources.

Using the above example, we will now look at the program/service grid for your agency's three basic programs (see Exhibit 7–1).

Across the top of the program/service grid you will notice the primary categories that describe most corporate and foundation funding (see also the section on national statistics on giving in Chapter 1). Down the side of the grid are the three major pro-

Exhibit 7–1 The Program/Service Grid: Basic Analysis

	Public—Society Benefit	Arts	Environ.—Wildlife	Human Services	Internat. Affairs	Health	Educat.	Religion
Family Counsel.				X			X	
Child Counsel.		X		X				
Substance Abuse Teens				X		X	X	

gram areas of your agency. The grid shows (the Xs) that your social service agency's programs and services can be classified by more categories than just the human services category of funding. The particular components of each, as described above, can also fall into the arts (the theater/drama component of the program for emotionally disturbed children), education (the substance abuse and family violence prevention components) and even health (the substance abuse component). In terms of potential funders and your research, you now realize that you can move beyond foundations and corporations that fund only social services and can start to explore those that fund education, the arts, and health (possibly related to prevention and/or substance abuse categories). As you look at possible sources and indexes in various foundation and corporate giving directories, you will notice that, within the broad funding categories above there will also be subcategories, such as "education—substance abuse—adolescents" or possibly even "arts—art therapy—children." These subcategories can help direct you to additional possible sources and resources.

The program/service grid can enable you to take a much more creative approach both to understanding your organization and to finding potential corporate and foundation funders. The grid can also be a useful tool in working with program staff, particularly as new programs, projects, and services are developed. Using the grid will help most organizations realize that, whatever they do, they may actually be working in several different areas and are not just a social service agency, a museum, a health care agency, etc.

The program/service grid can also be taken a step further. Some organizations use this model not only to generally classify their programs and services, but to also break out the various costs associated with programs, services, and projects. Exhibit 7–2 is an example of how the model can be used to do a more detailed budgetary analysis, using one of the basic program areas from the program/service grid.

Notice how the analysis in Exhibit 7–2 was done. Staff time, using percents, was allocated to the two major program components. These percents were applied to salaries and benefits to calculate the dollars from each that would be assigned to the two programs. All other direct costs were allocated to the programs, as shown (administrative overhead will be discussed as part of Chapter

> **The program/service grid can enable you to take a much more creative approach both to understanding your organization and to finding potential corporate and foundation donors.**

Exhibit 7–2 Emotionally Disturbed Children's Program: Budget Analysis

	Arts	Human Services	Totals
Personnel (salary and benefits)			
Program Director	$8,000 (20% of time)	$32,000 (80% of time)	$40,000
Counselor I	-0-	$30,000 (100% of time)	$30,000
Counselor II	-0-	$32,000 (100% of time	$32,000
Counselor III	$4,500 (15% of time)	$25,500 (75% of time)	$30,000
Theater Program Coordinator	$28,000 (100% of time)	-0-	$28,000
Administrative Assistant	$10,000 (50% of time)	$10,000 (50% of time)	$20,000
Contractual Services			
Contract with Community Theater for space, equipment, actor services	$35,000	-0-	$35,000
Supplies			
Office	$2,000	$3,000	$5,000
Theater Program	$2,000	-0-	$2,000
Equipment			
Office	$1,000	$3,000	$4,000
Theater Program/ agency supplied	$2,000	-0-	$2,000
Telephone			
Services/share of equipment lease	$1,000	$3,000	$4,000
Services/local and long distance	$200	$300	$500
Duplicating/Copying	$1,000	$800	$1,800

continues

Exhibit 7–2 continued

Miscellaneous	$200	$300	$500
Totals	$94,900	$139,900	$234,800
Administrative Overhead @15%	$14,235	$20,985	$35,220
Grand Totals	$109,135	$160,885	$270,020

12). The Arts Program's total costs of $109,135 need to be raised from corporate and foundation sources. Breaking down the actual direct and indirect expenses in this manner gives a clear indication of needs. The detailed breakdown also can be used to target specific arts-related funding prospects.

Taking this process a step further, the budget analysis will enable fund-raising efforts to be even more tightly focused. For example, the specific components listed in the expenses of the arts program may—or may not—be appealing to some foundations. For example, the contract with the community theater group may appeal to a foundation that normally would not fund a social service agency but that has funded community theater groups in the area. From their perspective, a grant to your agency for this portion of the project is actually an additional way they can continue to fulfill their interest in the arts. Also, by recognizing this as a component of the program and identifying its costs, you can better target foundations that fund community groups and that may make only smaller size grants. In terms of this component of the total program, one specific place to begin your research is on funders of community theater, including funders of the theater group your organization will be contracting with to carry out the program.

analysis of some of the specific programs at an agency, but also how to use this information and analysis to move beyond what may at first appear to be the initial pool of potential funders. Understanding and actually analyzing each program and project at your organization can help reshape your thinking about potential funders. An analysis like this can also help direct you to specific funding sources.

Strategy Tip: Budgets! More and more frequently an essential skill for a professional development person is knowing how to read, analyze with a critical eye, and even prepare budgets. When you are handed a project or program budget to include with a proposal, you need to be able to look at it and ask the same basic questions the foundation and corporate staff and decision makers will probably ask when they examine it. If you are not familiar with budgets and budgeting processes, if you don't know the difference between a line item and a line drive, if you don't have a basic understanding of how a programmatic budget should

Strategy Tip: The above example shows not only one way to do a more detailed

look, find some resources in your area and use them. There are many books on budgeting, including budgeting for non-profit organizations; there are also courses, seminars, and workshops on budgeting for nonfinancial executives, and similar programs. Some of these are offered through community colleges, four-year schools, graduate schools, and adult education programs, which may be in your area; others are offered through traveling seminar series. If you're not sure what is available, check with your local educational institutions, or even your organization's accounting firm. Budget skills, once acquired, will serve you well for your career enhancement and growth.

The Case Statement—Putting It All Together

Let us assume that you have applied to a foundation or corporation for funding. They invite you in to present your organization's "case" for funding (an unlikely procedure in reality) to the decision makers. What are you going to say? What should you cover? Should you talk about the mission and history, the plans, what you specifically want funded? The case statement or case for support is a means of putting together all of the information about your organization, including all of the categories of information listed under the major headings in this chapter. It may also include information on larger trends and needs in society or other information related to the purposes of your organization and the causes or people you serve.

The case statement literally presents in great detail the "case for support" of your organization. A well-presented case statement is, in a sense, an argument to encourage people, foundations, corporations, and others to support your organization either through their involvement or through their gifts, or both. In some ways it is a written version of what might be presented in a court or to a group of funding decision makers. But it is a very detailed

and comprehensive approach; in fact, the strange part about a case for support is that a good case is so detailed it rarely gets used in its entirety outside the organization!

The purposes and uses of case statements are difficult for some people to understand. As a consultant I have frequently prepared draft case statements for organizations. Their first reaction, when I present them with a 30- or 40-page document that typically makes up a case statement, is usually "who's going to read that?" I see the case statement as primarily an internal document and a resource, which can be drawn upon for a variety of purposes. I have heard the case statement described as a "core" document for the organization. It can and should become central to many of the functions of the organization, including fund raising (annual and major campaign efforts), planning, evaluation, operations, public relations, and other areas. It also can become the information source for publications and other materials, such as annual reports, brochures and pamphlets, fund-raising letters, proposals to potential funders, presentations, marketing information, etc.

But the case statement and the process of developing one are highly strategic. Development of a case statement is usually an organization-wide process, which can involve the board and many of the staff and even, at times, those who are served by the organization. An outside consultant or writer may be used to pull together the needed information and to prepare the initial drafts. Program, operations, fund-raising, and other staff frequently are involved in drafting or reviewing drafts of the case statement. The board of the organization may direct the staff to prepare the case statement and will probably review and approve the final version.

Developing the case statement and involving different segments of the organization in its creation, review, and approval creates not only a document; it also creates a common basis of understanding about the mission, roles, plans, and needs of the organization. Remember some of the key questions that might be asked of board members and staff by potential funders? A good case statement and a good case statement development process will help ensure that key board members and staff will know the answers to these questions and that there will be a consistent message and image presented by the organization, no matter which staff member or board member is doing the presenting. A good and accepted case statement also lends a consistency to materials developed by the organization, no matter what their purposes.

Example: As a consultant, I frequently review all or most of the current materials and publications of the organizations I am assisting. I have often taken all of the major external materials (publications and other items sent out or handed out by the organization) and put them on a table in front of someone who knows little or nothing about the organization. I ask the person to look at the items, but not read them, and to tell me if all of the items are from the same organization; all too often the answer is "no." Do your materials have a consistent look and feel about them? If you have a logo or symbol, is it used consistently on your materials and is it located where it will get noticed? Are the colors and textures used, if any, consistent or is there such a mix of colors and textures that each item could be from a separate organization? Do you have, as some places do, an expensive folder filled with poorly done copies of things, or is there a consistent "feel" about everything? And, most importantly, are the messages presented by your organization clear, consistent, and concise? Or are they, too, a jumble? Remember, your materials and publications always present both "direct" messages (the content) and "indirect" messages (the overall look and feel of the materials). The direct message may say "we are a vital, important, well-run, efficient, and effective organization." The indirect message may say, through badly prepared materials, typos, and inconsistent appearance, "we really aren't all that we say—we don't even care very much about how we present ourselves."

Now I should point out that not everyone would agree with me on what a case statement or case for support is or should be. Some see it as exclusively a document prepared for fund-raising purposes. Others believe it should be short and to the point. Some see the case for support as a document that will be used externally and as almost a version of an actual proposal minus the specific request. Some see the case as a document that need

only be prepared by staff, especially fund-raising staff. These more tactical views of the case remove its role in promoting an organization-wide common basis of understanding of and knowledge about the organization. If I were to interview several of your organization's board members right now, would they give me consistent answers about what your organization is and what it does? Would I get a clear image of the organization from them? Once the case is developed, it, like the strategic plans of the organization, should be a "living" document that is revisited, updated, and used over and over.

What are the contents of a case for support? If you read this chapter, you should have a fairly good idea of what the contents should be. Here is a quick summary list of the possible contents (your organization's particular circumstances may require additional items or that some of these areas be changed):

- needs ("out there")

- mission

- history

- present services and programs

- structure, board, and staffing

- operating budget and sources of support

- organizational needs

- organizational plans

- past history with funders

- strong points and weak points (the organizational evaluation issue)

Some case statements use a theme or central image to bring together the various parts of the

> **Once the case is developed, it, like the strategic plans of the organization, should be a "living" document that is revisited, updated, and used over and over.**

case. Some case statements are elaborately printed with graphics, pictures, special layouts, etc. But others are simple documents that, because they will mainly be used internally, are set up in the most basic possible form. While appearance may be important for other documents and publications of the organization, the important point of the case statement is that it is a document to be used. When organizations have case statements, I like to see them well thumbed and worn rather than pristine. It tells me a lot about the organization and its commitment to the case statement process.

Chapter 8

Researching Funders: Reading between the Lines

Foundation Leaders Urge Grant Seekers to Do More Homework

Los Angeles—Too many grant seekers send applications to foundations that have no interest in supporting their causes, according to survey findings released at the annual meeting of the National Society of Fund Raising Executives here.

In a survey of 40 grant makers, almost half said that the No.1 step grant seekers should take was to read foundation application guidelines carefully and do extensive research to be sure they understand what a foundation is willing to finance.

The Chonicle of Philanthropy

If you've followed along so far, you should have a good understanding of your organization and its needs, or at least you have the framework to develop this understanding. Again, it is important to remember some key points:

- Successful fund raising from foundations and corporations is a long-term, strategic process.

- The starting point for this process is not the potential funding sources but your own organization and its needs.

- The key to the process is in the "operational art" coupled with overall strategies and specific tactics.

- Research, like proposals, meetings, phone calls, and many other factors, is only a part of the overall process.

You are now ready to move on to the next phase: research on funding sources. Chapter 9 will discuss the variety of different sources on foundation and corporate funders and how to use them. This chapter is more concerned with helping you develop the critical and analytical skills you will need to carry out your research. It will try to explain what to look for and how to approach the information resources you will be using. On the surface, researching funding sources can appear to be a relatively straightforward task, especially if you know your organization and its needs. All you have to do is list your needs and match them up with potential funders' areas of interest. Easy!

Example: I was doing some research on potential funders at the Washington, D.C., Foundation Center, the excellent resource of funding information with offices and cooperating collections in several cities around the country (more on the

Foundation Center and its resources will be presented later). Seated at the table near me were two individuals who were apparently working for an organization that served people with disabilities. The conversation went something like this:

Person #1: "I've got *The Foundation Directory*—it's got a whole lot of foundations and corporate funders in it."

Person #2: "How are they arranged?"

Person #1: "It looks like they're arranged by states and then alphabetical within each state."

Person #2: "That's no help. Is there an index?"

Person #1: "Let me look . . . yes, there is."

Person #2: "Look under 'Handicapped'—see what you find."

Person #1: "Wow! Look at all those funders! There must be 200 or more!"

Person #2: "Hey—that's our list. Let's just make a copy of the index and we can have someone come back later to get the addresses so we can send all of them proposals. That was easy."

The copy of the index was made and they left smiling. I stayed another few hours to look at one particular foundation.

Good research is obviously not that easy. It should be intensive, directed by the particulars of your organization and the need for which you are seeking funds, and wide-ranging. With the right attitude and approach it can also be fun and rewarding in the literal as well as the spiritual senses. It appeals to the detective or puzzle solver in many people, especially when it is viewed as exploration and discovery. It is worth repeating what was said earlier—that research is like taking snapshots of possible funders:

The more time you spend carefully analyzing prospective funders and understanding each one you have initially tar-

> **Good research should be intensive, directed by the particulars of your organization and the need for which you are seeking funds, and wide-ranging.**

geted, the better will be your chances of developing strategies for successfully approaching them for grants. Each piece of information you collect about a given prospect helps you form a picture of that particular prospect. I like to think of the information as "snapshots" taken while walking around the outside of a building. The snapshots will give you some ideas about the building before you enter it—and maybe help you decide whether or not you even want to enter it. The snapshots may tell you some things about what happens inside the building, but they will not be able to tell you all that happens inside.

After you've found as many pieces of the puzzle as possible—the basic information—you then need to put them together in ways that make them meaningful for you and for your organization so they can become the basis for specific fund-raising tactics for that source, and for the other sources being explored. This is where the real skill comes into play: making sense out of all of the information. The skills part of research does not involve merely copying an index out of *The Foundation Directory*.

Many people who are new to the fund-raising profession at first think there are only limited resources available on foundation and corporate funders. Few of them realize how many potential sources there are. After their first exposure to The Foundation Center, a cooperating collection, or even a single copy of a foundation directory, they are usually so overwhelmed by the number of resources, they feel uncertain about where to even begin looking.

Each time you find a piece of information on a foundation or corporate funder—an individual snapshot—what are you looking for? The following key areas and discussion should help give you a frame of reference for your research. Each of these areas should help guide your review of the materials, whether you are reading foundation-published or corporate information (such as an annual report or guidelines); directory information (such as what is contained in *The Foundation Directory*); press releases; newspaper articles; or anything related to potential funders. Also discussed will be the importance of each area to your research. You will also notice some parallels with the list of areas you should be familiar with at your own organization. And maybe you will start to be able to see inside the foundation or corporate funder, even beyond your basic snapshots.

The Reading between the Lines Skill

The real key to the approaches below is what I call learning to "read between the lines." Developing this skill will enable you to better interpret what all of the information means, especially as it relates to your organization and its needs. "Reading between the lines" means you compare and contrast the information you review to see what it is really saying and what it means for your organization and your approaches to the foundation or corporate funder. In a sense, each piece of information enables you to form a hypothesis or theory about the foundation or corporate funder, which you then test against the next piece of information. This is an extremely important skill to develop, because the information you get, even if it is directly from the source, may not tell the whole story unless you learn to "read between the lines."

A discussion of the primary areas to look at in your research follows, accompanied by examples to clarify the concept of reading between the lines.

Purpose or Mission

What does the foundation or corporate funder see as its mission or purpose? Some foundations have clear statements of their missions or purposes, while others may not be very clear. In some cases you may have to interpret the mission or purposes from other information on the possible source. And, of course, it may be difficult to even find the mission or purposes for many foundations since there is little information on them. Sometimes, especially in the materials published by foundation or corporate funders, the purpose or mission may be contained in the discussion of the founding and history of the funder. For example, a statement might be included that says something like: "The Smith

family established the Smith Family Foundation in 1947 to help meet the broad health care needs of the people of greater Smithville" or "Mr. and Mrs. Jones had a lifelong devotion to the arts and left their estate to the Jones Art Foundation in 1955. The Jones Art Foundation has continued this tradition by funding major performing and visual arts organizations within the six-county metro area."

Let's look at some examples of possible foundation and corporate funder mission statements and what they *might* mean (the hypothesis you will test against other information):

Example 1: "The foundation was established to help support the educational, charitable, social service, cultural, and health care needs of the greater metropolitan area."

Hypothesis: This foundation seems to fund many types of organizations across a broad spectrum of categories. It has a somewhat defined geographic area of where it funds, but the borders are not certain.

Example 2: "The foundation is interested in supporting agencies and organizations that serve children and youth, especially those in poverty areas."

Hypothesis: This foundation is fairly narrowly focused on children and youth agencies and organizations, but the types of agencies (social service, educational, cultural, health) are not clear nor is the geographic area served defined.

Example 3: "The foundation was founded to address issues of women and minorities."

Hypothesis: This foundation seems to be focused on a specific service area—women and minorities. But the types of agencies, organizations, and programs are not clear, nor is the geographic area served. Possibly it funds many types of agencies as long as they are working in one or both of the two defined program areas.

Example 4: "The foundation funds national programs related to three priority areas: family violence; abused and abandoned children; and children in the judicial system."

Hypothesis: The foundation is interested in broad-scale programs by national organizations focused on the three areas listed. It may have a broad interpretation of what it will fund within these three categories, including possibly prevention efforts and ways to deal with the results.

Example 5: "The foundation was established to promote world peace, nuclear disarmament, and international cooperation."

Hypothesis: The foundation is focused on major international issues and concerns.

Example 6: "The foundation gives to social service and health agencies, including AIDS support, the fine and performing arts and other cultural programs, youth and child welfare agencies, civic affairs and community development groups, education, and minority programs."

Hypothesis: The foundation has defined several somewhat specific areas of interest and is probably primarily focused on local agencies and organizations.

Example 7: "The foundation only funds preselected agencies."

Hypothesis: The foundation has essentially closed its doors to funding other than those organizations it wants to support.

Example 8: "The foundation only funds those organizations and agencies that the donor supported during his lifetime."

Hypothesis: Another closed-door foundation.

Example 9: "The foundation is interested in supporting new initiatives related to the alleviation of hunger and homelessness."

Hypothesis: The foundation has a very narrow focus in terms of the purposes of programs and projects and may supply start-up money for approaches it feels are creative and innovative.

These are just a few examples of the mission or purpose statements you may find. Remember that these statements may be clearly presented as the actual mission or purposes in foundation-published materials, or may be buried inside the information without being clearly designated. Alternately, the statements may be included in a foundation directory or other such source and may represent someone else's interpretation of what the foundation does, based upon what is known about the foundation. The statements can also be part of guidelines or instructions on how to apply to the foundation.

Not all foundations have a sense of mission or purpose. Sometimes when a new foundation is starting up, it may have to wrestle with what it is going to do with its grant-making funds, especially if the purposes or instructions left by the primary donor are vague or nonexistent.

Example: One of the country's largest foundations was in the process of being established. The primary donor had left no specific instructions for the purposes of the foundation when he passed away, except that he wished it would do good and help people. Soon after it was established, I heard the senior vice-president of the foundation speak to over 400 area development and fund-raising officers. His opening comments were something like this:

"Well, we don't know what we're going to be doing yet, so why don't you send us some proposals and maybe we can get some ideas about what we should be funding."

I thought the room would clear immediately as the over 400 people left to get their proposals together and sent to the foundation. Of course, the upshot was a press release about two months later stating the foundation had declared a moratorium on receiving any further proposals until it could better sort out what its priorities were. I seem to remember one line of the press release as saying: "Due to the unexpectedly large numbers of proposals received during the last two months, the foundation has found it necessary to ask that it not receive any proposals for a period of six months."

Publics Served

What does the foundation or corporation view as the publics it serves? ("Publics" is used here in the broadest sense of any group or set of interests.) Is it serving a broad spectrum of people (usually typical of a community foundation) or does it serve some selected groups, such as women and minorities, the disabled, abused children, etc.? Or does it serve its own interests first (as with many corporate funders)? Remember from earlier discussions that, except for usually larger general purpose foundations and community foundations, many foundations are likely to narrow their views of who they serve. Also remember that many corporate foundations may primarily serve their corporate bottom lines, their stockholders, or the interests of their leadership.

Rarely does a foundation, especially a private foundation, have a clear statement that says "publics served include. . . ." Again, you may have to interpret this information from mission statements or purpose statements, guidelines, or even from grants made. But each foundation and corporate funder has a definite view of who—or what—it serves. The two primary ways that you can classify foundation and corporate views of who or what they serve are:

1. External: the funding source is focused on something or some group beyond itself

2. Internal: the funding source is primarily focused on its own interests, although, of course the funding is externally directed.

These classifications may seem arbitrary in that most funders state some external interests and also have their own internal interests and priorities, whether stated or not. Maybe another way to think of who or what the funder serves is to see it as another straight line or continuum (see Figures 8–1 and 8–2).

Figure 8–1 depicts a foundation or corporation that is primarily focused on those it serves. Its mission statement may or may not reflect this, but its overall attitude seems to be that it has a genuine interest, within its dollar and other limitations, of serving the publics it has chosen as most important and needing support.

Figure 8–2 depicts a foundation or corporation that is primarily focused on internal interests. Again, the mission statement may or may not reflect this focus. However, a foundation that has closed its doors to any unsolicited proposals, or that only funds preselected organizations, is probably a candidate to be included in this category.

Please understand that the above classifications do not negate the charitable intent of a corporate giving program, corporate foundation, or other type of foundation. It is more a matter of emphasis. But it is very important to try to understand where the

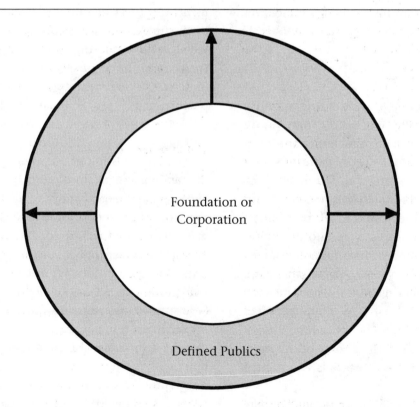

Figure 8–1 An Externally Focused Foundation

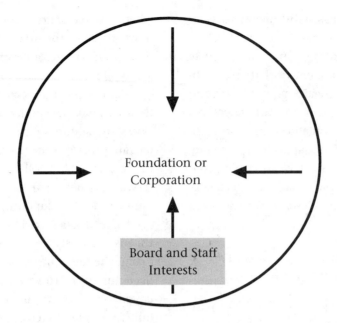

Figure 8–2 An Internally Focused Foundation

Guidelines

emphasis is. And, when it comes time to develop approach strategies to each potential source, your understanding the prospect's perceptions of who it serves will offer your organization ways to better match your needs with that particular source's focus and interests.

Guidelines

Guidelines usually provide information on what foundations will and, increasingly, won't fund, but can also include other important information about limitations, special grant programs or initiatives, or other areas. In foundation and corporate funding directories the guidelines may be summarized in the "Purposes" or the "Grants For" or "Funding Priorities" section of the information. Some directories do not usually list out the organizations, areas, or types of programs the source has stated in its own materials it will not fund. The guidelines are usually a narrower interpretation of the mission or broad purposes of the foundation or corporate funder as well as some of the more specific information that *may* be related to actual grant making.

The funder's own published information may include the guidelines in its annual report (fre-

quently guidelines and other grant application information is toward the back of the annual report if it is a fairly extensive document), or as part of grant application instructions on a separate document, or even in an entirely separate piece printed by the funder. Guidelines can be short or very detailed, at times running on for several pages when there are a number of special grant programs and initiatives. Sometimes the guidelines can be almost purely negative ("The foundation will not fund the following types of organizations and programs"); in these cases you should refer back to the foundation's mission or purposes to get some understanding of what it will fund. If you are looking at the guidelines of a family foundation (and often those of other types of foundations) and a statement about what will not be funded seems to be very specific, there may be an interesting story behind that prohibition. For example, one family foundation I am aware of will not fund any drug- or alcohol-abuse treatment program despite having otherwise fairly broad guidelines. I will not go into the story I have heard about why this prohibition exists, but it does.

Guidelines are a very important part of the total picture you are trying to develop of each potential funding source. The foundations and corporate funders themselves realize this and, as has been discussed, many are trying to make their guidelines even more specific in order to filter out inappropriate or unwanted proposals and other contacts. But guidelines are not the entire story of what the funder will and won't do. The guidelines are one more "snapshot" you are using to try and assemble the best possible understanding of the foundation or corporate funder before you actually approach it.

Why is your best approach when reviewing foundation and corporate funder guidelines to "read between the lines"? Even guidelines that, on first glance, seem fairly explicit need to be read with the attitude of "this is what they say they are interested in funding, but is this really what they do?" If you have already read or interpreted the mission or broad general purposes, review the guidelines and compare them to the mission or purposes. Ask yourself some basic questions, such as: Do the guidelines and the mission or purpose of the foundation or corporate funder seem to "fit" together? Or are there some apparent differences when comparing guidelines to the mission? One hypothesis you can make is that the foundation or funding program might have had one vision of its purpose when it was founded, but the original purpose might have evolved over time and the evolution is reflected in the guidelines. Remember, in the discussion of types of community foundation funds, the fund originally set up for "the humane slaughter of packing house animals in Chicago"? Over time this fund, like many foundations, had to be redefined—in this case more, rather than less, broadly—to adjust to changing circumstances. For example, there were probably a fair number of foundations set up prior to the 1950s that, in some way, focused on polio but that now are more generally interested in funding organizations and programs for children and others with disabilities.

> Even guidelines that seem fairly explicit need to be read with the attitude of "this is what they say they are interested in funding, but is this really what they do?"

You should also examine the guidelines as they relate to the publics served and ask similar questions, such as: Are the publics served consistent with the foundation or corporate funder's guidelines? Or are differences apparent? For example, if your information seems to indicate the potential funder serves a wide variety of publics, you might notice that the guidelines are considerably more restrictive. Again, you may have to make some hypotheses about the reasons for this. Possibly the foundation's grant-making funds are more limited than its vision of the publics it serves. A corporate funder might see its publics as those communities in which it has plant operations, but limited funding resources due to a lack of sufficient profits might mean the guidelines limit grants to scholarship funds for the children of employees. Again, your objectives include making some educated "guesses" or establishing some hypotheses about each particular funder.

The mission, publics served, and guidelines also offer the opportunity to start to match your organization and its needs to particular potential funding sources. Knowing your organization and developing the program/service grid, even in its basic version, can help bring some structure to your research process as you read through and between the lines of the materials from the foundation or corporate funder or review the summary information in directories.

Example: Let's take one of our earlier examples and work through it in more depth:

"The foundation was established to promote world peace, nuclear disarmament, and international cooperation."

Initial Hypothesis: The foundation is focused on major international issues and concerns.

Publics Served: Reading through the foundation materials, you find a brief section that states the foundation is primarily interested in providing funds for programs and services in the New York metropolitan area related to the foundation's purposes.

Your "reading between the lines" question: Does this statement support or not support the initial hypothesis? The foundation could continue to be focused on international issues and concerns through its support of New York-based organizations and groups concerned with the same issues the foundation states it is interested in funding. However, the foundation has at least narrowed the geographic area somewhat.

Guidelines: The foundation's published guidelines state that:

> The foundation primarily supports organizations and agencies in the New York City area that provide basic assistance, such as food, shelter, and medical care, to those most in need. Organizations and programs outside the New York City area will not be supported, nor will organizations based in New York City but which provide services primarily or wholly outside of New York City. The foundation does not provide operating, capital, scholarship, or debt-retirement support and only funds existing direct service programs and projects that meet the basic needs listed above.

"Reading between the Lines" Analysis: The initial hypothesis that the foundation is focused on major international issues and concerns is *probably* wrong. There is a disconnection between the mission/purposes of the foundation and its guidelines; the "publics served" could apply to either the guidelines or to the mission. If your organization is concerned with the issues of "world peace, nuclear disarmament, and international cooperation," the foundation, based on its guidelines, would probably not be interested in considering a proposal from you. But if your organization serves some of the basic human needs of people in New York City, you might be eligible.

Do you have any guesses at this point about what is going on inside the foundation? Possibly since this is a family foundation, the original donor(s) or people who founded it had a much bigger vision of what the foundation should or could be doing than those now operating the foundation. Maybe those now operating the foundation see more immediate needs but keep the mission and purposes as they were when the foundation was established. Or there may be one or two very strong individuals on the board of the foundation who have managed to convince the other board members this is where the foundation should be putting its grant money. Or something else happened internally, such as a personal experience of one or more of the board members, or a strong appeal from some of the human service agencies to some of the individuals on the board of the foundation who also serve on their boards.

Something external may also have happened. Possibly the organizations related to international issues and previously funded by the foundation are no longer operating or receive sufficient funding from elsewhere. Or possibly the end of the "cold war" helped influence the foundation board to move to a more local level of support. At this point, these are all guesses. But this example (based on a real foundation but changed somewhat) shows both what can happen and how to start your analysis. Of course, this example was selected to emphasize the point that each foundation and corporate funder requires a careful reading and analysis by "reading between the lines" and interpreting what really happens at the funder, especially as key findings relate directly to your organization and its needs for support. Many times the guidelines, mission/purposes, and publics served are very consistent. But this does not mean you should stop there. There are other key pieces of information that will give you additional snapshots of the funder and thus add to your understanding of each prospect. The strategies and approach methods you develop will not be based on any one or two of these snapshots, but on the best possible total composite picture you are able to build of each possible source—and your professional judgment, based upon both your analysis of the source and your knowledge of your organization—as to whether or not a particular source is appropriate to pursue.

Assets

What are the assets (the permanent funds) of the foundation? Most foundation directories and most foundation annual reports or other published information list the assets of the foundation. When looking at asset figures, always note the fiscal year of any financial figures. As we shall see in our later discussion of specific information resources, the financial information in directories can be two, three, or even more years out of date. Foundation-published information, such as annual reports, can be six months to one year out of date, or even more if annual reports are published on two- or three-year cycles, as some foundations do.

What do the asset figures mean? A general rule of thumb is that the greater the size of the assets, the greater the flexibility of the foundation or corporate foundation to take new or different approaches to its grant making. This does not necessarily mean the foundation or corporate grant maker will move beyond its mission or guidelines, just that there may be some additional flexibility possible. Assets, especially at a private foundation, are almost always related to the ability of the foundation to make grants. At corporate foundations and corporate giving programs there may be only limited or no permanent assets and the yearly transfers of pre-tax profits sustain the grant making. Here the more reliable measure of the potential of your organization for support may well be the grant dollars given out the previous year.

A foundation with a large or very large asset base (for the sake of a number, $50 million or more) can do much more than a foundation that has a very limited asset base. A private or corporate foundation with $50 million can (and has to, according to the Internal Revenue Service rules governing private foundations) give out at least 5 percent of that base, or about $2.5 million per year in grants. A small family foundation with about $1 million in assets can only give out about $50,000 per year; this may go entirely to organizations the primary donor supported during his or her lifetime. So if there were 10 organizations he or she supported, each might now get a yearly grant of $5,000—and that closes out the grant making unless the foundation has an exceptional year in terms of its investments and asset growth. A small foundation can also help keep things simple for its board and staff (if any) by making a few larger grants rather than a lot of small grants. The basic paperwork and review process may be almost the same for the small requests as for the larger ones, so why not simplify the process with a few larger grants?

The above example included a very important point: permanent assets of foundations are invested and can grow, but also can shrink, depending on such factors as the stock market, other investment results, the general economy, and other factors. A considerable growth of assets during a foundation's fiscal year can mean it is "asset rich"—and needs to make more and/or larger grants to keep up with the 5 percent IRS rule. Thus a foundation that one year ended up with $50 million in assets and the next year ended up with $60 million due to wise investments and strong stock market growth could move from a foundation that makes $2.5 million in grants to one that makes $3 million in grants. Community foundations, through a combination of current asset growth through investments and the addition of new permanent funds, can grow even more dramatically. This kind of growth and the additional funds available for grants can encourage a foundation to move into new areas for its grant making, to try some grant making the staff and board always may have wanted to do but didn't have the resources for, or to take some risks the funder had not taken previously, such as starting a small grants program for new organizations.

But remember that there is another important factor related to the assets of community foundations. Community foundations, as you read in Chapter 5, have different types or categories of funds. A community foundation can, on first view, be asset rich; it can have substantial assets. But the key to its grant-making flexibility will not be only the size of its asset base but also the particular mix of types of permanent funds that make up the asset base. For example, a community foundation might have $50 million in permanent assets. If 80 percent of these are in designated funds, it means that only 20 percent of the income from the other categories of permanent assets (about $10 million) can be used for grants. Based upon 5 percent yearly earnings on this $10 million base, the community foundation can make restricted, unrestricted, and advised fund grants of about $500,000, not the projected $2.5 million in grants it would first appear the foundation can make based on the $50 million of total assets. Thus the foundation has little flexibility in what it can do with the funds available for grants.

The opposite side of asset rich can be a reduction in the size of the asset base due to investment market downturns, bad investment decisions, etc.

Foundations with decreased asset bases are less likely to take risks, and more inclined to not overcommit their grant money or make any exceptional or large-scale grants. For private foundations especially it all becomes somewhat of a balancing act as they try to grow, manage their available grant funds, and make good grant decisions. Also remember that even the largest foundations do not have unlimited funds or unlimited flexibility. No matter where the power and decision-making ability is placed, there are usually controls and constraints on what can and can't be done. An exceptional year in terms of asset growth does not mean the party hats come out and the foundation suddenly takes a drastic change in direction. Foundations still take time to evolve, but substantial assets and good asset growth can encourage evolution.

A larger asset base also gives the foundation the ability to hire staff (professional, support, or both) as well as develop a mix of larger and smaller grants. It also can enable the foundation to make multiple-year grants (grants paid out over more than one fiscal year), with somewhat less fear of overcommitting funds and not having anything available for new requests for the next year or two. Of course, this too is a balancing act, which some foundations become very good at and others never seem to master. But having the large asset base can "open up" the foundation to different and better ways to do things.

Now, as you look at the asset base for a particular foundation, review the mission/purposes, publics served, and the guidelines and using the "reading between the lines" approach, start asking some key questions, such as: Is the asset base consistent with these other components or snapshots of the foundation? Or does the foundation seem to have a very ambitious mission, such as "world peace, nuclear disarmament, and international cooperation," but less than $1 million in assets? Maybe the guidelines are "too big" for the asset base. If the guidelines seem to list out many areas of inter-

est and types of organizations, programs, and services that may be considered, but there is only a $1 million asset base, the foundation may find it necessary to further narrow its guidelines or even to rotate its emphasis among the different program areas listed in its guidelines. For example, a small foundation with six major program areas of interest (children and youth, senior adults, the arts, environmental organizations, international policy, and disaster relief), may select one or two areas to emphasize for a period of some years, and then move its focus to other areas. The foundation may clearly state this is how it is doing business, or it may choose not to make this information public.

Board Composition and Backgrounds

Foundation directories are increasingly including more than just a listing of the names of foundation board members. Each board member may also have listed his or her employer, other for-profit and nonprofit affiliations (such as other board memberships), and other useful information. Review this information carefully and again "read between the lines." At the most basic level, even the last names of the board members of the foundation or corporate foundation can be useful. From our earlier discussion of family foundations you will remember that, even if you don't immediately know if a potential funding source is a family foundation, the last names of board members can be a strong clue. If the foundation is the Wealthy Foundation and almost the entire board is made up of people with the last name of Wealthy, except for one Wealthy-Jones, you can be fairly certain it is a family foundation. Knowing this should give you some ideas to test out as you continue to review the foundation's information, such as: Does the foundation seem to favor supporting several particular organizations or does it seem open to supporting other organizations that may not have received previous funding, as long as there is a fit with the guidelines?

If the foundation is a family foundation, find out how many generations are currently on the board and how far removed in time the board is, especially its leadership, from the founder(s) of the

> **Foundations still take time to evolve, but substantial assets and good asset growth can encourage evolution.**

foundation. Information that might help answer some of these questions includes the founding date of the foundation, the ages of people on the board (most directories and foundation-published materials will not include ages, but sometimes other resources with biographical information might be useful to find out ages), the relationships of people on the board (are there spouses on the board, for example), and how close the mission matches up with the guidelines (the mission may have been created by the founder or primary donor to the foundation while the guidelines might have evolved over time or been redefined by the newer generations on the board). When you start to explore actual grants made (see section below on grants) and look back at the board composition, do you see a split in the types of agencies and programs funded (such as some "conservative" groups or causes and some "liberal" groups or causes)? This split might be due to some differences of opinion among the foundation's board members, possibly reflecting family members versus other board members, generational differences, or other factors. Or do you see a mix of organizations that are funded, including some that seem to get somewhat consistent funding and others that seem not to be the "regulars"? This might again reflect family members supporting the traditional organizations of interest to the donor or founder and the interests of the newer, younger, or more distant relatives on the board. You may only be making an educated guess about what happens internally at the foundation at this point, but you will want to test it out as you continue to review information.

Grants and Grant Patterns

Next look carefully at the grants actually made and also the patterns of grant making of each foundation or corporate funder. Some sources, such as the more comprehensive foundation and corporate annual reports and some directories, list all grants made for a given fiscal year or at least (in many directories) examples of recent grants made. Be sure to notice the year that the information covers; like the fiscal information, the guidelines, and other information, the grants listing can be two, three, or more years out of date.

Looking only at the grants listing or the examples of grants and using your "reading between the lines" approach, try to see if there are patterns in the grants actually made. Also, if the specific purposes of the funding as well as the agency or organization name are listed, examine these carefully. Do the grants actually made seem consistent with each other in terms of the types of organizations and types of programs or projects funded? Or are there a few grants that don't seem to fit the general pattern? Or does there not appear to be any pattern, just a collection of grants?

If possible, try to acquire the foundation or corporate donor's annual reports for two or three years. Again compare the foundation's or corporate donor's grant patterns over time. Is there consistency, or do there appear to be major shifts in where and what the donor supports? Sometimes shifts in patterns of funding can be caused by planned changes in the program emphasis of the funder. At other times the shifts can be caused by a board member or members making a strong case for a change or board members responding to particular proposals that might normally not receive funding but, due to the personal appeals of some board members, receive grants.

Look also at the levels (dollar amounts) of grants actually made by the foundation or corporate funder. Again, "read between the lines" to look for patterns or consistencies, or even a lack of a pattern. Are most grants within a reasonable range or are there a few that seem much larger—or smaller—than most of the other grants? Foundation and corporate giving directories often give ranges and/or average amounts for grants from each listed source, and some also list the size of the maximum grant made. When looking at this information, you might see something like: "typical grant range: $25,000–$100,000; maximum grant: $1,000,000." This disparity may mean something exceptional happened in the foundation's or corporate grant maker's process. Finding out where the maximum grant went and what the purpose of the grant was may help you determine what happened. A series of smaller grants may indicate what I call "payoff" or "don't bother us" grants. These are grants given to help support the charitable interests of one or a few board members (the "payoff" grant), or grants given, sometimes without an actual request or proposal being submitted, to show support for an organization without making a major commitment of dollars.

Keep in mind that foundations can divide their grant-making funds in many ways. A given foundation or corporate funder can deliberately decide it will make grants within a given size range, or it can simply respond to the requests it receives. The grant range cited in a directory may be very broad (typical grant range: $100–$1,000,000) or very narrow (typical grant range: $5,000– $10,000). But the range gives you some indication of where the amount of your particular request should fall. Always keep your request reasonable as it relates to both the organizations' actual needs and the usual range of grant making by the foundation. And if there are a few exceptionally large grants made by the funding source, the nature and background of these may help you determine if your organization should go in for such an exceptional grant or should keep in line with the usual amounts given.

Strategy Tip: Remember our discussion of how foundation staff members try to manage their workloads? One of the easier ways for a program staff member to eliminate your proposal from consideration is for your organization to make a grant request at an inappropriate dollar level. What does this mean? Supposing the Wealthy Foundation's typical grant range is $5,000–$25,000 and the largest grant the Foundation has ever made is $50,000. If your proposal requests $100,000, and especially if you have never received funding from the Wealthy Foundation (or even approached the foundation before), the program officer need only get to the request line of the proposal to know you haven't done your homework. The decision to remove your proposal from further consideration by the foundation usually becomes easy. So try to fit the amount of your request to

what is appropriate and usual for each particular funding source.

Strategy Tip: If you are approaching a foundation that has never funded you before or that your organization has never even applied to before, you might want to seek a grant amount at the lower end of their grant range. Asking for and successfully obtaining a smaller grant from a given funder, while it may not totally meet the funding needs for your project or program, can accomplish a few other very important things. The funder may feel there is less risk involved in a smaller grant to your organization, especially if it is the first grant it has made to your organization (what I sometimes called a "get-acquainted grant"). Your organization has increased its credibility among other potential funders by adding another foundation or corporate donor to your list of funders. And you have acquired some funding for the program or project, which can be used as leverage with other possible funders.

If the materials or the directory you are using lists the agencies and organizations actually receiving the grants, your next step is to review these carefully. Using your "reading between the lines" approach, see if there are organizations similar to yours that have received grants. Are there organizations similar to yours located in your organization's geographic area that have received funding? If any details of the type of program or project funded are listed, look carefully at these to see if there is anything similar to what your organization is seeking to get funded. Maybe your examination will show that your organization's "new and innovative" program or project is not so unique. Or maybe your program or project is just different enough, or will serve those who are otherwise underserved, or has some other characteristic that

> Using your "reading between the lines" approach, see if there are organizations similar to yours that have received grants.

will set it apart from others already funded by that particular source. Here again having a complete knowledge of your organization can be of great benefit as you go through the funder information.

Example: An organization's planning committee developed a program designed to work with women in prison who were substance abusers and who were pregnant. The organization approached a private family foundation, which had made previous grants to other groups for issues related to women in the justice system. At the meeting with the director of the foundation, the program was explained to the director; he stated that the foundation had funded several similar efforts by other organizations during the last five years and had decided to move away from funding programs related to pregnant women in prison.

Strategy Tip: In the above example the director of the foundation gave the organization the names of individuals and organizations that had similar programs or projects and were funded by this particular foundation. This type of information can be of great value to you and your organization if efforts are made to contact these groups and individuals. How might they help? They may provide leads to other possible funding sources that would be interested in your project or program, give help and advice based upon their own experiences with similar programs, provide you with additional information and advice on approaching the specific foundation or corporate funder who gave you the referral, or in some cases work with your organization on collaborative efforts to develop programs or projects.

Strategy Tip: Funders are increasingly looking to collaborative efforts or cooperative ventures where two or more organizations with similar or complementary purposes work together to address a particular problem or concern. For the potential funder the advantages include avoidance of duplication, a stronger project or program based upon the combined experience and expertise of the participant organizations, and more efficient use of the grant funds. For the participants themselves there are also the advantages of using their respective resources and skills, learning from each other, making a whole greater than the sum of the parts, and developing cooperative rather than competitive approaches. But beyond these obvious advantages to each of the parties, there can also be a strategic fundraising benefit. Let us suppose a smaller and less well-funded organization develops a cooperative venture with a larger, well-funded organization. The larger organization has a strong track record of receiving support from several major foundations and corporations for its other programs and services. By combining with the larger organization the smaller organization can get access to these potential funders for possible support of the cooperative project— and, in doing so, it also has introduced itself to these funders and can reapproach them for future support of other projects and programs. In a sense, the smaller organization has had the larger group open the door to its funders for future additional support, while at the same time creating a cooperative effort with immediate benefits to both and those they serve. So be prepared to look at cooperative and collaborative ventures, which may have both immediate short-term benefits to those in the partnership and long-term strategic benefits for future fund raising by each organization.

Also look at the geographic locations of the grant recipients. If the other information you are examining specifies a geographic area served by the foundation or corporation (see some examples in the mission statements presented above), are the actual geographic areas in which grants were made consistent with any statements about what geographic areas the funder serves?

Example: A foundation's mission statement says it was founded to provide support for ". . . organizations, programs, and services in the Greater Washington, D.C. Metropolitan Area." In the list of organizations funded during the previous year you notice one agency in Tucson, Arizona, received a substantial grant. All of the other agencies and organizations funded seem to be located in the Greater Washington area. What happened? Of course, you may never actually know, but you might be able to make some fairly good guesses. One theory or hypothesis might be that a board member of the foundation is on the board of, or has some other connection with, the Tucson agency. In order to test this, you might go back and review the board involvement information. You may find a board member listed who is also serving on the board of the agency in Tucson or is part of a committee of that organization. Or possibly, the foundation board member had a family member, relative, or even a friend who was served by that agency. Or the foundation board member merely might have heard some "good things" about the agency during a vacation in the Tucson area. The key point is that, for some reason that may be obvious or not so obvious, the foundation board was willing to make an exception to its usual practices and procedures and made a grant outside of its usual geographic area.

Another area to look at when you are examining the actual grants is the time period of the grants. Some foundation and corporate grant maker annual reports list not only the amounts of grants, the recipients, and possibly the specific purposes of the funding, but also the grant period or length of time over which the grant will be paid. This information can be listed in several ways, for example:

- A three-year grant of $75,000 ($25,000 per year)

- Total Grant: $75,000. To be paid FY 1997: $25,000. To be paid FY 1998: $25,000. To be paid FY 1999: $25,000

- Total Grant: $75,000. Paid FY 1997: $25,000. Unpaid: $50,000

Why is it important to know if a foundation or corporate funder will pay out grants over more than one year? The program, project, or service you are seeking to have funded will probably extend over more than one year, so finding out which foundations could provide multiple-year funding can help eliminate or at least decrease having to find new funding sources for each year of the projected budget. If, in fact, your organization has a project, program, or service that will require funding over a period of more than one year, your priority potential funders list should include near the top any sources that can give multiple-year grants, especially at the levels needed.

Strategy Tip: Does your organization have a program or project that needs start-up funding, but, once it is up and running, will generate other funding or income (such as fees for service, etc.)? The fact that a program or project will generate its own support or be self-sustaining in the near future can be a strong selling point to foundations and corporate funders, especially those that make multiple-year grants. If appropriate, examine the possibility of seeking a "declining grant" from a funding source; the amount paid on the grant each year should decrease as new income sources phase in.

Example: An example would be the creation of a new fund-raising/development function at your organization. Suppose that there had never been a development function in place, but the board and staff were committed to establishing a fund-raising office. The initial start-up costs are projected at $75,000. At the end of the first year it is projected that the newly hired development staff member will have been able to raise approximately $25,000 in new funds; at the end of the second year approximately $50,000 will have been raised, and at the end of the third year approximately $75,000 will have been raised (these are very conservative figures). An approach might be made to a foundation, especially one that has provided previous support, to make a grant to provide start-up funds for the development function. The rationale would be that, by having an in-house development function the organization can help sustain itself into the future by identifying new funding sources (rather than returning over and over to the current sources) and developing a broader base of support. Specifically, your organization might request a three-year declining grant of $80,000, payable as follows: first year: $50,000; second year: $25,000; third year: $5,000. Notice how during the first two years the grant amounts make up the difference between the needs and the funds that are expected to be raised. In the third year the $5,000 might be used for salary and benefit increases. The basic idea is that the development staff member will be producing gifts to the organization in excess of his or her expenses within three years and the foundation or corporate funder can get out of the business of supporting this function.

Now, admittedly, the above example might take an approach to a somewhat enlightened funding source. But a previous funder might feel this investment would help the organization sustain itself into the future and thus the funder's investment would have been well directed. It should also be mentioned that a major and long-term individual donor could be another potential source for supporting the start-up costs of the development function. Again, the strategy would be to stress to him or her that having an effective development function will help ensure the future of the organization and therefore "protect" his or her investment.

Another area to examine carefully is the types of grants made. While the guidelines may give several possible areas (such as "The foundation will consider requests for program and project support, research, and operating support . . ."), are the grants actually made representative of these areas? Or do most fall into only one or two areas? If the latter, it may mean that proposals sent to the foundation or corporate funder reflect only a few areas. Or it may mean that the foundation or corporate funder has elected to keep its guidelines fairly broad but narrow down the actual areas it will fund, as in the example below.

Example: A smaller family foundation includes in its guidelines that it will consider requests for capital support (construction, renovation, "bricks and mortar"). During the previous year the foundation committed to a major capital grant to an organization; this grant will be paid out over a period of three years. In order not to overcommit its current and possible future grant funds, the foundation internally decides not to make any capital gifts for two years, since capital gifts are usually of substantial size. However, the foundation also decides not to alter its guidelines, as it will return to considering capital grant requests after the two-year period. This example illustrates how foundation and corporate grant makers can have internal policies and procedures that might be different from or modify their more public external statements and guidelines. Some funders may add a note to their usual guidelines to reflect such a change, such as "Note: Capital requests will not be considered for a period of two years." Or "Please note that capital requests will only be accepted for consideration after September 1, 1998." Other funders may elect not to do so.

Now, the next step, which was hinted at in the above section, is what I consider to be one of the fun parts of research on corporate and foundation funders. After you have read through the actual grants made, or at least examples of the grants, and after you have examined the dollar amounts, payment periods, types of grants made, recipients, geographic areas, and other factors listed, review the foundation's mission and guidelines again carefully. The key question to ask yourself, as you read between the lines, is "Are what the foundation or corporate funder *says* it does and what it *actually* does with its grant dollars consistent?" In some cases the answer will be "yes." All of the other information provided by the foundation seems to support its actual grant-making practices. But in other cases there may be several grants or even patterns of grants that seem inconsistent with the guidelines, mission, and other information on the foundation or corporate donor. Let us go back to an earlier example and expand upon it:

Example: "The foundation was established to promote world peace, nuclear disarmament, and international cooperation."

Initial Hypothesis: The foundation is focused on major international issues and concerns.

Publics Served: Reading through the foundation materials, you find a brief section that states the foundation is primarily focused on providing funds for programs and services related to the foundation's purposes in the New York metropolitan area.

Your "Reading between the Lines" Question: Does this statement support or not support the initial hypothesis? The foundation could continue to be focused on international issues and concerns through its support of New York-based organizations and groups concerned with the same issues the foundation states it is interested in funding. However, the foundation has at least narrowed the geographic area somewhat.

Guidelines: The foundation's published guidelines state that:

> The foundation primarily supports organizations and agencies in the New York City area that provide basic assistance, such as food, shelter, and medical care, to those most in need. Organizations and programs outside the New York City area will not be supported, nor will organizations based in New York City but which provide services primarily or wholly outside of New York City. The foundation does not provide operating, capital, scholarship, or debt-retirement support and only funds existing direct service programs and projects that meet the basic needs listed above.

At this stage your "reading between the lines" analysis is: The initial hypothesis that the "foundation is focused on major international issues and concerns" is *probably* wrong. There is a disconnection between the mission/purposes of the foundation and its guidelines; the "publics served" could apply to either the guidelines or to the mission. If your organization is concerned with the issues of "world peace, nuclear disarmament, and international cooperation," the foundation, based on its guidelines, would probably not be interested in considering a proposal from you. But if your organization serves some of the basic human needs of people in New York City, you might be eligible.

Next you review the foundation's listing of actual grants made and recipient organizations; the foundation information includes brief descriptions of the projects and programs funded at each agency. These generally support your hypothesis that the foundation generally is following its guidelines rather than its mission and your "best guess" as to why this is so might be that the foundation does not have the resources or possibly the interest to move toward more mission-directed funding. Another hypothesis might be that the board of the foundation sees the more immediate needs in the New York area and has chosen to support these.

But when you look carefully at the actual grants listing, you notice some major differences between the foundation's guidelines—especially the areas of support and geographic locations information—and the grants it approved during the previous period. Here are some of the grants from our hypothetical example that don't seem to fit the guidelines and restrictions stated in the foundation's own information:

- A three-year capital grant of $600,000 to Harvard University for the Harold G. Wealthy Center addition to Adams Hall.

- A grant of $25,000 to the Marion, Illinois, Senior Center in honor of Mrs. George Wealthy, Jr.

- A grant of $10,000 for the Medical Institute of Oshkosh, Wisconsin, for its cancer research program.

What is happening here? On one hand the foundation seemed to clearly state it wouldn't make these types of grants (out of geographic area, capital, and research grants), but on the other hand it went ahead and approved the grants. Now is the time to really apply your "reading between the lines" skills by going back over any of the information you have available on this foundation. As you review the background biographical information on the board members of the foundation, you notice that the board chair is Harold G. Wealthy, who is listed as a 1939 graduate of Harvard University and a member of the Board of Harvard. His personal connection with Harvard (you notice several other members of the Wealthy Family who serve on the foundation board are listed as graduates of Harvard) and the board's willingness to both honor and support him through a grant to Harvard were probably the incentives needed to ignore or make an exception to the guidelines in the case of the capital grant.

The second grant also is clearly tied to some family interest. The foundation's founder, according to your information, was George B. Wealthy, Senior. The foundation was established in the 1930s, so Mrs. George B. Wealthy, Jr., the wife of the founder's son, must now be fairly old. Your "best guess" is that she is presently residing at the Senior Center and this would indicate again that the board of the foundation made an exception to its stated guidelines to honor her.

The third grant is a little more problematical. There doesn't seem to be a clear connection to any of the Wealthy family members on the foundation board, but the research grant obviously is not in keeping with the guidelines. Checking some other biographical reference sources, including a news clipping, you notice that one of the Wealthy family members not associated with the foundation recently passed away after a long bout with cancer. Possibly this grant was, in a sense, a memorial gift to help with cancer research; but you can only guess.

We now know several key pieces of information or several "snapshots" on this particular foundation. We know the foundation has a very broad mission, but has chosen a considerably narrower focus in its guidelines. We know the foundation

generally does follow its more narrow guidelines and has also narrowed its geographic area considerably. We also know the foundation's board is willing to make exceptions to the stated guidelines, apparently when there are other family involvements or the board wishes to act on behalf of family members.

We can now make several hypotheses, which can be tested out based on the foundation's own information, foundation directories and other reference sources, other references, and the experiences of colleagues at other organizations. Here are some possible hypotheses:

- The foundation operates as we would expect a family foundation to operate, with emphasis on family members, their priorities, and support of the "home" area of the foundation and the family.

- The foundation is very board-driven, even if it has a staff, and the board is willing to make exceptions to its own guidelines to benefit family interests and concerns.

- The mission of the foundation has probably been refined over the years, but is too broad to support the specific interests of the current board members; guidelines therefore reflect these narrower interests.

Why are these hypotheses important? Because as you develop your approach strategies to this foundation, you will need to ensure that your organization's needs and the strategies themselves match up with both the interests of the foundation and the way it operates. For example, if you wish to approach the foundation for support that falls outside the areas specified in its guidelines, you will probably need the support of one or more

> **You will need to ensure that your organization's needs and the strategies themselves match up with both the interests of the foundation and the way it operates.**

of the family members on the board of the foundation in order to move beyond the restrictions stated (see later section on approaching board members of foundations directly). The grant exceptions also indicate possible approaches to the foundation based on some special interests of the family or at least some of the family members. Harvard University obviously has a strong pull on the family's interests, but senior centers and senior care as well as cancer research and cancer/health care issues might appeal to the foundation if they can be presented in the right way. One of the "tricks" of the approach will be to get some or all of the board members to move their interests from personal, specific, family-related concerns to a more generalized approach to an area or issue.

Example: The foundation provided a grant for a senior center out of its usual geographic area. While the grant was most likely a reflection of the fact that a family member is a resident of the center, your organization might build upon the positive personal feelings board members have about the care of their family member at the senior center by helping them develop a more generalized concern about the needs of senior citizens and how your organization will help meet those needs (if, in fact, these services and programs are appropriate to your organization's mission and purposes). A proposal or meeting with the foundation staff or board members should combine the program description and request with a strong overview of the needs of seniors in the area. The strategy would be to educate the key decision makers at the foundation about the needs of the elderly as well as the numbers in the area, local agencies currently serving the elderly, and the uniqueness of your organization and the proposed program. The idea is to move the foundation's key decision makers from focusing on their personal concerns in a way that goes against the current guidelines to a broader position that elderly needs and services should be supported by the foundation.

Your hypotheses can—and should—help guide your strategies. In the analysis above, the foundation's exceptions to its own guidelines means that there may be a slightly open door to other possibilities. To summarize the above discussion briefly, to "read between the lines" you will:

1. Look at the foundation's overall mission or purpose.

2. Look at what the foundation says it does (its guidelines or similar information).

3. Compare the mission to the guidelines.

4. Look at what the foundation actually does (its grants).

5. Compare what it actually does to what it says it does.

6. If there are exceptions or discrepancies between what the foundation says it does and what it actually does and/or its mission, review other available information (such as backgrounds on board members) to develop your "best guesses" about the reasons behind these exceptions or discrepancies.

7. Use this information to develop your specific approach strategies to each foundation.

Some foundations have actually formalized the concept of making exceptions to their usual grant guidelines by having an area called "out-of-program grants" or "general grants," or "unclassified grants" or even just "other." The usual place to find out if the foundation has a formalized "exception" policy is in the grants listing section of the annual report or other published information from the foundation. At the end of the listing of grants in various categories (such as health, education, social services, etc.) there might be the "other" listing of grants. Also, at times at staffed foundations the exceptions can happen because staff want to "try something different" or test out new possible areas of funding, or meet a new or emerging need in the community. Staff may, or may not, be successful in getting approval from the board for these exceptions. As the foundation evolves or the needs become clearer, the exceptions may be developed into new program areas and incorporated into the guidelines. This is one obvious way that foundations can change what they do.

The Foundation Filter

We've discussed in detail the situation where there are exceptions or discrepancies between what the foundation or corporate donor says it does and what it actually does. While this occurs fairly frequently, what about the more common situation when the mission, guidelines, and actual grants all seem fairly consistent? For these foundations "reading between the lines" may not reveal much more than what is on the surface and your "snapshots" may all seem to fit together rather well. Despite these appearances, you should still proceed through the testing process. One way to think of this testing process is to compare it to a funnel with different filters at each level of the funnel. The filters range from the one at the widest part of the funnel (the broad mission or purpose of the foundation) to those at the narrowest end of the funnel (the actual grants made). As you put your organization through the funnel of the foundation or corporate foundation information, you want to see if you can successfully get through each filter by asking a specific question and, if you get a "yes" answer, moving to the next level. If you get a "no" answer to your question at a given level, you then need to look for exceptions through the process outlined earlier. Sounds a little complicated, doesn't it? Table 8–1 should help.

The above represent the most basic areas that need to be examined carefully. While most of these have been covered earlier, there are a few areas in the foundation funnel that should be expanded upon as well as some additional areas of information that may be available. These will now be discussed in detail.

Timelines and Meetings

Almost all foundations, corporate foundations, and corporate giving programs have decision-mak-

ing timelines. This is the period between when your organization actually submits its proposal or request and when the final decision is made by the foundation or corporation. A decision timeline can be extremely important to your organization's planning and strategy development processes, especially if the funding you are seeking is time sensitive. For example, if your organization anticipates starting up a new program or project in six months and you will be seeking corporate or foundation support for the program or project, you will need to seek out potential funding sources that will decide within six months or less.

Foundation and corporate decision-making groups usually have scheduled meetings. Scheduled meetings can be monthly, every other month, quarterly, every six months, yearly, or even "as necessary." The information on the frequency of meetings is often included in foundation-published information and/or foundation directories and other references, but not always (especially for smaller foundations). The basic message is that, even if you go through your proposal creation and strategy development process, and have actually submitted your request, several months or even a year can pass before a decision is made. So it is important to tie your timelines and plans to the decision timelines of the funding sources when you are seeking support. A foundation that meets once a year and whose next meeting is 11 months away, even if it matches up in most other ways with your needs, is probably not a good prospect if you want to start your project within six months. On the other hand, it might be wise to keep that particular foundation in mind for continuation funding of the project once you get the start-up funding in place.

One way to think of the testing process is to compare it to a funnel with different filters at each level.

Strategy Tip: Be sure your organization's senior staff and board members know how long the foundation and corporate decision process can take so they can plan and anticipate funding requirements considerably in advance. Board and staff need to know that turnaround on requests and proposals will not be imme-

Table 8–1 The Foundation Filter

Filter	Question	Answer	Next Step
Foundation's Mission or Purpose	Does the mission seem to include organizations or programs such as my organization?	Yes No	Proceed to next filter Review other information, especially grants made for exceptions
Publics Served (if not included in mission or purposes)	Does the foundation see itself as serving those we serve or organizations like ours?	Yes No	Proceed to next filter Review other information, especially grants made for exceptions
Geographic Area	Does the foundation make grants, regardless of its location, in the area in which we are located?	Yes No	Proceed to next filter Review other information, especially grants made for exceptions
Grant Types	Does the foundation make grants in the areas or of the types we are seeking (program, operating, capital, etc.)?	Yes No	Proceed to next filter Review other information, especially grants made for exceptions
Usual Grant Size and Time To Make Decision after Proposal Received	Does the foundation make grants of the dollar size and over the time period we need?	Yes No	Proceed to next filter Review other information, especially grants made for exceptions; develop alternate strategy of seeking smaller grants if usual grant size or maximum grant is not what is needed, especially if it is a new prospect
Deadlines and Decision Process	Are the deadlines for proposals and the timelines for the review and decision-making process appropriate to the needs and plans of our organization?	Yes No	Proceed to next filter Possibly seek other more appropriate sources that can decide within your needed time frames
Actual Grants Made	Has the foundation funded organizations, programs, and services similar to ours?	Yes No	Develop strategies and approaches Review other information again and look especially for other exceptions and why they might have been made by the foundation
Other Areas	Does the foundation provide other ways to assist my organization that could also meet our needs (noncash assistance, technical support, special expertise, etc.)?	Yes	Determine how proposed project or other need could be met all or in part through alternative (other than cash grant) means; develop approach
		No	Seek other sources

diate. They also need to know that the foundation and corporation cultivation process, which, in most successful cases, precedes the actual submitting of the formal proposal or request, can itself take a long time. A rule of thumb is to allow at least six months between the time you first contact a foundation or corporate funder and the time you hear its decision—and this is the bare minimum!

Deadlines for applications and proposals are almost always tied to meeting dates. If the foundation has a staff, they will need time between the receipt of the proposals and the actual meeting date in order to carry out their review processes, prepare their recommendations, and get the materials to the board members in sufficient time to allow each person time to review the materials prior to the meeting.

Example: It was my first board meeting at the foundation where I had just started as a program staff member. Each board member sat with the meeting book on the table in front of him or her. The meeting book contained about 300 pages of materials—the agenda for the meeting, the foundation's financial reports, and the proposal write-ups and staff recommendations for the approximately 80 requests that were being considered.

The meeting was called to order by the chair. Almost immediately one of the board members picked up his meeting book in both hands and started to slam it repeatedly and violently on the table. The first loud "crack" as the book hit the table startled everyone. Over the repeated "crack, crack, crack" noise his voice rose in a crescendo of anger: "I got this book on Friday! We're meeting on Mon-

> **A decision timeline can be extremely important to your organization's planning and strategy development processes.**

day! If we don't get this book at least two weeks—not two days—ahead of our meeting, there will be no meeting!" The staff, almost in unison, shuddered—it would be a long and difficult session. But we had learned our lesson and the meeting books were always in the hands of our board members at least two weeks before the meeting date, even when we had to hand deliver them to board members' homes at night.

There are two basic systems that foundations and corporations have for dealing with incoming proposals. The first is the deadline system, which we have been discussing above. In the deadline system the foundation or corporate source has a specific deadline or series of deadlines prior to its decision-making meetings. Generally, all proposals and requests that come in prior to the deadline will be considered at the next meeting of the decision-making group. However, there are a number of "ifs" tied to this system. Proposals will be considered at the next meeting of the foundation board or other decision-making group:

- if the foundation's or corporate donor's basic requirements as to purpose of the request, geographic location, type of organization, size of the request, etc., are met

- if all the necessary materials are submitted with the proposal

- if the staff person (if any) responsible for reviewing the proposal had time to do so

- if the staff person feels he or she is sufficiently prepared to make a recommendation to the decision-making group

- if funds are available for new grants

- if the docket of proposals is not already full or reaches what the board and/or staff sees as the capacity for a given meeting

When one or more of these "ifs" is not met, the proposal may be "held" or "deferred" until the next meeting, which could be anywhere from a month to a year away.

The second basic system for dealing with incoming proposals is what has been described as a "rolling" system. In the rolling system there are usually no deadlines; proposals are taken on a "first in—first out" basis up to what is judged to be the capacity of the next decision-making meeting. When this capacity is reached, all subsequent requests are held for the subsequent meeting. Thus the foundation may judge that its board can effectively review about 50 proposals at one meeting. The first 50 proposals that come in, again assuming the "ifs" above have been met, are covered at the next board meeting and all others, if they also meet the "ifs," are held for the following meeting.

The deadline system, in a sense, rewards meeting the deadline with a good chance for consideration, whereas the rolling system rewards getting your proposal in early; the earlier your proposal is submitted, the more likely, if it meets all other requirements and the "ifs," it will be considered at the next meeting.

Of course, there are exceptions to these broad categories. The first exception can be the staff discretionary grant-making ability that was mentioned earlier. In cases where staff can make decisions without going through the board, grants can be approved much more rapidly. A staff member of a foundation or corporation, if he or she can decide without any further staff involvement, may be able to turn around a request and give a decision within a few days or a few weeks. Always remember, however, that where staff are able to do this there will be an upper dollar limit on the size of the grants that staff can decide.

Another exception is where the foundation or corporate foundation decision-making group meets on an "as needed" basis. Frequently this arrangement means that a staff member or board member decides to call a meeting when there are enough requests to consider. Depending on the inflow of proposals, meetings might be held fairly frequently or very infrequently. In such cases planning on receiving a decision by a certain date can be very difficult. The "as needed" arrangement for decision-making meetings is sometimes used by small family foundations, especially those without staffs.

Example: A small, unstaffed family foundation primarily funds national organizations. The foundation's board includes a husband and wife, who jointly established the foundation, the brother of the wife, and the husband's business partner. Once or twice a year the wife of the co-founder, and possibly one other board member, travel around the country to meet with organizations that have submitted proposals to the foundation and that fulfill the basic guidelines and interests of the foundation. These trips are usually scheduled when sufficient proposals have been collected to warrant a trip or in connection with other family business-related travel. Within a few weeks after each trip is completed, the board meets and makes its grant decisions. The entire process is deliberately informal and unstructured, with no real deadlines or scheduled board meetings.

A third exception can be emergency requests. While many foundations and corporations don't tend to respond too well to an internal "emergency" situation at an organization ("Help! We can't pay our bills!"), some will respond to an emergency when it is not something the organization itself can or should control. Examples might include natural disasters, major crises in public funding, or other situations beyond the control of the individual organizations. In such cases foundations and corporate funders may not wait for their usual scheduled meetings to occur and may respond with rapid funding decisions to meet the emergency needs. But again remember this is an unusual exception to unusual circumstances. At times, a crisis, such as a suspension of city, state, or federal funding, can overwhelm organized philanthropy's ability to respond to all of the agency needs and issues.

Strategy Tip: If a foundation or corporate funder's decision-making cycle is not clear from the published materials or other information, ask. At the same time, find out as much as you can about the decision-making process for each potential funder: what are the steps they take, how is the final decision made and who makes it, who is involved in their review process, and other related questions.

Noncash/Noncharitable Assistance

Another area to examine in your review of foundation and corporate giving information is the roles of noncash assistance and noncharitable corporate giving in each source's support program (see earlier discussion of giving from corporations). Information on noncash contributions may be included in source-published or directory information along with the data on charitable cash contributions. However, information on noncash giving and, to an even greater extent, noncharitable giving by corporations may not be as easily obtainable in your research sources, including the company's own published information.

Noncash and noncharitable giving may flow through areas of the company (such as marketing, public relations, etc.) other than the charitable giving program area (such as community affairs, or a corporate foundation). While the charitable giving or corporate foundation may have its own information and publications, information on these other possible sources of support might be not be included in the materials, but might be found in the general corporate annual report, or only in the company financial statements. So it can become difficult for you to find out if the particular company you are approaching for a cash gift also has the potential to provide your organization with noncash support and/or noncharitable support.

Some companies are beginning to see advantages in developing more centralized approaches to their charitable corporate giving, noncash support, and noncharitable support of the nonprofit sector. Such companies, usually under direction of senior management, are "packaging" their various ways of supporting the nonprofit sector in order to better utilize all of their resources and to get more of a bottom-line return on their investments. This approach has yet to be widely used, but with the overall trends in the corporate sector, it will probably become more popular.

Example: A number of large technology-related companies, working through their national industry association, meet together to discuss types of projects or programs they will support. While the amount and nature of the support will be defined individually by each corporation, all will

"adopt" a single cause or organization, which will become the focus of their attention. The companies see advantages to this arrangement if the "right" cause or organization is selected, in that it will help promote a positive public view of the entire industry, enable each company to work on a local, regional, and/or national level as it desires, and also help build public awareness of the new technological product all will be selling or supporting. The companies plan to support the selected cause or organization in several ways, including providing charitable grants, giving noncash support (equipment and services), providing noncharitable support through marketing and public relations areas of the companies, and providing volunteer assistance.

How do you find out about noncash and noncharitable support if the information available is unclear on the types of support offered? If you are targeting a particular company and its charitable giving information or the directories you are using do not cover these other areas, find out what other publications the company has available, such as the corporate annual report, or reports to shareholders. Get these materials and read them carefully, again using your "reading between the lines" skills. See if you can determine, from the information, what people or areas at the company might be responsible for these other ways your organization can achieve its financial and programmatic goals.

Strategy Tip: If the materials are not helpful or you cannot find the needed information elsewhere, the best advice is to ask. If the company has a corporate giving officer or there is a corporate foundation with an identified staff member, ask that person about other opportunities for corporate support, who to speak with to get more details, and how the process works. And don't forget that some foundations also can provide noncash assistance, although this is less common than in the corporate sector. Foundation staff, at times, can help direct you to likely corporate sources for your organization's special needs or for assistance that could be provided by other than cash gifts.

Messages

There are other important pieces of information often contained in foundation- and corporate-published materials you should always carefully review. Two of these are the board chair's message and the chief executive officer's or executive director's message (the latter may be called the president if the head of the board has the "chair" title). Foundation, corporate foundation, and corporate annual reports, especially for larger sources, often contain these messages. Why is it important to read these? Because the messages often contain such key information as:

- new funding initiatives the foundation or corporate funder is undertaking

- completed funding initiatives

- new areas of interest for the funder

- significant changes in the guidelines

- new ways the funder will operate

- featured grant programs, projects, or funded organizations

- board changes

- staff changes

- other information that may help you better understand the potential for achieving success with the funder

Examples of Reading between the Lines

Let us together, using the "reading between the lines" skills, or "RBL," as we will call them, look at and analyze a hypothetical but somewhat typical board chair's message as it might be presented in the annual report of the Harvey J. Colson Foundation:

"During 1996 the Harvey J. Colson Foundation continued its long tradition of supporting worthy local charitable organizations."

RBL: Check the guidelines and grants made—does the Colson Foundation actually only fund local organizations?

"The Foundation made 160 grants totaling $2.4 million, of which $2.2 million was paid during the fiscal year."

RBL: A little simple math: $2.4 million divided by 160 grants gives an average grant size of about $15,000. Remember to check a foundation directory resource to see if this average is close to what they reported; don't forget to check the fiscal year for the directory report and look at how it compares to the information for the Foundation's Annual Report. Also note that the Foundation did not pay out all of its grants during the fiscal year—does it make multiple-year and/or challenge grants? Check the guidelines and other information.

"Among the most notable grants was the special capital grant of $500,000 to the Museum of Art toward the new Harvey J. Colson Early American Art Wing."

RBL: Check the guidelines again—they state the foundation will not consider requests for capital support. Check the board members' biographical information. Timothy Colson, the board chair, is on the board of the Art Museum. Best guess at this point: the capital grant, an exception to the Foundation's usual practices, was most likely a result of this connection. Timothy Colson is also on the board of the United Way—this could be a plus for your agency as it receives United Way funding. Check other biographical sources, such as *Who's Who*. Timothy Colson is the son of the Foundation's original donor. His wife serves on the board of a local theater company; this probably indicates a family interest in the arts and culture. She also serves on the board of the local child abuse agency; family seems interested in serving the community beyond their foundation roles. See how many other family members are on the board and check their biographical information. Also note that the original estimate of the average grant size may not be as high as you first thought.

"Other notable grants by the Colson Foundation included a two-year, $100,000 grant to a collaborative effort by six child care agencies to better coordinate their services and programs to underserved children."

RBL: This confirms the Foundation makes multiple-year grants. Also, the Foundation supports collaborative efforts. Colson family members seem interested in children and children's issues. Check guidelines and interest areas again, as well as other grants made to further confirm this.

"The Colson Foundation also recently completed its three-year grants program to support the introduction of computers and technology into public schools that would otherwise be without these resources."

RBL: The foundation directory you are using referred to the start of this special grants program, but that information is obviously out-of-date. The program does reaffirm the foundation's interests in children, especially those most in need of education and services. Do the current guidelines indicate any support of education or is the connection again the underserved children interest? Check and find out. Does the Foundation show any other technology-related interests through its grant making? If so, in what ways and how might these be applied to your organization's needs?

"In a new initiative the Colson Foundation will focus some of its grant funds on the growing incidence of child abuse and especially on those agencies that have innovative or new approaches to helping abused children and preventing further abuse of children."

RBL: This is strong evidence of the family's commitment to children's services and children's issues. It also shows the probable influence of the wife of Timothy Colson (see discussion of biographical information above) on the direction of the Foundation, even though she is not on the board. The statement also shows that the Foundation is open to new ideas and approaches to issues, possibly even in its other funding programs. The statement shows that the Foundation is interested in not only treatment, but also prevention—again,

this might be useful information for other programs beyond the Foundation's expressed interest in child abuse.

"In order to implement this new grant focus, the Colson Foundation has hired Dr. Anthony Grey, a leading national expert on child abuse and formerly head of the State University's Department of Child Psychology, to become Vice-President for Special Programs."

RBL: This information provides the contact person for any grant requests related to child abuse treatment and prevention. Remember to check board and staff members at your organization to see if any of them know Dr. Grey and can therefore be a link to him. Will he handle other special grant programs and, if so, what are they? Check other information on the Foundation.

"In other areas, the Foundation's Board of Directors, at its Annual Meeting, decided to now meet monthly in order to better respond to the large number of proposals being received."

RBL: This will change their deadlines and processing procedures; if the information is not contained elsewhere in the Foundation's information, remember to call and find out what the new deadlines are.

"The Foundation's Finance Committee also informed the Board at the Annual Meeting that the Foundation experienced substantial growth in its permanent assets."

RBL: Review the Foundation's fiscal information to see how substantially the assets did actually grow. A considerable increase means there will be more funds available for grants. Using a little simple math again, figure about five to seven percent of the total assets will probably be given out as grants.

"Finally, the Board was saddened by the death of long-time Board member Anna Colson. Her 25 years of service as a member of this Board and her long commitment to the local community through her numerous civic and personal philanthropic activities were an example to us all. Anna's position on the Board will be filled by Robert Risker, President of First City Bank."

RBL: Find out more about Anna Colson, using other biographic and press clip sources. What organizations was she involved with and did she support through her "personal philanthropic activities"? What seemed to be her patterns of interest and support? How do these fit or do they fit with those of the Foundation? Were these activities substantial? If so, this may indicate a portion of her estate might be going to the Colson Foundation, thus further boosting its assets and making more funds available for grants. Check on biographical information for Robert Risker. Find out if he is a board member of other organizations, both corporate and nonprofit. What are his other activities? Call and ask the bank if they can send you a biography or press release about him. Does the bank have a charitable giving program? Are your organization's accounts maintained at this bank? Some banks may be more responsive to requests for support from their nonprofit customers than from others.

The above example shows how an analytical, questioning approach can help develop and confirm information about the foundation. This information can be the basis for developing and refining your organization's approach strategies to each funding source so that you can create better chances for success.

Staffing

Foundation- and corporate-published information may also contain information on staffing of the funding source. Some annual reports, especially for larger foundations and corporate giving programs, provide detailed information on staff but most list only staff and their titles. Whatever information you can obtain on the staff of a particular foundation or corporate funder can be useful in several ways. For foundations and corporate funders where staff are assigned to different areas of the foundation's grant making, such as health, education, etc., the staff information may be a useful

> An analytical, questioning approach can help develop and confirm information about the foundation.

guide as to the specific people that should be approached. This can help you go directly to a specific individual or individuals rather than just calling "the foundation."

But other foundations' materials may not be much help in identifying who does what on the staff if there is more than one staff person. Remember earlier we discussed the concept of "generalists" staff versus "specialists" staff. In most of the smaller foundations and even in some of the larger foundations staff are all considered generalists and can be given the job of handling any proposal that comes in, regardless of the type of organization or type of program for which support is being sought. Some foundations may have a few specialists to handle requests that have a very technical nature or require in-depth understanding of an area or issue (see the example of the Colson Foundation's Board Chair message above), with the rest of the staff functioning as generalists.

When reading through staff listings in foundation and corporate materials, see how much you can learn, even if only names and titles are given. For example, do there appear to be several different levels of staff (such as executive director, program directors, and other program staff), or just a few levels (such as executive director and associate directors)? Several levels of staff might mean the foundation has somewhat compartmentalized how it operates, and compartmentalization might also be a sign of a more staff-driven foundation with some autonomy of each area. A smaller staff with fewer levels might mean the foundation staff operate more as a unit with group consensus decision making and grant recommendations. Do staff members have advanced degrees? If they do, this might indicate some specialization or at least some areas that they see themselves as knowing more about than some of the other areas they might be responsible for when reviewing incoming proposals.

When looking at staff listings and titles, also notice if there is a person responsible for processing incoming proposals. This person might have the title of "Proposal Manager" or "Grants Applications Manager." The existence of such a position means that the foundation (it is usually a foundation that has this position) has centralized its processing of proposals. This individual (or, in a few cases, the office) may be responsible for reviewing all incoming requests to ensure that they meet the foundation's basic guidelines, that the needed materials are included, that proposals are logged in and necessary control forms set up, that acknowledgment letters are sent, and that proposals are assigned to appropriate staff for review. In some foundations the person with these responsibilities can have considerable power and can send proposals back if they don't exactly meet the foundation's stated (and sometimes unstated) requirements. In other foundations the individual or office acts more as a processor and cannot make decisions about whether or not proposals meet requirements; it is up to program staff to make decisions about returning proposals for not meeting requirements or for other reasons.

The proposal manager or grants application manager may also serve as the primary contact point when a person calls the foundation for information or to inquire about the status of a proposal already submitted. He or she may help control direct contact with the foundation's program officers unless or until they are ready to be spoken with by applicants and others. This helps filter out the calls from those only requesting information from the foundation, people calling to set meetings when program officers are not yet ready to meet, and people and organizations that clearly fall outside of the foundation's purposes and guidelines. In other foundations the receptionist or the support staff of individual program staff may also serve this "gatekeeper" function.

How do you deal with gatekeepers at foundations and corporate funders? Accessibility to foundation staff is seen as a growing problem by those of us who are outside the foundations trying to get in. Foundation staff are increasingly perceived as not returning phone calls, unwilling to meet, or simply shutting themselves off from those they are "supposed to" communicate with, regardless of who those people are or what they want. Foundations and corporate grant makers have varying ideas about how open and accessible they should be. To make a broad generalization with many exceptions: the degrees of openness and accessibility by types of foundations and corporate donors range from community foundations (usually fairly to very accessible) to small family foundations (usually fairly to very closed), with general purpose foundations, special purpose foundations, corporate foundations, corporate funders, and larger family foundations falling in between in approximate order of openness. Just remember that each case is unique and that, while in the past some foundation staffs saw themselves as overworked, now many are probably really overworked.

Assume you are on the program staff of a relatively small foundation. You have approximately 40 to 50 proposals to review over a period of about two and one-half months, as your board meets quarterly. All materials have to be ready for the board books at least two weeks ahead of the meeting date (or you may get a repeat of the book-slamming incident mentioned earlier). You are expected to meet with most or all applicants once you have reviewed their proposals. You are also responsible for doing your homework by making the necessary calls and other inquiries to verify information on new applicants as well as speak with other past and current foundation and corporate funders (in my experience, this checking process usually involved an average of about 10 to 15 calls per proposal). You have staff meetings to attend, other activities and meetings outside the foundation but related to your work, and so on. You get frequent calls from people who start off the conversation by saying "I have a great idea . . . all you have to do is get me a grant!"

What do you do? The first step is probably to have someone filter your calls first so that only serious or appropriate callers are directed into your office. You seek to hold meetings with those who have proposals already submitted, followed by those who meet the foundation's basic criteria and guidelines. You also try to control your workflow by processing only those proposals that include all the necessary information, meet the guidelines and deadlines, and clearly show that the applicants have done their homework. Other applications get returned. To the outsider you may appear difficult to reach or inaccessible; from your viewpoint you're just trying to control the volume of your work.

This is not to excuse the arrogant, rude, or totally inaccessible foundation staff person. Yes, there are those types loose in the foundation world. Some delight in what can be a "power trip" as a foundation officer; others always give the attitude that they are too busy to see you or that you and your organization may not be worthy enough or important enough to see them. That is unfortunate but it does happen. The best advice is to be persistent without overdoing it and, if the door stays shut after you've done your homework and put together what you feel is the best possible strategy, after several trys, go elsewhere.

What else might be contained in a foundation's or corporate donor's annual report and other published information? Larger foundations might have discussions of what happened during the previous year within each of their major grant areas. Again, this information can help you see what types of programs, projects, and other supported activities the foundation or corporate funder felt very positive about and thus is featuring in the report. Sometimes foundations or corporate funders will include profiles on selected funded organizations; corporations may include information on their volunteer efforts, such as participation in community clean-up campaigns, charity golf tournament sponsorships, or other activities that reflect well on the company and its commitment to the community. Some foundation annual reports can have a particular theme or focus each year, usually on some major issue and how the foundation's grant-making program and other activities are addressing this particular issue. Community foundations may fea-

> **In reading between the lines, your primary intent should always be to match up the interests of funders with your organization's needs.**

ture their nongrant activities in working with their communities on particular concerns or issues.

All of this information can provide useful clues to identify those areas and concerns the selected funding source sees as paramount in its own work. In reading between the lines, your primary intent should always be to match up the particular interests and concerns of each funding source with your organization's own needs in ways that will benefit both the funder and your organization—and of course, those you serve. In the best sense of the word, you and your organization are truly seeking a partnership with each funder, whether it be an individual, a foundation, or a corporation. A partnership is an exchange of benefits between the partners, not giving a check to an organization so it can do something that would otherwise not be possible or to do more of something it is already doing. As we shall see, developing relationships with funding sources is a very special kind of a partnership. But first, we need to examine other sources of information on potential funders.

Reference

"Foundation Leaders Urge Grant Seekers to Do More Homework." *The Chronicle of Philanthropy,* 4 April 1996.

Chapter 9

Researching Funders: Other Sources of Information and What You Need to Know

The preceding chapter, although it included some discussion of other information sources, primarily focused on "reading between the lines" of foundation and corporate primary (printed or published by them) sources of information. But we have also mentioned other sources, such as foundation directories, electronic resources (desktop computerized databases and on-line information), biographical directories, and even press clippings. What do you need to know about these resources and how to use them?

There are many secondary resources of information on corporate and foundation funding. Some people are surprised at just how many sources there are. I have often watched people come into the local office of the Foundation Center; they are frequently overwhelmed by the fact that there is an entire library of information on potential fund-

ers. And, if they see beyond the full bookshelves and the computer terminals and the file cabinets in the typical Foundation Center, they will know additional resources are being added almost daily.

This chapter is not intended to provide an in-depth discussion of each possible source of information, whether it be printed, electronic, or even word of mouth. Rather it is intended to give you important concepts and guidelines for reviewing and using the information, no matter what the source. The following sections discuss the major generic categories of secondary sources of information.

Printed Foundation and Corporate Funder Directories

Types

Foundation, corporate foundation, and corporate funder printed directories are published by a growing number of sources, including The Foundation Center, The Taft Group, and others. Directories can be categorized in a number of different ways. There are national directories, which list many major foundation and corporate funders throughout the United States. There are also regional, state, and even local directories of funding resources. National and other directories may list funders alphabetically by the name of the funder, or may use the state name as the first classification basis, with funders listed alphabetically within each state listing. Printed directories usually provide several indexing systems with extensive cross-referencing. Indexes can include:

- types of areas, programs, and services funded (health, disabled children, women's issues, etc.)

- names of foundations and corporate donors (if another basis is used for the general listing)

- names of board and staff members of foundations and corporate donors (often useful if you find an individual who serves on more than one foundation board)

- a geographic index of foundations and corporate donors

- types of funding provided (operating, project/program, etc.)

- grant recipients and their geographic locations

- major products and locations of corporate funders

- funders providing multi-year and operating support

- new foundations listed since the last publication

- foundations deleted from the current edition

Strategy Tip: When using printed foundation directories, you will need to develop good "flipping" skills. The numerous indexes in most major foundation directories require you to flip back and forth between them and the primary information. So, no matter which directory you are using, always become thoroughly familiar with the indexes for that particular source. But it is also important to remember that the indexes are just one of many ways to classify information on funders. Each index, while it can direct you to other information or resources, also provides a very limited view. Remember our example of the dialogue at The Foundation Center when two people saw

the subject index as the only necessary resource to examine? Indexes are helpful, but only in directing your exploration of other information, not as the final word.

These basic directories, especially the listings containing foundations and corporations throughout the United States, are supplemented by other printed resources, which frequently take the same information provided in the source directory and list it in different ways or amplify it. For example, corporate funders and corporate foundations may also be listed in a separate directory solely focused on corporate giving. Foundations making grants over a certain dollar size or providing certain types of grants (operating support, funding for technology, etc.) might also be listed in separate directories. Some directories provide information listed by types of programs actually funded and the names of organizations receiving grants. Again, these may be listed geographically or in other ways.

I find these specialized directories particularly useful because they tell me what the foundations and corporate funders are actually doing, rather than merely describing what they say they do. Even the large national directories are now including examples of grants made in their listings of foundation and corporate funders, rather than just giving the general information on the funding source. It is always helpful to see both what the basic information about the particular source says as well as what happens when grant decisions are made. The directories containing listings by area or issue funded can be valuable tools for finding out what grants were made to programs, projects, and agencies that might be comparable to what you are specifically seeking to have funded at your organization.

Also, don't overlook the more localized information increasingly available in separate directories. Directories can contain listings of funders located in your geographic area. For example, if your organization is headquartered in Washington, D.C., a localized directory of this type would give you the names of and information on corporate and foundation funders in the D.C. metropolitan area.

But, while most of these may in fact fund in Washington, D.C., some may not, or may have a much more national focus in their grant making. For other directories, "localized" might mean the primary listings are of organizations receiving grants in your area, regardless of the location of the funding source. Thus a social service agency operating in Washington, D.C., might be listed along with all of its major corporate and foundation funders, the purposes of the grants, and the amounts of the grants received for a given period. This information, as we shall see, can be extremely helpful when you move beyond published sources to the "word of mouth" category discussed below.

Trends and Issues

Before we move on to the next type of information resource, we might examine some of the major trends and issues for printed resources on foundations and corporations. One of the most obvious trends is related to the size of these volumes. No printed directory can contain the 40,000 plus foundations and corporate funders that probably exist. The major national directories are increasingly large and some publishers are moving to two-volume sets ("A–P, Q–Z + Indexes," or supplements) just to accommodate the information. In order to keep size somewhat under control, each publisher must define the specific criteria for inclusion in the particular directory or directories it issues. These criteria are usually presented in the front of each directory. An example of the criteria might be only listing foundations and corporate giving programs that made at least $2 million in grants for the reporting period (usually the fiscal year for which information is included). It is very important to know what the criteria are for the particular directory you are using. The criteria, by definition, place some limitations on the directory information and may exclude some key funding prospects that could be a resource for your organization.

Another facet of foundation and corporate funder directories is the comprehensiveness of the information included on each funding resource. As those using the directories have become more sophisticated in their research and thus in their need for information, the directory publishers have included more information on each particular source. For example, several printed directories now include brief information on other activities of foundation and corporate board members, some analysis of grants on each source (average grant size and dollar range of grants are typical), and examples of recent grants, sometimes even divided by program funding areas and with some brief descriptions of what was actually funded.

Of course, the provision of more information on each particular source places some limitations on the number of sources that can be included if the total size of the volume is to be kept within reasonable limits. Some publishers work around this by printing supplements, or by including much of the more detailed information in some of their other directories. The advantage gained by going to a regional or even local focus is the ability to include many more sources and/or much more information on each resource without exceeding reasonable length limits.

Another area of concern is the costs of the printed directories. Directories, as they have grown over the years, have become fairly expensive, especially for smaller organizations. An individual directory might cost between $100 and $200, with a complete set of directories from one particular publisher running several hundred dollars. For some organizations, this is a major expense and, considering that most directories come out on yearly basis, the long-term expense for a complete set of references can be substantial. But, compared to the costs for electronic databases, the printed directories are still a less expensive alternative.

There is also the issue of the timeliness of the information contained in the directories. The major printed directories contain information on each source that can be two, three, or even four years old. This is not a reflection on the publishers of

> **It is very important to know what the criteria are for the particular directory you are using.**

the directories but rather on the simple facts of the data collection process. The foundation or corporate funder's annual report information and/or audit and other grant information may not be ready until four to six months after the close of its fiscal year. Depending upon when this is ready and how it matches up with each publisher's cycle to turn out the next volumes of its directories, the reasons for the time lag can become quickly obvious. Some foundations also may not provide timely information anyway or may be on a two-year cycle for their general reporting beyond the basics of their audits; in these cases the information provided can quickly move into the three- and four-year-old categories.

But the timeliness of the information is a critical factor to take into account when you are conducting your research on particular funding sources. It is also yet one more reason to seek out the foundation or corporate funder's own information if any is available. Foundations and corporate funders, as was noted, can and do change their purposes, grant interests, guidelines, and other significant ways they approach their funding. Also, assets can substantially increase over a short time (especially at community foundations as new gifts and funds are received, but also at family foundations as additional family members may give or leave funds to the foundation). Leadership and staffing can change, foundations can even relocate somewhere else in the city or even to another area entirely. In short, many of the key pieces of information you need to know to be successful with potential funders can change dramatically over a two- or three-year period. If you assume that the information in a directory reflects the current situation of a particular funder, the result can be wasted energy and even turned-down requests. Most directories provide dates for the information they include, especially the fiscal information on assets and grants. Other information on areas of funding interests, board members, guidelines, and procedures may or may not be from the same period as the fiscal information. If you have no other guidance, assume that the date for the fiscal information is also the date of all other information provided in the directory.

In looking at foundation and corporate directories a key question you should answer is how the

information was collected. Most major directories state up front specifically how the information was obtained. Most also attempt to use a variety of resources in compiling the information, such as the foundation-filed Internal Revenue Service 990PF forms, foundation-printed materials, articles and other print media information, questionnaires, phone surveys, and other sources. Some directories clearly state they send the compiled information to each foundation for verification. Given all of these information collection methods and the probable great range of how the funders respond to the requests from directory publishers for information, the quality, timeliness, and even the accuracy of what is published can vary. Some foundations, as you will see in their entries, are not very responsive. My favorites are where contact people and even the foundation's phone number are not listed; a few give only a post office box number for mail and the most basic descriptive information.

Finally, as with all resources including databases, on-line resources, printed secondary source information, and the foundation's own published materials, always keep in mind the "snapshot" and "reading between the lines" concepts discussed earlier. Each piece of information is only a small snapshot of the potential funding source. Your task is to get as many snapshots as possible, fit them together by using one piece of information to confirm (or refute) another piece of information, try to make your best guess on what is there and what is missing, and create the most accurate "picture" possible of that particular source upon which you will develop your strategy for approaching it.

Desktop Computer Database Directories

Given the growing volume of information, growing numbers of foundations and other funding sources, and the growing numbers of people like you and me who want to get to these sources, it was almost inevitable that the computer and information revolutions, much like the chocolate truck and the peanut butter truck, would collide with the need to know more about funders and result in—Reese's Cups (or the database equivalent of these little joys).

Orca Systems, The Taft Group, *The Chronicle of Philanthropy*, and The Foundation Center have led the way by providing desktop databases of foundation and corporate funder information, which you can access from your personal or office computer. The obvious advantage of the computer foundation and corporate funder databases is the ability to sort through the huge volume of data to quickly pinpoint potential sources. Databases, by letting you enter selected key words, phrases, or codes (such as "grants/social service/Washington, DC, >$50,000" for those of you into Boolean operators), can quickly pull up the information you are seeking, assuming, of course, it is there. Databases also have a much greater information capacity than the printed pages you can accommodate on your bookshelves. For example, CD-ROM technology (those small silver disks that look like music CDs) can now accommodate about 300,000 pages of text on one CD-ROM. The digital video disk, which will be available soon, will enable your personal computer to have storage capacities several magnitudes larger than the 300,000 pages of the CD-ROM, but will be the same size and work much the same way. Now, imagine lugging around a printed foundation directory with 300,000 pages or 3 million pages! The mind and the back both boggle!

While the technology is impressive and the storage capacity of CD-ROMs is immense, there are still a number of key areas you should explore when using these reference materials. The most obvious question is how many sources are contained on each particular product. Is it 14,000 foundations and corporations or, in the case of The Foundation Center, is it "43,000"? Next, how complete is the information? Does it include information on foundation and corporate board members? Does it include information on grants actually made? Remember how important it is to know what each funder actually does. What else is included? Remember again that, no matter what the source you are looking at, you are still only getting a snapshot of each particular funding source. Some of these snapshots may not include much detail while others may include considerable detail. How current is the information? Most information, even in the foundation's own published materials, may be over one year old. Another area to explore is the sources of the information. Was it obtained from Internal Revenue Service 990 forms, direct contact with the foundations and corporate grant makers, and/or other sources? I am aware of at least one producer of electronic foundation and corporate reference resources that used a combination of foundation-published materials (if available), Internal Revenue Service 990 forms, written surveys to foundations, and follow-up calls.

A very critical area to examine with these electronic resources is the ways you are able to search the data. Given the amount of information available, you want to be sure that you have considerable flexibility in how you can structure information searches. What are the criteria that you can use for your searches? Can you search by location of the foundation and corporate grant maker and location(s) where grants are made? Can you search by purposes of grants made? By size of grants? By types of agencies funded? Can you cross-reference board members to see what other foundations and corporations they might be affiliated with?

Beyond these and other similar questions, you will also want to be sure that, as with all software, there is good documentation with the product, including a clear user's manual. Even a quick thumb-through of the manual can probably tell you if it is clearly written and understandable or if it resorts to computerese. More and more frequently the software itself has a built-in help system, which enables you to learn how to do basic procedures with the software while you are using it. Does the product you are looking at have this feature?

Another area to examine is the ability of the software to generate reports and other printed information. It is frequently very nice to have colorful screens full of information, but how does the product enable you to tie this information together and print it out in ways that you and others can use? For example, can you select several complete individual source records easily and print them out as a continuous list? Possibly you want board mem-

> **No matter what the source you are looking at, you are still only getting a snapshot of each particular funding source.**

bers or other staff to look through the detailed information on several prospects. Is this the type of report that can be easily prepared? Also you will want to find out how flexible the report and printed output systems are. Can you, for example, export files and reports into other software programs, such as your organization's word processing program? Can names, addresses, and phone numbers be exported into contact software files? These are important areas to look at when considering electronic database resources.

I once attended a demonstration of some fundraising software and the representative of the company made an interesting claim about people purchasing software. She stated that "... the first time people buy software, they buy it for the features. The second time they buy software, they buy it for the service." I don't know if that is true, but anyone who has had to deal with computer software knows the frustrations of: being put on hold for long periods of time ("Each call will be handled in the order in which it was received; you are caller number 177" or "Thank you for your patience; there are 27 calls ahead of yours"); working through elaborate phone systems to reach a real person ("If you need some help, push 1; if you need a lot of help, push 2; if you have just smashed your computer and thrown it out the window, push 3; if you are about to follow it out the window, push 4"); or leaving phone messages and not getting them returned. Good support services, or "technical support," can be one of the keys to a happy relationship with your software. So be sure to ask about service and support. Is it available 24 hours a day or only at certain times? Computers and software have built in the capacity to know when you need them the most—and that is when they fail! So can you reach technical support at 7:30 PM when your software locks up in the middle of the report for your 8:30 AM board meeting the next morning? Or, for those of you on the Pacific Coast, are they on Eastern Time and already watching *The Tonight Show*?

Related to the technical support issue is the question of charges for technical support. Some software comes with "unlimited free technical support," while other products come with limits, such as "60 days of free technical support from your date

of purchase" or "your first five calls to technical support are free." Of course, after this statement the fee structure for additional technical support may be presented. Some software companies now have "clubs" you can join to get a higher grade of technical support, get continued technical support, or, in a few cases I've seen, to actually talk to a real technical support person! Always be sure, when looking at corporate and foundation database software, to know what the potential costs are for technical support beyond what may be initially provided at no cost. Talk to others who have and are using the particular databases you are exploring and ask them what their experiences have been on the issue of technical support. Have they generally been pleased with the service they got? Were their questions answered? Were they actually "talked through" procedures or problems so they had a better understanding of what happened or what they need to do to avoid that problem the next time? Sometimes good and readily available technical support is worth a considerable amount—and when those reports are due, its value can be priceless.

Strategy Tip: And, finally, always register your software, no matter what it is. This alone can save you considerable trouble and countless hours because you will get the most current information on upgrades (which can be issued to bring you new and better features—but also can be issued to help solve "bugs" or problems in the previous version), options, other new products, usage tips, technical support, and other vital information you will need to know to keep your relationship with your software a happy one.

On-Line Resources

Earlier in the book I made the statement that whatever I tell you about on-line resources on corporate and foundation funders will be out of date between now and when the book is published. Those most familiar with the on-line world say that the resources available, the ways that information is delivered, and the number of users are all expanding geometrically. The resources are growing increasingly varied and have moved well beyond printed information and pictures to sound, interactive materials, downloadable software, movies, e-mail, and other fascinating and even, sometimes, useful things. If you are not familiar with the Internet and the World Wide Web, if you don't know about news groups, chat rooms, "flaming," and all the other terms associated with on-line resources, if you've never received a free America Online software disk, then you may be living in a cave.

The purpose of this section is not to acquaint you with the on-line systems, but to discuss some of the specific on-line resources that can help you in your search for potential corporate and foundation funding sources. However, I will attempt to give my own definitions of a few terms you should be familiar with when you read this section:

The Internet

The "net" is a loose "confederation" of small and large computers all over the world that are linked together to share information. The Internet is not controlled by any one person or place, is not structured in the usual sense of the word, and is a dynamic network that is constantly growing and changing. It can be accessed by computer, and now by "boxes" hooked up to television sets.

The World Wide Web

The Web is a part of the Internet where individuals, companies, universities, government agencies, nonprofits, and others can each have specific locations or "home pages" presenting in both text and graphics their products, services, data, or anything else they want. Home pages are usually linked to other resources so that, by clicking on a picture, words, or other objects displayed on your screen, you can immediately move to that new resource, which can be a part of the original resource or connected to an entirely different resource.

Search Engine

A search engine is a type of software that is used specifically with the Internet and the World Wide Web to find information according to criteria specified by the user. Search engines help you move through the jumble of information on-line and go to (hopefully) the resources you are looking for, although much of your success will depend upon which search engine you are using, how you are able to specify the criteria, and what criteria you actually use. In the desktop databases discussed above, your search may have to deal with only 40,000 or 50,000 pieces of information, but when you are on-line the search engine must be able to deal with millions of pieces of information, which are literally scattered all over the globe. So on your desktop with your CD-ROM running you might have entered "disabilities" as a search criteria and found which foundations and corporations provide funding for disabilities-related programs and organizations. But on-line you might enter "disabilities" and end up with multiple thousands of references ranging from legislation to advocacy groups to articles in publications to places selling items and services for the disabled to nonprofit agencies that serve disabled people and even to people who are against the whole idea of disabilities.

URLs (Uniform Resource Locators)

URLs are the "addresses" of World Wide Web sites. By entering a URL into your Internet software, you are connecting your computer with the World Wide Web pages on a computer that could be down the block or halfway around the world. Clicking on words, a picture, or a button on your screen may shift you to another computer and, invisibly, move you to another URL.

On-Line Services

Although not the same as the Internet, these enable you to get onto the Internet through the service. On-line services are (usually) commercial providers of news, information, entertainment, and resources, including, in many cases, access to large databases of information. Some of these databases may also be accessible on the Internet while others may be exclusive to a particular on-line service. You become a member of an on-line service and pay a monthly fee while you are a member. The fee may be time/usage-based or a flat rate per month. Examples include CompuServe, America Online, Prodigy, and others.

But what is on-line that is useful for your search for potential corporate and foundation funders? It is both impossible and imprudent, given the fast-changing nature of the Internet, on-line services, and the World Wide Web, to try to provide a definitive list of resources. However, I will try to pinpoint some resources that can be valuable and also give you categories of other resources that will be helpful, no matter what develops. I will also include URLs or addresses for specific resources. Some of the organizations on the World Wide Web enable you to contact them directly through the use of electronic mail (e-mail) using their Web pages. Very few foundations and corporate donors have developed their own World Wide Web pages so far, because typically the nonprofit sector and particularly organized philanthropy has been slow to adapt to major changes in the way things are done. As more people have access to the Internet and other on-line resources, the numbers of foundations and corporate donors using these methods of distributing their information will very likely start to grow rapidly. If you want to go beyond the basic information below, please refer to the excellent article "Using On-line Databases for Prospect Research" by Miranda D. Scott in the October 1995 issue of *Fund Raising Management* (pages 44–49).

Specific World Wide Web Resources

A General Directory to the World Wide Web

World Wide Web Yellow Pages—(http://www.yellow.com) This is a reference resource, much like the phone book yellow pages, to the World Wide Web.

Foundation-Related Organizations with Links to Foundations

Council on Foundations—(http://www.picnet.com) The Council on Foundations is the "trade association" of the grant-making world. Its over 1,000 members include private foundations, community foundations, corporate foundations, and corporate grant makers. The home page for the council provides information on its services and programs, but also has links to other home pages for individual foundations. At this point not many foundations—corporate, private, or community—have home pages up and running, but this is expected to change.

The Foundation Center—(http://www.fndcenter.org) The Foundation Center is a national network of libraries with resources on foundations, corporate donors, and general materials on fund raising and nonprofit organizations. Headquartered in New York, it has several facilities around the country and also has established a number of "cooperating collections" of resource materials in public libraries in other locations. In addition, The Foundation Center is one of the leading publishers of directories of corporate and foundation funders and other materials related to obtaining funding from these sources. Foundation Center sites also frequently conduct seminars and workshops on fund raising, proposal writing, researching funding sources, and other topics. The home page for The Foundation Center also provides links to foundation home pages.

Resources for Corporate Information

If you want to find out if a particular company has a World Wide Web home page, either use a search engine (but be careful—typing in "IBM" might bring up thousands of references), or try using http://www.companyname.com. Some companies' Web sites are purely gimmicky ads for their products while others actually contain useful information. Some companies may have several Web sites for their different branches or product lines. Also remember that the information resources below will give you only snapshots of the companies and may often not be very helpful in terms of the specifics on the corporate foundation or corporate giving program. But these resources can often help you learn more about a company, who runs it, what they do, where they are located, and even their financial status.

Wall Street Journal—(http://bis.dowjones.com/bizpubs/wsj-interactive.html) *The Wall Street Journal* is a primary resource on what is happening in corporate America.

Dow Jones News/Retrieval—(http://bis.dowjones.com/) This is the parent company of *The Journal* and provides a clip service with access to many databases on businesses and to business-related publications. This is not a free service.

Hoover's Profiles (http://www.hoovers.com/) This service gives useful information on corporate officers, where to contact the company, some basic financial data, locations, etc.

On-Line Services: CompuServe, America Online, and other on-line services provide extensive access to databases and other information on corporations. The Scott article mentioned earlier provides excellent information on the resources available through some of the on-line services.

On-Line Publications Related to Philanthropy

American Philanthropy Review—http://205.198.215.242/

Chronicle of Philanthropy—http://chronicle.merit.edu

Nonprofit Times—http://haven.ios.com/~nptimes

Other Resources On-Line

The following is a general grouping of other resources that might be helpful in your search for information. The best way to learn more about them is to try them out and see how useful they will be for your particular needs.

National Society of Fund Raising Executives—(http://www.nsfre.org) This is the international professional organization of fund raisers. While the Web home page is primarily geared to information about membership and for members, members of NSFRE can access the NSFRE Resource Center by phone at their national headquarters in Alexandria,

Virginia. This on-line service is truly "on-line" as you get to speak with a real person who can be very helpful in locating information for you. Just remember: a) you must be a member of NSFRE to use this service, and b) the service is not intended to substitute for your own research. So do not call the Center and ask for a list of 10 foundations that fund senior citizens' services in your area!

On-line Funding Search Tools—http://www.uic.edu/depts/over/nonprof.html

Philanthropic Links—http://www.duke.edu./ptavern/pete.philanthropic.html

Prospect Research Page—http://weber.u.washington.edu/~edu/~dlamb/apra/APRA.html

Print Media Resources

Besides the directories, foundation- and corporate-published information, the on-line and electronic database resources, there is also a wealth of other materials that can be helpful in your research efforts. Popular magazines, newspapers, and other publications sometimes feature items on foundations, corporate giving, and other resources. If your computer is down, or you don't have on-line access, or your search engine ran out of steam, the reference section of any reasonably good public library can provide you with excellent resources and ways to track down information on organized philanthropy. There are a number of publications that provide topical references to articles and other written pieces in major publications. The Foundation Center, if you have one available near you, also maintains clip files of articles in the print media related to corporate and foundation giving. Newspapers are often the first source to publish information about the establishment of a new private foundation by some local citizen who recently passed away. Local newspapers, especially in smaller cities, may sometimes run features on prominent individuals serving on foundation boards or on the foundations themselves.

In some cities a local newspaper or other source may publish a yearly directory of information on the major manufacturing companies, other major businesses (such as law and accounting firms), major service providers (such as hospitals), and even foundation and corporate donor information. I was providing consulting services in a city of about 260,000 people and found that a local resource put out a publication every year that provided detailed information on all of these sectors, including a complete listing of all of the foundations in the area. This list and the details it contained were more helpful than a foundation directory because foundations were included regardless of their size. The foundation directory would have only included the largest three or four foundations in the city.

I believe that the best single periodical printed resource currently available on foundations and corporate philanthropy is *The Chronicle of Philanthropy*. This newspaper-style publication, which is published approximately twice a month, contains grant listings, highlights of foundation and corporate giving annual reports, staff changes at foundations and corporate giving programs, and many articles on trends, issues, specific happenings, and other useful information related to philanthropy. Why is this the best resource currently available? The information is timely (more so than foundation annual reports and certainly more so than the information in the directories), well organized, and very useful for developing strategies and approaches to foundations and corporate funders. Of course, it is not comprehensive, but the index published by *The Chronicle* helps guide you to many resources in previous issues. Also note that *The Chronicle* publishes The Chronicle Guide To Grants, a computer database focused on grants made by foundations and corporate funders.

Beyond this resource, there are many publications, including newsletters and magazines devoted to all aspects of the nonprofit world, such as giving by and getting grants from organized philanthropy. A variety of special purpose newsletters focus on specific aspects of grant seeking, such as getting grants from corporations, foundations, or the public sector. Many of these resources can be located through using electronic or printed reference sources.

Reference sources that at first might seem unrelated to philanthropy can be useful supplements to your other research materials. *Who's Who* and other similar biographical sources can help you track down useful additional information on corporate officers and board members of foundations. Some of these are now on-line either through an on-line service such as CompuServe or through other sources. You need not be computer literate to search them out at your local library.

Foundation Internal Revenue Service 990 Forms

Have you heard somewhere about a foundation but can't find anything else about it? The single most comprehensive resource on private and separately organized corporate foundations is the Internal Revenue Service 990PF (for "private foundation") form each is required to file every year. Community Foundations must file an IRS 990 form like other public charities. The 990 forms, like everything else we've discussed, are snapshots. The single advantage is that almost every foundation has filed its 990, so this may be the one source to go to if no other information is available. The 990 forms contain basic information about the foundation, such as its name, address, phone, a list of board members, fiscal information (assets, expenses, grants paid), and, usually, a list of grantees and amounts paid to each. Remember that the 990 forms are also one of the basic source documents for many of the foundation directories.

Where are 990s found? Currently, the best sources are the Foundation Center sites around the country, which maintain these files on microfiche (miniature photos of the filed forms). Special viewers enable you to read the forms and to print hard copy, if you wish. The process can be slow and hard on the eyes, but the results can be information that may not be obtainable anywhere else. I always see the 990s as a last resort when there are no other sources of information on a particular foundation prospect, or when the foundation has only minimal information in its listing in a directory. I expect that shortly this information will become available on CD-ROM or possibly on the Internet, which will make it more user-friendly. Although I have not seen the Foundation Center CD-ROM because it has just been issued, the fact that it contains over 40,000 foundation references may negate the need for the 990 forms—depending on how much information is listed on each source.

Other Sources of Information

We've covered foundation-published or printed information, printed directories, desktop databases, on-line services, other printed media, and foundation IRS 990 forms. So what is left? Sometimes I find one of the best resources on a particular foundation or corporate funding source can be other organizations that received grants from that source. If, in my research, I see an organization or program that appears to be somewhat like the organization or program I am at and am seeking to have supported, I contact the executive director or chief development officer at that other organization. What do I ask? Here are some of the basic areas I cover:

- What, generally, was your experience with that particular funding source? Did they "make you jump through a lot of hoops" or was the process fairly straightforward?

- What was the process you went through? Did it seem to follow the way the foundation described it would work?

- Whom did you work with on the staff there? What was that person like? What questions were asked?

- How long did the process take from beginning to end?

- What do you think your organization did right that made the process successful?

- What, if any, were the problems you had with the process or what would you do differently the next time around?

- Do you have any other suggestions or advice about that particular funding source that might be helpful to our organization if it is to pursue a grant from that source?

When I present this strategy in classes I teach, often some of the people in the class don't believe an organization's staff will answer any of these questions. But, in my experience, many senior staff and development officers are willing to share information, although there may be some limits on how much detail they give you. I view using this process as one more way to compile information on each funder I am researching. Many people are surprised how much development officers will share their corporate and foundation experiences with each other. I like to believe that this sharing is an indication of how far the profession has come and also an acknowledgment that there is a strong feeling that "we're all in this together." I hope the growing funding pressures will not dilute much of this spirit.

There is a final resource, and it can be an excellent one that can help shortcut some of your research work. It is also a resource that few people use, which can make it even better for your organization when you use it. That resource is the topic of the next chapter.

> **Many senior staff and development officers are willing to share information.**

Chapter 10
Approaching Funders: An Overview

What are foundations and corporations, as far as most nonprofit organizations are concerned? "Sources of funds" is the common and all-too-frequent answer. But, as we have already seen, some corporations and a few foundations can provide other resources to nonprofit organizations. If asked, some of the resources they can provide include: equipment, supplies, volunteers, special and technical expertise, facilities, printing, production, public relations, accounting, graphics and design, and other services. The availability of these resources means we all need to think beyond the narrow view of the corporate sector as merely a source for funds.

But what about the foundations? Aren't they primarily sources for funds? I believe this view places strong limitations on what you and your organization can achieve when working with foundations and their staff members. I have heard foundation staff say, both in public presentations and in individual discussions with them, "I wish people would see us as more than a source for a check." Isn't that their purpose—to process your materials

and grant requests and make grants to the organizations they select? What else can they possible do for you?

Role of the Funder

As a program officer I sometimes found my relationships with staff and board members of organizations were productive and fulfilling for me when I was seen as something beyond a source for a grant. When I first arrived at the foundation, I was somewhat unsure what my role was supposed to be. On the surface, I, like other program staff, was a processor of information in the proposals we received and in the meetings we held with potential grantees. I would read the proposal, do my homework and checking, meet with the applicants, and write up the information for presentation first to the program staff and, if there was general consensus on the part of the staff, to the board. In the board meetings I would answer questions about the applicant, the proposal, and the specific recommendations, and the board would make a decision; possible decisions included approving the recommendation for each applicant as it was presented (provide a grant in the recommended amount or decline to support the request), modifying the amount of a grant and adding or changing the grant terms and conditions, or even reversing the recommendation and providing a grant when none was recommended or not approving a recommended grant. As long as I did my homework and was well prepared for the board's questions and possible reactions, the process was not difficult.

That was the surface appearance—and, for some foundation staff members, that well may be all there is to the process. But about a week or two after I started work at the foundation, I met with a program staff member who had been there for several years. He and I reviewed what I saw as my roles and responsibilities, which basically followed the description above. He nodded and said, as I best remember our discussion: "Yes. That's part of it, but that's not the whole story. We're really advocates for the organizations. Our role is more than to process the applications, sit in the meetings, and see what happens. We're here on their behalf. Sometimes we may help them in other ways but they may not get a grant. And sometimes they get the grant and that's one way we help them. But we're really here because of them and to help them as best we can."

At first I thought he was talking about an ideal situation; after all, how could our foundation and staff help an organization we decided not to fund? The people at the organization usually did not see us as helpers and advocates! But that brief discussion helped start a major change in my thinking about my roles as a foundation program officer, and, much later, about the working relationship between those seeking funding support and the staffs of foundations.

Soon after this conversation I had a particular proposal to review. The organization clearly met our basic guidelines, although the particular program for which they wanted support was not something our foundation found exciting. I did my homework and met with the director of the organization, prepared my summary and recommended the program not be funded. At our board meeting the recommendation was approved. Although our board meetings never ended at exactly the same time, I could never figure out how many of the people at organizations that had proposals up for consideration seemed to know exactly when our board meetings ended. The phone would be constantly ringing the moment we left the meeting room!

Almost the first call I received was from the director of the organization that had submitted the proposal our board had just turned down. The conversation went something like this:

Director: "Hello. This is George Smith at the CEF Agency. Can you tell me what happened with our request?"

Me (somewhat guiltily): "Um, yes. Our board decided not to fund your request." Note: one of the little in jokes at the foundation was that it was the staff's hard work and extra effort that resulted in grants, but it was "those guys" on the board who turned down requests.

Director: "That's it—we're dead! I might as well send the staff home and close the doors right now!"

Me (very guiltily): "Hey! Wait a minute! That's not the end of everything. Your request was only for support of one program. Your agency does a lot more than that."

Director: "Yes, but we were counting on your grant."

Me: "Well, there are other places in town that do funding. We're not the only source of support."

Director: "Maybe what I need is some help. Could I come in and meet with you again? I'd like to see how we could improve our proposal and when we can come back to the foundation. Also, you could help me by telling me more about those other foundations that might be interested in supporting our program."

Me (somewhat relieved): "Sure. I can do that. Let's set up a time now."

What happened here? First, the director initiated the call rather than merely waiting for the letter announcing our decision. Now, of course not all foundations will tell you their decisions over the phone; some will insist you wait for the "official letter." But at least the director tried. The second thing to notice about this case is the director caught me at a time when I was feeling a little guilty about our decision to not fund his organization's request. The agency had done its homework and the proposal was entirely appropriate for our consideration. I had spent time on reviewing the request and had found the agency was doing a good job of delivering its services and was well thought of by people in the community. The services were needed and overall the agency had a good track record. Every time we turned down a request, I did feel some guilt, especially where overall the agency seemed to be a good one. Again, I know that not every foundation staff person will feel guilt about agencies that are turned down. Some might even be said to enjoy this part of their job because it confirms a sense of control or power. But I have met enough program officers to know that many feel this way, especially when the request was an appropriate one for them to consider.

What else happened in this case? The director immediately asked if I would be willing to help and advise him on what to do next. Now, since I was already feeling guilty, this request was a way to help alleviate some of that feeling. Instead of being the ogre, I could help the organization in other ways. The director had also moved beyond seeing me and our foundation as merely a source of money and was moving toward establishing a different kind of relationship with us, maybe something more in keeping with the "advocate" role the staff member had discussed with me earlier.

The end results of this case included the director coming in to meet with me. At the meeting I told him some of the reasons for our decision to turn down the request, made several suggestions about how the proposal could be improved, and told him our procedures about reapplying. He also reminded me of the other part of our conversation and asked for my suggestions about other foundations that might be interested in the agency and this specific request. I suggested a few other foundations and also gave him the names of the staff people that I knew at each. He asked if I would be willing to talk to them about the agency and their request, which I offered to do. I certainly felt better and he felt a lot better. Subsequently, the agency received funding from one of the other sources I had recommended, and later returned to us with another proposal for a new program, which we funded.

Not all of these stories have happy endings, but there are some lessons to be learned from this case. Most foundation staff are human and take their jobs seriously. Turning down requests is not their favorite thing to do (unless they see themselves as "protectors" of the foundation). Some foundation staff can be helpful in many ways besides just being the processing point for a potential grant. If those seeking grants believe that one of their goals should be to develop ongoing relationships with foundation staff—to create partner-

ships based upon complementary goals—and if they believe that foundation staff can help in many ways, then there can be benefits beyond the approval of a grant.

If asked, foundation staff can be helpers, advisors, sources of information on other funders, guides to the ins and outs of their own foundation, and even advocates for the causes and needs addressed by the organizations seeking support. But all too often they are simply seen as "someone who can get us a check." This reduces the basic approach to a potential funding source to: "Make our case. Wait for a decision."

Approaches to Funders

I believe there are three basic approaches that are used with foundations and corporate donors. These are: the "beggar" approach; the "superior–inferior" approach; and the third, which is focused on developing a long-term partnership. Here is how I see each of these three basic approaches.

Beggar

Most people have been approached on the street by someone asking for money. Although "beggar" may not be a fair characterization of these people, it does usually describe their approach. In my role as a foundation staff member I was often approached in a similar manner by organizations. Although the words were different, the approach sounded like this:

"Oh, please help us. We're just a small organization and anything you can do will help."

The attitude was generally that the organization was desperate and any amount would help it survive a little longer. We quickly tired of this approach. We knew there were many organizations that needed help. That a grant would only help them survive a little longer was not sufficient rea-

> **Foundation staff can be helpers, advisors, sources of information, guides to the ins and outs of their own foundation, and even advocates.**

son to provide them with support. This approach was also known as "Would you like to buy a cabin on *The Titanic*—after it hit the iceberg?"

Superior–Inferior

This method of approaching foundations is probably somewhat more common than the "beggar" approach, at least among the more sophisticated organizations. If it had to be put into words, they would basically be:

"We're a good organization and we do good things. If you give us a grant, we can do more good things."

What is wrong with this approach? From the standpoint of a foundation, this style of approach has a basic weakness. Of course the organization could do more good things with more money. Couldn't we all do more things if we had more money? "Doing more good things" was usually not a compelling reason for the staff to recommend or the board to approve a grant.

My favorite example of the superior–inferior approach was the organization that came to us with an "innovative, can't fail" proposal. The basic idea was we would provide them with a grant of $15,000, which they would use to send out a mass mailing. This mass mailing, according to their figures, would generate about $50,000 in new contributions to the organization. This $50,000 would again be used to do another mass mailing, which would bring in about $250,000. Again, the $250,000 would be used for yet another mailing, and, surprise, this would generate over $1 million. And so on, and so on. In a relatively short time, about a year or less, according to their timetable, this small organization would be generating large amounts of money, thanks to the foundation's initial small grant of $15,000. What, aside from some ethical issues, was wrong with this idea? On the surface, our little grant would enable them to become big-time fund raisers in less than a year. Of course, they had overlooked the fact that the usual return rate on "cold" or "acquisition" mailings was likely to be less than 1 percent. So the $50,000 in initial returns was about as unlikely as, well, the rest of their expected returns. "We do good things, and, if you give us a grant, we can do more good things, such as raise a lot of money."

Negotiated Partnership

This is what I see as the most productive approach to foundation and corporate funding sources. First, it focuses on something longer term than merely getting a grant. The basic idea is to create a long-term relationship—a partnership—with each funding source and particularly with the staff (or with board members, if there is no staff). Why call this relationship a partnership? Because a partnership has, in my view, several key characteristics.

- There is a recognition that the goals of the partners, while they may be different, are complementary.

- Each partner sees that the other partner can play many—and changing—roles in the relationship.

- Each partner receives different benefits from the relationship—these, like the roles, can change over time.

- Each partner is committed to continuing the relationship for its mutual benefits to both parties as long as it is practical.

- Each partner is committed to keeping a high level of sharing, honesty, and trust in the relationship.

All of this assumes that you have done your homework and that the foundations where you are seeking to develop partnerships do, in fact, have goals (or a mission or purposes) that complement those of your organization. But the partnership approach is more than something you try to do—

> The basic idea is to create a long-term relationship with each funding source and particularly with the staff.

it really represents an attitude you should take in all of your relationships with foundations and corporate funders. On the corporate side it is much more obvious that a partnership is required; in fact, as we have seen, corporations are increasingly seeking partners where there is a clear bottom-line impact for the companies. But the partnership approach is also the best approach to the foundation world because it emphasizes the multiple roles that each foundation and its staff can play in helping your organization achieve its goals while meeting its own. The partnership approach also emphasizes that you need to strive for a long-term, continuing relationship with the foundations and their staffs, always being mindful not to overwhelm each staff member with maintaining the relationship.

But notice I used the words "negotiated partnership." What do I mean by including "negotiated"? To me, the word implies the continuous give and take that are necessary to maintain the relationship. Including this word also demonstrates that the relationship is dynamic—it is constantly changing in response to the changes at each foundation that occur over time (such as shifting funding interests, new areas that will be supported, and general changes in direction and focus) as well as the changes at each organization. The partnership is "negotiated" on a continuing basis as these changes occur. The partners must recognize this fact of change and continuously renegotiate the terms of the partnership based on the changing circumstances at the foundation and the organization. The limits on the relationship also have to be worked out and clearly understood by both parties to it. For example, a foundation or corporate staff person who feels extremely pressured by the workload may only want limited contact; your task becomes one of using those limited contacts in the most efficient and effective way possible. At times, the partnership can be strong or intense, such as when the purposes of a foundation or corporate funder and the organization mesh, or when there is a grant made. But at other times the partnership can be less strong or less intense, such as when a foundation's funding interests shift away from the needs of your organization or when your organization's specific needs may no longer have a close fit with the purposes of the foundation or corporation. This does not mean the relationship ends. It should mean that the partners merely agree it will move to a lower level of intensity. In practical terms, this can mean the foundation staff member's roles focus on helping and guiding you and your organization to other, more appropriate sources. And your roles include keeping that foundation staff member informed of your successes (and failures) with the sources that were recommended to you, as well as keeping that person up to date on other activities at your organization.

So, based upon my experience as well as discussions with others (both fund seekers and foundation staffs), the negotiated partnership is the most productive approach to foundation and corporate funders. The primary goal for you and your organization is not merely to acquire a grant, but to maintain and enhance the relationship with each and every foundation or corporate staff member who seems willing to do so. But the major driving force for creating and maintaining negotiated partnerships has to come from you and your organization. In most cases it will not come from the foundation or corporate staff person, at least until you initiate it.

Strategy Tip: In any of your contacts with foundations and corporate funders, always keep a long-term perspective. If you have done your homework and strongly believe that you have found an appropriate match between your organization's needs and a particular foundation, develop a commitment to persistence. Don't overdo your contacts and, if the clear message back to you from the potential funding source is "we're not a place you should continue approaching,"

> **The negotiated partnership is the most productive approach to foundation and corporate funders.**

then don't continue to pursue it. But if there seems to be some interest in your program or your organization and what it does, keep at it, even if you are turned down the first or even second time around. One of the people I work with uses a rule of thumb "three strikes and you are out" with foundation and corporate funders. I don't necessarily agree with that, but there does come a point in time when you should probably put your energies elsewhere. However, as we shall see later, even a turn down by a foundation or corporate funder can be an opportunity to start to develop a negotiated partnership, if you have not been able to create one prior to the turn down.

Staff Types

Just as there are styles of approach to potential corporate and foundation funders, there are also styles of behavior of foundation and corporate staff members. Based upon my experience, I place foundation staff members into three distinct categories. Again, please remember that these are generalities, and not every foundation or corporate program officer you meet will necessarily fit one of these categories. But the categories can be a guide that will help you as you develop your strategies and approaches.

The Blocker

This type has the attitude that he or she is there to prevent you from getting access to the foundation or corporate funder. The blocker is characterized by unreturned phone calls, non-responses to letters, an unwillingness to meet, and, frequently, an effective "assistant blocker" who is skilled at keeping you away from the staff member. Some staff members with the blocker attitude feel this role is part of their job. Other staff members with the blocker attitude use it as a means for controlling their work flow. And, unfortunately, others have

the blocker attitude out of a sense of their own perceived importance (and, consequently, you and your own organization's lack of importance). A foundation staff member can easily feel an elevated sense of importance, especially when many organizations use either the "beggar" style of approach or the "superior–inferior" style. In both cases the foundation staff person is treated as a power and authority figure—and probably soon comes to believe it.

Blocker types also can see themselves as gatekeepers to the foundation's or corporation's giving, even when they may not be actually making any funding decisions. Because they see themselves as "controlling" the purse strings of the foundation or corporate funder, they may only want to meet with "important" people and organizations. Sometimes the way to successfully approach them is by having one of your board members who may be seen as a "high status" individual by the blocker make the approach to the potential funder. But realistically blocker types can be very difficult to connect with, and, once you have connected with them, they can continue to be difficult.

The good news is that at least at some foundations there is more than one staff member. If you run into a blocker, try to develop a strategy to approach another staff member, if one is available. The foundation I worked at had several program officers, including a few blockers. Because we were all generalists, proposals could be assigned to any one of us. I am almost certain that some organizations withdrew their proposals when they found out they were assigned to a known blocker; they would reapply at a later date and hope to get assigned to a different staff member. But sometimes, when and where you can, you need to take a more active approach to problems accessing a foundation or corporate giver when you run into a blocker type.

Example: An organization I was consulting with had been approaching a major foundation without much success over a period of a few years. The organization had been meeting with a staff person at the foundation about once a year to review planned programs and projects. This staff person oversaw the program category that seemed to be the best fit for the organization and its programs.

But each time they met, the staff person, a blocker type, would be very negative about the possibility of receiving a grant for any of the described programs or projects. We strongly felt the programs and projects were entirely appropriate for the foundation's consideration based on extensive research and analysis of the foundation's grant patterns. But the negative responses continued at each meeting. After our third year, the executive director of the organization and I reviewed the staff structure of the foundation. Without too much stretching, we found a second program area of the foundation that might just fit the programs and services of the organization. Mindful of any potential problems that might occur if we were seen as "making an end run" around the blocker, we decided to approach the two staff members responsible for the second program area. In the letter requesting a meeting the executive director informed them of the previous contacts with the foundation, including the name of the staff person we had been meeting with; our reasons for approaching the second program area (in part, this was recommended to us by a staff member at another foundation); and also of the fact that the organization had received funding from the foundation several years ago.

We subsequently met with the two staff people. The particular program for which we sought support was not quite the right fit for their program interests, but we also developed a clearer understanding of their specific interests as well as two new staff contacts at the foundation, both of whom seemed more receptive to the organization and its work.

The Process Administrator

The second type of foundation staff is what I call the "process administrator." This person sees his or her job as almost entirely focusing on the proposal review process and ensuring that you go through each of the steps in the process. While the process administrator does not usually try to block contact with the foundation, he or she is usually a strict enforcer of the process steps. If you should attempt to stray outside of these steps or seek advice or help from the process administrator, he or she will quickly make it clear to you and your organization that this is inappropriate. Your job is to provide the process administrator with the information needed for the foundation or corporation to make its decision; the process administrator's job is to collect the information, analyze it, and present the recommendations to the decision makers. In the view of the process administrator, the rules, procedures, and guidelines of the foundation establish what it can and can't or won't do, and these become the boundaries inside which you must fit your organization and its needs. The process administrator truly serves as an intermediary between those seeking funding and those making the decisions—and this is how he or she sees the position. Unlike the blocker, the process administrator does not generally actively hinder your contact with the foundation, but the process administrator will probably not actively help you, either.

Process administrators focus primarily on procedures and probably like order and consistency. They also are clearly willing to return proposals that indicate the applicant has not done his or her "homework" on researching the foundation and its mission and guidelines. When you encounter a process administrator, be sure the attachments to your proposal are exactly what the foundation or corporation wanted, and everything is neatly packaged and in keeping with the foundation's or corporate funder's specifications. Process administrators are usually less concerned with their personal status and sense of importance, at least when compared to many blockers. They usually seem to enjoy their role in the middle and tend to recognize that the power really does rest with the decision makers, not with them.

The Helper

The third type of foundation or corporate program officer is the "helper"; my associate at the foundation would have called this type the "advocate," but that may be somewhat too narrow an interpretation of the roles this person fulfills. A helper type can be genuinely helpful but still might not serve as a true advocate for your organization and its needs. And an advocate can only advocate within the general boundaries of what the foundation or corporate funder can or can't do, even though advocates often try to stretch those boundaries when new areas or special needs arise.

The helper can, if asked, provide assistance in many ways (see also earlier) including:

- providing additional and possibly unwritten information on the helper's own foundation or corporation and what its current interests are

- giving insights into the foundation's or corporation's review and decision-making processes

- giving assessments of the strengths and weaknesses of your request for support

- guiding or referring you to other potential sources for funding

- discussing ways to make your request more appealing to the decision makers

- providing referrals to organizations that have carried out similar projects or programs

- sharing some estimate of your chances with the helper's decision makers and what their concerns might be

In short, the helper type is the ideal person for the establishment of a negotiated partnership, because his or her commitment is to both the foundation or corporate funder, and to those seeking support. The helper's most valuable function, at times, may not even involve a grant to the organization, but may be the result of the referrals, advice, information, and connections that emerge from your relationship with the helper. If you find a true helper, seek to develop a long-term relationship within limits acceptable to both parties. Be sure to let that person know what the outcomes of his or her advice, referrals, etc., were. Be willing to bounce new ideas and concepts being developed at your organization off the helper, if he or she is also willing. As has been indicated, program officers, especially those assigned to particular program areas, can have considerable expertise and knowledge of their particular areas and the major emerg-

ing developments in their field, so the helper may be able to provide you with needed expertise.

This somewhat simplified approach to foundation types is only intended as a guide. But it is important that you develop a clear understanding of the many roles foundation and corporate program officers can play and the ways they can be helpful, often only helping when asked to do so. Even in your first meeting, as we shall see in the next chapter, it is possible to start to test out whether or not the staff person you are meeting with is interested in helping or merely wants to be a process administrator or even a blocker. Be sure not to focus just on presenting your proposal and waiting for a reaction. Create a dialogue. Take some initiative and ask some questions focused on such areas as other possible funding sources, other places doing work similar to that done by your organization, getting some additional information of how the decision-making process works at that particular source, and any other helpful information that can open up doors for you and your organization.

Often, people I speak with about approaching foundations and corporate funders have come to believe that most program officers are blockers or, at best, process administrators. Many of these people feel discouraged about even continuing to seek support from foundations and corporations, believing that they will always be turned down or not even ever have access to staff. In some cases I know the lack of response reflects their own minimal preparation and failure to do the necessary homework before making an approach. Foundation staff, no matter what type or category they fall into, do not want to do the basic homework for organizations interested in seeking funding. Falling back into my old program officer's role, I remember seeing many of the applicants that clearly fell outside our areas of funding, our geographic area of service, or our other guidelines and restrictions. Surely we were not capable, as one memorable request asked of us, of providing funds to pay for the purchase of weapons to be smuggled into a Central American country so that the government could be overthrown! Clearly not within our guidelines!

Where the homework is done properly, where the strategies are in place, and where the approaches are made in the best possible ways, there may often be found the helper types that can benefit you and your organization, even beyond the possibility of grants. Thinking over my several years of experience in working with clients and helping them develop their foundation and corporate contacts, I believe that the ratio of helpers to process administrators and blockers has been about two to one. This perception has been based upon careful homework and strategy development, matching up of foundation and corporate interests and funding patterns with the needs of the organization, the use of referrals from other foundation and corporate officers, and the development of networks of long-term relationships with key foundation and corporate staff members.

Much of the above view developed out of a point in my life when I was seeking to change careers. After several unsuccessful attempts with job interviews, I asked a person what to do. He said that going to ask people for jobs is one method, but the more successful one is to go ask people for help and advice and suggestions from them about others who also might be helpful to you, and, as you expand this network of helpers, the job will come. After about four months I had developed a network of about 45 people; at times, I felt I would have many helpers and advisors, but not the career change I had been seeking. One of the people I met was called right after I left his office by someone seeking to hire a new staff member for a foundation—and a few weeks later I had the job.

Tracking Information

This overview of approaching foundations and corporations would be incomplete if it focused only on preparing you for the external factors you will probably face. Internally, you also need to be ready to make your approaches, even beyond knowing your organization. Are your internal systems and procedures ready for making multiple foundation and corporate approaches through a variety of methods, and keeping track of all of your contacts? Will you be able to know:

- what your research showed about each source and where you got that information

- when you called or wrote to each potential funding source for information

- where you've already received the information

- where you've scheduled meetings and what has happened or needs to happen prior to those meetings

- where you need to schedule meetings and include the executive director and a board member from your organization

- where you have proposals pending and when the decision dates are

- where you need to send additional information although you've already sent your proposal in

- which foundation or corporate staff officer referred you to another foundation or company, and who you should contact there

- which foundations and corporations have approved grants, turned down grants, and where requests are still pending or decision dates have been deferred

- which foundations and corporations have interim or final reports due to them, and when these are due

- when payments will be received from foundations and corporations that have approved grants

- which foundations and corporations still need more research before strategies can be set

- which foundations and corporations have not been contacted for over a month and need to have follow-up calls

As you can see from the above, merely keeping track of all of the information, research, contacts, and next steps can be a daunting task. It can be somewhat of a problem if you have 5 or 10 foundations you are pursuing; it can be a major problem if you are going after 40 or 50 foundations at the same time.

Aside from not knowing their own organizations and failing to do the homework needed before undertaking serious approaches to foundation and corporate funders, one of a grant seeker's biggest failings can be lack of preparation to track all of the foundation and corporate contacts and potential contacts. The range of techniques for accomplishing this task can go from sophisticated over-the-counter computer fund-raising software through custom-designed software using standard database programs to elaborate systems of forms and files, and, at the other extreme, 3" × 5" cards or even a marked up yellow pad and a wall calendar. I believe the key is not which system you use, but creating a system that will work for your organization and its needs and that can be expanded to meet changing needs. A good system is also simple to use and understand and can easily be learned or used by others. Whether it is on a computer or on paper, your tracking system needs to be highly flexible so you can pull information out in a number of different ways, yet sophisticated enough to avoid the frequent problem of merely copying information, much of it the same, from one form to another.

You should carefully think through the development of your tracking system and consider the minimum information you will need and how you can best organize it. You should be very analytical and be sure you are covering all the areas you will potentially want to include; it is often very hard to change a system when you find information must be presented or recorded in some way you hadn't anticipated. Also take into account your organization's reporting needs and expectations. Does your organization's board and/or management want or require periodic update reports on approaches to foundations and corporations? If so, what type of information do they prefer?

Will your system enable you to extract information in other ways or in more detail if the board or management wants it? For example, I find it very useful to be able to get information on when I last contacted a prospect, so I can develop a reminder or "tickler" file to ensure I stay in contact with all of my prospects at appropriate times. You'll also want to ensure that any entries in your record system can be traced back to the person entering them, so that, for example, if your executive director receives a call from a foundation, this fact will be recorded in the system.

Basics for a Record System

Here is some very basic information for any corporate/foundation record system:

- foundation contact information (name of foundation, address, phone number, fax number, e-mail address, contact people)

- date the file was started

- basic research information and sources of information, including dates entered, areas will and won't fund, funding limitations, special interests, grant size/type information, meeting dates and deadlines

- additional important information (previous grants to your organization, key contacts between people associated with your organization and the foundation or corporation, even information on previous requests sent to the potential funder that were turned down)

- project or program for which support appears most likely

- current status. I usually use these categories: Prospect, Active, Proposal Pending, Grant, Inactive. Prospects are funding sources that have some potential for support, based on research and other information, but have yet to be met with or directly contacted about a particular funding need. Active means that the cultivation and contact process is underway (strategies have been developed, meetings have been held with the foundation or corporation, inquiry letters have been sent to the funding prospect, etc.). Proposal Pending means a proposal has actually been submitted. Grant, of course, means a grant has actually been received. Inactive means that either more information is needed or there is some other reason to hold the particular source

- amount and purpose of request. If a three-year grant of $75,000 ($25,000 per year) has been requested for the XYZ program, this information would be recorded in this area

- amount of grant, payment period, purpose, restrictions. If a grant is approved, the amount, time period (and specified payment dates, if any) will be recorded here along with any special restrictions or conditions placed upon the grant by the foundation. The actual funder-approved purpose of the grant should also be recorded, especially if it varies at all from the request you made (such as restricting funding to only one part of the program's expenses). Restrictions might include the filing of progress reports before payments will be released, meeting challenge grant conditions within a specified period, etc.

- dates items are due to the foundation or corporate funder, and/or key deadline dates

- contact information. This information is one of the keys to developing and keeping a successful negotiated partnership with a foundation or corporate funder. Please see below for more details on recording contact information.

Contact information—when anyone in your organization last had contact with a potential funder and what has to happen next—is, of course, critical to your fund-seeking process. I believe that contact information can be kept in a relatively easy manner, such as shown in the following example (Exhibit 10–1 below) of a foundation/corporate contact sheet with examples of information.

In Exhibit 10–1, the second column represents the initials of the person making the entry or providing the information. The "Notes" section is fairly flexible, enabling you to record meeting information, letters sent, calls made, and other important information and items in brief form. The "Next Steps" keeps track of what has to or should happen

as a result of that particular note. This can be a convenient way to remind yourself of things you need to do. And, of course, the "By" column can be used to track actual deadline dates as well as target dates for you and others to achieve particular tasks and actions.

This may seem like a lot of trouble, but, no matter how you record the information, it is vitally important to keep track of each and every key foundation and corporate contact as well as other data and information for each source. How important is it? Suppose you miss a proposal deadline date for a foundation that only meets twice a year. You have now set your organization's funding plans with that particular source back by at least six months. Information, as in Exhibit 10–1, can be collected in a brief but efficient manner. Internal records systems do not have to be complicated to be effective. The systems should be easy to understand and use, or the chances are they won't be used or kept up to date properly. Systems should also avoid excessive duplication of information, multiple forms, hard to understand categories, or the use of complex classification systems.

How simple can a foundation/corporate record system be? The basic categories of information listed above and the contact record can all be placed on the front and back of a single sheet of paper. The front can contain the basic information listed, and the back of the same sheet can contain the contact record, with additional contact sheets following. In fact, I've used similar systems for many years without any major problems—even without computer systems. Here is how the relatively simple paper system has worked for me:

- Each sheet (one per funding source) is set up with the basic information on the front, and the contact record on the back, using the column headers listed in Exhibit 10–1 above. I don't like using boxes and prefer column headers because they give me the flexibility of having a lot or a little information in each note.

- I next get a three-ring binder and several dividers. Five of the dividers are set up as follows: Prospect, Active, Proposal Pending, Grant, Inactive (see definitions presented

Exhibit 10–1 A Sample Contact Record

Date	By	Notes	Next Steps	By
1/14/96	EAS	Called and had foundation annual report, guidelines, and other materials sent.		
1/25/96	EAS	Information received and reviewed. To active prospect for disabled children program.	Further research; determine any board/staff connections	Deadline for proposal: June 1
2/1/96	JW	Board Chair knows Chair of foundation board through church.	Meet with Board Chair and Executive Director to brief them	ASAP
2/7/96	EAS	Meeting with Board Chair, Executive Director to discuss strategies. Board Chair will call foundation Board Chair to arrange possible meeting.	Check with Board Chair in one week	2/14/96
2/13/96	MV	Board Chair set meeting with foundation staff member Bud Smith for 2/26/96.	Brief Board Chair, Executive Director on strategies for meeting, prepare draft materials	2/23/96
2/22/96	EAS	Briefing held with Board Chair, Executive Director; basic script developed.	Revise budget; finalize materials and script for meeting	2/25/96

above). Within the Active and Grant dividers, I have 12 dividers, one for each month of the year.

- Each funding source sheet is filled in with as much information as I have on each prospect and punched to fit in the three-ring binder.

- Each sheet is then placed in the appropriate section of the binder (Prospect, Active, Proposal Pending, Grant, Inactive) in alphabetical order by the name of the foundation or corporate funder, and, if Active or a Grant, within the appropriate month when some-

thing next has to occur. For the Proposal Pending section, I don't use the monthly dividers, as these are the places I want to give the most frequent attention, at least reviewing them on a weekly basis to see if I should be checking back with each prospect about the possible decision or the need for more information. This setup thus becomes my "tickler" or reminder file for due dates, when I have to do things, or when I have to check on actions or next steps.

- As contacts are made, sheets in the Active section are moved into the next monthly divider where something has to occur, based, in part on dates in the "By" column of the contact record. However, if I want to pay special attention to a particular prospect for some reason, I may elect to keep it in the current month's section. Sometimes I put sheets in the monthly divider ahead of the month something is due to help remind me to get to work on it or check on that item early in the process. For example, if a final report is due to the funder in mid-May, I will put that information sheet in my April divider to remind me to get started on the report in April, not when it is due in May.

- As the contact record on the back of the sheet gets filled up with information, I merely duplicate the back form, attach it to that particular sheet, and continue to fill in the contact information as it occurs.

- I put the sheets for funders that have provided the organization with current grants in the Grant section and either within the month when they will next send a check for a grant payment (some foundations and corporate funders provide you with a schedule of payments on their grants) or in the month when a report is next due to the funder (or possibly in the month before, to help remind me early).

- The sheets can easily be duplicated for planning meetings with other staff at the organization, or for meetings with board members. The system also provides a quick way to answer such management questions as:

How many proposals do we have for that project and where are they pending?

What is the total amount in grant requests we have pending right now?

How many grant decisions will be made in May?

Do we have anything active with the Brown Foundation?

When is the fiscal report due to the Martin Foundation?

- The sheets can also be used to prepare summary and status reports, as references for the actual files on each potential source, and for a variety of other purposes.

Using the one notebook, I have on my desk almost everything I will need to keep track of where everything is, what happens next, and how successful we are being in our corporate and foundation fund-raising efforts. Over the years this system, or minor variations on it, has worked successfully for me. In some cases this paper system has actually outlasted or replaced elaborate computer software systems. In other cases it was incorporated into the computer and data processing system. With some adaption, it has always worked. But be sure not to simply copy this system. It is better to analyze and address your own and your organization's information needs and working styles and develop a system that will meet these. Exhibit 10–2 shows the front page of a sample Foundation/Corporate Contact Form.

Exhibit 10–2 Foundation/Corporate Contact Form

Date File Opened: _____

Date Closed: _____

Foundation/Corporate Name:

Address:

Phone #1:   For (Person):

Phone #2   For (Person):

Fax: E-mail:

Current Status (date current status)	Prospect	Active	Proposal Pending: Request: $_____ Date Sent _____	Grant $_____ Date: _____	Inactive	Special:

Type: ___ Family   ___ Gen. Purpose   ___ Special Purpose   ___ Community
            ___ Corp. Fdn.   ___ Corp. Giving   ___ Other/Special (Explain):

Primary Contacts:

Name: Title: Salutation:

Contact Information:

Name: Title: Salutation:

Contact Information:

Proposal Due Dates/Meeting Dates/Other Key Dates:

Key Information and Strategy Notes:

#Item Information   **By   Date**

Chapter 11

Approaching Funders: Specific Methods and Strategies for Each

Chapter Overview

One of the key components of the "Custer Assumption" (that no one survived)—a common but wrong point of view of the foundation and corporate funding process—is that an organization approaches potential funders by sending them proposals. As you have undoubtedly noticed, despite all that has been presented so far in this book, there has been little mention of proposals. Proposals are only a very small part of the process of obtaining funding from corporate and foundation funders. If you follow the steps outlined in this book and have done your homework—knowing your organization, researching and reading between the lines, and preparing your internal systems and procedures—you have probably completed about 60 to 70 percent of all the preparation work you will need to

do. This chapter will cover much of what happens next: the various methods for approaching corporate and foundation funders and the strategies that should guide you as you make your approaches.

One method for approaching foundations is obviously sending a proposal. But this is only one of many that will be discussed. Any given corporate or foundation source may require several different methods of approach over a period of time. And the specific strategies you use with each may also vary for each potential funding source. Review the methods and strategies carefully. All too often, people and organizations put little emphasis on, for example, contacting a foundation or corporation by phone even though that phone call can be a critical part of the total approach.

Strategy Tip: Although it took me a long time to come to this point of view, I now believe that committing your organization to a written proposal requesting a specific amount for a particular purpose should be kept low on your list of approach priorities as long as possible. The exception is, of course, when the foundation or corporate funder requires a written proposal before other methods of approaching the funder can be used. Once your organization is committed in writing to a particular request, you are very limited in your ability to discuss other options or ideas for foundation support. A proposal, in a sense, locks your organization into a particular course of action and gives the potential funder a much narrower frame of reference for viewing your organization. Wherever possible, use as many of the other approach methods as you can before committing yourself to the written proposal.

Inquiry Letters

Increasingly, foundations and some corporate funders are requesting or requiring the use of an inquiry letter as the first means of approach. An inquiry letter is a relatively short (many foundations specify a length of two to three pages) letter explaining in brief terms what your organization is, what it does, what the grant will be used for, and, in some cases, why your organization believes there is a fit between the purposes and guidelines of the foundation or corporation and your organization's needs.

More foundations and corporations are specifying they require an inquiry letter rather than a full proposal, and there are many reasons for this. The first and most obvious is that the inquiry letter process is one very specific way a potential funder can control the amount of written material it receives. Thus the inquiry letter process is a simple method of cutting down the volume of work for program staff. Instead of having to read through 10- or 20-page proposals with additional pages of attachments, the program staff need only review a short letter form each organization.

But there are other, less obvious reasons for a potential funder to specify the use of an inquiry letter. An inquiry letter must show the potential funder that the organization submitting it has clearly done its homework and has a good understanding of the mission, purposes, guidelines, and

> **More foundations and corporations are specifying they require an inquiry letter rather than a full proposal.**

specific funding interests of the foundation or corporation. Program staff can easily separate out the inquiry letters of organizations that don't understand that particular potential funder, or have not done their research and review of the funder's materials, from those that have done all of these.

Another reason inquiry letters are becoming a more popular method for corporations and foundations is that the letter quickly (because of the length restrictions specified by many foundations and corporations) gets to the heart of the matter for them: what is it your organization wants funded? The program staff person does not have to wade through pages of background information, data, long histories of the organization and the needs, or other material, which a typical proposal might include. The inquiry letter, if it is well written, tells the program staff member much of what he or she needs to know to decide if the funder wants to further pursue the particular need by having a meeting or inviting a full proposal. Again the inquiry letter process offers a quick and easy method to separate much of the chaff from the wheat—to remove organizations and projects from consideration prior to having to review full proposals, bringing them to the decision-making body of the funder, and doing all of the other things associated with the steps necessary to make a grant or to decline to make a grant.

Some potential funders resort to inquiry letters because they believe these letters put less of a burden on the applying organization. They believe the proposal process involves enormous amounts of staff time and energy at the organization and, rather than have all of this put into creation of a proposal that might well be turned down, it is better to require only a short letter. However, if 60 percent to 70 percent of your work seeking potential funders is spent in the areas of knowing your organization and research, the proposal—or the inquiry letter—are only relatively small parts of the total process. And, as we shall see, once you have prepared your first few proposals, the proposal development process can proceed fairly quickly.

But what are the pluses and minuses of inquiry letters for your organization? At first glance, one plus is you obviously don't have to prepare a full proposal to a particular potential funding source if all it requires is an inquiry letter. Or do you? The inquiry letter is much like a miniproposal, except for one major distinction that many (but not all) potential funders make between the inquiry letter and a proposal. A proposal usually must include a request for a grant in a specific amount and for a specific purpose related to the organization's needs, such as a program or project. In many instances the foundation or corporation will state that your organization is to include in its inquiry letter a description of the program, project, or other funding need for which you will be seeking support, but the foundation or corporation will not require that the inquiry letter include a specific grant request and amount of the grant. Thus, for example, a proposal might, in its Grant Request section (see Chapter 12 for a detailed discussion of the proposal's components) state "The XYZ Agency requests a two-year grant of $50,000 ($25,000 per year) for support of the child care project of the disability outreach program." The inquiry letter may describe the disability outreach program and list each of the major parts of the program, including the child care project, but there will not usually be a grant request and amount specified. The potential funder may also ask that a program or project budget be included with the inquiry letter, but most make a distinction between the inquiry letter and a proposal.

But why was it implied above that, while it appears that one advantage of this approach method is you don't have to prepare a full proposal, you might in fact have to prepare one anyway? The processes for preparing the inquiry letter and preparing a full proposal are much the same. And, with the exception of the Grant Request section for the proposal, the content of the inquiry letter is usually similar to, but not as long as, that of the full proposal. The inquiry letter will probably represent a summary of your full proposal (again, minus the grant request) and can be used as a guide in preparing the full proposal when the time comes to do so. So, in a sense when you are writing the inquiry letter, you are developing the core for your proposal. The areas covered, the needs or what your organization plans to do or is doing, the background on your organization, and the specific program or project for which you will possibly be seek-

ing support are all in the inquiry letter, just as they are contained in the proposal. The only difference is they are in a more abbreviated form. When you write the inquiry letter you really are writing a shorter version of the full proposal. The inquiry letter must therefore contain the key or essential points and "messages" to build your case. You want the potential funder to see why they should give your organization and its needs full consideration and thus enable you to move into the next phase of the approach process. The full proposal will amplify these key points and messages and support them with other information.

Strategy Tip: Sometimes I find that writing a clear and concise inquiry letter is much easier if I start by developing a draft of a full proposal first. This may seem to be going backwards, but developing the full draft proposal enables me to include all of the details, amplifications, background information, and other areas that I think could conceivably be important to the potential funder. Getting all of this in one place helps clarify my thinking and sorts out those elements that are probably, based upon my understanding of my organization and my homework on the potential funder, of primary importance for an inquiry letter to a specific foundation or corporation. I have the advantage of already having my draft proposal in place, if a potential funder gives the organization the go-ahead to submit a full proposal based upon the inquiry letter.

Another advantage of drafting a full proposal first is to help build understanding and consensus within your organization around the specifics of the proposal before you make any contacts with potential funders through inquiry letters or other approach methods. Be sure your executive director and other key staff know what a proposal will look like—and why it will look that way—as well as what it contains and the specifics of the request that will be made. By doing this review in advance and explaining the process and reasons behind it, you can avoid problems such as having to redefine a request to a foundation or corporation after you have already sent them an inquiry letter, or, worse, having to modify or withdraw a proposal because it was not exactly what your organization's management and leadership wanted or what the program staff needed. So the best advice is to get your plans and the reasons for them understood and get the necessary OKs before any inquiry letters go out, or other direct contacts are made.

Example: Following is an example of a somewhat typical inquiry letter to a foundation; the organization and other information is for illustrative purposes only, and any similarities to any existing organizations are coincidental. If a particular foundation or corporation specifies the format or content of an inquiry letter or a proposal, or even gives a suggested outline for you to follow, disregard the examples presented here and use whatever it suggests or specifies. Not doing so may result in the removal of your organization from consideration, even if the particulars of your request are appropriate to that foundation or corporation. The following example of an inquiry letter will be "dissected" (the sections in italics) so that you can see the rationale behind each part.

Tom Wright, Program Officer
Alexander Jones Foundation
3750 Business Center Road, Suite 234
Monmouth, New Jersey 34752

Dear Tom:

Thank you for taking the time to speak with me on the phone yesterday about the work of The Johnson Center and the possible interests of the Alexander Jones Foundation in supporting it. As I mentioned in our phone conversation, we

> **Be sure your key staff know what the proposal will look like, as well as what it contains and the specifics of the request.**

were referred to you by Bob Patterson at the Smith Foundation (a current funder) in New York City. As you requested, I've enclosed information on The Center and other materials on our current programs and projects.

Analysis: The first sentence immediately reminds the foundation staff person you have spoken with him and when this happened. Foundation and corporate staff receive many calls every day; it is always a good idea to remind them of any previous contact you have made with them or with others at the foundation. The second sentence reminds the staff person that one of the reasons you are calling his foundation is that another foundation staff person gave you the contact. This helps build some credibility for your organization, especially if the person at the Smith Foundation knows the Program Officer at The Jones Foundation. The sentence also builds credibility for your organization by showing that the Smith Foundation is already a funder. The next sentence starts "As you requested . . ." to show that the enclosed information is being sent because the Program Officer asked for it; again, it is useful to remind him that he initiated the request for the information.

To give you a little background on The Johnson Center, we were founded in 1979 as the only comprehensive child abuse treatment center serving Monmouth and Ocean Counties in New Jersey; we continue to be the only comprehensive center in the area. Our mission is to provide a full range of educational, treatment, legal, and medical referral services to abused children and their families so that the healing process can begin. As you may know, reported child abuse cases have grown at an alarming rate nationally and at a rate exceeding over 32 percent over the past five years in the bi-county area. There is substantial evidence that in many cases, the abusive parent or relative was also an abused child; our goal is to break this cycle.

The first sentence points out the service area of the center and affirms it is still the only one in the area providing a full range of services. Homework on the Jones

Foundation has indicated it does fund in this geographic area (regardless of its location, which happens to also be in the area). The next sentence gives the basic mission of the center. Next a few basic facts about the extent of the problem nationally and in the service area are presented. Finally, the overall goal—breaking the cycle of child abuse—of the center is presented.

Our major programs include:

Educational Services: The two primary components of our educational services are our public awareness/outreach program "SANE" (Stop Abuse Now Everywhere) and our day care/schooling program. SANE provides public information activities and materials designed both to increase public awareness of the issue and to give people specific ways to recognize child abuse and to take steps to report it to the appropriate agencies. SANE includes a publications program, which has distributed over 40,000 brochures to school teachers, family members, attorneys, law enforcement officials, and others. SANE also includes a series of seminars, conducted in conjunction with local school systems, designed to build public awareness of the issue and our services and programs.

The Center also operates a combination day care center/school program for children who have been identified as abused and referred to us by the courts. Our day care and educational program is integrated with our therapeutic services so that children, especially those who are severely abused, can continue to receive care and education appropriate for their particular age levels. These programs and their staffs are fully accredited by appropriate agencies.

Treatment Services: The Center offers individual child therapy by a staff of professional therapists and social workers, as well as a full range of family and crisis intervention services. Our crisis intervention teams are on call 24 hours per day and are used by local and county law enforcement officials and members of the court system to provide immediate needed assistance. Each team includes an attorney, a professional child and family therapist, a social worker, and a doctor. Each team completes a standard orientation program both to our agency and other legal and social service providers as well as to the specific needs and problems of abused children and their families.

These paragraphs briefly outline the basic services of the Center. Notice that mention is made of the accreditations of the Center's programs and staffs. This is important because it tells the potential funder that the Center has had outside, objective evaluations of its staff and work.

The Center is currently financed by several income sources, including county and state funds (20 percent of our total operating budget), United Way funding (20 percent), fees for service (20 percent, based upon each participant's ability to pay), individual contributions (20 percent), and corporate and foundation operating and restricted grants (20 percent). Our current operating budget is $1.85 million. We have a total staff of 27, including 18 professional staff.

The Center next presents a very brief overview of its budget's size and the sources of its income. Notice that the Center shows it has a diverse base of support. This is important to the potential funder, who may be concerned if an agency is relying too heavily on only a few sources of support, some of which may not be very stable. The size of the staff is also given, including the number of professionals.

We are currently exploring possible foundation and other support for start-up costs related to establishing an office in Ocean County. The establishment of a second site for the Center was recommended in the recent report "Ocean County 2000" prepared by the Ocean

County Government and the United Way of Ocean County. With the exception of a site Director, the Ocean County office would be staffed by reassignment of existing Center personnel. The advantages of the new Ocean County office include: providing a more accessible location for those we serve in Ocean County (some of whom must currently drive 30 or 40 miles to our present location), providing a day care and schooling program closer to the children in Ocean County, and serving as a second core site for our crisis intervention program. The needs and plans for a second site have been fully approved by both county governments, by our United Way funding sources, and by all other appropriate agencies. We have obtained donated office space and facilities, which meet all applicable requirements.

The Center has briefly outlined the project for which it will be seeking support from the foundation. Notice that the Center shows the need for a second site was verified by other agencies. Some of the basic advantages of the second site are also given, and the plans for staffing the site are presented. The Center is providing clear evidence that it has done its homework in seeking resources, such as the contributed space, needed to establish the site.

Because our plans involve substantial use of existing resources, the start-up costs for the second site will be minimal. Also, current funding resources will provide most of the needed operating support for the second site. However, we will require outside funding for providing the necessary office equipment for the second site, as well as initial funds to cover the salary and benefits of the new site Director. The United Way of Ocean County has indicated it will provide sufficient funds after the first year of operation to support the salary and benefits of the site Director. Additionally, our Development Office is seeking other ongoing sources of support for these needs, including the creation of a second Corporate Advisory and Support

Committee focused on Ocean County. We expect that the total financial needs related to the start-up of the new site will not exceed $55,000.

In this paragraph the Center presents its basic needs, which it would like the foundation to consider. Notice that the Center shows that it has already explored ways to sustain support for the new position, so that the foundation will not need to be reapproached for support once the start-up costs are met. The Center also demonstrates it is developing a back-up source of income for the new site—the Corporate Advisory and Support Committee. The final sentence gives the upper limit of the total needs; the strategy may be to ask only for part of this need from the Jones Foundation, but that is something that has yet to be determined.

As you know, many years ago the Jones Foundation was very supportive of the initial establishment of the Johnson Center. The Foundation's latest Annual Report and Grant Guidelines indicated the Foundation's renewed focus on child abuse treatment and prevention efforts as well as an intent to provide more grant funds in the Monmouth and Ocean County areas. The Foundation's recent grant to the Monmouth County Bar Association for its Child Abuse Legal Assistance Training Seminar enabled several members of our crisis intervention team to serve as trainers for area attorneys. We are hopeful that the Jones Foundation will be willing to consider a full proposal from the Center for support of this important step to better serve abused children and their families.

This paragraph first reminds the foundation that it was a past supporter of the establishment of the Center; the foundation's original "investment" helped the Center reach its present state. The paragraph goes on to demonstrate that the Center has done its homework by reviewing the current Annual Report and Guidelines of the foundation and that, based upon this review, the foundation is an appropriate place to submit a request for support of the expansion to a new site. Next, the Center shows that some of its staff participated in an-

other foundation-funded project, again helping to build its credibility.

I have enclosed a brief Fact Sheet as well as a copy of our most recent Annual Report. Also enclosed is the Executive Summary of the Ocean County 2000 Plan—I have highlighted the section referring to the establishment of a second site for the Center. I will be glad to send you copies of the relevant approval letters as well as the United Way's letter committing future support for the site Director position. Our present plans call for opening the new site within one year. We are also exploring support from other possible funding sources.

This paragraph covers the key enclosures. Notice that not everything is included so that the foundation staff member will not feel overloaded with materials, but the offer is made to send other relevant items. A brief one- or two-page Fact Sheet summarizing the organization's mission, history, programs, services, staffing, budget and sources of support, and plans is a useful reference document for the foundation staff member. Highlighting a relevant section of the Ocean County 2000 Report helps the foundation staff member pinpoint the important information without having to read the entire Report summary. This paragraph gives the timeline and presents the fact that the Center has a fund-raising plan and has identified sources other than just the Jones Foundation.

Mary Jacobs, our Board Chair, and I will be glad to meet with you to further discuss our plans and a possible proposal to the Jones Foundation. I will be calling you in the next few weeks to see if we can arrange a meeting. In the meantime, if you have any questions, please do not hesitate to give me a call. Also, we will appreciate your suggestions and advice about any other possible sources of support for this important project. Thank you and we look forward to speaking with you.

Sincerely,

Alice O'Brien, Executive Director

The final paragraph accomplishes several things. First, the commitment of the volunteer leadership of the Center to this project and to obtaining support for it is indicated by the mention of the Board Chair's willingness to be part of the team meeting with the foundation. The Executive Director offers to meet; as will be seen when we discuss meeting strategies, meeting before the proposal is actually submitted can help better shape the final proposal to the particular needs and interests of the foundation. The Director also says she will call the foundation staff member; rather than taking the passive role of waiting to contact the foundation, she will take a more active role by following up with the next step. She does plan to allow some time to pass before making the call; this is done to allow the foundation program officers to review the materials that were sent. But she also invited the program officer to call her if he has any questions or needs additional information. Finally, the foundation program officer is placed in the role of helper and advisor by being asked for ideas on other potential funders.

The inquiry letter above is only an example of how these can be used to build your case to potential funders. However, the key "messages" conveyed in the above letter should be a part of any inquiry letter and, as we shall see, of any proposal to a foundation or corporation. Presenting your entire organization—its mission, history, current programs and services, finances, and plans—as well as your understanding of how your request will match up with the foundation's or corporation's specific interests and guidelines in a brief two- to three-page document may at first seem difficult. Perhaps one way to accomplish this is to develop, with other staff, the key "messages" you wish to convey to each funding source. Notice that some of these messages also relate to your organization's own efforts to develop both realistic plans and alternative approaches to ensure their success. Messages might also include the outside endorsement of your agency and its plans by other organizations; the defining of the needs by a third, more objective party, rather than merely by your agency; the development of a fund-raising strategy involving multiple potential funders for a particular project, rather than the "all or nothing" approach of seeking support from only one funding source; and the presentation of the ways that the project or program will be sustained over the long term.

The inquiry letter is best understood when it is seen as both a presentation tool and an educational device. In the letter your organization presents itself in a way that is hopefully appealing to the interests of the foundation or corporation. The letter must demonstrate that you clearly understand to the best of your ability what these interests are and how what your organization does or plans to do fits with these interests.

But the letter also seeks to educate the potential funder about the important aspects of your organization and to create a sense of credibility for your organization. The focus is not just on the immediate needs for which you are seeking support from that particular source, but rather on the full range of what your organization is, what it does, and how it fits with the other organizations and needs in the area it serves. In a subtle way, the inquiry letter, by describing the organization and what it does, presents some other possible options that the potential funder might consider. Thus, while the particular project may or may not be of interest to the foundation, the discussion in the meeting might focus on the broader needs of the organization as well as some of its other planned programs and projects.

The inquiry letter places the foundation program officer in the role of a helper and advisor, not just a dispenser of funds. Even if the foundation decides it is not interested in pursuing support for this particular project, the letter has opened the door to using the staff member as a resource and a referral point. The follow-up call, no matter what the program officer's specific response to the inquiry letter, should pursue this strategy. The letter thus becomes one basis for creating the negotiated partnership that was discussed in the previous chapter. Each of the approach methods discussed in this chapter is a part of the overall strategy of seeking to build long-term relationships with foundation and corporate staff.

Meetings

I have heard it said that an organization has a 70 percent chance of getting a grant from a corporate or foundation funder if it meets with the potential funder, but only a 30 percent chance if it does not meet with the funder. I have no way of knowing if this is true. I do believe, based upon my own experiences on both sides of the desk, that meetings can be a very effective way to present your organization and its case to a potential funder. Meetings, as with the other approach methods discussed, can be part of an overall strategy for creating and maintaining a negotiated partnership with a foundation or corporation. But I also believe that going into a meeting without proper preparation and planning can hurt your organization's chances of getting support. Knowing your organization and doing your research are only part of the preparation work that should go into planning your strategies to meet with potential funders.

Two Scenarios

There are basically two scenarios for meetings with foundation and corporate funders. In the first, your organization has not yet submitted a full proposal to the potential funding source. You may have submitted an inquiry letter or merely sent some basic information, such as an annual report. Or you may have only sent a letter confirming the meeting and who from your organization will be attending (always a good idea). Or, in some cases, there may only have been a few brief phone conversations. In the second scenario your organization has already submitted a full proposal. For some foundations and corporations this may be the only circumstance under which your organization will be able to meet with the potential funder.

What are the differences in the basic approaches under these two scenarios? In the first, where there is not yet a formal submission, you can have a more flexible strategy to "shop" the foundation or corporation and see what will best fit both your organization's needs and the particular funding interests of that source. Of course, you

> **Meetings can be part of an overall strategy for creating and maintaining a negotiated partnership.**

still need to have done your homework and have a good understanding of both that particular funder's primary interests and the most likely programs and projects or needs of your organization that might fit the funder's interests. But, because you are not tied to one particular project, program, or need (unless this is all that you have that might make a good fit), you are free to explore some possibilities with the foundation or corporate staff member. Your overall objective, in addition to creating a basis for a negotiated partnership, is to reach an understanding of which of your needs will be the best fit and have the most likely chance of getting funded. You will want to come away with a good understanding of not only the nature of your specific proposal or request, but the amount of the request that you will be making. Also, you will want to leave with a better understanding of that particular funding source and staff member. And, finally, you want to have obtained suggestions and advice about other possible sources of support for your organization and its programs and needs, including those that may not be of direct interest to that particular funder.

Strategy Tip: There are some differences in the preparation work needed when you are planning to meet with a potential corporate funder. If your preliminary research indicates the corporation you will be meeting with prefers to work in partnership arrangements with nonprofits, prior to your meeting you and other key staff should discuss what it is your organization can offer the corporation in return for its support. The most basic question you should seek to answer or at least have thought out prior to your meeting is "can our organization help benefit the corporation and its bottom line in some way?" Are there specific ways your organization would be willing to "partner" with a corporation? What are some specific benefits this partnership would bring to each of the parties? How far is your organization willing to go in such partnerships? What dollar levels do

you require in order to give major recognition to a corporation? For example, if you are seeking a corporate sponsorship for a golf tournament benefiting your organization, at what level of support will your organization be willing to call the tournament "The XYZ Corporation/ Children's Agency Golf Tournament"? When approaching corporations always have some options to present in terms of the benefits of a partnership to the corporation. But also remember not to be so presumptuous as to tell corporations how a partnership will be of benefit to them. They will probably have some clear ideas about possible options for arrangements with your organization. Be prepared to negotiate these so that your organization's interests and needs are met as well as the company's interests.

In the second scenario, where the potential funder has already received a specific proposal, you and your organization are usually much more likely to be locked into discussing that particular approach. Thus, while part of the discussion may focus on your organization and its general needs, the foundation or corporate staff person will probably be more interested in discussing the proposal and how it fits the funder's interests. The conversation will usually be more focused on details of the request and your organization, in part because the program officer or other staff member already has considerable specific information on your organization (and presumably has read it and done his or her homework). In terms of the amount of your request, if you have done your homework, it should generally be in line with what is appropriate for that particular funder, but the program officer may make suggestions (or even just tell you) to change the amount of the request. In part, this may be based on the level of risk-taking the foundation or corporation is willing to accept and the funder's "comfort" with your organization and what it is doing as well as other internal factors. These can include the level of the grant the program officer feels the decision makers might approve, your proposal as compared to other pending proposals, and other concerns, which may not be obvious to you.

But before we get into more details about meetings and specific meeting strategies, let's discuss some of the major issues related to meetings with potential funders. How many people should attend a meeting with a potential funder? My recommendation is that your team consist of a minimum of two people. Only rarely should more than two attend. Circumstances might include a meeting with a potential funder where you know in advance several staff and/or board members of the funder will be present at the meeting and additional people from your organization will give some balance to the numbers, or where there is more than one person from your organization with strong professional or personal ties to that particular source and/or those who will be at the meeting. Another circumstance might occur when you need to have someone from your organization with special technical expertise in the area for which you are seeking a grant. But never try to overwhelm the potential funder with numbers just for the sake of doing so. And always be sure you have clearly told the person(s) you will be meeting with at the funding organization exactly how many and who is coming from your organization.

Who Should Attend?

There are many opinions on this, but my general feeling is that at least one member of the board of directors or trustees and one senior staff person (usually the executive director or president) should attend meetings with foundations and corporations where funding is being sought. Now, before all of the directors of fund raising and development start hopping up and down in anger, let me explain why I say this. I realize there are differing circumstances, depending upon the institution and how it operates its fund-raising program. For example, many hospitals, colleges and universities, and other large institutions rely upon their senior development/fund-raising staff person to make the foundation and at least some of the corporate contacts, with the president of the organization making only the

calls where the largest requests will be or have been made. In other organizations only staff, including possibly the chief executive officer and the chief development officer, make these calls. Sometimes program staff from the organization are involved in the calls. And in a few cases only board members make the foundation and corporate calls, especially where there are strong peer relationships.

But, generally, I think the most effective strategy is to have one representative of the volunteer leadership of your organization and the senior staff person serve as the team for meeting with at least the major potential funders. This is certainly not a hard-and-fast rule, and, in each case, the best possible team should be the one that is used for each particular source. But when your organization uses a board member and a senior staff member, this approach conveys some specific and very important "messages" to the potential funder, as well as enabling each member of your team to play very different but equally crucial roles in the meeting.

What are the "messages" you send to a potential funder by having both your volunteer leadership and senior staff be part of the meeting with the funder? The first is that the volunteer leadership, as well as the staff, are committed to the organization and its major fund-raising efforts. More and more funders see the critical importance of involvement of volunteer leadership as well as staff in all of the major areas of the organization, although most of these same funders see the need to have a clear differentiation of functions between board and staff. If the potential funder sees or believes that the board of the organization generally has a "hands off" attitude or does not want to be involved, except in a very limited way, then the funder may feel that the risk factors are much higher; the result may be an organization that is less likely to receive support. A second message sent by having volunteer leadership involved is that the particular need for which support is being sought—or if a proposal has not yet been submitted, the fund-raising needs of the organization—are very important to the board as well as to the staff. Remember our earlier discussion of cases where board members were not even aware of major funding requests or of new major projects and programs of their organizations? By having a board member at your meeting with a potential funder you are clearly saying "our board not only understands what we are doing or planning to do—they are a part of it."

But why should at least two people from your organization be part of meetings with potential corporate and foundation funders? Having two people there enables each, in turn, to play a particular and different role, while at the same time ensuring one person can listen, observe, and take notes while the other is presenting or responding. Having a two-person team also enables the team members to evaluate each other's skills in presenting and responding so the team can benefit from its experience in productive ways and can become more effective on future calls—"learning by doing." The team can also, after the call is over, compare notes and get a clear understanding of what happened in the meeting and what needs to be done next as follow-up steps. And, finally, using a team enables your organization to match up the particular individual strengths of your team members and to present some indication of the diversity and experience of those who lead your organization.

Where is the director or vice-president of development/fund raising in this mix? Here is where I usually get into trouble with my development colleagues. In many cases foundation and corporate staff members see development officers as the "hired guns" of the organizations that are approaching them. Now, I'm not agreeing with this assessment and with what follows; I'm just saying it is a fairly common perception on the funding side. Development staff are sometimes seen as primarily interested in getting another notch on their guns by obtaining a grant from a foundation or corporation. Their interest—again, from the funder's point of view—is not in the particular program or project for which support is being sought, nor in the big picture of the organization and how it fits into the needs of the community, but only in getting the dollars. There are, of course, many cases where this does not apply. Other foundation and corporate staff members have close relations with development staff of organizations, and others just see them as part of the team at a particular organization. But be aware that there are other attitudes and opinions that exist and that it is always im-portant to put together the best possible team to do the job, regardless of who is on the team.

Roles of Team Members

What roles should the team members play when meeting with a potential funder? Again, these can vary with circumstances but generally there are two different but integrated roles that team members have in these meetings. The volunteer leadership team member is there to present and discuss the "big picture" items: the needs of the community, why your particular organization is the best organization to meet these needs, and the commitment of volunteer leadership to the organization and to meeting these needs. The senior staff team member is there to present and discuss the organization's operational side, including such areas as sources of support, programs and projects, staffing, and the specifics of the proposal, if one is under consideration. If a proposal is not under consideration, the senior staff person is there to help narrow down the organization's specific funding needs to those that best match up with the interests of the particular funding source. He or she is also there to answer specific questions about the organization, its needs, and the projects or areas for which it is seeking support. Both members are there to listen, take notes, observe the reactions of the foundation or corporate staff member to what is presented, and, afterward, reach consensus on what was heard and the next steps they are to take. One team member can play a key role filling in gaps in the conversation so that a dialogue is maintained, or providing needed information not available to the other member of the team. And, remember it should be clear to all team members that they are also to evaluate each other's performances as well as their feelings about their own performances. Out of this latter process can come considerable refinement and improvement of the skills and abilities of team members so that each call is more effective than the previous call.

Rehearsal Sessions and Evaluation

Unfortunately, some teams see their role(s) as merely to present, and then wait for a response from the foundation or corporate staff member. As a consultant, I worked closely with an individual who, in her first few meetings with foundation and corporate funders, saw her role as making a 15- to 20-minute presentation "at" the funder's staff member, and then to wait for his or her response. At times, this approach involved actually cutting off the staff member as he or she tried to ask a question or make a point! After seeing one or two of these sessions, I worked with her on ways to create an immediate dialogue with the funding prospect, rather than to present 20 or 30 key points about the organization and its needs. One way to avoid this and similar situations is to script out the presentations by developing the key points or messages you wish to convey to the particular potential funding source. Once this is done, team members should actually rehearse the call on the prospective funder. Possibly another staff member or board member can play the role of the funding prospect's representative; it may also be helpful to have two to three other observers for the rehearsal session. After the rehearsal session, all involved should evaluate the session, including such key questions as:

- Was a dialogue created?

- Did each member of the team convey a good understanding of your organization and its needs as well as of the funder?

- Did team members listen carefully and respond appropriately?

- Were questions answered in a way that showed a high degree of knowledge of your organization and how it serves the community?

- Was the team taking a strategic "negotiated partnership" approach to the session, or was it only interested in the potential grant?

- If a specific proposal was not already submitted, did the team shape the discussion in a way that clearly presented several potential programs or projects that might appeal to the potential funder, based upon the funder's own particular interests?

- Were efforts made by the team to have the funder's representative suggest an amount to request or a range for a request (if no proposal had already been submitted)?

- Did team members show they had a good knowledge of the organization's budget, funding sources, fund-raising efforts, the budget for the project(s) or program(s) being explored with the funder, and plans to raise the needed funds?

- Did team members effectively deal with any sensitive or difficult questions in a way that indicated honesty and openness?

- Did team members effectively use any materials, such as fact sheets, budgets, etc., in the presentation?

- If team members were not able to answer specific questions, did they respond in a way that indicated they would get an answer back to the person as soon as possible?

- Did team members thank the funder and review next steps with him or her, including what additional materials, if any, the foundation or corporation needed and any deadlines at the end of the session?

Each team member should, prior to the rehearsal session, be thoroughly briefed on the potential funder and provided with the research and background information developed by staff. Any previous contacts with the foundation or corporation as well as any other history with the potential funder should be reviewed with each team member. Team members should read any materials from the funding source, such as annual reports, grant guidelines, etc. These materials should be discussed by team members and other staff involved in developing the strategies for each potential funder.

In reality, it may not be possible to conduct rehearsals with team members prior to each meeting with a potential funder. But, wherever possible, the rehearsal technique should be used prior to the first meeting a particular team will have with a potential funder. After actual meetings, team members and others from the organization should debrief, using the questions outlined above. In the debriefing session team members and other staff should review not only the particulars of each meeting and what the follow-up steps are (and who will be responsible for carrying them out) but they also should review what was learned about their overall preparation, their presentation and discussion techniques, and their responsiveness to questions and comments of the potential funder.

Focusing on the Funder

A few paragraphs ago I mentioned the individual who initially saw her role in meetings with foundations and corporations as talking "at" them rather than creating a dialogue with them. How do you create a dialogue? There are many ways to do this, but one of the easier ways is, after the initial introductions and thanking the individual for taking the time to meet with you, to ask some key questions. These key questions can focus on your organization, such as "Did you get a chance to review the materials we sent to you?" If the individual did, your next question might be "Do you have any questions about our organization and what we do?" Or the questions can focus initially on the foundation or corporate funder. When appropriate, I prefer the latter approach for a several reasons. First, good questions about the foundation or corporate funding source can clearly demonstrate to the potential funder that you have done your homework. Second, good questions can help clarify particular points of information or issues that may not be clear in the funder's printed materials or in your research. And third, good questions can help focus attention on the funder's particular interests as well as your organization's needs, and how these fit those of the funder.

What are some examples of questions focusing on the funder? Here are just a few possible examples:

- "When we read your materials we noticed that the foundation has a new initiative to better address the needs of children in the community. Since that is one of the primary service areas of our organization, could you tell us more about how that initiative evolved and what the focus will be in terms of your funding?"

- "We noticed the foundation recently increased the number of grants it was making to children and youth agencies. Was this a deliberate decision on the part of the foundation or just a response to needs in the community?"

- "Have the recent cutbacks in public funding for children's programs had any impact on the foundation and its funding priorities?"

- "The foundation's guidelines indicate it is supportive of new initiatives to better serve children. Could you explain a little more specifically the interests of the foundation?"

- "The corporation guidelines state you fund only agencies that benefit the communities in which your company has operations or agencies that directly benefit employees of the company. Could you explain more specifically what that means?"

- "After we reviewed your most recent annual report, we were not sure about the decision-making process the foundation uses to make grant decisions. Could you explain in a little more detail how grant decisions are made?"

These are just a few examples of questions that can lead to developing a more complete understanding of the foundation beyond what you may have gathered from written materials and other research. After you have collected basic information, these questions help move the focus of the discussion from centering exclusively on your agency to centering on both the funder and your organization. One of the goals is to create a dialogue focused on more than just your organization's specific needs and getting a grant to meet those needs.

At times, a more personal approach may be appropriate. For example, if the individual you are meeting with has common friends or professional acquaintances with you or your organization, it might be good to open with a comment such as "Barbara Smith over at CYC said to say hello when we meet with you" (if in fact Barbara Smith is more than a passing acquaintance of the person you are meeting with). Alternately, if you know something of the background of the individual you are meeting with, you might want to open with some reference to this, particularly if there are logical connections to your agency and those it serves. In such cases you might want to open with, "I noticed from your biography that you worked with the YMCA in Cleveland before you came here. I'm always interested in how people get into foundation work; how did you end up here?" The objective is to make some real connection with the person you are meeting with, rather than just seeing the meeting as a chance to present your case.

Creating a Dialogue

Why is creating a dialogue so important in these meetings? Creating a dialogue breaks away from the "beggar" and "superior–inferior" approaches discussed in Chapter 10. A dialogue helps create a sense of equality and partnership in your relations with potential funders and keeps the focus where it should be: on the interaction of the mission and interests of the potential funding source and on the mission and needs of your organization—and those your organization serves. A dialogue designed to recognize that there are mutual interests held by both the potential funder and the organizations seeking support, that there is a higher purpose to this process (serving the greater needs of the community or country), and that the potential funder's representative is more than a possible source for a check can help start the "negotiated partnership" you should be seeking.

Strategy Tip: Learn to listen. Many people are good or excellent presenters. Few are good listeners. Yet listening is one of the essential skills to create a dialogue and to build a relationship with an individual. Learn to hear both what is said and what is meant, as well as what the person is really thinking or feeling. In your meetings with potential funders pay attention to what they are really saying. Take careful notes (this in itself can indicate to the person speaking that you are listening carefully). When a foundation or corporate staff member says "I'm very busy—I can only give you a short time for our meeting" what else is he or she really saying? Possible meanings might be: "I'm feeling very pressed today," "Be brief and to the point," "Respect my time and workload," "I'm always busy," or something else. Or when the person says "Are you familiar with a similar project we funded for the XYZ organization?" he or she might be checking to see if you have done your homework, or might be asking you to explain in more detail how your project or program is different from the other project or program, or might be really saying this is an area the funder already has supported—do you have anything different to offer? The tendency in meetings with potential funders is often to focus almost entirely on your organization and its needs, rather than on what the person is really saying. Practice your listening skills as well as your presentation skills.

When a proposal has already been presented to the potential funder, the nature of the meeting will change. Because the person (or people) you are meeting with will have much more specific information in front of him or her, the discussion will be more focused on the details of the match-up between the foundation's or corporation's interests and the needs your organization is seeking to address through funding. But even in these situations it is important to create a dialogue and to move away from the somewhat natural tendency to make a presentation. As a program officer I frequently saw organizations send people to meetings who were primed to make a major presentation (sometimes involving displays or even videotapes). I often felt their approach could be summed up by the phrase "If we keep talking, maybe he won't ask us many questions!" But, at other times, the approach was much more passive—more in line with the "beggar" style we've discussed. In these cases it was almost as if they were relieved that I took control of the meeting and initiated all of the questions and discussion.

Strategy Tip: Be careful about how you use materials in meetings with potential funders. My belief is to keep it simple and to limit the materials you bring with you. Give the potential funder only a few key items. Avoid having the person sit through a long—or even a short—videotape, or watch an overhead transparency presentation; videotapes and other elaborate materials should either be sent before the meeting or be left with the person to view later when the meeting is over. And, unless the materials are absolutely essential to making your case, the best approach is probably to explain what they are and ask if the foundation or corporate staff person wants to review them before you send them. Don't hand out large quantities of materials that will require the funder to find different pages and items of information you are referring to while you make your case; this can result in major parts of the meeting being devoted to such "key" questions as "did you say that was the third paragraph on page 42 or the second paragraph on page 43?" One of my favorite approaches is a simple Fact Sheet printed on two sides of one sheet of paper. The Fact Sheet can be an outline of the full proposal, and thus can follow the same general set of categories as the proposal (or letter of inquiry) (see the next chapter on proposals). The Fact Sheet can also help keep your team focused on the key points that should be covered in the meeting with the poten-

---

tial funder and can be left with those you meet with to provide them with a quick summary of both your organization and its needs.

One strategy to help create a dialogue with a potential funder who already has a proposal is to very briefly present some background on your organization and who it serves as well as what led up to the particular need (a new program designed to respond to an emerging issue in the community, an expansion of a program to meet increased needs, etc.) that you are seeking to have supported. But again, stay away from the tactic of making a presentation. Wherever possible, seek the potential funder's opinions about your key points and other areas. Make some initial statements but then move into some dialogue-creating questions. Dialogue-creating questions can start off with such openings as "Are you familiar with . . ." or "Do you see this as a major need of the community . . ." or "Did you know that our agency . . ." or even "Are you aware of—or has the foundation funded—any similar approach to this issue by another agency in our community?"

Always assume that the person you are meeting with has done his or her homework and has thoroughly read your proposal and the attached materials. This may not always be the case, but it is better to assume it than to assume you have to review everything in the proposal during the course of the meeting. It is often a good idea to assume that the person you are meeting with may have a better base of knowledge—or may believe he or she has a better base—about major issues and needs in the community than you do. This assumption is more likely correct if he or she is a "specialist" assigned to a particular program area at the funding source. Often foundation and corporate staff members do have a good overview of what is happening in the community or area they serve, at least in terms of funding requests they are receiving. When the funder has program staff with different specialty areas (such as "Children and Youth," "Cultural Arts," etc.), these staff members may meet from time to time with their counterparts from other funders to discuss the major issues and trends as well as innovative new grants or initiatives.

Some foundation and corporate staff members may be actively involved in the communities they live and work in, either because of their professional interests or for personal reasons. They may be active with the United Way or the local school board, or they may serve on the boards of other nonprofit organizations. They may have a long history of involvement in the community, even aside from their corporate or foundation roles. So their knowledge—and often their opinions—about the community and its needs may be extensive. These may be tempered by the interests and leadership of the foundation or corporation they serve. A staff member of a grant-making organization may have a strong opinion about particular issues in the community, but, if the foundation or corporation has its own stand on these same issues or is not interested in or supportive of these issues, the staff member may elect to reserve his or her opinions or defer to the corporate or foundation views. In creating a dialogue, try to get a sense of where that particular staff member stands on the issues you are addressing, especially if these issues may be controversial. Also, try to get a sense of the potential funder's organizational views on these same issues—and see if you can determine the differences between the staff person's view and that of the funder.

But also realize that it may be necessary to educate the potential funder not only on your organization's particular plans, but also on the particular issues and needs the organization is trying to address. This approach assumes that there is some logical connection between the interests of the foundation or corporation and the particular needs or issues for which you are seeking support. This "educational" approach may be necessary, especially when the service or program for which you are seeking support is particularly innovative or different from the areas which the potential funder usually supports.

Example: An organization I was consulting with frequently developed innovative, "cutting edge" programs and projects. But the innovative nature of these programs and projects became a drawback when we approached potential funders, because they rarely, if ever, had funded anything similar. In one case we were meeting with the executive director of a medium-sized family foundation. After we explained the project to him, he responded: "You know, this is an area I really think we ought to get into and start funding. We've talked about it a lot at the staff level; maybe now is the time to try to sell it to the board. But I'm just not sure it will be acceptable to them yet. Let's give it a try." We later found out he did indeed try to sell the concept and the specific proposal to the board members, but they were not ready to move into funding this new area. Nevertheless, we had a new friend who was supportive of the importance of the program—and who could be helpful in many ways, such as referral to other potential funders.

Ground Zero Approach

However, in other situations you may have to take a totally different approach to the foundation or corporate staff member. Whereas in some cases, the needs your organization addresses may be easy to understand, in other cases even the need itself may not be understood by the funder. Feeding hungry children, helping the elderly, and better education are all relatively easy to understand. But where do educational programs for members of the judiciary fit into the list of needs? Why is doing this important and, if it is done, what will be the impact of such a program? In cases such as this, you may have to move back a few steps and educate the prospective funder on the importance not only of your particular program or project, but on the importance of the need itself. This is what can be called a "ground zero" approach. Before you can begin to convince the potential funder of the value of your program or project and why it should be funded, you need to start at the zero point of ex-

> It may be necessary to educate the potential funder not only on your organization's particular plans, but also on the particular issues and needs your organization is trying to address.

plaining the need. Built into this process is the assumption that the potential funder is already making grants in areas somewhat related to what it is you are doing or planning to do. In the example of judicial education, all the foundations approached had been providing grants for justice- and court-related projects and programs. The task became connecting what they currently funded to the need to better educate sitting judges on certain key issues so that they could improve the quality of their judicial decision making.

The ground zero approach needs to be used with great care and must be based on excellent research on the prospective funders. It also requires the development of a strategy that will clearly connect the current funding interests of the funder with the need your organization's project or program is addressing, and thus with your particular project or program. Think through your key points carefully. List what the objections from the funder might be, such as: "We've never done anything like this before," "I'm not sure I can convince my board to do this," "How does this fit with our current funding interests," or, "What's the real benefit, especially in terms of our usual funding, of doing this?" How would you respond to each of these and other possible objections? Why and how did your organization come to believe that this particular need was one that should be addressed? How can you help give the person you are meeting with the necessary points to help him or her move it through the decision process?

The ground zero approach also involves more risk in terms of your organization's raising support for a new project or program. Whereas when you are seeking sources of support for most needs of your organization, your research and approaches can focus on matching potential funders' interests and actual grants for these needs, the ground zero approach means you must attempt to build bridges where none have existed before. But there are many potential benefits to using this approach when it is required. One benefit is that you and your organization can help move funders into new and exciting areas that they may not have even considered before. Also, you have the potential to develop new allies for your programs and projects if foundation and corporate funding staff accept the importance

of the new areas of need that are being addressed by your program or project. These individuals, even if, at times, they are not able to convince their own boards or other funding decision makers of the need to support the program or project, can help direct you to other potential funding sources and may even make the case to these potential funders.

Example: A member of the board of a small family foundation was approached by the executive director of an organization for support of a new project. It quickly became clear that the foundation's board would not support the project, even though it fell within their general guidelines. The board member stated that the area was too controversial and had too many unknowns for the board to feel very positive about making a grant. But the board member himself was very interested in the area, in part because he was an attorney and had some basic familiarity with the legal aspects of the issue. He admitted to wanting to know more about it. The executive director asked him if he had any suggestions about other potential funders who might be interested in the project. He gave the name of another funder, offered to call the staff member there, and sent the director over immediately to meet with him. He also described in detail why the funder would have a strong interest in supporting the project. The result was a $25,000 grant toward the project.

Some time ago I prepared a short piece on asking for and getting major gifts from individuals. Below I've excerpted part of this unpublished piece; many of the steps apply to meetings with foundations and corporations as well as individual solicitations.

The Meeting—Ten Easy Steps

There are many variations on ways to conduct a gift prospect meeting. Each individual session must reflect the organization, the team selected, and the uniqueness of each prospect. Typical steps in a prospect meeting include:

1. Opening. Introduce everyone, if necessary, thank prospect for the opportunity to meet, ask if he or she received the materials, stress importance of the meeting, affirm session will

be kept brief and team is there to listen as well as present.

2. Presentation. Brief background on the organization, but focus on the needs and the future. Stress the more emotional components of the appeal but also present the facts. Talk about the uniqueness of the organization and why it is the best place to meet the needs. Cover the campaign plan and the need to create a feeling the campaign will succeed. Present possible ways people will be able to contribute to the campaign. Also cover gifts or pledges made, if any, and how the prospect will be part of a large effort.

3. Questions and Comments. Provide the prospect with an opportunity to respond to the presentation with any questions or comments. Listen carefully to what these are, and respond to them as directly as possible. Is the general tone of the questions and comments positive, neutral, or negative? Does the person seem interested in the presentation or merely listening? Use body language clues as well as the verbal comments. Adjust the next steps as necessary.

4. Move to the Personal Level. What role(s) can the prospect play in achieving the goals of the organization, making the campaign a success, and/or better meeting the needs that exist? Why was he or she selected to meet with early in the fund-raising process?

5. The "Ask." At this point the request for the gift is made. The "ask" usually begins "We would like you to consider . . ." or "We would like you to be one of our lead supporters by. . . ." Again, the importance of the prospect and his or her gift to the success of the campaign should be stressed. The "ask" should be brief and should end with a question or statement such as "Can we count on you?" or "We're counting on you to be a significant part of this."

6. Prospect Reactions. Give the prospect the fullest opportunity to respond, to ask questions,

and to examine alternatives. Answer all questions as directly as possible.

7. Responding to Objections. Be prepared to respond to objections, concerns, and comments. Reinforce positive comments the prospect has made about the organization and his or her relation to it. If the prospect is hesitant about giving an immediate decision, agree to a time frame and set who will contact him or her. Stress the specifics of how a major gift can be given and how it can be paid over time. If the answer is a "no," first ask for the specific objections to giving, if not already stated, and respond to these. Ask if the prospect would be willing to consider at any future time. If the answer is still "no," offer alternative ways the person can assist, such as identification of other prospects, providing advice and suggestions on the campaign itself, or assisting the organization in other ways. If the answer is "yes," congratulate the prospect on being one of the leaders of the campaign, thank him or her, and reinforce the positive impact the gift will have on the total effort and the organization.

8. Closure. Close out the session, again thanking the prospect for his or her time, reaffirming the next steps and who will contact the prospect.

9. Follow Up. Immediately after the meeting the team should review the results, the prospect's reactions, areas that can be improved in future presentations, and the follow-up actions required with the prospect. Within a few days after the meeting the prospect should be called and thanked, preferably by phone for being willing to meet and for any contribution or assistance he or she has made. This should also be confirmed in writing, preferably by the head of the campaign committee or the chair of the board or both. If the prospect has not made a decision, keep him or her informed of other key gifts and pledges made, other campaign developments, and be sure to recontact the prospect at the agreed-to time.

10. Donor and volunteer recognition. Key donors and anyone else who has been helpful in the campaign effort should be recognized in a way appropriate to the level and importance of their contribution.

Key Questions to Ask

There are some specific, critical questions that should be asked in every meeting with a potential corporate or foundation donor; some of these have been mentioned earlier, but are included here as a summary of these points. These questions and the reasons for asking them are:

"Could you explain (or review, if it is clearly presented) the review and decision-making processes for your foundation (or corporation)?"

Reasons: Few foundations and corporations clearly spell out their review and decision-making processes. It is very important to get the best possible understanding of how these processes work and the roles that staff members, the board, and any other review or decision-making bodies play in the processes. Some foundation staff, when asked this question, will put much of the authority and responsibility with the board, while others will stress the key roles they play as staff. At the most basic level, though, you should come away with a clearer understanding of how the processes work at that particular foundation or corporation as well as who is involved in the review and decision making. Asking this question can also lead to the next key question, which has also been discussed earlier.

"Do you have staff discretionary grant-making ability?"

Reasons: The answer to this question can help lead to the development of specific approach strategies to the potential funding source and may also help provide direction for the rest of the meeting. If the staff member you are meeting with indicates that he or she does have the ability to make grants, or if there is a staff-driven grant process, your next question should be: "What is the maximum level at which a grant can be made by staff?" If this is the case and the staff member seems genuinely in-

terested in your organization and its projects and programs, you might begin to shape your request (if a proposal has not already been submitted) toward a goal of obtaining a level of support consistent with a possible staff discretionary grant from that particular source. Thus your task becomes one of "winning over" that particular staff member. Even if you have submitted a proposal, if the staff member indicates staff discretionary grants are permitted, you might consider redefining your request to fit within the limits on the amounts of staff-approved grants. This may also mean redefining your other fund-raising approaches to make up for any differences between the amount of your original request and the probably lower level of your redefined request. The best advice may be, once you have learned there is a possibility of a staff-approved grant, to discuss the option of redefining your request with the foundation or corporate staff person. This in itself might give you a clearer understanding of how he or she feels about your particular proposal or the project or program for which you are seeking support. Remember also that if you are approaching a potential funding source for the first time, the "risk factor" for the foundation or corporation in making a grant through a staff-only process might be considerably lower for the funder than that of going to the full board.

"Do you have any suggestions about other places where we might seek support (for this program or project)?"

Reasons: This question reflects what should be your expanded view of the foundation or corporate staff person as something more than the possible source of a check. An earlier example showed that asking this key question resulted in a grant from another source. But it also clearly places the staff member in the roles of advisor and helper and can be an important step toward developing a negotiated partnership. This question should always be asked, and it becomes especially critical if it appears that the particular corporation or foundation you are meeting with may not be inclined to proceed further with exploring support for your organization. At this point shifting to how that person might help your organization in other ways may make that person feel like he or she can in fact do something for you rather than just say "no" or "we're not interested." The "guilt" factor may be operating in this situation to some extent (as we shall see in a later chapter, it can also operate at other times) and falling back on many people's tendencies to want to be helpful can move the meeting toward a more positive direction. Regardless of how the meeting is proceeding, always ask this question.

Many foundation and corporate staff are well aware of other potential funding sources, especially in the areas that they specialize in or that are a part of the funder's interests. This is especially true for private and community foundation staffs, many of whom periodically meet together with their colleagues from other corporations and foundations to discuss current trends, issues, and funding. So, if the person you are meeting with does suggest other corporate or foundation sources, be ready with another question (if the person only gives you the names of the foundations or corporations): "Can you recommend someone there I should speak with?" If you are given a name or names, your next question should be "May I tell that person you referred me to him or her?" Getting contacts at other potential funding sources should be one of your key goals whenever you are meeting with any potential funder. And getting permission to use that person's name when making your next contact can help open up other doors and options much more quickly than "cold" calls.

If you did explore the sources being recommended by the staff person, but your research indicated that a particular recommended source was not a likely prospect, you might indicate this in your discussion in order to get that person's views on why he or she believes it may be a good source. You might discuss your reasoning as to why you feel the recommended source was not a good possibility. Be sure to understand the reasoning behind what the staff member is recommending; you may well need to present this same reasoning to the recommended source when you approach it.

In some cases the foundation or corporate staff person you are meeting with may be willing to actually make the call to set up a meeting with the recommended foundation or corporation. It is probably a good idea not to ask the individual to do this, but be aware it can happen. Keep in mind there are many ways that each individual you meet with can be helpful; don't be afraid to explore options with each person.

"Could you give us your assessment of how our proposal compares to others submitted here?"

Reasons: If you have submitted a proposal, this question becomes your opportunity to get some real feedback from someone who probably has experience in looking at many proposals. Be prepared to see any feedback as helpful, even what you may at first see as negative comments. It is best not to get defensive, but see that the person is trying to help you better shape your future proposals. Be sure to ask follow-up questions to get more detailed explanations of both the strengths and weaknesses of your proposal. And, as in other areas, always thank the individual for the suggestions and advice.

"Is there anything else you need from us at this point?"

Reasons: If, in the meeting, you or the person you are meeting with has not clearly established what other materials are needed to take the process to its next stage, this question can help define what materials should be sent. It is important to ensure that the foundation or corporation has everything necessary to continue its process.

"May we submit a proposal for support of the XYZ program or project?"

Reasons: If you have not yet submitted a proposal, but have been working in the meeting toward defining a proposal, it is always a good idea to be sure there is a mutual understanding of the next step. Ideally, you and the staff person should also have discussed the level of the request that seems acceptable; the level should be presented as part of the above question in order to again confirm the understanding reached. Thus the question might become: "May we submit a proposal for $25,000 toward support of the XYZ program or project?"

Strategy Tip: Does your organization have problems? It is the rare organization that, at some point in its existence, does not have problems or difficulties.

But what happens when your organization is in a difficult situation and you are in the process of approaching potential funders? The problems can be strictly internal, with little outside awareness, or, often the more difficult situation, external and well known to the public. Much earlier, an example was given of an organization that had major problems—large financial debts—but was eventually successful in getting a grant and even succeeded in getting some financial assistance to start to solve its problem. The best advice, especially when dealing with potential funders, is this "problem–solution" approach. If your organization has a problem or a difficulty, the least desirable approach is to merely present the problem or difficulty to the potential funder, or, even worse, pretend it doesn't exist. The absolute worst case is to attempt to conceal the problem from the potential funder and hope it won't be discovered. This approach can and will raise serious ethical questions about your organization, including its leadership and management. And, since many foundations and corporations speak with each other, you may face a situation of being turned away by several potential sources based on your organization's negative reputation. Foundations and corporations can know more about your organization than you think they do, and if they find out your organization is intentionally or even unintentionally concealing information, the results may be disastrous.

So, if your organization has a problem or difficulty, be sure the organization develops possible solutions to resolve that problem or difficulty.

Strategy Tip: Suppose someone on your organization's board or staff knows or has some connection to the board member of a foundation. Should that connection be used to approach the foundation? I frequently asked this question in a workshop I taught for The Foundation Center. In several cases members of the workshop responded with examples of problems caused by approaching board members of foundations that also had staffs. In some cases board members known to people associated with an organization had been given proposals before they were actually submitted to the foundation. In other cases board members had been asked to "champion" the organization's proposal or planned proposal. And in some cases the foundation board member had only been asked to provide guidance or suggestions and advice on approaching the foundation. How could these strategies cause a problem? If you are not familiar with the internal workings and procedures of the foundation, you and your organization's seemingly innocent attempt to get additional help with your approach may be seen by the staff of the foundation as an effort to "go around" them, or to actually avoid their usual procedures. The results can include delayed processing of your organization's proposal, a decline of your organization's request for support, or a returned proposal. Some of the members of my class recounted cases where approaching a board member of a foundation resulted in one of these consequences.

Some foundation boards have agreed that they will not accept any proposals nor can they be approached individually by organizations wanting support for their requests. Any board member who is approached individually would respond that the organization should follow the usual procedures by first contacting staff or by submitting a proposal to the foundation. But, as we have seen, some foundations are very board-driven and may not have any restrictions on what board members can and cannot do. Even in these foundations staff may become resentful if board members take a direct role in bringing proposals to the foundation or acting as "champions" where they have been asked to do so. The best advice, if your organization is approaching an individual board member of a foundation, is to open with a statement such as "We are planning to approach the ABC Foundation for support of our organization and I know you are on the board there. Would you mind if I discussed our approach to the foundation with you?" Using this opening or something similar gives the individual board member a chance to define the limits of your interaction with him or her and to let you know immediately if there are formal or informal restrictions on the roles the individual can play. But again, be cautious; even a board member who is very open to being approached individually may not be aware of how the staff of the foundation might feel about this approach.

Other Ways to Prepare

What else should you know or be prepared for when meeting with a foundation or corporation? Remember the earlier discussion of different roles—advocate, blocker, etc.—that foundation and corporate staff members can play? The advocate, if he or she sees that you have indeed done your homework and that there may be a match with the foundation's or corporation's purposes and guidelines, may want to work with you to develop the rationale that will be used to recommend a grant to the board or other decision makers. The advocate may also want to help your organization strengthen its proposal, if one has already been submitted, or help shape the request in a way that will make it even more appealing and likely to get approved. But, if there doesn't appear to be a good match or the risk factor seems too high, the advocate may recommend approaching the foundation with another program or project that will be a better fit, or possibly even holding off on a formal approach or going elsewhere for support. In most cases the advocate will seek to be helpful and will offer constructive advice and suggestions. He or she may also discuss similar projects the foundation or corporation has funded elsewhere, or even suggest additional people to contact who are at other organizations working on similar issues.

The blocker, if you are able to meet with him or her at all, may ask a series of detailed questions about your proposal and may challenge the assumptions underlying the proposal or your organization's plans, or the uniqueness of what your organization is trying to accomplish. The blocker, in essence, may be doing exactly the opposite of the advocate; he or she may be seeking reasons to turn down your proposal or at least to discourage you from continuing to approach the foundation or corporation. The blocker may also be reluctant to offer suggestions about how to improve your proposal or where else to seek support. Developing the ideal of the negotiated partnership with the blocker is usually difficult or even impossible. The best approach, as with all approaches to foundations, is to be open and honest, and, as always, to be prepared by doing your research. If you believe, based on the available evidence and information, that the particular foundation or corporation is indeed an appropriate potential source of support, say so and give your reasoning. Possibly the blocker will be impressed that you have done your homework and that you do know the foundation or corporation. And always remember that some blockers, in fact, may be presenting you with the same questions and raising the same issues that the board of the foundation or corporation or other decision makers may raise prior to acting on your request. The person you are meeting with may be a blocker in attitude but an advocate in terms of the real purpose of the approach he or she is taking in the meeting.

There is also a third category of individual you may encounter when meeting with a foundation or corporation. I call this person the "neutral." This type falls in between the blocker and the advocate. He or she may ask good questions and be somewhat helpful, but gives no clear indication of the pluses and minuses of your organization's proposal or potential request, or of the chances for success with that particular funder. You often come away from a meeting with a "neutral" with no better idea of what will happen with your request than when you went into the meeting. The "neutral" may be taking this approach because, in fact, he or she is accepting the role of processor without any real decision-making authority, or he or she may merely feel more comfortable in not encouraging—or discouraging—your organization by seeming to appear positive or negative. Some foundation and corporate staff are very effective at being "neutrals." And some may fall into a category of "helper neutrals"; these individuals may have helpful suggestions and advice about other places to approach and/or other people and organizations to speak with about similar projects or programs, but will still give your organization no clear reading on how they or their foundation or corporation view your request.

What You May Be Asked

What will the program officer or other foundation or corporate staff member cover in the meeting? Be prepared for anything! Questions asked might be very specific to your organization and its proposal, or might have a broader focus on issues and concerns of the foundation or corporate funder. Corporate funders in particular may ask you if any employees of the corporation are involved in or served by your organization, and/or what would be the benefits of a partnership between your organization and the corporation. One corporate funder I heard speak stated firmly that nonprofits should not presume to tell a company what the benefits of a possible partnership would be; the company itself would decide. Other corporate staff I have met with or heard discuss this issue are not quite so dogmatic and are open to various approaches. But, with corporations becoming increasingly concerned about the bottom-line impact of their corporate philanthropy programs, corporate giving officers are increasingly asking organizations about the real or possible connections that will result in mutual benefit. Corporate giving officers may also ask about ways the corporation could benefit your organization through noncash support. Be prepared with some options if this question is raised. And, at times, the corporate staff member may also seek to determine if there are ways the

> **Be prepared for anything!**

company might support your organization through funding from another part of the corporate budget, such as marketing dollars, rather than through philanthropic giving. When preparing for your meetings with potential corporate supporters, think through some options for each of these possibilities and be prepared to give some examples of alternate ways a company might assist your organization (see also the earlier discussions of these strategies).

Strategy Tip: Is an employee of a corporation that you have targeted for possible support involved with your organization? Employees of companies could be serving on your board or on your organization's committees, or may be participants in events run by your organization or may be recipients of your organization's services and programs. Such employees, if they are at all familiar with your organization, can play key roles in opening the doors to their employers or in presenting the case for supporting your organization to the corporate decision makers. Many corporations value their employees' opinions highly and encourage active involvement in the community, as we saw earlier. It is also usually much harder for a company to turn down an approach on behalf of a nonprofit organization by an employee than it is for the company to turn down an approach by "outsiders." This can hold true despite the level of the position the employee holds in the company.

However, if the employee is or has been the recipient of services of your organization, there may well be some ethical and confidentiality issues involved in seeking out this person to assist with the approach to his or her employer. Information on where clients or service recipients are employed may be confidential and not open to general staff review. Or the types of service your organization delivers (such as treatment for substance abuse) may also discourage present or past clients from connecting themselves to your organization. How can you seek out employees of companies you have targeted without violating their personal privacy or your organization's confidentiality of information? One way is to publicize and build awareness of your organization's development plans through public meetings, newsletters, or letters to those involved with the organization as volunteers or clients, and other key individuals. These meetings and publications might list target companies from which support will be sought as well as other fund-raising plans. Examples might also be given of ways that people can help, such as by merely identifying the appropriate channels to go through at their companies, helping to set the meeting, or even being part of the call on the company. The intent, in part, is to allow people to self-identify their employers and their willingness to help with approaches to these employers. Thus each person can decide how comfortable he or she is in being identified with your organization and with approaching his or her employer. Once individuals have come forward and offered to help, the particular ways they can help and extent of their willingness to help can be determined for each person.

What are some of the other areas that may well be covered in your meeting with a potential funder or supporter? In Chapter 7 several areas were reviewed that, I believe, are critical starting points for preparing for your approaches to foundations and corporations. A complete and in-depth understanding of your organization, including its history, mission, goals and objectives, people served or issues addressed, current operations, budget, sources of support, staffing, leadership, future plans, the specific planned programs or needs for which support is being sought, and future support sources, will help you be prepared for many of the questions potential foundation and corporate funders may ask. But also you and your organization will need to be aware of what is happening beyond your organization, both in the community and even more broadly, that may impact what your organization does and how it does it. Examples of possible broader focus questions you might get when meeting with potential funders include:

- "Your organization is heavily reliant on United Way funds. What are your plans if these funds decline or are shifted to other priorities?"

- "Given possible changes in public sector support, how does your organization plan to help ensure you will continue to get your share of public dollars or how will these shifts change its funding strategies?"

- "How does your organization plan to respond to the changing demographics—and the resulting changing needs—of our community over the next several years?"

- "What do you see as the biggest external factors that will affect your organization and its services over the next few years?"

If the particular person you are meeting with is a "big picture" person, the above questions and others may well be included in the conversation.

Be aware of who your organization's "competition" is, what they do, and how what your organization does is different. It is important for some foundation and corporate staff members to find out how your organization is different from other organizations, which may on the surface appear to be doing the same things. In some cases the staff person you are meeting with may be trying to help build justification for supporting your organization. In other cases the staff person may not really have a clear understanding of what the differences are between your organization and others. Even if you have a proposal submitted, the person you are meeting with may not see these differences. Be sure to understand and be able to present the clear differences, not the "surface" differences such as "we have a bigger budget," "we're the oldest agency of this type in the city," or "we serve more people." Here are some examples of statements that might be used to establish the clear differences between your organization and others:

- "We are the only full-service family and children counseling agency in the six-county metro area."

- "We're the only agency in the city that is fully accredited to provide our services."

- "Based on our research, no other agency in the area is providing this service, yet there are an estimated 25,000 people who could benefit from this new service."

- "We are the only agency with six service sites outside the city limits plus our two centers in the city."

Staff questions will usually also focus on the particular project, program, or need for which you are seeking support. It will help if you have some idea of the uniqueness or differences of your program, project, or need as compared to others that might be seen as similar by the staff member. As with the questions about your agency, the staff member may be trying to help build the justification for supporting your request, or may just want to differentiate your plans from others that he or she may see as similar. At times, the unasked question might be "If I support funding this particular request and our board approves funding, are we going to get swamped with requests for support of similar programs or projects?" Be particularly careful when describing your program or project as "unique," "innovative," "original," etc. Many staff, as was mentioned earlier, are often aware of the major innovations in their field or area of expertise, or, if they are generalists, of what is happening in the community the funding source serves. In your view that which is "innovative" may well be something the foundation or corporation funded three or four years ago. Some questions related to this area of inquiry might include:

- I'm familiar with the XYZ agency and what they do. How are you different from them?

Be sure to understand and be able to present the clear differences, not the surface differences.

- We funded a program like this about three or four years ago at the XYZ agency. Are you familiar with what they did there?

- We have a similar request from the ABC agency. Are you familiar with them and with their plans?

Another key area for staff questions may be how funding will be obtained in the future to support the needs your organization is presenting to that particular foundation or corporation. In some cases, such as where fees for service will be generated or where a project or program has a definite and short-term (1–3 years maximum) time span, continued funding may not be an issue. But many funders want to see clear evidence that a program's survival is not based on a strategy of receiving a continuing flow of grants (especially from that particular source) or that ongoing support is expected to be generated through overly optimistic strategies or high-risk methods. Be sure to have a well-thought-out plan for generating continuing support for a project or program before you meet with any potential funder. Here are some possible questions related to this area of inquiry:

- If we make a grant, it would probably be for a maximum of two or three years. How do you plan to support this program (or project) after that?

- How would you incorporate the expenses for supporting this program (or project) into the operating budget, once the initial funding is over?

- How did you arrive at the income projections for supporting this program (or project) after the initial grant support would end?

A growing area for questions from a potential funder is evaluation: how will your organization evaluate the effectiveness of the proposed program or service for which you are seeking support and/or how will your organization measure the impact of the grant made to support this program or project? It is no longer sufficient to merely believe that a program is good or effective. Even just showing the numbers served in a new or expanded program, or for capital campaigns, that the available facilities have been increased, is not usually sufficient for most evaluation purposes. Evaluation methods are becoming more quantitative and complex, and often, for large-scale programs or projects, outside specialists are hired to carry out evaluations and to make formal reports to the organization on how effective the program or project was in achieving its objectives. Sometimes the evaluation method itself can help make a stronger case for support from a potential funder.

Example: A small national organization offered, as one of its primary activities, educational advancement workshops for the group of professionals that it served. The workshops were to provide those attending with sufficient information and a variety of opinions so that the basic individual frame of reference used for decision making would be changed or enhanced. In most cases, the travel, lodging, and meal expenses as well as the costs of the workshop itself needed to be covered by the organization. It was necessary to seek support from foundations for the complete costs, including all of the travel, room, and board for each attendee.

The first foundations approached had some record of providing partial support for similar programs, but had never been asked to fund the complete costs associated with the workshops. Their somewhat logical reactions included: "So we give your organization a grant that enables several people to go to some nice location for three or four days. They attend a few meetings, probably sit around the pool or play some golf, have some nice meals, and go home. What's changed?" The organization took this as a challenge and sought to answer the basic question raised by the potential funders: "What's changed?" The Executive Director designed a brief survey of participants' basic attitudes on the issues that each of the workshops would address. The survey was actually designed in two parts; one was given to each participant and completed at the start of each workshop. The second part was administered at the end of the workshop. This "before and after" format showed that

there was a clear change in the basic frame of reference of most of the participants as well as a much more complete understanding of the complexity of the issues being addressed. The survey technique and the results demonstrated the effectiveness of the workshops in achieving their goals. Additionally, the survey results and the many positive comments provided in the open-ended survey items were effectively used to help convince other potential funders, including some that required a "ground zero" approach, to support the workshops.

Some possible questions about evaluation methods might include:

- What have other organizations done to evaluate similar programs or projects?

- Given the scale of this program or project, do you think you might want to use a more rigorous evaluation method and possibly hire any outside evaluation specialist?

- What are some of the alternate evaluation methods your organization considered before selecting this method?

- How does your organization plan to use the results of the evaluation internally?

Potential funders will also be likely to ask about both project or program budgets and organizational budgets. If your organization has already submitted a proposal with a project or program budget, their primary focus may well be on that information. If your organization has only submitted an inquiry letter and/or has sent basic information on the organization, the focus of the questions may be on your operating budget or fiscal year-end information. Project or program budgets not only should include the projected expenses for each category (see the following chapter on proposals) but also should include in the body of the proposal or attached to the budget itself the justification for each expense item, and preferably how the cost figure was projected. For a few brief examples of budget items and justifications, see Table 11–1.

What are some of the questions a foundation or corporate staff member might ask in reviewing

Table 11–1 Budget Items and Justifications

Item	Expense	Justification
Salaries: Executive Director (@ 10% of time for 12 months)	$5,000	Oversight of program, meetings with Program Director
Copying	$3,500	300 Workshop participant manuals, 200 pages each @ $.05 per page plus miscellaneous additional copying of letters, memos, etc.
Equipment Purchase	$2,400	Installation of 2 additional phone lines @ $75 each; purchase of 2 additional phones @ $75 each; purchase of printer @ $450; purchase of computer system at $1,650

the budget items in Table 11–1? Questions might include:

- Is it necessary for 10 percent of the executive director's time to be supported by a grant for this program?

- What will be included in the miscellaneous costs?

- Should the computer system and printer be leased rather than purchased, since this is a time-limited program?

While some of these questions or similar questions may seem picky, remember that the person you are meeting with may have to understand in detail the justification for each of the items in your budget, since he or she will probably need to be able to explain the budget to the decision makers if a grant is being recommended.

Strategy Tip: It is a good idea to be open to negotiating on various budget items, if the person you are meeting with indicates there are some probable difficulties in getting approval for certain parts

of the budget. Some foundations or corporations, for example, may not want to provide support for the purchase of equipment for a project or program that is time-limited. Others may take issue with supporting "indirect costs" or "administrative overhead" (see the following chapter for a more complete discussion of this issue). If there are specific items or budget areas a potential funder may prefer not to support, be willing to discuss with the staff person the best way to present your organization's needs to the foundation or corporation in a manner that will be consistent with its interests and restrictions. Recognize that, in so doing, you may be helping to build the "negotiated partnership" relationship that you are seeking.

The staff member may also ask you a series of questions about his or her foundation or corporation. Sometimes these questions may be rhetorical, such as "do you know how our decision-making or grant approval process works?" or "do you understand my role as a staff member in our grant process?" The intent is to be sure that you receive necessary information about the internal operations of the foundation or corporation, including information that may not be available in the printed materials from the source. But also, at times, the staff member may be checking or testing you to be sure you in fact understand that particular funder. Some possible questions that might be asked to "check" your knowledge of the funder could include:

- Why do you think our foundation (or corporation) might be interested in funding your organization (or your program or project)?

- How do you see your organization (or this program or project) as fitting our guidelines?

- Are you aware of our new funding program for . . . ?

- Do you know about our recent grants in this area?

The staff member may well ask you about other foundations and corporations that are also being approached for support of the project or program. The usual intent is to determine if your organization has in fact developed a plan for raising funds for the program or project or if the organization is just seeking any possible source that might be interested. The staff member asking about other potential funders will want to ensure that your organization has done its homework, including having researched other specific possible funding sources and developed strategies for approaching them. But the staff member may have another reason to ask about other places that your organization is approaching. The staff member may want to speak with his or her counterparts at the other funders you are applying to or meeting. The conversations could well focus on what each staff member thinks of your organization and its possible or already-submitted proposal, and how each views your plans in terms of community needs and priorities. As was explained earlier, this is a fairly common practice among foundation and corporate funding staff members. Some of the questions you might be asked include:

- Who else are you approaching for support of this program (or project)?

- Have you found out which other foundations or corporations might be interested in supporting this program (or project)?

- Have you talked to the ABC Foundation about this program (or project)?

Sometimes staff may also ask for "references," especially if they are not very familiar with your organization. Here the intent will be to have additional contacts who might give a somewhat more objective assessment of your organization and its effectiveness. At times staff may also give you the names of individuals, possibly "experts" in a particular related area, with whom they may recommend you speak about the proposed program or project. The dual effect of giving you these names is to provide you with assistance and an outside assessment of what is planned, but also to give them someone they can speak with about the plans once your organization has presented its plans to that person. Some of the questions related to this area might include:

- Is there someone I can speak with about your organization who knows what you do but is not directly tied to you?

- Who is your contact person at the United Way and may I speak with him or her?

- Have you spoken with Dr. Bell at the university about your plans? He's an expert in this area of services.

Strategy Tip: Frequently the staff member or another person associated with a potential funder will recommend your organization speak to a particular individual about your proposed program, project, or other need. You should first ask why he or she is recommending that particular person if the reasoning behind the recommendation was not clear. Always thank the staff member for the recommendation. If the recommendation seems at all reasonable or appropriate, follow through with it and contact the recommended individual. When contacting that person, be sure to indicate who referred you to the individual and the reason for the referral, including how it was suggested that person could assist your organization. When speaking with that person, it might also be useful to find out his or her relationship to the staff member of the funding source. Be sure to ask if the individual has other possible funders he or she could recommend and review your list of other prospects with the person to get additional suggestions and advice on each. Be sure to keep that individual informed of what happens with the fund-raising effort for the program or project and keep him or her "in the loop." Sometimes these referrals can become valuable resources for your organization. Part of your negotiated partnership strategy should also include informing the foundation or corporate officer who gave you the referral about the outcomes of the contact with that individual.

Closing the Meeting

The meeting is reaching its end. The staff member has asked several questions about your organization and its services and programs that might be of interest to the foundation or corporation, and your team has presented your organization and its case. As the meeting is ending, regardless of the outcomes, it is always a good idea to do several things:

- Review with the staff member the specific next steps that are to occur. These might include submission of a full proposal (if one has not already been submitted), submission of additional supporting materials, revision of the proposal or parts of the proposal (such as the

budget) and resubmitting it, or providing other information to the potential funder. If the staff member suggested a specific strategy or a specific amount to request, reconfirm this information with him or her. It is also a good idea to reconfirm any foundation or corporate deadlines for materials and the date of the next meeting when grant decisions will be made.

- Review with the staff member any suggestions he or she made about contacting additional potential funders, other organizations, or individuals and indicate your organization will follow up with those suggestions and will let the staff person know what happened.

- Thank the staff member for his or her time, suggestions, and advice.

Strategy Tip: Suppose your organization has submitted a proposal to a foundation or corporation and you meet with the potential funder. During the meeting it becomes obvious to you that the potential funder is not likely to fund your request for support. The staff member may indicate the request will be submitted to the board or other decision-making body, but gives it little likelihood for success. What should you do? First, explore the reasons the staff member believes the proposal won't get approval. It is not a good idea to become argumentative about the reasons given to you; the staff person will probably have better insights than you into the inner workings of the foundation or corporation, and the opinions of board members or other decision makers. Ask the staff member if there are alternative approaches that could be taken (such as funding specific components of the proposed program or project), or if there are other programs or projects at your organization that might be considered for support. If, after exploring other options, it still appears unlikely your organization's proposal will receive positive consideration, you should consider withdrawing the proposal. "Withdrawing" a proposal is usually understood as meaning the submitting organization asks that the proposal not be considered further by the potential funder or that the proposal not go forward for a final decision by the board or other decision-making body of the funder.

Why should your organization consider withdrawing a proposal rather than letting the potential funder go through the complete review and decision-making processes? One reason is to simply accept the fact that support for a proposal will probably be turned down or declined, based upon the initial impressions you receive from the potential funder. But beyond that it may be you can make a stronger case to that particular source by presenting the foundation or corporation with an alternate or reworked proposal. Also, a formal decision—and a "no" to your request—on your organization's proposal may prevent you from re-applying to that particular source for some specific period of time. Remember from our earlier discussions that many foundations and corporations have specific rules about how soon an organization can re-approach the potential funding source for support, once action has been taken on a request. In some cases the time period before your organization can re-apply may be as long as one year. If your organization's proposal is withdrawn before a formal decision is made, you may be able to reapply much sooner. But be sure to check with the foundation or the corporation on its specific rules about re-applying when a request has been turned down.

After the Meeting

Your meeting with the foundation or corporate staff member ends. You have reconfirmed your organization's next steps, any deadlines, the approximate or specific time frames for the decision, and any changes in the proposal or additional materials needed by the potential funder. You and the other members of your organization who attended the meeting have left the offices or other location where the meeting was held. What happens next? The best advice is to find a place to sit down with your colleagues and review the entire meeting, including the following areas:

- How does each member of your team feel your organization and its case for support were presented in the meeting? What were the strong points and the weak points of the presentation? Did each of you participate and were the roles clearly defined? How could the presentation and your various roles be improved the next time? Did your team seem to convey an understanding of that particular funder's interests and guidelines? Did your team strive to create a dialogue and treat the staff member as a potential helper and advisor?

- How did the staff member respond to your group and its presentation? Was a dialogue created? Did he or she seem interested and involved in the discussion, or was he or she more standoffish and not very interested or involved? Did he or she seem genuinely interested in helping and providing advice and assistance? What was his or her body language saying versus the words? Was the staff member a blocker, a processor, a helper (and potential partner), or merely neutral?

- Who will compile the notes of the meeting and, if necessary, prepare a brief report on the meeting and the next steps for the records?

- What specific new information was learned about that particular potential funder in the meeting? What other insights were picked up about the potential funder, its areas of interest, and how it operates?

- What were the specific questions asked about your organization and its proposal? How effectively did the members of your group answer these questions? How did these questions compare to other questions asked in meetings or conversations with other potential funders, if any? Were there areas of discussion or questions that were unexpected or that were not answered effectively or at all?

- How were materials, if any, from your organization used in the meeting? Did the members of the team feel the materials were effective in supporting the case for funding the organization? How did the staff member respond to the materials and their use? Do the materials or the use of the materials need to be changed in any way?

- What were the staff member's specific comments about the proposal and its potential to fit the interests of the potential funder? Were these comments generally positive, negative, or just neutral?

- What are the specific next steps your organization should take or that the staff member recommended be taken? What were the timelines for these steps that were spelled out by the staff member? Who will be responsible for coordinating the next steps to ensure they are taken, and who will carry out each task?

- How does each member of your team assess the overall chances of success with this particular potential funder? Why does each member of the team feel that way about the chances of success?

- How effectively did the team and each of its members work together during the meeting? Were those attending appropriate for that particular potential funder or should the team have had a different "mix"? Are there other ways the team could be improved? Did each member feel comfortable with the role(s) he or she played in the meeting?

- Who will prepare the thank-you note (which should be sent a few days after the meeting and should be separate from any other follow-up or the submission of additional materials) and send it to the staff member? Who will sign the thank-you note? (Usually it should be signed by the most senior staff person or volunteer attending the meeting, but this may not always be possible or appropriate.)

- What, overall, should be done to improve the effectiveness of the organization when meeting with the staff of potential funders? Is there additional training of others or even of this particular team that should take place? How can the insights and suggestions from this meeting be conveyed to others in the leadership of the organization?

- Do team members have other comments, reactions, concerns, or suggestions as a result of the meeting?

This review session should be held as soon as possible after the meeting so that the immediate impressions and reactions won't be lost over time. It is always a good idea to include the review session in your team's schedule so that, for example, a one-hour meeting with a potential funder would immediately be followed by a review session of approximately one-half hour to one hour. This can be especially important if your team has more than one meeting with a potential funder scheduled for that particular day or over a period of a few days. Reviewing each meeting will help your team better prepare itself for the next meeting as well as raise the overall level of performance.

Within a few days after the meeting and the review session, as was mentioned, a thank-you note should be sent to the staff member you met with at the potential funder. It is best to just send a brief thank you and to separately forward any requested materials or additional information. If you have been asked or plan to submit other materials, the thank-you note can briefly indicate this will be done, but the primary purpose of the note is just to genuinely thank the individual you met with for his or her time and help. Too many organizations and individuals forget a simple "thank you" is still appreciated.

If other materials or additional information has been asked for by the staff member or has been promised by your organization, it should be sent to the foundation or corporate staff member as soon as possible. If, after reviewing your notes and those of your colleagues, you are uncertain about what was being asked for, call the staff member and inquire rather than guessing what he or she wanted. The cover letter for the materials should start something like this:

> Thank you again for taking the time to meet with Mary Jones, our Board Chair, and me on October 25. As you requested in our meeting, we are enclosing the following additional materials in support of our request for a grant toward our new youth outreach program.

The materials enclosed should be listed in the cover letter and briefly described. The letter should always close with an offer to further discuss these materials and your proposal, and also your organization's willingness to submit anything else that will be helpful to the staff member in his or her review of your request.

If the meeting was held prior to the submission of a full proposal, and the staff member you met with requested your organization submit a proposal, you should do so as soon as possible. The thank-you note should indicate a proposal will be forthcoming soon. Please refer to the following chapter on proposals for more specifics.

If there are no clear follow-up steps resulting from your organization's meeting with a foundation or corporation, it is still a good idea to continue to develop and maintain the relationship with the staff member. Here are some specific ways to do this:

- If your organization has a newsletter, send it to the staff member. Personalize the process a little by sending the newsletter with a brief note. If there are articles of relevance to the request being considered by the foundation or corporate funder, refer the staff member to these articles in your note.

Too many organizations and individuals forget a simple "thank you" is still appreciated.

- Ensure that the staff member receives your current annual report or the newest version when it is issued.

- Notify the staff member of any significant developments at your organization, such as an award being received by the organization, or the selection of a new board member. Keep these brief and personalized with a note from you or one of the other individuals from your organization who met with the staff member.

For additional suggestions, also see Chapter 13 on what you should do after your proposal has been submitted to a foundation or corporation. And always remember to record all contacts with the foundation or corporation, including the sending of materials and additional information on your organization.

Phone Calls

The importance of phone calls as strategies for approaching foundations and corporations for support is often overlooked. Making phone calls also tends to be taken for granted; it is something many of us do almost automatically without thinking too carefully about what we will say or do on the call. Yet phone calls can be used very strategically when making contact with potential funders. Unfortunately, most people don't think of phone calls as part of a major approach to a funder and often are underprepared for what may happen during the call. Here are just a few examples of what can happen with phone calls to potential funders:

Example: You call a potential funder for information, expecting to get a receptionist. Instead, the board chair of the foundation answers the phone. What should you say?

Example: You call a potential funder to try to set a meeting. The person answering the phone says, based upon the name of your organization, the staff will not meet with you. How should you react?

Example: You call a potential funder to try to set a meeting. You get a program staff member on the phone who asks you to briefly explain what your organization is and does, which you do. The staff member then asks why the funder would be interested in providing support to your organization. What should your reply be?

These are just a few real examples of what can happen when you call a potential funder. The examples also should be clues that it is best to prepare and think through each phone call before you make the call. Phone calls can and should be used effectively as part of an overall approach strategy for each potential funder. But, in order to do so, you must do your homework and prepare carefully for each call. It is easy to delegate to a member of your support staff the task of calling each foundation and corporation on your prospect list for information. But it may be more effective in terms of overall strategies for you or another senior staff member to make these calls. The examples above can point out some situations that may occur when calling. Having a senior staff person make the calls can help ensure there is better preparation for each call and also that situations such as those above can be more effectively handled. And, having a senior staff member make the calls sends the message to the potential funder that contact with that funder is important to your organization, even at the most basic level of just asking for information. Should you end up speaking with a program staff member, officer, or even a board member of the potential funder, you also have the opportunity to begin to develop a relationship with that source and can begin to assess their interest in your organization.

Example: Based upon initial research for a client, I had identified a moderately sized national foundation that appeared to be a prospect for support of one of the client's programs. I had used foundation directories for my preliminary research, and subsequently wrote to the foundation, as they specified, to get the printed information. After reviewing this information, the executive director and I decided to try to meet with a staff member of the

foundation, which did not require a proposal be submitted prior to such a meeting. We identified, from the foundation's published information, the staff person responsible for the area of interest that most closely matched the planned program at the organization.

I was given the task of calling to see if we could get an appointment for a meeting. After a few tries, I was able to speak with the staff person. After explaining who I was and my relationship to the organization (always a good idea), I briefly summarized the purpose of the organization, who it served, and the purposes of the planned program (remember, this is a "cold" call with no previous contact with this individual or the foundation). As in the earlier example, the staff member asked me "why do you think our foundation would be interested in funding this program?" I had in front of me a listing of grants the foundation had made (including the names of the organizations receiving the grants and the specific purposes of the grants) over a period of about four years and had pinpointed a few of these that I felt were relevant to making the case for the organization. I replied: "When I was reviewing the list of grants your foundation has made over the past few years, I noticed these grants for similar purposes. However, here are some of the differences between the planned program and what you previously funded. . . ." After listing these differences, I proceeded to point out in a sentence or two why the organization believed the program was a better and more comprehensive approach to the issues addressed by the other organizations the foundation had previously funded. My entire discussion of the organization and the program probably took about three minutes. The staff member paused, and then said "You're right; we should meet. Let's set a date."

Why did this call succeed? There were several things that were done before the call was made:

- The program development committee of the organization reviewed what had previously been done in the area and designed the new program based upon the experiences of other organizations, but with several unique components focused on both the mission of the organization and its previous work in this area.

Phone calls can and should be used effectively as part of an overall approach strategy.

- The overall purposes and various components, including the target audience of the proposed program, were detailed out.

- The foundation, including its grant guidelines and specific grants made over the past several years, was initially researched using secondary resources (foundation directories).

- The foundation's own published information was obtained and reviewed.

- Grants made by the foundation for purposes similar to the proposed program were identified using the foundation's published information and the secondary sources.

- The appropriate staff member was identified.

- A call "script" was developed, with a brief description of the organization and of the program, and a brief description of the foundation, including the relevant grants it had previously made. The total script was timed to last about four minutes.

One of the key questions to consider prior to calling a potential funder is: can you explain what your organization is and what it does in about two minutes or less? Even when making a seemingly basic call to get the foundation's or corporation's printed information, as we saw in the examples above, you may need to be able to present your organization in a few brief words to the person on the other end of the line. If you were asked to tell anybody about your organization and were restricted to three to four brief sentences, could you do it?

Strategy Tip: Develop a brief three- to four-sentence description of what your organization is and what it does. Base the statement on the mission of the organization, the specific programs or services, and who it serves. Test the description on your staff and board to see if it distills the essence of the organization into the briefest possible words. Then try the description out on some people who don't know your organization, such as friends or other acquaintances. Do they understand the organization and what it does, based on your brief description? Do they see how it differs from other organizations that may have similar purposes? Based upon the reactions of both the "insiders" and the "outsiders," refine your brief description until it is distilled to the essence of what your organization is and does.

After You've Been Turned Down

"Wait a minute" you're probably saying to yourself. "I thought this chapter was about 'approaching foundations and corporate funders.' What does getting turned down have to do with approaching potential funders?" Assuming you've done your homework, identified a foundation or corporation that seems to match up well with your organization and its needs, sent in a proposal (since they told you they would not meet), done your follow-up calls, and chewed your nails about as far down as you can, you eagerly await a response. The letter arrives and, upon opening it, you learn that your organization's request for support has been turned down. What do you do next? The usual answers might involve some type of self-inflicted injuries or over-consumption of certain substances. But there is a better and more productive approach, which is rarely used. Call the funding source and see if you can discuss what happened and what should happen next. Again it is important to see the foundation or corporate staff member as more than the source of a check—or even of a turndown letter. If you have already met the staff person, see this as another opportunity to continue to develop a negotiated partnership. If you have not met the staff person, see the turn down as an opportunity to begin to develop the negotiated partnership.

Example: As a foundation staff member, I met with an executive director after a turn down and he covered several areas with me, all at his initiative. These included:

- Sharing with him the specific reasons why the proposal was turned down. In some cases this was not possible, but here the reasons were fairly clear. The executive director agreed with me that the organization had not made a very strong case for its new program, especially when he realized that similar programs already existed at other nearby agencies.

- Giving him my overall reactions to the proposal and ways it could be improved. I made several suggestions, including the obvious need to present what other agencies were doing that was similar and to better justify the need for the program.

- Reviewing with him the timelines and process for reapplying to the foundation. He specifically asked if there was a required time period the agency must wait to reapply, since its request had been turned down, or if it could reapply immediately. I suggested the staff first review their needs and priorities before reapplying.

- Suggesting to him other foundations and corporations that might be interested in funding the organization and its existing programs and services.

After the meeting, I thought about what had happened from my standpoint. The executive director had "used" me (in the positive sense) very effectively. First, he had caught me at a time when I in fact did feel somewhat guilty about the decline of his organization's request. Second, he had used this as an opportunity to get additional help and advice rather than just accepting the "no" or taking his frustrations out on the foundation or the staff. In this sense he was treating me as a partner and an advisor rather than as the source of a check or the turn down. And third, he was keeping the relationship going. I subsequently spent additional time assisting him with regrouping and reformulating his plans, and later with reapproaching our foundation for support. By the end of the entire process, which did result in the organization's obtaining a grant from our foundation, I calculated I had spent more time with the executive director of that organization than I did with many of our grantees.

In the above example it is important to realize that the executive director—not the foundation staff member—took the initiative and set the agenda about what would happen next. The emphasis was on getting help, and advice, and keeping the contact going in a productive way. While the executive director may have happened on this technique by chance, it can be an effective means to approach a foundation or corporate funder even when you have been turned down. And, in some cases, it can help make your first personal contact with the foundation or corporate staff when all other contacts have been through correspondence or phone calls.

Now, it is important to realize that foundation and corporate staff members are not always going to be helpful and willing to share what "really" happened with your proposal. But you should always see the turn down as an opportunity to try this approach rather than as the end of the world or even of any possibility of achieving success with that particular source.

Requests for Proposals

Some of the larger foundations and even some of the smaller foundations and corporate funders are using the "request for proposal" or "RFP" approach with increasing frequency. Strictly speaking, this is not a technique for your organization to approach a foundation but rather the potential funder "reaching out" to organizations asking for proposals related to some defined issue or area in which it has an interest. RFPs have some advantages in that they usually clearly spell out the specific area of interest and possibly even details of the types of programs or projects that will be considered for funding. Usually the application procedures, other requirements, and the timelines are fairly specific, even though the same foundation or corporate funder may otherwise not be as clear on what it is interested in with its regular grant programs. RFPs are also usually directed to specific organizations that the foundation or corporation believes may have the experience and the capability to carry out the program or project.

But there are also some disadvantages to RFPs. While an organization may generally be capable of meeting the requirements that are stated in the RFP, fulfilling the specifics if the organization is awarded the grant may mean a diversion of time and resources into an area that may not be directly related to its ongoing programs, services, and general operations. There can be a strong tendency for organizations, especially those that are already operating on tight budgets to try to "go after the money" when they receive an RFP from a potential funding source, regardless of the consequences or the actual appropriateness of the proposed project to their organization. When the foundation or corporate funder gives a general outline of the program or project that they are seeking to support, the applying organization may also try to promise more than it can deliver. For example, an organization that has staff who are already working at their maximum capacity may believe this same staff can also carry the burden of the additional program or project.

Another issue related to the use of RFPs by foundations and corporate funders is the way the RFPs are distributed. In many cases the funding organization may draw up a list of organizations that it feels are appropriate to receive the RFP, due to the particular nature of the project area, and send the RFP only to these organizations. The criteria used by the potential funder may not be as inclusive as they could be, or the funder issuing the RFP may not have an up-to-date list of organizations that would be appropriate to receive the RFP. The RFP may get sent only to organizations that the foundation or corporation has previously funded, or the funder may simply not know about your organization and its appropriateness for meeting the requirements of the RFP. The end result may be that your organization does not receive an RFP when in fact the program or project described in the RFP might be something that is appropriate to your organization.

If you become aware of an RFP that your organization did not receive, you should see it as an opportunity to start to build a relationship with the potential funder or to strengthen an existing relationship. You should contact the issuer of the RFP to find out if in fact your organization is eligible to receive an RFP. You can also possibly determine what the criteria were for selecting organizations to receive the RFP, and, if appropriate, get on the funder's list for future RFPs. If you are not already familiar with that particular potential funding source and what it does, your contact will also be an opportunity to learn more about it, to obtain the basic information, and to begin to develop some relationship with the staff there, even if you are clearly not going to be a part of this particular RFP process.

To summarize this chapter briefly, each method of approaching a potential funder should be seen as an opportunity to enhance your overall strategy of creating and maintaining a long-term relationship with that particular potential source—another means toward creating the negotiated partnership, which is one of your goals. It is also important, while keeping in mind the overall goals, to prepare for and use each approach method carefully. Again, planning is the key to success. Even phone calls, as was discussed, need to be planned out and thought through before they are made.

Meetings with potential funders are particularly critical and should be planned and rehearsed. Each meeting is also an opportunity to refine your skills and the skills of others from your organization who participate. All of the approach methods discussed should have a strong underpinning of research and reading between the lines. Approaching funding sources that are in fact not appropriate is usually not a good use of the time and energy of your organization. But approaching those potential funders that are good prospects can have both short- and long-term rewards for your organization.

> **Each method of approaching a potential funder should be seen as an opportunity to enhance your overall strategy of creating and maintaining a long-term relationship.**

Chapter 12

Proposals: One Means of Approach

In looking back over this book you will notice that much material has been covered but there still has been little discussion of proposals. Many other books on corporate and foundation funding focus almost entirely on the proposal. But remember, the central point of this book is that proposals are only one means of approaching foundations and corporate funders. The proposal is part of a total process that begins with having an overview of the components of the process and why each is important toward the overall goals of getting funding and building relationships. Once you have the basic understanding, knowing your own organization is the first step in the process. Research is also key. Following good research and "reading between the lines," you can use the various methods to begin to build relationships with potential funders.

Although proposals are part of the process, their importance should not be underemphasized. When your organization prepares a proposal, it is committing itself in writing to the specifics of a course of action. The proposal is the written case your organization is presenting to a particular potential funder as to why there is a good match between the interests of that funder and the needs of the organization. The proposal and the results of the review of the proposal are usually the two primary bases upon which funding decisions will be made.

Internal Uses of Proposals

Staffs of organizations, especially development staff, often overlook the fact that a proposal and its development can serve important organizational purposes as well as being a vehicle for obtaining outside support. Here are some of the internal functions a proposal can fulfill:

- Because the proposal will be a document that will be seen by those outside the organization, it can be a vehicle for building consensus internally about the particular purpose for which support is being sought. Staff—including pro-

> When your organization prepares a proposal, it is committing itself in writing to the specifics of a course of action.

gram staff and senior staff and board members, especially for major new initiatives—need to have a common vision of the purposes for which funding is being requested. Involving staff and appropriate board members in the defining and reviewing processes for the proposal can help build this consensus.

- For new programs, projects, or services, program staff members should prepare the initial description of what each is and what each will accomplish. Development staff should provide program staff with an outline of the basic areas that will be covered in the proposal so that program staff can prepare both the necessary descriptions and can also develop related components, such as the evaluation methodology, budgets, etc.

- Proposals can also force staff to look outside the organization to see what others are doing that might be similar. Sometimes what may appear to be a brilliant new idea or concept is something that has been tried and proven—or even tried and discarded—elsewhere. Duplication in itself is not necessarily a sin, but being short-sighted and not knowing what is going on "out there" can be major sins in the eyes of potential funders.

- The proposal can also help the organization ensure a strong sense of its mission and purposes. Often, in the day-to-day work of an organization, staff and even board members can overlook the real reasons the organization is there and does what it does. The proposal development process offers an opportunity for the organization to revisit its purposes and mission and to ensure the proposed program, project, or service is in line with the mission.

- Board members, especially when there is a board development or fund-raising committee, can review the basic descriptions or the full proposal. The board members can help ensure the descriptions are clear and more likely to be understood by outsiders; they can help eliminate jargon and help keep the proposal focused on the bigger picture while emphasizing the overall strengths of the organization and its qualifications to carry out the proposed program or project.

- Others in the organization should also be involved in the process. The business office or the administrative area can review project or program budgets to help ensure that cost projections are realistic in terms of the organization's other expenses, staff salaries, etc. Support staff can not only help proof the proposal but can also provide significant input as to the clarity of the proposal and the strength of the case being presented. Other volunteers can also provide a more objective opinion of the proposal's strengths and weaknesses.

- Finally, the proposal can help the staff better define the specific components of the planned program or project and its uniqueness or appropriateness to the organization's mission and goals. Many times new programs or projects start out as sketchy ideas. Staff and even board members may all agree to proceed with the implementation of the new program or project without seeing all the specifics clearly spelled out. The development of the proposal requires that the details be thought through carefully and that most of them be clearly stated. At times, it is these gaps in the details that become the basis for the questions raised by foundation and corporate staff.

Overview

When discussing proposal formatting and content, it is also important to remember that the content of proposals can run the gamut from being fully defined by the potential funding source (through an application form) to being entirely the creation of the applying organization with few or no hints about what the potential funder actually wants. While much of what follows in this chapter is focused on a particular recommended basic format and content, there is no magic formula for proposals that will always work, no matter where they are going to be sent. Here are the basic rules to follow:

- If the potential funding source has an application form or a proposal form, use it and follow it exactly. If you have questions about what is being asked for on the form, use your questions as an opportunity to contact the foundation or corporation. Failing to use a provided application at best can result in some embarrassment to your organization for not following the funder's stated procedures and at worst can mean your organization's disqualification from further consideration.

- If the potential funding source gives you an outline to follow when submitting a request, follow the outline and disregard what follows. The outline is the funder's way of telling you what is expected in the proposal and the order in which it should be presented.

- If in a meeting with staff of the potential funder the staff member has given you specific instructions on applying, such as "send me a three- or four-page letter asking for . . . ," do so, even if the foundation has indicated in its published materials that it wants a full proposal.

- If the potential funder gives you a series of key questions that it would like answered in your proposal, answer them. These key questions can even be used as headers in a section of your proposal.

- If the potential funder provides a form such as a proposal summary or a proposal cover sheet that should be submitted along with your proposal, use these. In some cases the proposal summary may be what the board actually sees when it makes its decisions. The cover sheet may be used by the foundation or corporation to organize your materials when they are submitted.

The proposal is closely related to the case statement or case for support (see Chapter 7). In fact, a well-written case for support can make the development of specific proposals a relatively easy proc-

ess. Whereas the case for support is "making the case" for support of the organization and all of its needs, the proposal is really a subset in that it is making the case for support of one of the organization's needs. But the case for support should already contain much of the information that will be contained in the proposal, such as general needs addressed by the organization, the organization's mission, its services and programs, etc.

The proposal also is more closely tied to the funding interests of the particular source that you are approaching and must make a clear and specific request for support for a stated purpose and in a stated amount. At this point it is appropriate to point out that the word "proposal" will be used in this chapter in two ways. First, there is the proposal in the sense of the specific document making the request to the funder. But second there is the proposal "package," which contains the specific proposal, the cover letter, the cover page, and the attachments, all of which will be discussed below. These elements, as shall be explained, are part of the proposal in the more generic sense; all are part of the case your organization is making to that particular funder to provide support, and each should be designed to reinforce the case.

So, what follows below is a list and detailed discussion of each of the components of the proposal package. All of these components should be considered as essential *unless* the funder tells you otherwise or specifies in the materials exactly what is wanted (see the "rules" above). Also remember that some of the components may have to stand on their own for the person reviewing them. Decision makers may see all of your materials, some of the materials, or merely a summary of your request, which was prepared by the staff of the potential funder. You can never be sure what will be seen by whom, once the materials arrive at their destination.

Strategy Tip: Many organizations, when they are assembling their proposals, use various binding systems such as spiral binders, loose-leaf covers, sliding clip binders, or other methods. I recently moderated a panel of staff from three foundations. All of the panelists said not to use fancy or elaborate binding methods. One stated she was able to supply her daughter's school with a variety of binders since she immediately dismantled any bound proposals she received. At the foundation where I worked all incoming proposals were immediately stripped of their bindings so the various parts could be easily used by the staff. I remember seeing wastebaskets full of elaborate binders at the end of the day. The best advice is not to spend money on elaborate binding systems. Simple metal binder clips or folders containing your proposal and supporting materials can work very well in most cases. But be sure each page contains your organization's name in case the pieces get separated.

The Cover Letter

The cover letter is one of the most critical parts of the proposal package, but in many cases it gets relegated to the same level of importance as phone calls to potential funders. Yet the letter may be the only part of your entire package that gets read, especially if the proposal package is the first contact with the foundation or corporate funder. The staff member may well decide, based on the letter, if he or she wants to proceed further with a full review of your entire proposal package. If the letter is merely cursory (basically stating "here's our proposal") or if it does not show a clear understanding of the foundation or corporate funder and its priorities, the staff member may elect to read no further.

The letter should be designed to draw the reader into the case your organization is making for fund-

> **The cover letter is one of the most critical parts of the proposal package.**

ing. Since it may be the only part read, and will probably be the first part read, the cover letter should be a miniproposal with all of the key elements contained in the full proposal. The letter should stand alone and essentially be the "executive summary" of the full proposal. The content of the letter should follow the proposal outline presented below and should usually move from the general (the needs or issues that will be addressed) to the very specific (the purpose for which funding is being sought and the amount of the request). The cover letter should also serve some additional purposes, which are summarized below.

Opening Sentences

The very first sentence of the cover letter should refer to any previous contacts with the foundation or corporate funder. Here are some sample opening sentences:

A. "As you requested at our meeting with you on September 16, we are submitting our request for support of . . ."

B. "As a follow-up to our phone conversation with you on September 16, we are submitting our request for support of . . ."

C. "After a careful review of the guidelines and other materials for the XYZ Foundation, we are submitting our request for support of . . . to the Foundation."

D. "At the suggestion of Mr. William Smith of the ABC Foundation, we are submitting our request for support of . . . to you."

What does each of these openings say to the person at the potential funding source who is reading the cover letter? Opening sentence A immediately reminds the staff person that your organization met with him or her and that the proposal is being submitted in response to a specific request (if this was actually the case). If the staff member did not actually request a proposal but was met with, the opening sentence might be changed to "As a result of our meeting with you on September 16 we are submitting our request for support of. . . ." Foundation and corporate staff meet with many people, and it is usually a good idea to remind the person that your organization did indeed meet and to list the date.

Opening sentence B reminds the staff person that there was contact with the foundation or corporate funder and that, if it was actually the case, the staff person initiated the request for the proposal. Opening sentence C says that your organization has done its homework and is not just sending out shotgun proposals. It indicates that you have reviewed their materials and carried out other research. Opening sentence D says that you have discussed your plans with another foundation and that individual referred you to this particular foundation. In your conversation with the ABC Foundation person you should have determined if that person actually knows someone at the XYZ Foundation or just knows of the Foundation. If the person does know someone there, your next sentence might be "Mr. Smith suggested we contact you directly about our request."

Notice in each of the opening sentences except C "you" is used instead of the name of the foundation. This helps make the approach more personalized and indicates your organization is responding to something—a specific request from a staff person or the suggestion from someone—rather than just sending out proposals.

Content

If, during your meeting or phone conversation with the foundation or corporate staff person that person made specific suggestions about the content of your proposal or asked that specific issues be addressed in the proposal, the first paragraph should be a recap of the staff person's advice and, if there was to be follow-up, what happened. This helps put some responsibility for what follows on the staff person's shoulders. Here are a few examples of "recap" and follow-up results:

> During our meeting on the 16th you suggested we contact Dr. Mary Robbins at the State University about her research on the availability in our area of services similar to that which we are proposing. Her study (see her summary in Appendix VI) indicates there are no similar services within our service area.

During our meeting on the 16th you asked about the need to purchase additional computers, which was projected at $3,400 in the original budget we submitted with our letter of inquiry. We followed up on your suggestion to contact the GEF Corporation about surplus equipment and were able to obtain the needed computers at no cost. Thus we have removed $3,400 from the project budget (Appendix IV). Thank you for your suggestion.

During our meeting on the 16th you suggested we also contact the MNO Foundation and the EFG Corporation about their possible interest in supporting this initiative. We met with Joan Roberts, Program Officer at the MNO Foundation, who encouraged us to submit a proposal for this project, which we are currently preparing. We also have a meeting scheduled on November 3 with Bill Kenniston, Corporate Affairs Officer at the EFG Corporation, to discuss a possible approach there.

In each case your letter is saying "We listened to your advice and followed up on it and here is what we did about it or what happened." This clearly shows you valued the advice and followed through with the suggestions. In each case you should also say what the outcome was. If the foundation or corporate staff person made suggestions or gave advice, and you were not able to follow up on it (such as the person you were referred to never called you back) or the results were inconclusive, you should say so in the cover letter; doing so will again put the staff person in the roles of helper and advisor and the person may be willing to make alternative suggestions. He or she may even make an effort to call someone who was suggested as a contact but whom you were not able to reach.

At other times the staff person may have suggested revisions in the proposed program or project.

If your organization feels justified in not following through with these, it is often best to briefly recap what was suggested and your organization's rationale for not proceeding in that direction. In most cases the staff person will respect your honesty, although he or she may not agree with the rationale. Your rationale may also be a sign that your organization is not willing to do anything just to get a grant. In every case where a suggestion is made or advice is given, be sure to thank the person offering the advice or making the suggestion.

What should be the length of the cover letter? There are no hard and fast rules but as a general principle the letter should be kept to a maximum of three pages. Remember it is a summary of the proposal, not the full proposal. It needs to be as brief and concise as possible, while still covering all of the main points of the proposal. It is usually best to write the cover letter after the proposal and to follow the general format of the proposal down to and including the specific purposes for which the grant is being sought and the amount of the request. For the specific content of the cover letter, refer to the detailed discussion of the proposal content below.

Who Signs and Why

A key issue—and one often overlooked—is who signs the cover letter. This may not seem very important when there are so many other considerations related to the proposal process. But the signatures at the bottom of the cover letter say much about the organization and its commitment to the grant request. My general recommendation is that the cover letter should be signed by the chief operating officer (executive director or CEO) of the organization as well as the board chair or president of the organization. Having the chief staff member and the chief volunteer sign the letter indicates that the request represents an organizational commitment and that the commitment is supported by both the staff and the board. It also correctly says to the volunteer leadership that they are an important part of the funding process and have key roles they can play to help make it successful.

Of course there are many exceptions to this principle. In some cases, such as at colleges and universities, the chief development officer is known to the foundation or corporation being approached and can sign the letter. In other cases where there is an existing relationship between someone at your organization and the foundation or corporation, it may be a good strategy to have that person co-sign the letter. For smaller scale projects and programs, or other small requests it is often acceptable for the executive director to be the only signer of the letter. But for major new programs or projects, proposal cover letters should be signed by the board chair and the chief staff person. The example below indicates one reason the signatures—and their implications—can be very important.

Example: I received a proposal for a major new program initiative at an organization; if I remember correctly, the total amount of the request was in the neighborhood of $300,000. While reviewing the cover letter I noticed that it was signed by the executive director of the organization, but by no one else. I decided to call the board chair, who was listed on the stationery, to get his opinion of this major new undertaking of the organization. When I reached the board chair and explained that I was a staff member of the foundation, he started the conversation like this:

"Yes. What is this about?"

"I'm calling about the proposal we received here asking for $300,000 toward the new outreach program at the IJK Organization. I see you are the chairman of the board and I had some questions I wanted to ask you about the plans and the proposal."

"What plans for an outreach program are you talking about? And what $300,000 proposal?"

I explained briefly what we were being asked to support. He continued:

"That never came to the board! I never heard a thing about it. But I'm planning to find out!"

My reaction was this: Here was a major new program, which would increase the total operating budget of the organization by about one-third if it was established; it also involved new staff and a number of other changes in the organization and its operations. Yet the board of the organization apparently had never seen or heard of it, and had not approved the decision to move in a new direction or to seek outside support. This told me that the leadership of the organization was not fulfilling its oversight and approval roles and that the staff were not taking the responsibility of ensuring board involvement when major new initiatives were being planned. This opened the questions of what the board members were involved with and what they saw as their roles and responsibilities. I called the executive director of the organization and, after explaining my conversation with the board chair and the major issues I saw in our review of the proposal, suggested he withdraw the proposal from further consideration, which he did.

There is also another consideration related to the signatures on the proposal cover letter, and to the example above. Be sure anyone signing the proposal gets a copy before it goes out, and try to ensure that each person getting a copy reads the proposal. One way to help this happen is to tell each person he or she may be called by a foundation or corporate staff person to discuss the proposal in detail.

Strategy Tip: In this era of word processing, mail merge, and other sophisticated techniques, it is interesting to hear foundation staff members say they are still getting many proposals addressed to "Dear Sir or Madame." It is relatively easy to find out to whom you should address each of your proposals. Having a specific name in the salutation helps create a feeling that this was not one of 50 generic proposals sent out by your organization. Also, since cut-and-paste is an established technique, be sure that you have not cut and pasted everything, including the name of the "other" potential funder to which you are addressing your proposal. Staff members have told me with amusement how they are reading through a proposal addressed to them at the ABC Foundation, but the body of the cover letter and/or the proposal keeps referring to the XYZ Foundation. So, the message is: proof everything very carefully. If, like me, you have great difficulty proofing your own writing, find someone else who is good at proofing and have that person review the materials before they are sent out. It is probably an even better idea to have at least two people proof anything as major as a grant request.

Strategy Tip: If a staff member of another foundation or corporation referred you to the foundation or corporation you are sending your proposal to, and especially if you mentioned that person's name in your introductory paragraph, send them a copy of your cover letter and indicate on the original cover letter that a copy is being sent to that person. If there are other key people outside your organization who should receive copies of the letter or the complete package, such as the head of the local United Way, indicate on your cover letter that these people are receiving copies.

The Cover Page

Following your cover letter, you should usually have a brief cover page. The cover page presents the most basic and most critical information in a concise manner and in one easy-to-find place. As a program officer I often wished more proposals had a cover page; it would have saved me considerable time and energy when I was looking for basic information, such as who should I contact about the proposal, or how much was being asked for, or what was the purpose, stated briefly, for which a particular organization was seeking support.

The cover page is just that—a cover page. Exhibit 12–1 is the typical cover page layout I use or recommend, although there can be several varia-

Exhibit 12–1 Sample Proposal Cover Page

Request To: The David and Helen Smith Foundation

Amount Requested: $100,000 over three years ($50,000 the first year, $30,000 the second year, and $20,000 the third year)

Purpose: Toward initial start-up costs (staff and equipment) of a new family counseling outreach program

Submitted by: The Middleton Family Services Center
Address: 1228 Center Way
Middleton, MD 20918
Contact Person: Jo Patterson, Executive Director
Phone: 312-555-3388
Fax: 312-555-3399
Date Submitted: November 4, 1996

tions on the basic layout. The important point is that the information listed below be included; the precise formatting and other details are up to you.

Let's review the contents of the cover page carefully. The first item is the name of the foundation or corporation to which the proposal is being submitted. This at least gives some indication that the proposal is not one of 50 "Dear Sir or Madame . . ." proposals. Next is the line indicating both the amount of the grant being requested and the timeline being requested by the organization for payment of the grant. This section is very important for a number of reasons. The amount of the grant being requested can be one of the indicators to foundation and corporate staff that you have—or haven't—done your homework. Spelling out the timeline, especially when you are requesting grants be paid over a period of more than one year, is always helpful to the foundation or corporation because it must, like most organizations, do financial planning. A major issue for some funders is future grant commitments (grants that have been approved, but that will be paid out in future fiscal years). Foundations, and corporate funders to some extent, that make multiple-year grant commitments must be careful not to overcommit against future income on their assets. If earnings on the investments are not as high as were projected and if a number of multiple-year grants must be paid off, the foundation or corporate funder can find itself in a situation where it has few or no funds available for making new grants. Occasionally in your research you will find a listing for a foundation or corporate funder that will read "all funds committed"; this probably reflects the situation described here.

The "Purpose" line gives a one-sentence description of how the organization will use the funds, if granted. Many proposals I reviewed had much to say, but few were able to give me a one- or two-sentence capsule description of what it was they really wanted to do. At our foundation, and I am sure at others, the board required that each proposal write-up prepared by a program officer contain a capsule description of the purpose for which funds were being requested. The details of what was planned and why were included elsewhere, but the capsule description was a critical part of the infor-

mation. Notice in Exhibit 12–1 that the statement includes several key words, which can send important messages to the foundation or corporate staff member reading it. "Initial start-up costs" indicates the organization probably anticipates the ongoing costs of the program, once it is underway, will be coming from other sources. "Staff and equipment" states specifically what the funding will be used for by the organization. "New . . . program" says to the potential funder that the funds will not be used for the expansion of an existing program but to add a new service that has not been provided by the agency before. "Family counseling outreach" briefly describes the nature of the new program. This, of course, will be elaborated upon in the proposal. Essentially what this one sentence has accomplished is to concisely present several of the key elements of the proposal in the briefest possible way.

Next the name and address of the organization submitting the proposal is given. This is followed by one of the most important elements, the name and phone number (along with the fax number and, in a growing number of organizations, the e-mail address), of the contact person. The contact person may be different from the persons who sign the cover letter. In some cases the contact person may be the program director or the development officer. However, the contact person, no matter who it is within the organization, should have received a copy of the full proposal package before it was sent to the potential funder and should be thoroughly briefed on each funding source that has been sent a proposal. The individual should also have a good understanding of the total organization and its needs. Usually it is a good idea to have a senior-level person, if not the CEO or executive director, listed as the contact person. In this day of elaborate and sometimes frustrating voice mail systems, it is also a good idea to list the most direct phone number for reaching the contact person.

> **Many proposals I reviewed had much to say, but few were able to give me a one- or two-sentence capsule description of what it was they really wanted to do.**

Finally, the date the proposal was submitted should be listed on the cover sheet. Again, foundation and corporate staff have sometimes remarked how many undated proposals they receive from organizations. Dating your proposal is not only a way to record when it was sent, but also is helpful to the potential funder in terms of its deadlines and processing. When there are deadlines, the importance of dating your proposal—and verifying when it was sent—can become critical if you are sending it in close to the deadline. If the foundation or corporate funder is on the "rolling" system of taking as many proposals as possible for decisions at the next meeting of its board, and then deferring consideration on the remainder until the following meeting, the date on your proposal may well help the funder decide if it will fall into the group for consideration at the next meeting, or the deferred group.

Strategy Tip: It is relatively easy to add headers and footers to your proposals. Because foundations and corporate funders frequently unbind proposals and sometimes separate the various parts, always try to have a header on each page of your proposal with the name of your organization on it. If the pages get separated, the staff at the foundation or corporation will be able to identify which pages belong to your proposal. The footer should include the page number for each page and the date of the proposal.

The Main Body of the Proposal

Length and Formatting Issues

How long should the main body of your proposal be? If the foundation or corporate funder specifies, recommends, or even suggests a length or length limitations, the best advice is to follow the recommendations. Some foundations and corporate funders are very specific about their limitations, even to the point of saying, in a few cases

"we will accept no proposal longer than five pages" or something similar. But many funders only suggest a length. If the potential funder does not say anything about length, five to ten pages should be the limit. Remember that this is the body of the proposal itself and does not include the cover letter (one to two pages), and any attachments, which will be discussed separately below. One way to view the proposal is as falling between the expansiveness and inclusiveness of the case statement and the brevity and precision of the cover letter.

To format, use one and one-half or double spacing between lines to help make the proposal more readable, and use a reasonable font and type-face size (some of us older types prefer 12 or 14 point type). Double spacing the lines and using fairly wide margins enable the reviewer to make notes and comments, as some prefer to do. It is increasingly easy to use graphics when preparing documents. Although it is a fairly conservative approach, I believe there should be minimal or no graphics included in the body of the proposal, unless a chart or graph can help make a point more easily than a long explanation. Even then, having the chart or graph as an attachment might be the more appropriate route to take. Using graphics only for the purpose of breaking up the document or marking off sections can get to be distracting while at the same time lengthening the document. Given the five to ten page length, it is best to focus your attention on the key messages you want to convey and strive to make your case rather than impress the potential funder with your design and graphic skills.

Inclusions and Exclusions

Some people have asked about the inclusion of pictures in proposals. Again, with the growing availability of scanners and high-quality printers, it is becoming easier to include pictures in the body of the proposal or as attachments. However, the tendency of some organizations to show the "warm and fuzzy" side of what they do, especially when it involves children or animals, should generally be held in check when it comes to proposals. The attachments can be appropriate for inclusion of pictures, if you and your organization believe they are essential to making the case. Annual reports, for example, often contain pictures and are appropriate to include as attachments. But using pictures in the hopes that they will better make your case may not be a wise assumption. Foundation and corporate staff can be somewhat hardened to pictures and strong emotional appeals, especially those staff who have been in the ranks for a long time and have, as one person said, "seen it all." Besides, while a picture can be worth a thousand words, if your choice is having a picture or having a thousand words in your proposal, it is better to go with the words.

Introduction to the Content Elements

It would be nice to tell you that there is a proposal formula that will always be successful at getting grants for your organization. But if you believe that, then you obviously have not been reading this book! As has often been pointed out, a proposal one foundation or corporation sees as "appealing" may well be seen by another foundation or corporation as "appalling." Much depends upon the foundation or corporation itself, the staff reviewing your proposal and their experience, the types of proposals they typically receive, and many other factors. For example, one foundation staff member I am familiar with was a writer and a reporter before she became an officer of the foundation. Her stated approach to proposals is the reporter's time-honored rule of story writing: who, what, where, when, and why and, for proposals, how. A staff member at another foundation, which is heavily focused on funding smaller social service agencies, might overlook a lot of "sins" and focus entirely on the concepts or plans presented in the proposal.

The message should clearly be that there is much you cannot control once the proposal is received. As we shall discuss later, there are still many things you and your organization can do once the proposal is sent in. And, as you should already know at this point, there are many things you should have done before the proposal was submitted. If, for example, you had created a negotiated partnership prior to submission of the proposal with the staff member of a potential funder, you should have

been able to better shape your proposal to the funder's needs and interests.

Key Areas

The content of the proposal should always reflect three key areas:

1. your organization and its needs

2. the interests of the potential funder

3. the larger needs and issues in society that your organization's mission is focused upon

Most proposals focus on the first area. Some focus on the first and second areas or the first and third areas. Few proposals manage to cover all three areas effectively. Many organizations, when they are preparing proposals, start off presenting their programs and services, often speaking of their history or the quality of their work. There sometimes is an underlying assumption that there is inherent value in what they do. Of course, no proposal ever started off: "We're a meaningless and pointless organization"! Foundation and corporate staff do tend to get somewhat immune to all of the "innovative," "creative," "original," "outstanding," and other adjectival organizations and programs that ask them for support. But, as a colleague of mine who also worked at a foundation says, "The central question really is 'who cares?'" Does the content of your proposal really address the issue "who cares"?

The content of any proposal should take an educational approach in presenting your organization. It is always wise not to assume that any potential funder—even one that funded your organization in the past—knows who you are and what you do. Staff at funding organizations change, files get lost, and even someone who handled your previous proposals or grants may not completely remember your organization. In cases where you are reapproaching a foundation or corporate funder where your organization already has a staff contact, it is appropriate to ask that person if you should send in a full proposal or if he or she would prefer something shorter. If the staff member feels comfortable with something shorter, he or she may ask just for a brief letter outlining your plans and needs.

The educational approach implies your proposal is structured in a way that leads the individual reading it through a series of "lessons" about your organization and the needs or issues your organization serves. But the "lessons" are always geared to the specific interests of the "learner"—the potential funder. That is why I believe the best proposals start off with the general and move to the specific. Some organizations turn this approach on its head and believe it best to start the proposal presenting the specific program or project for which support is being asked, make the grant request, and then get into the background information on the organization. A few potential funders also prefer this approach. But I believe most staff at funding organizations would prefer the general to specific approach, as long as the proposal is concise. If you were trying to get somewhere using a map, would you first want to see a small piece of the map showing you just the block where you are trying to go, or would you prefer to see the entire area map first, so you have some idea of the big picture?

Moving from the general to the specific in your proposal has another advantage. It is in the proposal's discussion of the more general aspects of your organization and what its plans are that the foundation or corporation may begin to see the connection with its own particular interests. Foundations and corporations, by their very nature as we have seen, have categories of interests that they seek to support through their funding. Their categories might be as generic as "supporting education" or more specific such as "serving the educational needs of disabled children." A proposal that starts out by presenting broad needs or issues in society, which match up with the interests and funding patterns of the particular funder receiving the proposal, is building its case on a strong base.

> The educational approach implies your proposal is structured in a way that leads the individual reading it through a series of lessons about your organization.

If the proposal next presents the organization and shows why, in terms of both its mission and its services it is an appropriate organization to address these needs, the case becomes stronger. And if, finally, the specific program, project, or other funding need is presented, the organization has built what I believe to be the best possible case by leading the reader of the proposal from the common territory of shared interests to the specifics of what the funder is being asked to support. If all of this sounds either a little murky or too academic, it will hopefully become more realistic as you continue on. Here is a real example of the concept.

Example: A small social service agency has plans to carry out a renovation and expansion of its facility. Part of the plans include a bowling alley, which was estimated to cost about $500,000. The initial budget for the capital campaign listed the bowling alley with the projected costs, but no explanation or justification. The executive director, board chair, and others met to discuss the budget. A key question was "How can we justify the costs of a bowling alley—almost 16 percent of the total goal—to anyone?" The discussion moved to the mission of the agency and the area it served.

The agency was the only one that provided a variety of educational, recreational, health, and cultural programs in an otherwise vastly underserved area of the city. The area was characterized by some of the highest unemployment levels in the entire city and by, according to a United Way survey, a much greater need for human services than almost any other part of the city. Except for the programs provided by the agency, there were no other opportunities for family recreation within several miles of the neighborhood. The closest bowling alley was approximately three miles away. Gradually the group came to see that the value of a bowling alley would not be the bowling alley itself, which was only a means to an end. The bowling alley would be the only place in the neighborhood where families, neighbors, and friends could get together for recreational purposes in a positive atmosphere. For many of the families, it could well be the only place the entire family could get together, since many of the children spent most of the nonschool day at the agency. It could also help draw people to the agency who could benefit from the other services that were offered there. So the bowling alley really was something more; and it was directly tied to the central mission of the agency.

In general, the easiest way to think of the content of a proposal is to think of an inverted pyramid (see Figure 12–1). The widest part of the pyramid is at the top; it is here you are presenting the broad needs or issues in the world "out there" that your organization serves through its mission and programs. It is also here that you are seeking to have the potential funder begin to see the relationship between the corporate or foundation mission and its funding interests and the essential purposes of your organization: who or what it really serves. As you move down the pyramid you next present the mission of the organization, which is tied to the broad needs or issues above it. Then you present a brief historical perspective on your organization. As you move toward the tip of the inverted pyramid, your presentation of your organization becomes more focused. There is a discussion of the organization's current programs and services and those served (or the issues addressed), followed by information on sources of financial support and uses of funds. Next you move into the specifics of the program, project, or other need for which

you are seeking support from that particular funding source. Then you cover how the planned activity will be evaluated. You also present a brief discussion of other potential sources of support you are approaching for the particular need. Next, you present information on timelines and how the need, if it is to become an ongoing part of the organization's programs, will be supported in the future. Finally, you present a few sentences in which you make the actual grant request of the foundation or corporation; this is the shortest section of the proposal and you have now both literally and figuratively (in terms of the inverted pyramid model) reached the "point" of the proposal.

A Proposal and Analysis

In order to make all of this clearer, I will present a "walk through" of a proposal for a fictional organization. As each part is presented, it will be analyzed to show what is being said and why. As with any such exercise, remember that this is only an example. Your actual proposals should reflect all of the key elements presented here and should accurately reflect both the funding interests of the particular source you are presenting your case to as well as the particulars of your organization.

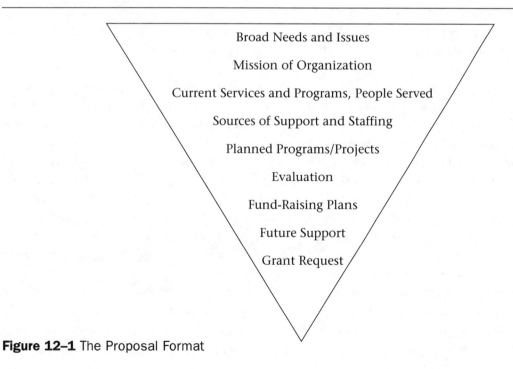

Figure 12–1 The Proposal Format

Metro Family and Children's Services
Request To: The Robert A. Ardsley Foundation
Purpose: Support of New Family and Children's
Outreach Counseling Program Based in Area
Schools
Amount Requested: $100,000 Over Two Years
($50,000 Per Year)

The Need

There is a major need in the metro area for high-quality family and children's counseling services and related family assistance programs. Working and single-parent families are under growing stress and pressures, as is indicated by the 25 percent increase in the divorce rate in the metro area over the past five years, the 32 percent increase in court-adjudicated family violence cases, and the 28 percent increase in child abuse by parent cases (all information from county court system data reports for the past five years).

According to the latest available census data, the metro area includes over 25,000 families in which both parents work or which are single-parent families with the parent having a part-time or full-time position. The data also showed that over 80 percent of these families are lower-middle or lower income. The 1996 United Way Needs Survey indicated that these same families rated "family stress" and "job stress" as the two most critical issues they were facing in their day-to-day lives. Over one-third of those filling out the survey said that such stress was having a "significant" impact of their lives and their relations with other family members as well as their work performances. This same group indicated that there were few or no resources in their immediate area that could provide counseling and other related services to assist them with these issues. Many also noted that work and family schedules prevented them from using the counseling and assistance services that were available.

The conclusion drawn by a recent study by Dr. A.J. Smith, Dean of the Department of Sociology at the State University, was that a high-quality counseling program focused on the families and children who are most "at risk" for potential family

breakdowns and conflicts could help prevent many of the situations that ended up in the court system. Heading off these problems in the early stages could help move families toward more normal functioning and better ability to deal with everyday stress. The cost savings of an early intervention and prevention approach would be considerable, especially in terms of the use of public funds and programs to deal with dysfunctional families through the court systems, foster homes, incarceration, and other expensive measures.

But the same families that are most at risk have the least access to quality family counseling services and, even if services are provided in their area, have limited available time to use such services due to work and family obligations.

Analysis: The "Need" section of the proposal example above sets the basis for everything that follows. Notice that there is no mention of the agency yet; the information presented is primarily factual and based upon outside sources. This information shows there are specific and mostly unmet needs that, if met, could help resolve a number of problems, both for individuals and for the community. Also, if the needs were met, there are potential cost savings that could be realized in such areas as the legal system and the delivery of human services. One conclusion is that preventative approaches could help head off later major problems that could be much more difficult to deal with effectively. But the "Need" section also raises some unresolved questions centering on the availability of the needed services and the limited time those who need the services have to use them.

Now it is obvious that not all "needs" are as clear-cut and supportable by data as the need presented here is. But the proposal should make the case for whatever your organization is trying to accomplish "out there" in the real world before it gets into who you are and what you specifically plan to do. Suppose the proposal was for a capital need, such as a grant toward the costs of a new building. As we saw with the "bowling alley" example above, the building is only a means to an end. By constructing the building, the organization is going to fulfill a broader purpose than just creating a structure. The "Need" section of the proposal should always speak to that broader purpose—it should answer the question "what is beyond the organization that can be—and should be—changed, corrected, or improved?"

But the "Need" section can do something more. As was presented in the earlier general discussion section on content of the proposal, the "Need" section can be the first point within the proposal itself where the foundation or corporate person reading the proposal begins to connect the mission of your organization with the funding interests of the foundation or corporation. Let us assume that you have done your homework and have thoroughly researched the fictional "Robert A. Ardsley Foundation." Its guidelines, previous grants, and other information you review indicate:

- The Foundation primarily funds in the local metro area.

- One of its Board members is also on the board of the local United Way.

- The Foundation has funded a number of programs related to family violence and child abuse cases in the court system.

- Much of the funding has gone toward programs that assist lower-middle and low-income people.

- The Foundation has not provided many grants to human service agencies, except those related to the court system and family/child violence and abuse cases.

- Your agency has not received any previous grants from The Foundation during the last five years.

- The Foundation had provided past funding to the Dean of the State University for some of his research projects on area needs and issues.

- The Chair of the Board of the Foundation, in the most recent Foundation annual report, cited a need for The Foundation to increasingly focus its grant making on measures ". . . that can demonstrate cost effectiveness and efficiencies in resolving the major issues faced by the residents of the metro area."

- The Foundation has made a number of two- and three-year grants with an upper range as high as $75,000 per year.

- The staff member who reviews requests from human service agencies previously worked at a children's service agency.

Let us also assume that you have not been able to meet with The Foundation and that they require a proposal be sent before a meeting can take place. What has the "Need" section accomplished in the light of the above information you have collected on The Foundation? Here are some of the "connections" you may have made in the "Need" section to this specific foundation:

- The use of United Way information helps build some credibility for your case both because it is an outside source of information and because of the involvement of a board member of The Foundation on the Board of the United Way.

- The reference to the study by the Dean of the State University also helps build the case for support, since he has been a grant recipient of The Foundation.

- The reference to the court system statistics also helps build the case because these numbers, and hopefully your organization's planned program, tie into a direct interest of The Foundation.

- The "Need" section begins to make the argument that the proposed program will help alleviate some of the high costs involved in court cases related to family violence and child abuse, an area The Foundation is probably directly familiar with based upon their guidelines and actual funding patterns.

- Dr. Smith's conclusions about the potential cost savings of preventative programs tie in with The Foundation's expressed interest in cost-efficient and effective programs—and with the specific plans for the new program for which your agency is seeking support.

Also notice that the header of the proposal includes both the name of the foundation to which the proposal is being addressed as well as the purpose of the grant request and the amount and time period of the grant request. The amount being requested is in keeping with the grant-making capabilities of The Foundation, as is the request for a two-year payment period on the grant.

Mission

The mission of Metro Family and Children's Services is:

. . . to improve the functioning and effectiveness of metro-area families by being the leading provider of family and child professional counseling services and related assistance, including referral services, and by providing training and support to other professionals dealing with families and children.

The mission statement was reaffirmed at the recent Metro Family and Children's Services annual board and staff retreat during which progress toward the goals and objectives of the agency's current three-year plan was evaluated according to the criteria developed with the inception of the plan.

Analysis: In a few brief sentences the agency has accomplished several key objectives related to presenting its case for funding by The Foundation. First, it has presented its mission statement, which will help The Foundation better understand how the specific programs and services, as well as the planned program, fit with the general purposes of the organization and relate to the specific interests of the potential funder. Second, the agency has shown that the mission statement is not just something on a piece of paper but is the guide to the agency's planning and evaluation of its effectiveness. Third, the agency has shown that it does indeed have a long-range plan and that the board and staff are engaged in the planning and evaluation processes. From the potential funder's point of view, this is an agency where there is board involvement, and mission-driven planning and evaluation do occur. The Foundation may begin to feel that, although it has not funded this agency recently, the risk of doing so might not be as high as it would be for some of the other agencies applying for support.

Background

Metro Family and Children's Services was founded in 1904 as The Children's and Orphan's Welfare Agency. From its inception, the agency has been committed to improving the lives of children living in the immediate urban area, with a strong emphasis on serving those most in need. The original agency primarily provided residential services for area orphans, limited health care to families

without other resources, and free meals to poor families living within the area of the agency.

As adoption and foster home services became more widespread and available, the agency ceased providing residential services to orphans and began to provide services focused on poor and lower-income families. These services continued to include the food and pantry operations, but also included language and citizenship classes for new immigrants, job training and placement, housing assistance, and supplemental educational and recreational programs for children. The era of the Depression saw the agency considerably expand these services and the creation of the first agency "outposts" in different area communities to better meet the needs of people in these areas. During this period the agency changed its name to the Family and Children's Agency to better reflect its revised mission and programs.

The coming of World War II saw many major changes in the nature and purposes of the agency in response to the changing needs of area families and children. Many area families in effect became single working parent homes as fathers went off to war and mothers were employed in the defense industries located around the metro area. Most of the traditional services of the agency were either no longer needed or were needed only on a much-reduced scale. But staff of the agency began to see the need to provide counseling to families and children who were having difficulty adjusting to an absent father, a working mother, and often unsupervised children. At the same time, the staff and board of the agency recognized that the traditional services it had been providing were readily available through a number of other local agencies. In 1943 the Family and Children's Agency became the first area agency committed to providing counseling services to families in crisis or under stress and to providing one-on-one and group counseling services to troubled children. Services included psychological testing and referral to other area agencies for related needs, such as health care, legal assistance, etc. These basic services continue to form the core of the current programs of Family and Children's Services, which was renamed in 1955 to better differentiate it from other area organizations.

Analysis: The brief history recounts the development and evolution of the agency from its start. But the history also demonstrates the willingness of the agency to change in response to the changing needs of the people it serves. This history thus shows the agency is flexible and responsive, rather than stubbornly trying to cling to an outdated service model and mission.

Current Services and Programs

The current services and programs of Family and Children's Services are:

- Family Counseling: Working with all family members as a group, counselors provide short-term crisis intervention and long-term ongoing counseling services to families at risk. Families come to the agency through referral (60 percent) or at their own initiative (40 percent). Family groups are seen on the average of once per week, although for crisis intervention situations families may receive the services as much as three to four times per week.

- Teen Groups: The agency currently is maintaining 37 teen groups, each of which meets two times per week. Groups average about eight to ten members each and focus on personal relationships, dating, substance abuse, sex, stress, school, and other issues. Groups are staffed by two professional counselors each. Especially troubled teens may also receive separate individual counseling.

- Teen Drop-In Centers: The agency maintains four Teen Drop-In Centers; each is located within one to two blocks of the four metro high schools. The drop-in centers are staffed by professional counselors and trained youth workers and provide nonthreatening, safe, and confidential opportunities for teens to discuss concerns and issues and get unbiased information. The centers also provide a referral point to the teen group counseling sessions as well as the substance abuse program (see below). The four drop-in centers each average about 75–100 visits per school day.

- Substance Abuse Program: The substance abuse program is focused on teens and adults who

are engaged in substance abuse. Working with area hospitals and health care providers, Family and Children's Services provides both medical and counseling assistance to self-identified and referred substance abusers. Additional services, such as employment assistance and training, are provided through referral to other agencies. During the previous year the program worked with 150 individuals, each of whom on average was involved in 25 individual and group sessions.

- Child Abuse Intervention Program: This program provides intervention and assistance services to abused children and other family members, as well as referral to other appropriate agencies for legal, medical, and other assistance. The program includes a 24-hour hot-line service and also is closely tied to local law enforcement and court agencies. Working with the courts, staff of the program help remove children from abusive parents and violent family situations and place them in approved safe and secure living situations on a temporary or permanent basis, as required. During the most recent year the agency worked with 243 cases of child abuse.

- Family Violence Intervention Program: Like the child abuse intervention program, the family violence program is designed to assist victims of family violence as self-identified or referred by law enforcement and court authorities or other agencies. The program also includes a 24-hour hot-line service and provides counseling assistance, and referral to medical, legal, and temporary housing services. During the most recent year the agency assisted over 475 families through this program.

- Referral and Information Resources Center: Family and Children's Services is unique in having a referral resources center that is tied to all of its other programs but also acts as a referral and information resource for anyone in the area needing assistance or direction to particular types of services and agencies. The Resource Center also provides information to each of the hot lines maintained by the agency and to the program staff, and it serves as a back up information resource for other area hot-line services. During the most recent year the Center received over 42,000 calls.

Family and Children's Services is currently the largest single provider of family and child counseling and support services in the metro area. Of the three major nonprofit agencies providing these services, Family and Children's Services provided 80 percent of all the counseling and support sessions given in the area during the most recent year (all data based on United Way information). During the previous year the agency provided 15,400 individual and family counseling sessions, 3,200 group counseling sessions, and over 127,200 contacts and visits connected with its programs and services.

During the past year the agency commissioned an independent study of who uses its services and their general satisfaction with the effectiveness and delivery of the services. The findings of this study, which has been repeated every three to five years for the past 15 years, are incorporated into the agency's planning and review processes, as well as the ongoing evaluation of its work. The major findings of the most recent study are summarized as follows:

- Family and Children's Services clients include those from all economic levels and areas of the city. However, 74 percent can be classified as lower-middle to lower income and 53 percent represent single-parent families. About 80 percent of the adults served were employed and 20 percent were unemployed.

- Of those surveyed, 84 percent said they were highly satisfied or generally satisfied with the services they received; only 2.3 percent rated the services as unsatisfactory.

- Seventy-three percent of the respondents said the services they received had made a significant and positive difference in their lives and in those of their family members. Studies of court records indicated that families using the services of the agency are 87 percent less likely to end up in court or in the legal system than other families who had not received the services.

- Teenagers participating in agency programs rated the services highly, with the average number of visits per year per participant being 10–12 and 83 percent of those visiting the drop-in centers returning at least four times.

All programs record client information and visits, and each has a built-in ongoing evaluation component to measure its effectiveness and efficiency. Techniques used include periodic surveys, as was covered above, as well as exit interviews, mail surveys, follow-up phone calls by staff using standardized questionnaires, staff input and suggestions for program improvement, and other means. This information and other resources, such as the periodic United Way Needs Survey, are incorporated into the yearly and longer-term planning processes carried out by the board and staff working together at the annual planning retreat. Yearly goals and objectives for each program area are developed at the planning retreat, based upon program evaluations carried out as well as based upon the long-range plan. Each program is also evaluated as to its responsiveness to the needs of the community. Each year all program directors must respond to the challenge of whether or not their program should continue, thus helping to ensure programs continue to be tied closely to community needs rather than continuing to be supported because they already exist.

Analysis: Again, in a relatively short section the agency has presented what it currently does as well as how it evaluates its programs and how it plans. Notice that wherever possible the agency not only describes the program but gives the numbers served. Quantitative data, if it is available for whatever your organization does, can considerably enhance the building of your case as well as show more clearly the magnitude and outreach of your organization. However, if there are very large amounts of statistics or quantitative information, the information should probably be presented as an attachment rather than incorporated into the body of the proposal.

Notice also that information on the effectiveness of the services is included in this section. This again helps build the needed credibility for the agency's request to The Foundation. It demonstrates the agency's willingness to look carefully and frequently at what it is doing and also its willingness to have both staff and those it serves involved in the evaluation process. This raises an interesting question that you may have to face some day: what if the evaluation results are not as positive as those presented here? What if, in fact, the ratings are somewhat negative? Remember our earlier discussion of the "problem–solution" approach? Here again your agency should be prepared to apply this approach by showing what it plans to do to help increase the positive ratings.

The general impression the agency presents in the above section is that it is well managed continually evaluates (using a variety of resources) the effectiveness and the efficiency of its programs; and is willing to change and be flexible in response to changing needs in the community. Also notice that all of the programs and services are in keeping with its mission statement; the agency is clearly mission-driven and incorporates its mission into both the planning and evaluation functions.

Staffing and Sources of Support

Family and Children's Services is presently staffed by 34 professional staff (please refer to the organizational chart in the attachments, item D), and 18 support staff. Primary functional areas include administration and business services, client services, fund raising, evaluation, and volunteer services/community outreach. Additional support for the work of the agency is provided by the Volunteer Association, which includes over 220 individuals. Volunteers provide the equivalent of 27 additional full-time staff through their services, which include staffing the agency's three hot lines (after an intensive three-week training program), providing support for the Referral and Information Resource Center, and serving as support staff at the Teen Drop-In Centers.

Family and Children's Services most recent annual budget (see attached Audit, item E) was $1.87 million. This excludes donated and in-kind services and other items, such as the free use of space for three of the four Teen Drop-in Centers and the contributed services of the volunteers. Current sources of support include: fees for service and third-party payments (32 percent of the total budget), United Way funds (18 percent), a city government grant for the Drop-In Center Program (10 percent), a state grant to operate the Family Violence Intervention Program (8 percent), a separate state grant to operate the Child Abuse Intervention Program (12 percent), and gifts and donations through the annual campaign and special events (20 percent). The agency also maintains a small endowment fund of $520,000. The earnings on the endowment are currently placed in a preventative maintenance fund, which is used as needed for major repairs on agency facilities.

Analysis: The agency has presented a quick overview of the size and costs of its operations. Notice that not only are the numbers of regular staff given, but the numbers of volunteers are also included. Many organizations, in presenting their proposals, fail to mention the numbers of volunteers involved with the organization and the roles they play in helping to accomplish the organization's goals. Yet volunteers can substantially add to both the size and the effectiveness of an organization without adding significantly to the cost of carrying out its services or programs. By presenting how time given by volunteers would translate into equivalent full-time staff, the agency is demonstrating that it has, in effect, almost twice as many "staff" as listed in the actual staff numbers. The agency includes reference to donated space, which again shows it is taking appropriate measures to keep costs under control.

The agency presents figures for its total most recent operating budget. The use of percentages for sources of income rather than actual dollars gives a clear message that the agency has a fairly broad mix of sources of revenue. Why is this important? Potential funders generally feel there is a higher risk in investing in an organization when it only has one or two primary sources of support, especially if one or more of those sources has some probability of decreasing or being eliminated in the future. An organization that receives a substantial percent of its funding from one or two major grants that will end in a few years is seen as having a very high degree of risk in terms of investments by other potential funders; the organization may have to struggle to merely meet its core operating budget (the most es-

*sential staff and related expenses it needs to function),
much less operate special projects or new programs.*

The agency mentions it maintains a small endowment fund. The use of the earnings on the fund for preventative maintenance shows the agency is taking a responsible approach to its future.

Strategy Tip: The existence of endowment (permanent) funds, especially at some types of agencies, is often problematical when seeking support from a foundation or corporation. Development and maintenance of endowment funds is generally seen as a "good thing" for such institutions as colleges, universities, hospitals, and museums. But social or human service agencies are sometimes looked at somewhat askance, especially by some potential funders, if they have substantial endowments. I once worked with a human service agency that was fortunate to have a nine-figure endowment, but the executive director felt making this too public would be seen as a negative by the many contributors, especially those who gave small gifts every year. The agency's materials always tried to depict the agency as very frugal; the executive director wanted nothing that looked "too slick" or expensive.

And yet another institution I am familiar with received a highly publicized nine-figure gift restricted by the donor for use as part of its endowment. What was the result of this gift on other giving to this organization? The institution had its best year ever in terms of other giving after this major gift was announced. I would like to think that in this case donors—and even some like me who had never donated to the institution before—felt a sense of pride and responded with more and larger gifts.

So endowment funds can be a two-edged sword. Some foundations and corporations may see the existence of endowment funds, especially when they are substantial, as a negative when they are making their funding considerations. Others may see these same endowment funds as the organization's effort to help ensure its future. I believe any proposal should include mention of endowment funds as well as the intended uses of these funds. Potential funders who seem reluctant to make grants because of the existence of endowment funds should be educated as to the value of endowment funds in protecting the organization from fluctuations in annual support and helping to ensure it will have at least some stability in its financial base in the future. I would like to believe that the more enlightened funders believe that to be the case.

Planned Program

The Proposed School-Based Family and Children's Outreach Counseling Program (OCP)

The growing stress on working and single-parent families is clearly shown by the statistics presented in the first section of this proposal. Family and Children's Services has made every effort possible to improve opportunities for families to use its services, including extending hours of operation into the evenings, development of service sites in several locations, and adding staff. However, as was indicated in the United Way's 1996 Needs Survey, many of those families that are most under stress, and therefore most in need of the types of services provided by our agency, have the least opportunity to use our services because of family and work schedules and/or because of difficulty in getting to our existing locations.

In order to test these findings as well as collect additional information, Family and Children's Services carried out an informal survey of a sample of 142 children and their parents located in lower income and lower-middle income areas of the city, as described in the 1995 Metro Area Census Data Update. The survey was carried out using anonymous written questionnaires to both students and their parents. Four schools serving these areas agreed to carry out the survey through mailings and in-class completion of surveys.

The basic findings (see attachment, Item F for a complete summary of the results of the survey; the complete report is available upon request to Family and Children's Services) strongly support the need for services directed at "at risk" families and provided through a means of delivery that will supplement current services provided by the agency and other area organizations. Some of the key findings are as follows:

- Of the children and families responding to the survey, 81 percent were either families with both parents working or single-parent families.

- Of all those responding, 67 percent indicated they believed they had a medium to a high risk of family difficulties or were currently experiencing such difficulties.

- Of all those responding, 74 percent said they believed they and other family members could benefit from counseling services.

- Of the total number of parents responding, 71 percent said they had limited or no time available during the day to participate in family counseling.

- Of the total number of parents responding, 64 percent said that they "usually" drop their children off at school and pick them up every day. Of those dropping children off and picking them up, 92 percent said they do so in conjunction with before-school and after-school care programs. The survey also collected information on each respondent's usual drop off and pick up times at the schools.

This latter piece of information from the survey clearly demonstrated that there were two points each day when many of the parents and their children were in the same location. This fact, as well as the demonstrated needs, became the basis for the design of the School-Based Family and Children's Outreach Counseling Program (or OCP).

The central concept of OCP is to provide family counseling in school facilities prior to and after regular classes around the times when many parents are dropping off or picking up their children. This program would enable families, especially those most at risk, to receive counseling services at a location they are already visiting. Moreover, the services would be available prior to the beginning or at the end of their work day and thus will be much more in keeping with their schedules. Each session would last 45 minutes to 1 hour and would be with the members of one family at a time, although group sessions may be explored once the concept has become established and accepted. Under present plans, each family could have a maximum of two visits per week, although provision can be made for crisis intervention sessions as needed.

After the initial concept for the program was developed by the staff and presented to the board for its approval to proceed with exploration of the program, the four schools that participated in the survey were reapproached about the possible program. In each case, Family and Children's Services staff met with members of the administrative and teaching staffs to present and discuss the program. Following this, staff met with the parents' organizations to discuss the program. There was an overwhelmingly positive response from all parties, as is evidenced by the sample letters of endorsement (see Item G in the attachments).

All four schools have agreed (see Item H in the attachments for letters of agreement) to provide free space for the program, such as teachers' lounges that are not being used until school hours start. These schools, as was mentioned, are strategically located and serve areas where the cited studies show there are high proportions of families at risk. Where necessary, Family and Children's Services will provide refurbishing of these areas, including painting by agency volunteers, replacement or additional furniture, etc. Thus there will be an additional direct benefit to the schools in having the program located in their facilities.

OCP will be kept separate from school counseling and discipline programs both through written agreements with each school and through informational materials as well as maintenance of confidentiality of records and the emphasis on family-centered counseling. However, students themselves, teachers, and other school staff may act as referral points for OCP. The Program can also be publicized through parents' association newsletters, school bulletins, and other school-related means as well as through the current services and programs of the agency.

Because the focus of OCP will be on pre-school and after-school hours, and because it is expected that some of the current case load will be shifted to OCP, Family and Children's Services anticipates no need to hire additional counseling staff to operate the program. Present staff have indicated their willingness to be at OCP locations at the start and end of each day, and will return to their regular sites during the day. There will need to be some adjustment in the scheduling process to account for staff needing to start earlier or leave work later, but again discussions with staff have indicated this will not be a problem.

Preliminary estimates are that 16 family counseling sessions will be provided per day across the four school sites. Thus within one month OCP is expected to reach approximately 200–300 families (based upon more than one session per month for many families). It is also estimated that approximately 75 percent to 80 percent of these families would not be able to otherwise participate in Family and Children's Services family counseling programs due to their work schedules. Thus OCP would enable the agency to reach many of those "at risk" families that all available information indicates are most in need of family counseling services but least likely to be able to participate in the regular programs of the agency.

Family and Children's Services believes there are many other advantages to a school-based family counseling program. These include:

- providing opportunities for early identification of family problems in the one area outside the home where these problems may appear

- providing a relatively "neutral" setting for family counseling services

- enabling crisis intervention to take place rapidly and effectively when major problems or family issues make it necessary

- providing an entry point for referral to other Family and Children's Services programs and services as well as referral to other area agencies for specialized services and needs

- enabling promotion of the program through the cooperating schools as well as other means

- developing a model program that could be replicated in other schools and by other agencies

While the costs of operating the program are minimal, Family and Children's Services believes that the creation of a new position of Outreach Counseling Program Coordinator will enable the program to operate more effectively and efficiently. The OCP Coordinator will be responsible for oversight of OCP, including developing and maintaining relations with the staff, administration, and parents' groups at all four school sites; selecting and assigning professional counseling staff to each of the sites; coordinating work schedules; tracking data; promotion of the program; coordination with other program coordinators; ongoing evaluation of OCP; budget preparation and monitoring; and other related functions. The Coordinator will also be expected to have appropriate credentials to provide backup for the delivery of counseling services through OCP. Requirements for the position will include a minimum of five years' counseling experience with families and children, an advanced degree and appropriate certifications, three to five years' administrative experience at a similar agency, and proven effectiveness in working with diverse constituencies.

The OCP Coordinator position will be the only new staff position required to operate this program. The OCP budget (see Item I: Proposed OCP Budget and Income Projections in the attachments) includes $48,500 for salary and benefits for the OCP Coordinator per year as well as small amounts for supplies and office equipment; the total projected need for this position is approximately $50,000 per year. By the end of the second year it is estimated that OCP will be self-sustaining through the creation of sufficient income from fees for service and third-party payments as well as through increased annual support (presently growing at the rate of six percent to ten percent per year), as is shown in the attached income projections. Upon receipt of funding, it is expected that the OCP Coordinator will be selected and hired within a period of three months.

Analysis: Notice that it is here that the case is made for both the new program and for the specific needs that the foundation will be asked to support. Again the agency is presenting itself as carefully developing the plan for the new program. The program did not simply emerge as "great idea" but was taken through a series of steps to test its feasibility and cost-effectiveness. The program itself has been designed by the agency to maximize its current resources while at the same time not requiring too many additional resources. The program is focused directly on the specific needs that have been demonstrated to exist in the community and provides a unique solution to the issue of the limited availability for those who may be most in need of the planned services. The program is presented as a cooperative effort involving others in the community as well as having potential to provide further networking with other agencies and their programs.

Notice also the frequent referrals to the attachments. Attachments, as has been discussed, can play key roles in supplementing and complementing the body of the proposal without adding to the length of the document. Detailed information, such as budgets, letters of support, etc., can be included as part of the total package but will not break up the flow of information in the proposal itself.

The agency projects an image of having done its homework in thinking through and designing the new program. Even before the program has been implemented, the agency has gone out to get information and opinions so the program design will be the best possible. Planning and care are evident at every step of the way. But also the agency has not tried to develop the program on a massive scale that would preclude making major changes as it is developed and implemented, or that would require large levels of outside financial support.

The agency is showing that it is very cost-conscious. For example, the use of volunteers to fix up the existing school facilities indicates the concern of the agency with keeping costs down and developing cost-effective ways to meet the needs of the program. The use of existing professional counseling staff to provide the services also shows the agency is being creative in its approaches.

It is also in this section that the agency presents how it will continue to support the new position's costs once the funding from the foundation stops. The figures and rationale should assure the potential funder that it is unlikely the program will either have to be closed down due to a lack of continued grants or that the agency will be returning for additional support to keep the program operating in the future.

Overall, the agency has been using the proposal to build its case for funding the new program and has led the reader to the point of making the request for support. However, there is still one critical area that should be presented: evaluation.

Evaluation of OCP

One of the key roles of the OCP Coordinator is the continuing evaluation of all aspects of the program and reporting these to Children and Family Service's senior staff and board of directors. Families participating in the program will complete the agency's standard anonymous Client Satisfaction Survey on a periodic basis (the survey is usually administered after a client or group of clients have been in a program for a period of at least one month) and these results, identified by OCP, will be included in the agency's monthly Client Survey Results Report to the board of directors. All results of the survey are also provided to individual schools participating in the project as well as OCP staff.

Additionally, those not electing to continue in OCP will be contacted by the coordinator using both a mail survey and phone follow-up to determine their reasons for leaving the program. As with other agency programs, these results will also be included in staff reports to the board. According to agency standards, a program dropout rate exceeding 15 percent, due to dissatisfaction with the particular program, is cause for major concern and a rate exceeding 20 percent triggers a total program review process by the senior staff of Family and Children's Services.

Because OCP will be a new program for the agency, it will also be subject to Family and Children's Services benchmarking process. This process involves compiling of statistics on the program using the above two sources, an intensive review by the senior staff member responsible for programs, a detailed written evaluation of the strengths and weaknesses of the program prepared by the program coordinator with input from each of the staff members providing the services, and a three-hour staff review session devoted totally to discussing a single program. Benchmarking for new programs takes place at specific scheduled intervals: at the end of the first month of a new program, after the program has been operating for three months, after six months, and at the end of the first year. At this point a new program falls into the regular agency evaluation system. The intent of the benchmarking process is to build on a program's strengths while at the same time developing solutions to problems before they become major. The budget will also be closely monitored, as are all program budgets, by the agency's business office. Particularly important in this monitoring process will be measuring progress toward the goal of OCP self-sufficiency by the end of two years.

Because OCP will involve the development of close working relationships with each of the four schools where it will be housed, Family and Children's Services will seek the input of administrators, teachers, students, and parents as to the effectiveness of the program and suggestions for its improvement. The agency will develop a review committee with representatives from each of these groups to provide both opinions on the effectiveness of OCP as well as suggestions for its improvement. This concept has already been discussed with each of the schools involved and will be implemented when OCP is initiated.

Analysis: The evaluation plan presented by the agency includes several ways to measure success of the planned program while at the same time providing ways to correct potential problems and get input from the various constituencies involved with the program. Notice that the agency has a "benchmarking" process to measure progress and head off problems for new pro-

grams. Notice also that information on programs is given to the board of directors for its review, thus helping ensure that the volunteer leadership is kept up to date and has opportunities for input on agency progress and successes.

The agency also takes steps to ensure that program staff, even from other areas, are part of the evaluation process, and that evaluation includes opportunities for collection of objective information as well as subjective information. Overall, the evaluation process presented for this new program will probably be seen as comprehensive, extending beyond the agency itself (for example, through involvement of the school committees), and integrated with its existing evaluation process.

Grant Request

Family and Children's Services requests that the Robert A. Ardsley Foundation consider the agency's request for a two-year grant of $100,000 ($50,000 per year) toward the costs (salary, benefits, limited office supplies and equipment) of hiring a Program Coordinator for its school-based Outreach Counseling Program.

Analysis: We have now reached the "point" of the proposal: the grant request. Notice that the actual grant request is only one sentence long. If all of the other information and materials have already been presented, as they should have been, the grant request need not be any longer. However, if there are special conditions that the agency wants included as part of the request (such as challenge grant conditions, contingencies, etc.) these should be included in this section. Again notice that the time period for payment of the grant is spelled out as are the amounts to be paid each year.

Remember the inverted or upside down pyramid model presented earlier. The Grant Request section is bringing us to the point of the pyramid and should not be long on details or explanations. By now the agency should have presented the needs, who it is and what it does, how it operates and sustains itself, and the specifics of what it is requesting. Thus only the "ask" remains.

The example presented above is designed to illustrate several principles that have been discussed earlier. First, the proposal is part of a process of approaching foundations and corporations. The development of the proposal assumes that the organization, and especially the person or people pre-paring the proposal, have a complete understanding of the needs the organization seeks to serve, the mission of the organization, the current operations, and the planned programs, services, or other needs for which support is being sought. The development of the proposal also assumes that research, including a complete review of any available foundation- or corporate-published information, and "reading between the lines" have been done, and that preliminary contacts have been made with the potential funder whenever possible.

Second, the proposal is an educational tool designed to lead the reader from the "big picture"—the needs your organization is serving or plans to serve—to the conclusion, your organization's specific grant request. In the best sense the proposal should represent a self-contained and logical educational process. The reader—any reader—should come away from reading your proposal with a much better understanding of your organization and its purposes and plans.

Strategy Tip: One way to test out a proposal's effectiveness is to have someone who is not acquainted with your organization or who has minimal knowledge of the organization review the proposal. After reading the proposal, does this individual feel he or she has a much better understanding of your organization? Are the needs your organization serves clearly understood? Does the proposal make a compelling case for better meeting these needs through the planned program, services, or other activities? Are the individual's questions anticipated and answered in the document? Or are there possible questions that are not answered by the proposal? What further information would the person want if he or she was actually making the decision on your request? These are just a few of the areas you should cover with your informal reviewer.

Strategy Tip: When preparing your proposal, strive as much as possible to avoid jargon specific to your organization and its area of interest and service. Remember that the reader (or readers) of the proposal may be a specialist with broad experience in the field your organization serves; but it is at least equally probable that he or she may not have the depth of experience necessary to understand the terms and concepts unique to your area. In particular, family foundations or other small private foundations without staffs are likely to have board members with diverse backgrounds but possibly little knowledge of the special words or phrases that may be common usage in organizations similar to yours. Be particularly careful with scientific, medical, technical, "computerese," and legal terms or with words and phrases that may be interpreted differently based upon one's experience with and understanding of an area or profession. If you think there is a possibility that a key word or phrase may not be understood by a lay reader, either define the word or phrase or use a more common and more widely understood variation to make the point.

Using Attachments: An Overview

You have done your cover letter, cover page, and the proposal itself. Is your proposal package complete? The obvious answer is no. There are many other possible items that could be included, such as additional documents required by the foundation or corporate prospect, materials that could help amplify or support the case made in the proposal, or other materials related to the general need, your organization, and/or your organization's specific request. In my experience some organizations tend to use attachments carelessly or as filler. In these cases there seems to have been little thought given to what should be included and why.

Attachments can generally be placed into three broad categories:

1. required by the funder (even if at times the funder's guidelines don't specify certain documents are required)

2. required by the case for support made in the proposal

3. amplifying or supporting other information in the proposal, but not essential

Before exploring specific possible attachments and why they should—or should not—be used, it is appropriate to give an overview of attachments and their relation to the proposal. Attachments offer an opportunity to expand and amplify your proposal without adding to the length of the proposal. If used properly, they also can provide flexibility by allowing you to make changes in the information given to a particular potential funder. For example, if a potential funder's interests are fairly narrow and only include possible support for one area (such as equipment) of a planned program or project, the program or project budget can be amplified to better show the costs associated with the area most likely to appeal to that potential funder.

Attachments should always be used strategically and should be closely tied to your proposal and the specific purposes for which you are seeking support. Always ask yourself why you are selecting a particular attachment for inclusion; how does this attachment help the case you are trying to make in the proposal? Or, if the information is vital to your case, no matter who the intended audience, should the information be included in the body of the proposal itself?

Example: Some organizations are accredited by one or more groups. One approach to the use of accreditations and accreditation reports might be to include these as attachments. But this might involve the inclusion of lengthy documents, which the proposal reviewer might have to page through to find the parts relevant to your particular request. A better approach might be to list the accreditations held by your organization in the background section and to include brief excerpts of key parts of the accreditation reports relevant to the particular service or program for which your organization is seeking support. It is also appropriate in such cases to indicate, when mentioning or citing such reports, that the full report is available upon the request of the potential funder. As a general rule of thumb, avoid attaching lengthy documents unless the potential funder has specifically asked for them.

Attachments also provide potential funders with answers to some of the key questions they will have when reviewing your proposal package. Some of the attachments provide evidence from a source external to your organization, such as the Internal Revenue Service, in the case of your organization's 501(c)(3) letter, or the audit firm that conducted your organization's financial audit. Funders need or want this information to confirm you are, in fact, a 501(c)(3) organization and that your finances are in order. Other attachments provide evidence from the organization itself that it is functioning in a responsible and effective manner. For example, including a summary of your organization's long-range plan says to the potential funder that the organization does, in fact, plan for its future. Other attachments, such as the program or project budget, provide more details and information on the specific request being made to the potential funder.

Some people prefer or recommend that items such as program or project budgets be included in the body of the proposal. I prefer to include the detailed items and explanations as attachments with specific references to the attachments ("Please see Attachment B, Item 2") in the body of the proposal. However, keeping the attachments fairly minimal in number and length can help prevent unnecessary "back and forthing" between the body of the proposal and the particular attachments. Attachments should also be listed in the proposal's table of contents with both the letter or number

> **Avoid attaching lengthy documents unless the potential funder has specifically asked for them.**

designation and content of each attachment, for example:

- Attachment A: Internal Revenue Service 501(c)(3) Letter

- Attachment B: Fiscal Year 1997 Financial Audit

- Attachment C: Project Budget and Detail

Attachments should also be marked in some way to clearly separate them from the body of the proposal. Possible ways to do this include the use of tabs, colored divider sheets, etc. Whatever method you use, you should make it easy to move back and forth between the attachments and the body of the proposal. Avoid overly complicated systems (such as "Please refer to Tab C, Attachment C-4, Section C-4-7, Page 2, Paragraph 14"), which will only frustrate the reviewer as he or she attempts to find information. Keep the number and types of attachments simple to avoid complicated reference schemes.

Attachments should be placed in order of their importance to the potential funder. Those attachments that are clearly required by the potential funder should be placed first. For example, without your organization's 501(c)(3) letter, most foundations and corporations cannot proceed with consideration of your request. The next group of attachments should include the materials that directly support your case, such as the proposed program or project budget and other similar items. The final group of attachments should consist of any materials that are not essential but might be helpful to the potential funder. It is these materials that may be the most "expendable" if you need to keep the number and length of your attachments within reasonable bounds.

Finally, no matter what you are considering attaching, think first about how it will specifically help make your case. Attaching large quantities of materials, no matter what their content, may cause the reviewer to think "here is an organization that cannot say what it needs to say in a concise and clear way. It seems to want to justify everything and throw paper at me, thus wasting my time,

rather than getting to the point." Are the materials you are including relevant? Do they specifically address and help support the case? Or are they merely filler, such as ten-year old press clippings or standardized letters of endorsement from public officials (see also below)?

Attachments: Specifics

Following are the specific materials and items that you should either always attach or consider using as attachments.

The 501(c)(3) Letter

The first attachment should always be your organization's Internal Revenue Service Letter of Determination of Tax-Exempt Status—its 501(c)(3) letter. Most foundations and corporations require that this letter be included with your proposal, since they can only fund or usually only fund 501(c)(3) organizations. Some foundations and corporations do not clearly state this letter should be attached, but it is always best to do so. Even if your organization is applying to a foundation or corporation where it has recently received funding, it is wise to include the letter. Files can get lost, staff members can change, and other things can happen, so you should not assume the 501(c)(3) is still on file with the past funder.

If your organization has received a letter from the Internal Revenue Service reviewing and re-confirming its 501(c)(3) status, this should also be included with your proposal attachments. Review letters can be particularly important to the potential funder when your organization has an older 501(c)(3) letter (such as one dating back 20 or 30 years). The "no change of status" statement helps confirm to the potential funder that your organization is still, or at least was at the time of the review, a 501(c)(3) organization.

> **No matter what you are considering attaching, think first about how it will specifically help make your case.**

Some organizations fall under an "umbrella" 501(c)(3) designation. That is, the parent or larger group with which they are affiliated holds the actual 501(c)(3) status and the affiliation covers all of the organizations with this affiliation. Examples might include local chapters of national organizations as well as some religious groups where the national church organization's 501(c)(3) covers all of the associated agencies and organizations. In such cases, it is important to point out to the potential funder the "source" of your 501(c)(3) status and, if possible, to include a copy of the Letter of Determination from the parent organization or agency.

State Registration Documents

Increasingly, as has been pointed out, states have or are establishing their own individual requirements for the registration of nonprofit organizations headquartered or even operating within their borders. It is important to understand that these registration requirements are generally entirely separate from the Internal Revenue Service requirements. Be sure that your organization is in full compliance with any applicable state registration provisions both in states where your organization is located and in states where it does business (particularly fund raising). While some states do not have any such requirements, many do. Some states are also enforcing their registration requirements with penalties and fines for noncompliance.

While most foundations and corporations do not yet require the submission of state registration documents or materials, it is probably a good idea to include at least the letter or form confirming your organization's compliance with the state requirements as part of your proposal package. Inclusion of such materials may at least help alleviate concern on the part of the potential funder that its support may be going to an organization that could be cited by the state for noncompliance and could receive negative publicity for this problem.

Audits

Increasingly, potential funding sources want to see the most recent audit of an organization that is seeking their support. Many funders now require that an audit be part of the proposal package. The general reasoning is usually that an audit performed by a certified public accountant or a reputable audit firm helps provide an objective outside view of the finances and financial responsibility of the organization seeking support. Audit reports include both the financial statements and notes to these statements as well as the auditor's letter certifying the audit was carried out in accordance with generally accepted accounting principles and included the appropriate tests.

A knowledgeable reader can determine much information about an organization from its audit and the accompanying notes. Sources of support, cash flow, reserve and restricted funds, and other facts of the organization's "financial life" are revealed in the audit and by "reading between the lines" of the information. Notes to the audit also can be rich sources of information. The notes may make references to the need for tighter financial controls, major transfers of funds between accounts (such as shifts between reserves and general operating monies) that occurred, loans outstanding, etc. While audits are not perfect and reflect, in part, the information provided by the organization, they can be a vital part of the review process for any potential funder.

Strategy Tip: If the audit indicates a problem in the finances or financial controls of the organization, take the "problem–solution" approach. What types of problems or areas for concern might be cited in an audit report? Be prepared with a workable solution to any financial problems or control issues raised in the audit. It will be particularly helpful if the proposed solution(s) have been reviewed by your auditor or audit firm to ensure that the solution is practical and in general compliance with accounting standards and audit procedures. For example, a recent audit I reviewed indicated that the executive director had been making some loans to employees of the organization. The issue for the auditor was not that the loans had been made. Rather, it was that there was not an adequate system of controls in place to ensure loans were made with appropriate approvals and with assurances that they would be documented and repaid with interest. The board of directors of the organization reviewed the audit and put in place a system to ensure the controls, including a sign-off process by the board chair or the treasurer of the board, would be in place and appropriate documentation would occur.

Strategy Tip: One of the problems with audit reports is that few people pay attention to them, much less know how to read them. Be sure that anyone who will be involved in meeting with a potential funder is very familiar with the audit report and what the figures and statements mean. In my role as a foundation officer I estimate I would spend about 20 percent to 30 percent of my questioning time asking about information presented in the audit of organizations seeking support from our foundation. I sometimes found it embarrassing to watch people I was meeting with struggle to answer my questions about the organization's finances and particularly about the information presented in the audit. All too often, my questions would be answered with other questions from those I was meeting with, such as "I wonder why the audit does show that transfer of $150,000 from the reserve fund to the general operating fund." or "Loans? Do we make loans? I didn't know that myself." or "How do you interpret those numbers?"

There are some measures you can take to help ensure that those presenting to the potential funders are better able to answer specific questions about the fiscal and other information presented

in the audit. One approach is to have key board members and staff sit down with the auditors and completely review the audit, including the possible interpretations and implications of the numbers and comments in the audit report. One place this might occur is at a board meeting or the annual meeting of the organization. However, it might also be appropriate for the key board and staff officers to spend more time with the auditors in a somewhat smaller and less formal meeting to review the audit report completely. If this meeting has as its purposes reviewing the audit, ensuring that preparations are in place to help the next audit proceed smoothly, addressing concerns raised by the audit, *and* preparing for potential questions funders might ask when they review the audit, then the review process can give individuals within the organization a more in-depth understanding of what the audit is saying.

Another approach to this issue is to have yourself or another key staff member become the resident "expert" on reading and understanding audits, especially in terms of the possible implications to potential funders of the information presented. There are several ways to do this, including meeting with the auditor to get answers to key questions or concerns that might be raised based on the report information, or taking a course, such as one I took entitled "Reading Financial Information for Non-Financial Managers." The important point is to be sure that someone in your organization can both read and interpret the financial information presented in the audit reports.

What if your organization does not have an audit? Some potential funders still are willing to accept year-end financial statements instead of a full audit, especially for smaller organizations. But you might refer back to the strategy tip in Chapter 3 for suggestions about how to get your organization's first audit contributed as a service. Given current trends, it is probably good advice for every organization to strive toward having yearly audits carried out, no matter what its size or budget.

Annual Report

Does your organization have a published annual report? A good annual report can help provide an excellent overview of your agency, including its purposes, mission, current services and programs, major donors, board and staff, and, if audit information is included, its finances. Comprehensive annual reports can provide much of the information discussed here as separate attachments, except for materials related to the specific planned program or project for which your organization is seeking support. Review the contents of your organization's annual report carefully to determine how much of the information it contains will help meet the information needs of the potential funder. If the annual report contains the full audit report, for example, it is probably not necessary to attach the actual audit. But if the annual report contains only a summary, it is best to include the audit.

Project or Program Budget

The detailed project or program budget is an essential attachment unless your organization is requesting operating support. In the latter case, it is appropriate to include the current operating budget for the organization or the projected operating budget for which the grant is being requested. In all other cases the program or project budget should be included as an attachment. "Program" or "project," as used here, should be taken in their broadest terms to mean anything from a major capital campaign to a very specific need, such as a new staff member or a piece of equipment.

Remember that the program or project budget can be individually tailored to reflect the level of detail you wish presented to the foundation or corporation. For example, if your organization is undertaking a major capital campaign for construction or renovation of a building, but you are only seeking support for a specific component (such as computer equipment) from a particular funder, the best approach might be to present an outline of the overall budget for the project but a detailed listing of the computer equipment needs and projected costs. For another potential funder the entire project budget might be presented in detail if your organization is seeking a grant toward the total projected costs rather than only a particular part of those costs.

The project or program budget should also include both explanations of how the costs were arrived at (such as "two social workers at $26,700 per year base salary each plus 15 percent each for benefits") as well as the administrative overhead costs.

Strategy Tip: "Administrative overhead" or "indirect costs" are two terms used to describe the expenses not directly associated with and attributable to a program, project, or area at an organization, but which may still be incurred by the organization as a result of that program, project, or area. If that definition sounds a little murky, some examples might help clarify what is meant by these terms. Space in the organization's offices and equipment already owned by the organization might be used by a new program or a project. Also the program or project uses electricity and possibly other utilities. In some cases organizations actually calculate costs for such items and include the costs in the direct expenses for that program or project. Costs for space use might be established based on the square footage of the office space used for the program or project and the total cost of the organization's office space, for example. But other organizations prefer to include space, equipment, utilities costs, and other expenses in a single figure, which is called "administrative overhead" or "indirect expenses." Other items that might be included in this expense figure might include such things as the processing of paperwork associated with the program or project by the business or finance office, personnel office involvement with the program or project, meetings with and oversight by senior staff who are not directly involved in running the program or project, etc.

The overall idea of using an administrative overhead or indirect costs figure is to account for these indirect expenses without calculating every single expense—some of which might, in fact, be very difficult to actually project or tie back to the program or project. For example, how can the actual costs of electricity be calculated for a program housed in the organization's offices? Should a calculation be based upon the number of staff who are part of the program, the square footage of the office space used by the program, or the number of electrically operated items used by the program? As you can see, trying to figure every cost exactly may often be impossible.

Administrative overhead or indirect costs become a convenient way to try to account for such costs in a program or project budget. The usual method is to total the direct expenses for an actual or planned program or project and to apply a "reasonable" percentage to the total direct expenses to arrive at the administrative overhead or indirect costs figure. This figure is then added to the total direct expenses to give the total costs. But what is a "reasonable" percentage? The answer to this question can vary considerably depending upon the type and size of your institution, the nature of the program or project, and many other factors. The best rule of thumb is to use a figure of 10 percent to 15 percent for your administrative overhead or indirect costs calculations if you have no other basis for arriving at a figure. Some organizations, such as universities, have used administrative overhead or indirect costs percentages as high as 90 percent to 100 percent, particularly for major research projects. Using a 100 percent figure for administrative overhead and applying it to the direct costs of a program or project, which is projected to have direct costs of $50,000, would result in a total projected budget of $100,000! These levels of indirect costs are not as widely accepted as they once were, in part due to some widely publicized misuses of administrative overhead funds.

Let us take a more typical example to show how the calculation of administrative overhead or indirect costs can be shown. In Exhibit 12–2 a total direct cost figure for a project is shown (the budget details are not presented for this example, but would normally be included) and then the administrative overhead costs are calculated to arrive at the total projected costs.

A frequent question, when I have reviewed administrative overhead and indirect cost issues in seminars, is, "Should we present these costs to foundations and corporations when we are seeking support?" Some foundations and corporations have specific, stated policies about whether or not they will fund indirect costs or administrative overhead and, if they do provide funding, up to what level. For example, some foundations and corporations may fund up to only 10 percent of your total direct costs for administrative overhead or indirect costs. Other foundations and corporations have no stated polices. If there is not a stated policy, the best advice is to ask how they will respond to a budget that includes these costs. If you are not able to ask or to get an answer, you should include these costs as part of your program or project budget and let the potential funder make the decision on how it will respond. If you do include a calculation and a figure for administrative overhead or indirect costs, you should be ready to provide some justification of the factors or other types of costs included in that calculation. In most cases, I believe, there is justification for including some figure for these costs.

Exhibit 12–2 Administrative Overhead Calculation

Total Direct Costs	$147,300.00
Administrative Overhead (@ 12%)	$17,676.00
Total Project Budget	$164,976.00

Timelines

Projects and programs occur over time. One way to demonstrate how carefully your organization has planned for the implementation of a new project or program is to attach to your proposal a clear timeline showing the major events that need to take place and the approximate time points when these events will happen. What are examples of such events? The phasing in of new staff, evaluation points, the implementation of new systems, public relations/media efforts, future fund raising, and completion of construction are examples of some of the events that can be placed in a simple grid to show when these are expected to occur. Some timelines are presented on a monthly basis while others may be presented using quarterly checkpoints or other intervals. The easiest approach is to use a simple grid with the time periods across the top and the major events listed down the side.

Developing a timeline can help your organization plot out the essential steps and the key components of your project or program. The timeline, once completed, can also serve as a means of comparing actual progress to the planned progress of events. For the funder, the timeline helps define key checkpoints for its review and reporting progress. Some foundations and corporations, for example, require not only final reports but also interim reports on progress to date, the achievement of specific objectives as they were defined in the proposal, etc. In some cases more sophisticated grants may actually have grant payments tied to these progress reports, meaning that your organization may not receive the next payment on its grant until appropriate progress is shown through your report or through a review process. Project or program timelines may also be part of your organization's long-range plan.

General Long-Range Plan

Foundations and corporations, in increasing numbers, are requiring that an organization applying for funding provide them with its long-range plan or at least clearly demonstrate that there is a plan or planning process in place. Funders are often very concerned if the organization seeking sup-

port has no evidence of a planning component; such organizations are seen as riskier investments when compared to those organizations that do have plans. Does the organization merely plan to "do more of the same" in the future? Or does it tend to respond to whatever seems to be the latest concern or need without carefully thinking through the long-term implications of adding a new program or service? Or is the organization just operating on a day-to-day basis without any thought for the future? If your organization has a long-range plan, consider attaching the plan (if it is not too lengthy), a summary of the plan, or at least the major elements of the plan—such as key goals and objectives—to your proposal.

Strategy Tip: What if your organization does not have a plan? Remember our earlier example of possible approaches to take when your organization does not have a formal audit? Your organization might consider using a similar approach to begin the strategic planning process. However, unlike our earlier example where the strategy was to seek the donation of services for the first audit, your organization may have to obtain funding to pay for a strategic planning workshop facilitated by an outside expert. One possible exception to this might be asking a corporation that has a strategic planning person on staff to contribute his or her services to conduct the workshop. Be sure the individual selected is very familiar with the nonprofit sector and its differences from the corporate sector; the principles and techniques for strategic planning in the nonprofit sector can differ considerably from those in some areas of corporations, such as product planning.

Who might provide funding for a strategic planning workshop? The best possible sources include past or current funders, such as foundations, corporations, or even individuals. The basic approach when seeking support for a strategic planning process is to explain the importance of having a plan for both the future directions of the organization and for seeking additional funding from corporations and foundations. Those who have already invested in your organization should be able to see the considerable value in developing a long-range plan both in terms of the practical aspects, such as funding, and the longer-term benefits for the organization.

An effectively run one- or two-day workshop involving board members and staff can be a good starting point for your organization's planning process. The outcomes of the workshop should include an outline of a strategic plan as well as specific follow-up measures, action steps, responsibility assignments, and timelines.

Fund-Raising Plan Details

If the body of the proposal does not include a detailed fund-raising plan for the program or project for which you are seeking support, or if you want to expand on the plan presented in the proposal, you may consider attaching a more detailed plan. This might include timelines, prospects, strategies for approaching individuals for support, etc. Alternately, you might consider attaching a more detailed explanation of how long-term funding will be generated for ongoing support of the program or project. This might include detailed projections, explanations, and timelines for transitioning the project or program from corporate and foundation support to other sources, such as fees for service, funds from ongoing fund-raising efforts, United Way monies, etc.

Board List with Affiliations

If the materials on your organization do not include its board members with their professional affiliations, it is always a good idea to include the list as an attachment. Some organizations have a one- or two-paragraph listing of each board member's professional and volunteer affiliations as well as other brief background information, such as educational credentials (especially where these are relevant to the purposes of your organization), honors, or other items.

In Chapter 6 a brief discussion on foundations' uses of conflict of interest statements pointed out that some foundations have each board member fill out a conflict of interest statement listing his or her other nonprofit affiliations on a yearly basis. One way to collect information on the professional and volunteer affiliations of your organization's board members is to develop a brief form, which each board member fills out once a year and which new board members complete when they are appointed or elected to the board. Types of information you should collect are:

- Full name

- Title, employer, and nature of employer's business

- Home and office addresses, phone numbers, e-mail addresses, and fax numbers along with preference of where and how mail should be sent

- Brief biographical information

- Educational information (colleges attended, degrees, etc.)

- Other professional affiliations (association memberships, etc.)

- Volunteer involvements (other nonprofit boards, committees, and memberships)

- Hobbies, special skills, and expertise

- Churches or religious affiliations

- Club memberships

- Honors and awards

- Name and background information similar to above for spouse or significant other

- Names and ages of children

- Other significant information

All of this information can be very useful for fund raising and organizational development purposes as well as for such areas as public relations, internal newsletters, or other purposes.

Fact Sheet

Many organizations develop a one-page (usually printed on both sides) fact sheet (see also the earlier references to fact sheets in the discussion of proposal materials). The fact sheet includes brief sections on the mission, history, current services and programs, finances (including sources of support), staffing, and other key information on the organization as well as a contact person for additional information about the organization. Attaching a fact sheet can provide the reviewer with a quick summary of your organization. An additional advantage of including a fact sheet is that it can be duplicated and included in the materials going to the grant decision makers, enabling them to get a quick overview of your organization.

Other Information Relevant to the Project or Program

Consider attaching other important materials that are related to the project or program for which you are seeking support. Examples include short biographies of staff members who will be involved with the project or program, position descriptions for new staff positions associated with the project or program, technical information related to it, or other relevant materials. These types of attachments can help build your organization's case that it has done its homework when preparing its plans.

Letters of Support

Some organizations include with their proposals letters of support for either the entire organization or for the particular project or program for which they are seeking funding. While the inclu-

sion of such letters might be useful, there are some cautions associated with this practice. Letters of support from public officials, such as the mayor of your city or town, will probably not carry much weight in the funder's decision-making process, unless the public official is directly familiar with your organization. All too often such letters are prepared by aides or others with no real knowledge of the organization and in response to a request from the organization itself. The public official signing the letter may know little or nothing about your organization.

Letters of support from other major funders, such as United Ways, foundations, or corporations are usually not helpful if the letters are merely a general endorsement of your organization and its work. Many funders are reluctant to commit themselves in writing to endorsing particular organizations unless there has been a close and long-term relationship between the funding source and the organization. However, you should be aware that in some areas the endorsement of the United Way or other agencies might be required if your organization seeks to obtain funding for certain purposes, such as a major capital campaign. If this is the case, be sure to attach the endorsement letter from the particular agency to your proposal.

Letters from those served by your organization can sometimes make a powerful statement about its effectiveness and the impact your organization has on individuals' lives. A limited number of such letters can help support your case, but again remember that the decision makers will often see their final decisions as based on an objective review of your organization and its request, rather than on an emotional response.

If your organization's planned program or project involves other agencies, especially where there is to be a cooperative venture or your organizations are jointly seeking funding, it is of critical importance to attach letters of agreement between or among your respective agencies. These letters should clearly spell out which organization is responsible for what, which organization will serve as the fiscal agent for any grants, how the joint project will be overseen, how disputes or disagreements will be settled, the time period of the agreement, and any other related matters. Such letters or detailed agreements should be jointly signed by appropriate staff and board leadership of each organization.

And Some Other Considerations

If your organization has something other than the items listed above or something unusual to attach or include with the proposal package, the best advice is to call the potential funding source and ask if they would like to see or have that particular item. For example, some organizations have promotional or fund-raising videotapes. Rather than assume that a videotape is something the foundation or corporation would like to see, call the potential funding source and ask if they want it along with your proposal. Some foundations and corporations welcome such items, while others prefer not to receive them. This advice also applies to any lengthy publications, specialized fund-raising materials, or other items that may—or may not—help make your case. It is best not to include items that you or your organization feel will draw attention to its uniqueness, but which the potential funder may only consider an annoyance or inappropriate. Examples of such items are awards received by the organization (rather than just a listing of the awards), personal appeals to the potential funders from clients of the organization, petitions addressed to the funder, or other approaches that may be seen as mere gimmicks.

Overall, attachments should be selected carefully to help amplify the information in your proposal as well as to help build your case for support. Only the most essential attachments should be included. Do not include materials just to add to the length of the proposal package. The emphasis should be on amplifying key information and better educating the reader.

Appealing and Appalling Proposals

This somewhat lengthy chapter has explored the dimensions of the proposal process. Your proposal package should reflect all of the steps you have taken prior to the development of the proposal as well as your overall strategies for seeking support and the specific strategies for each prospec-

tive funder. Perhaps the best way to summarize this entire chapter is to present to you a brief piece, which I developed several years ago, entitled "Appealing and Appalling Proposals."

Appealing Proposals:

- speak to the real needs of the requesting organization

- speak to the interests of the potential funder

- are based on a complete review of the funder's printed and published materials, if any

- are based on a review of grants made by the funder

- are based on a review of other available materials and information about the funder

- are the result of specific strategies focused on each funder

- include a request for funds appropriate to the plans of the organization

- request funds at a level and over a time period appropriate to the grant-making capabilities of the funder

- demonstrate how a grant will make a difference in the effectiveness of the organization in meeting the needs of those it serves

- show the uniqueness of the organization

- have been preceded by contact with the staff of the foundation and/or an inquiry letter, when possible

- are submitted in accordance with the funder's decision-making schedule

- are brief (10 pages maximum with 4 to 5 pages ideal, excluding attachments)

- move from the general (overview of the needs served by the organization and what it does) to the specific (grant request)

- explain the importance of the project/program for which support is requested

- include discussion of how the project/program will be supported when the funding period ends

- include a listing of other funds received with sources, and fund-raising strategies

- include percentages for sources of income and expenses

- include a means of evaluating the success of the program/project and methods of informing others in the field of the results of the program/project, if appropriate

- include long-range plans and budget projections

- include as attachments the 501(c)(3), a one- to two-page fact sheet, a list of board members with affiliations, the current operating budget, the project/program budget, an audit or year-end fiscal statement for the most recent available year, and other appropriate supporting material

- include a cover letter, which can stand alone as an explanation of the organization and the request and which speaks directly to the foundation's interests

- are followed by a call to the funder to see if the request was received, answer questions, and arrange for a meeting, if possible

- are also followed by additional contacts updating the potential funder on progress, other grants received, etc.

- include a strategy to seek the funder's advice and assistance in locating other funding sources, especially if the request is declined by the funder

- are submitted with the knowledge of key board members as well as key staff

Appalling Proposals:

- assume all funders operate in the same way

- are submitted without regard to the potential funder's interests, past grants, and grant-making abilities

- are based on a crisis or an unplanned-for need

- request support for something that is not part of an overall organizational plan

- conceal vital information about the organization

- Include unrealistic project/program budgets or budgets that include inappropriate items

- present no plans for ongoing support of the project/program

- fail to state the need for the project/program and how funding will make a difference

- show no understanding of what other organizations are doing that is similar

- use a shotgun approach of mailing out several proposals to any source that might be interested

- have no follow-up

- say nothing about other requests being submitted or fund-raising strategies

- have a standard cursory cover letter

- include budgets in the body of the proposal

- include large quantities of unorganized information about the organization

- are lengthy

- are submitted by a junior-level staff member

- include no evaluation or dissemination plans

- have not been preceded by contact with the funding source

- assume the potential funder knows about the organization

- fail to reflect any past contacts with the funder, especially past grants received

- show no creative thinking about ways to leverage dollars

- reflect an appalling organization

Chapter 13

The Proposal: After It's Been Sent

There is a common mistake most people and organizations make after a proposal has been sent to a foundation or corporation: they do nothing but wait. Why is this approach a mistake? Waiting for the foundation or corporation to respond denies the emphasis on creating and maintaining a dialogue with the potential funder. Waiting says "we've done our part; now it is up to you." Even beyond that, waiting assumes that the foundation or corporation has received the proposal, that the potential funding source has everything it needs, and that the next step is a review, followed by a decision.

Below are listed several steps that can be taken to help ensure that the negotiated partnership with the potential funder remains central to your pur-

> **Waiting for the foundation to respond denies the emphasis on creating and maintaining a dialogue with the potential funder.**

poses. Each of these steps should be taken, wherever possible, to help establish or maintain and enhance the negotiated partnership. By taking these steps, you and your organization are doing as much as possible to ensure the success of your proposal to that particular source.

Strategy Tip: When sending your proposal, be sure that the total package is presented in a neat and orderly manner. All items should be in the order in which they are to be presented. But avoid the expense of fancy binders or other expensive methods of keeping the materials together; the chances are fairly good that your proposal will be separated into various parts soon after it is received. Send the proposal using a carrier that is reliable. If there is a due date, use a means of sending the proposal that will ensure it arrives on time. It is best to use a method of sending the proposal that enables easy tracking or includes a return receipt to the sender.

Calls

Once you have sent your proposal, allow about two weeks to pass. After this period, call the foundation or corporation and do the following:

- Confirm that the proposal was received.

- If you are not already speaking with the appropriate program staff person or do not know who it is, find out to whom, on the funder's staff, the proposal has been assigned (be sure to get the correct spelling and title for that person).

- Ask to speak with that person, if possible.

- Offer to send any additional information, if it is needed.

- Establish yourself or whomever is appropriate (and specified in the proposal) as the contact person, giving the specific phone number or extension of the individual.

- Offer to meet (or to meet again) to review your organization's request and the specifics in the proposal.

- If appropriate, invite the staff member to visit your agency, if this has not already occurred.

- If you are not already aware of the next date when the foundation or corporate decision makers will meet, ask when this meeting will be held.

- If there is any other information that you need about the potential funder, ask the appropriate questions on this call—but be sure you have done your homework first.

- Thank the individual for consideration of your proposal.

As is shown above, this phone call can serve a variety of purposes, all of which can be accomplished in a relatively brief time period. The purposes of this call include information collection as well as establishing and maintaining the more personal relationship leading to a true negotiated partnership.

Meetings

Because meetings were covered extensively in Chapter 11, we will not go into great detail about meeting strategies and techniques. Remember,

however, that meetings held with potential funders when they have received and reviewed your proposal are different and more focused than when your meeting occurs prior to submitting a proposal. You will probably not be able to use the "shopping list" approach when the proposal is already in the hands of the potential funder, unless that source is clearly not interested in the proposal but still seems open to considering support for other parts of your organization, or at least appears interested in the organization itself.

Strategy Tip: An "on-site" visit by foundation or corporate staff members and/or board members can play a major role in the potential funder's decision. Site visits by foundations and corporations are of particular value when there is something specific to see, such as active programs or services, special facilities, etc. But visiting a suite of offices, if that is all you have to show, has little or no value to most potential funders who would therefore prefer to meet in their offices. However, even where there is normally not much to see, because of the nature of the organization, there may be special opportunities to have a potential funder learn more about your organization by attending a special event, a workshop, or other activity conducted by the organization. If such activities are taking place during the period when your grant request is under consideration, and if your organization feels it is appropriate, invite potential funders to attend these activities. This is especially true when the activities are related to your funding request. For example, an organization I was working with as a consultant had, as its primary purpose, the carrying out of educational workshops. Because of the specialized nature of these workshops, it was often difficult to explain in detail the methods used and the materials covered. When the organization approached potential funders for support of these workshops, staff of the foundation or corporation would be invited to attend the next workshop. Some did attend, which considerably improved the success rate with grant makers.

If you are having a potential funder visit you "on-site," prepare carefully for the visit. If possible, a board member of your organization should act as a cohost for the visit. As with any meeting with potential funders, participating board members and senior staff should be thoroughly briefed on the purposes of the request and the interests of the foundation or corporation prior to the visit. Any members of your organization's staff who will meet the guest should be alerted to the possible time of the visit and should be briefed with appropriate background information on the request and the potential funder. All staff should be notified in advance about the visit and its importance for your organization.

If the foundation or corporate guest wants to observe services being delivered or your organization's programs "in action," be willing to cooperate, but always be mindful of the rights to privacy of those that you serve. For example, if your agency provides family counseling services, it would not be appropriate for a potential funder (or anyone else) to observe a family counseling session without the express permission of those involved. If observations of services or programs are to take place, always introduce your guest and have staff and others involved in the program introduce themselves to him or her. Explain what is being observed (such as the treatment therapies being used), if it is not obvious, and the reasons for this particular approach. Always be willing to have staff answer questions and, wherever possible, involve them in the explanations of what is occurring.

However, there is one caution that should always be kept in mind when a potential funder is visiting your organization: avoid "staging" events, activities, or other things solely to impress the potential funder. Most corporate and foundation staff will see through the artificiality of such activities and some may even develop a negative opinion of your organization and its fund-raising ef-

forts. The example below shows how staging can work against your organization and its grant-seeking efforts.

Example: A small museum was seeking a major grant from our foundation for the construction of new exhibits. The museum had an excellent reputation for its educational programs with area school children and was frequently visited on weekdays by classes of public and private school students. I was assigned to review the museum's proposal. Because I was not already familiar with the museum and also wanted to see some of the newly constructed exhibits, which were similar to those we were being asked to fund, I called the museum's director to arrange for a site visit.

On the day of my visit I arrived at the front door of the museum, only to find several teachers and their students waiting by the front entrance. They said the door was locked, which it was; some were angry because they had expressly come from their schools for a visit during class times. The posted hours indicated the museum should be open, but it was not. After knocking on the door without results, I went around to the back of the museum and found another entrance. After several rings on the doorbell, a staff member opened the door. The conversation went something like this:

"Yes?"

"I'm Gene Scanlan with the Chicago Community Trust. I have a meeting with Dr. Jones."

"Let me check; I'll be right back." (After waiting a few minutes) "OK, he's expecting you; come in."

"I tried the front door; it was locked, even though the signs say you're open today."

"Yes. We closed the museum for your visit."

I was astonished that the museum had closed just for my visit. I did not feel honored or important because they had closed the museum for me. Rather, I was upset that the museum would do this and leave some of their regular visitors literally out in the cold, just so they could give me the "red carpet treatment."

After being introduced to several staff members and a board member, the director, the development director, and the board member took me on a detailed tour of the museum and its exhibits.

At the completion of the tour, we moved to the main floor of the museum, where a small table had been set for lunch with key museum staff and the board member. The lunch was catered with a waiter, wine, and an obviously expensive meal. It was clear to me that the museum was taking every possible measure to impress me; but they were doing it in all the wrong ways.

As I sat there with my lunch, I couldn't help but think of the school children and their teachers who were probably either still outside the door or who had left in frustration. During the conversation with the museum staff and the board member, I said that all of this special treatment was not necessary and expressed my opinion that the museum should have been kept open. I saw no reason for closing it or for having a catered lunch. When I left the museum, there were still classes waiting outside. I was greeted with several angry stares and probably unspoken comments such as: "Why is HE so important that they make us wait outside? Don't we count for anything?" Several people did ask me why the museum was closed and when it would reopen, to which my only reply was "Soon, I hope."

Overall, the museum took the wrong approach to my visit. Rather than allowing me to see how some of their most important "customers"—the students—interacted with the unique exhibits in the museum, they decided to shut the doors and try and give me a false sense of importance. In doing so, they managed to offend their own customers, and to offend me, while at the same time preventing me from seeing what I really needed to see—the museum in use. My opinion of the museum and the attitudes of its staff and board was somewhat lower after my visit.

The message of the above example is to treat the potential funder as you would any guest visiting your organization. Allow him or her to see the organization and what it is really like in its day-to-day operations. Don't be afraid to show both the strengths and areas that need improvement. Sometimes, for example, the best case your organization can make for a capital campaign for expansion of your existing program space is to show the potential funder how crowded your present facilities are.

The example below highlights what can happen, at times by chance, when a visit by a potential funder is organized as it should be.

Example: An inner city private high school had struggled to stay open, but was beginning a large-scale campaign to raise private funds for many needs. The heart of the school's story was that 100 percent of the children graduating from the school went on to college, while other children from their same neighborhoods were ending up in gangs, using drugs, and, often, in jail.

A relatively small family foundation associated with a nearby company had provided the school with a mid-level grant. When the grant was made, the foundation head told the school that they could be approached one more time for a major grant. After considerable discussion by school staff, a request was made that the foundation make a grant of $500,000 to form the basis for an endowed scholarship fund, since many of the students could barely afford the $1,000 per year tuition costs, and others could not attend due to the lack of funds. Such a grant, while it would be a major commitment beyond that usually made by this particular foundation, would meet the foundation's objective of not having to be reapproached for a grant for some time. At the same time, the establishment of an endowed scholarship fund would meet a very real need of the school.

The foundation had not visited the school prior to making its first grant. Foundation leadership was invited to attend the school during a regular school day. As part of their visit, they were given the opportunity to sit in classes, speak with students, and have a tour of the building. They came away from the class sessions very impressed with the high caliber of the instruction and the eagerness of the students to learn and succeed. During the tour of the building, they noticed that the structure and interior of the aging facility were in need of major repairs. The staff of the school pointed out that these needs were also part of their fund-raising efforts, but they felt the educational priorities should come first. As the tour wrapped up, one of the foundation members remarked, "What good will scholarships be if the building falls down on the students?"

The unexpected result was a $1 million grant from the foundation—its largest ever. Of this amount, $500,000 was to be used for the establishment of the endowed scholarship fund and the remaining $500,000 for repair of the building. This visit certainly proved worthwhile.

Updates and Progress

Another way to build and maintain your relationship with a potential funder, once you have submitted your proposal and while it is still under consideration, is to update your contact on your organization's progress, particularly as it relates to the program or project for which you are seeking support. It is important not to overwhelm the individual with information and materials, but rather to focus on letting him or her know the key developments in your progress toward your program, project, or service objectives. When there is progress in major areas, such as the following, you should communicate to those potential funders where your requests are pending:

- hiring of staff for the program or project

- completion or preparation of other major components of the program or project, such as cost estimates and construction plans for a new building, or acquisition of new space for the program or project

- receiving of approvals, certifications, or accreditations, especially where these are required for proceeding on a program or project

- major recognition for your organization and its achievements

- receiving of other grants for support of the program or project

- any other critical information that will help make your organization's case for support.

One of the primary reasons for communicating such information to each of your potential funders, aside from the relationship-building as-

pects, is to show progress and give a sense of momentum. You want to clearly demonstrate that your organization is continuing to move toward its objective, and is not just waiting for the response of each of its possible funders. Also, in many cases when you submit your proposal not all of the key elements may be in place. It therefore becomes very important to show that these other elements are being worked on or completed.

When presenting my seminars, I am frequently asked about the issue of informing a potential funder where a request is pending about other funding received for the same program or project. The questions usually focus on the need to inform foundations and corporations, where requests are pending, of grants received for the same program or project, and on the possible responses of potential funders to such information. I believe that:

- Your organization is ethically obligated to inform potential funders, where requests are pending, of other funds received for the same project or program.

- Informing potential funders of funds received will usually help strengthen your organization's case and often help generate other grants from additional sources.

As was pointed out earlier, funders frequently talk with each other about specific requests they have received. If your proposal lists other funders you are approaching for support, as it should, it is possible at least some of these other funders will be contacted about your request. It is also possible that funders where your request is still pending will know about grants received from other sources for your program or project. So this is only one reason to inform the prospective funder about positive decisions by other funders.

I also think it is good ethics to be open and honest. Telling foundations or corporations that you have received partial or even total funding for a program or project they are considering also says your organization wants to ensure they know this important information and have it available for their own decision making. Telling them lets them know how much you still need to achieve your funding objective for the program or project.

Let's look at a "worst case" example ("worst" only in terms of your final possible action). Your organization is seeking a grant of $50,000 for a new program. You apply to four potential funders, all with different decision dates. One funder turns you down, but shortly afterward a second funder makes a grant of the full $50,000 needed for the program. What should you do about the remaining two potential funders where the request is still pending? The best advice is to immediately contact each and inform them that your organization has received full funding and that you would like to withdraw your proposal from further consideration. Also inform each that you are doing the same thing with other places the request was pending. Withdrawing your proposal under such circumstances is the "honorable" thing to do. It again shows that your organization has ethical standards and wants to be open.

You should also use this call, as with all contacts, to maintain and build the relationship with the potential funder. Explore with that person if there are other areas that the foundation or corporation might be interested in considering for support. If such is the case, offer to meet with the individual to further explore these possibilities. Or if the planned program or project could legitimately use additional support or may need funding for a second year, explore these possibilities with your contact. Always, no matter what else happens, thank the person for the foundation's or the corporation's consideration of your request and indicate you are looking forward to working with him or her on future projects, if this is a real possibility.

How can telling a foundation or corporation that you have received partial support toward a program or project help strengthen your case with that potential source and possibly encourage others to decide positively? As was discussed earlier, one of the characteristics of many funders is they are not high risk takers. Often, they are reluctant to provide support, especially to organizations that they have not previously supported; they prefer to fund previously supported organizations that they

are already familiar with because, in part, they see a lower risk in doing so.

But learning that another funder has provided partial support for your organization's program or project sends a signal that the funding for this program or project may well achieve the needed levels, and also that another source has taken the first step by providing a grant. Thus the possible risk factors may now be seen as smaller than they were when no one had "stepped up to the plate." By letting those places where your requests are still pending know that your organization has received partial support, you may well be lowering their perceptions of the risks involved and creating a sense of momentum and a belief that the funding effort will indeed succeed.

Strategy Tip: There is a different way to use the term "staging" from how it was used in the museum example above. When used with space technology, the term refers to the various groups of rockets, each of which provides a speed boost that the next rocket unit builds on in order to achieve maximum speed. The basic idea is that each stage takes advantage of the speed and momentum generated by the previous stage; thus the second stage may accelerate from the speed already generated from the first stage, rapidly adding to the overall velocity.

The principle of staging can be used in your proposal process to help build a sense of momentum. Wherever possible, you should seek to approach the most likely source for support of your organization's project or program first. Prioritize your possible foundation and corporate funding sources in terms of each funder's likelihood of funding your particular program or project. Also take into account the potential size of grants that could be made as well as each source's probable decision dates. Based upon your research at the top of your list, for example, might be a foundation that is given a fairly high probability of funding your organization because:

- it has previously provided support

- it makes large grants, compared to some of your other sources

- it will be meeting relatively soon, compared to some other potential funders

Use this foundation as the first "stage" of your fund-raising process, since you have a higher probability of success with it than with some of your other possible sources, and a grant from this source may well help trigger positive responses from some of the other prospects. Develop a group of prospects for your second and third stages (you may also have more than one source in your first stage). Use this technique to help create a higher probability of success by developing a sense of momentum and lowering the apparent risk for your second- and third-stage funders.

Dealing with Problems

Your organization has several grant requests pending with potential funders, and something goes wrong or causes a delay in the original schedule. What do you do? Let's first look at what could go wrong or cause a delay. In addition to such disasters cited earlier as "We Don't Know Who We Owe," many unexpected things may happen that could affect your organization's planned program or project and your fund-raising efforts. Examples, ranging from relatively minor to major, might include:

- Appropriate approvals (such as licensing, zoning, accreditation, United Way approval, etc.) for the program or project are not received when originally expected.

- New staff are not able to be hired as rapidly as originally anticipated.

- Space is not found or will not be ready on time.

- The costs of some of the items related to the project or program were projected too low.

- Construction planning had to be delayed.

- The program or project had to be given a lower priority due to other developments affecting the organization.

- Your organization receives a major cutback from other funding sources or an unanticipated downturn in revenue.

- A key staff person associated with the project or program or with your organization leaves.

- A public scandal emerges in the media and someone from your organization or your organization itself is involved.

In each of the above examples and in other examples you may think of or actually have experience with, the best approach is the "problem–solution" method discussed earlier. It is important to always inform any potential funder where your organization has a request pending that there is a problem, explain what the nature of the problem is, and describe your organization's planned or probable solution to the problem. In the case of major difficulties or where your organization has not yet come up with a clear solution, the best approach may well be to withdraw your proposal from further consideration until solutions can be achieved. This may mean your planned project or program may have to be placed on hold or canceled entirely until the more important matters can be resolved to everyone's satisfaction.

But, as with all contacts with any foundations or corporations, even dealing with things that have gone wrong or problem situations can help you continue to build your negotiated partnership with potential funders. Even in the worst possible crisis your organization might face, the advice and suggestions of your contacts at potential, present, and past funders may prove very valuable. Seek out their help when you have a major problem or concern. Ask about whether or not your organization's proposal should continue to be processed, and also ask for suggestions about other ideas, resources, and possible ways to deal with the problem.

When dealing with a highly public crisis or negative media attention, the best approach is to be open and honest, as well as to acknowledge real problems when they exist. But even in these cases experience seems to show that coming up with quick and effective solutions that are fair to everyone involved can help lower the degree of attention and negativism. Consider having an organizational crisis management team in place or ready to start seeking solutions, even if everything seems to be proceeding smoothly. Some organizations may even go so far as to work through simulated crises, so at least some preliminary thought has been given to possible constructive approaches and solutions.

If Your Request Is Turned Down

Our earlier examples clearly demonstrate the value of using even the turn down of your proposal as an opportunity to build or create a negotiated partnership. Somewhere around 1895, I estimate, someone drafted the first turn down letter from a foundation or corporate funder—and it is still used. It always seems to read something like this:

> We receive many requests for funding but only have limited funds available for grants. While your organization is certainly worthwhile and serves an important purpose, we are not able to provide you with a grant at this time. We wish your organization success.

As our previous examples showed, when you receive a turn down letter, you should always go back to the foundation or corporation that sent it to see if you can get answers to some specific questions. Try calling to see if it is possible to meet, or at least ask the key questions over the phone.

- What, if they can be revealed, were the specific reasons your organization was turned down? Was it that your organization did not clearly meet the areas of interest and published guidelines of the foundation, or were there other reasons that can be discussed?

- What was the staff member's overall opinion of your approach to the foundation, including your proposal and related materials? How could the approach, proposal, and materials be improved?

- If your organization can reapply to the foundation or corporation for support at some future time, how soon can that happen?

- Does the staff member have other recommendations about possible sources of support for this particular program or project and for your organization?

- Are there other suggestions or advice the individual has that might be helpful?

It is best not to try to argue with the foundation or corporate staff member, especially if you believe you can do so and turn the decision in your favor. Again remember that the person you are speaking with is probably an intermediary between your organization and the real decision makers at the funding source. Also, he or she may not be able to fully reveal all of the reasons behind the turn down of your organization's request. But seeking the help and advice of the individual can build or at least begin to establish the long-term relationship that should be one of your goals.

If the individual staff member does make suggestions or advice about other particular funders who may be interested in your program, project, or organization, keep that individual informed about your results with those particular sources and always keep the door open by asking for further suggestions or ideas. If the individual feels your proposal and/or other materials can be improved and offers specific suggestions, ask if he or she is willing to review your changes to see if they are on target. Always see that person as a resource, not just the source of funds. And always respect any limits he or she sets on the time, help, and all the advice the individual is willing to give you and your organization.

Chapter 14

After the Grant: Maintaining the Relationship

Your organization has successfully obtained the grants it needs for its program or project. The usual inclination, after the grant notification letter has been received, is to proceed with the plans and congratulate everyone involved on the success of the fund-raising effort. And what, according to some funders, all too often gets overlooked? A simple thank-you letter should be sent on behalf of your organization to the funder. Many grant makers have stories about major grants that have been made, but never even acknowledged by the recipient organization. Your organization's letter should acknowledge the grant, including the amount, purposes, and any grant conditions, and should be signed by your board chair as well as the chief staff officer. If the foundation or corporation has included any forms with its grant notification letter or check, these should be completed and returned to the funding source as soon as possible. If you are uncertain about the payment schedule for the grant, be sure to find out what it is from your funder. Be aware that some funders may make pay-

ments in several installments, even within the same year; the individual funder's policy on payments may be tied, in part, to the size of the grant as well as other grant conditions, such as challenge requirements, contingent grants (where your organization is required to do something prior to receiving a payment), or other special arrangements. Be sure your organization understands any such arrangements. And always ask the funder if you are uncertain about any aspect of the grant process.

Even after the grant is made, one of your organization's goals should be the continued development of the partnership with the funding source and your contacts there. All too often and even beyond the simple act of thanking the funder, it is the grantee that takes the relationship "for granted." Now that your organization is a grantee, it has a special obligation to be a true partner with your funder. Your organization's relationship is both a formal one and a financial one. Your organization has obligated itself to follow through as it intended in its proposal and in all of the conversations and other contacts with each funder. There are several key possible points where you can continue to build the partnership with the funder. These are discussed below.

> Even after the grant is made, one of your organization's goals should be the continued development of the partnership with the funding source and your contacts there.

Funder-Required Reports and Information

The first and most clearly established area for your continued relationship centers upon funder-required reports and information. Most funders, especially foundations, require, minimally, the submission of a final "narrative report" and a "fiscal report" at the end of the grant period.

Narrative Reports

Narrative reports may have specific length requirements placed upon them by the funder, or the length may be open ended. The content of the final narrative report may also be specified or outlined or may need to be submitted on a standardized form. Or the desired content may only be generally described. Usually, such narrative reports are intended to be a means for the organization receiving the funding to spell out the success (or failure) of the funded program or project and to directly show, as much as possible, the impact of the funding received from the foundation or corporation on the program or project, on the organization, and on those it serves.

Unless there are clear specifications from the funding source, the best approach is to use your original proposal to the funder, as well as any subsequent modifications in your plans or the program or project itself, as the basic outline for your final report. If there were changes necessary after you received the funding, explain what these were and why they were necessary. You should generally seek to inform the funders of major changes in your program or project prior to their implementation to help ensure the variations from your original plans are understood by the funder and are acceptable. The final narrative report need not repeat all of the information about your organization but should focus on the funded program or project as planned, what actually happened, the results of the evaluation process that was presented in your original proposal, "lessons learned" from this experience, general impact on the organization and on those it serves, and next steps, if any.

If no length is specified by the funder, five to ten pages should probably be sufficient for your narrative report. If you are using elaborate evaluation methods, such as data collection and analysis or even an outside evaluator, summarize the results in your report and include the more detailed information as an attachment at the end of the report. Also attach any other relevant information, keeping in mind that narrative reports and the related materials are usually intended to be fairly brief, even when no length is specified. Be sure to send an appropriate cover letter with the narrative report, always remembering to again thank the funder for the grant. The cover letter should serve to summarize the success of the program or project, and should be signed by the senior staff officer; for major grants, it is usually appropriate for the board chair to also sign the letter.

If you are uncertain about the requirements, content, or deadlines for funder-required final narrative reports, be sure to call your contact and determine what these are. This can be another opportunity to continue to develop the partnership. Wherever possible, meet the funder's deadline for receiving the final narrative report and any other required materials. If you see that your organization is going to be delayed in submitting the final information, let the funder know as soon as possible that the materials will be delayed and when your organization expects to send them. You should indicate the reasons for the delay.

Fiscal Report

In addition to the final narrative report, most funders require a final fiscal report. The purpose of this report is to show how the funds granted were actually used. Some funders have specific forms for collecting this information while others rely on each organization to supply the fiscal information in a manner appropriate to its own accounting and business processes. However, it is important for you and the business operations of your organization to be aware that all grant funding should be able to be tracked in terms of the specific program or project that it was given to support. Be sure your organization's accounting procedures can track income and expenses on a programmatic, project, or restricted fund basis and can even track detail for each program or project down to the line item (equipment, supplies, personnel, etc.) level. This is even more important when grants are made for particular components of a project or program, such as personnel expenses or equipment.

It is important to always refer back to the original budget submitted with your proposal when completing your organization's final fiscal report. If there are substantial variations in the actual expenditures as compared to the projected expenditures, the variations should be explained in the report. As was discussed earlier, it is also best to keep the funder informed when your organization anticipates any substantial variations from the projected budget prior to their actually being incurred, if possible, or, second best, as soon as they are incurred. Some funders have a process of actually approving your budget when a grant is made; this approved budget becomes the basis for the final fiscal report, and, at times, interim fiscal reports, submitted to the funder.

When a grant is received, it is best to contact the funder and ask for a copy of any final narrative report and final fiscal report forms. Having these at the beginning of the grant period can help ensure that the necessary systems and procedures are in place for tracking information and for meeting final report requirements in an appropriate manner. If there are not standardized forms for these reports, ask if is possible to get sample final narrative and fiscal reports. Also be sure that your accounting procedures can meet the funder's requirements for reporting fiscal information.

Interim Reports

At times, funders may also require "interim reports." In some cases these reports may be tied to future payments of the grant, while at other times the reports provide a means of monitoring progress. For example, the first payment of a grant for support of the salary of a new staff member may be contingent upon the hiring of that individual. The foundation or corporation may require the submission of a signed employment agreement or contract before it will release the grant or the first payment on the grant. Interim fiscal reports may be required if there are "challenge conditions" or "matching provisions" to grants. For example, if

payment of a grant is contingent upon the remaining funds for the project or program being raised, the funder may require certification from the organization that those funds are committed or in hand. If a grant is made on a dollar-for-dollar matching basis, the funder may require evidence that the matching dollars have been raised.

Interim reports can also be used to measure progress toward the goals and objectives of the funded project or program. These progress reports may or may not include a fiscal component and may or may not be tied to your organization's evaluation process. If your organization submitted detailed timelines for implementation or for carrying out the project or program, these timelines may well become the means for the funder to measure your organization's progress. Or the funder may only want reports at periodic check points, such as once every three or six months, to ensure that everything is moving smoothly. As with all areas related to the grant, if you are uncertain about what exactly is wanted and when it is required, check with your contact at the funder. And, as with other reporting requirements, if your organization is going to be delayed in submitting the required interim reports, let the funder know as far in advance as possible.

Problems with the Grant Program

Almost no program or project progresses exactly as planned. When funding support from foundations and corporations is involved, it is the responsibility of the grantee organization to decide what are merely minor problems and delays, and what are major problems. Problems can occur between the time the proposal is submitted and the time the grant decision is made, and after the grant is made, many things can occur and unanticipated problems can arise. The best approach is always to let each grantor know as soon as possible and to always present the problem–solution approach to whatever has happened. If there are to be major delays in the implementation or execution of the program or project, let each funder know and be sure to explain how the timeline will be adjusted. If funds will not be expended within the period that was intended, possibly due to delays in implementation or other factors, let the funders know and be ready with some alternative plans for the program or project.

In cases where there are major problems with funded programs, seek the verbal advice of your funding contacts before proceeding with a specific written course of action. Find out where each funder sets the limits on changes and responses the organization can make without formal approval of the funder, and determine actions that would represent a substantial change, and therefore may require formal approval. If it appears that a funded major program or project is not going to go forward at all or will be substantially delayed, the best advice is to let each funder know this is the case and offer to return the grant funds. It is always better to take the initiative on such matters rather than have the foundation or corporation find out about your organization's difficulties through other means and then be forced to withdraw ("rescind") the grant. While formal grant recissions are still somewhat rare, they do occur and can give an organization a negative reputation with funders, if this action was taken solely at the initiative of the funder.

Unexpended Funds

At the end of the grant period your organization may find it has unexpended grant funds. What should be done about this situation? Some organizations have made the major mistake of using these funds for other purposes beyond the restrictions of the grant and have failed to notify the funders that funds remained. All grant funds, unless they are specifically provided for general operating support or are totally unrestricted (in which case they can usually be used for any purposes of the organization), should be treated as "restricted funds" and must only be used for the purposes for which they were granted. Foundations and corporations, like any funder, are extremely concerned that their funds be used as intended. Misuse of funds, especially those funds that are restricted for specific purposes, can create major problems for organizations, especially when returning to those same sources for additional support.

As soon as your organization is aware that it will have unexpended funds from a particular grant, it should formally notify the foundation or corporation. The letter should include the amount of the unexpended funds and a specific offer to return these funds to the funder. Some foundations have clear policies that unused funds must be returned to them, while others tend to decide on a case-by-case basis. In any case, the foundation or corporation should give its clear authorization on what is to happen with these funds. If the funder does not have a stated policy on the return of funds, and if there is a legitimate use for these funds, such as extending the project or program by a few months or conducting a more extensive evaluation than was originally planned, outline in your letter these proposed uses for the unexpended funds as alternatives for consideration by the funder. Be sure that your alternatives are tied as closely as possible to the original purposes of your grant. No matter what the other alternatives are, the first option that should be presented is the return of the unexpended funds. Your funders will appreciate your organization's honesty in dealing with this issue.

Getting Ready for the Next Approach

If you have indeed developed a partnership with your funders, you will have informally been exploring with each one possible approaches for seeking further support when the grant period is over. In some cases you may not be eligible to immediately reapproach the funder for support because the foundation or corporation may require your organization to wait for a period of time before seeking another grant. Some funders, for example, require that an organization not reapply for a period of one year after it has received the second or third consecutive grant from a particular source. Others may ask that your organization not reapply after receiving only one grant, while still

> **In cases where there are major problems with funded programs, seek the verbal advice of your funding contacts before proceeding.**

others may have no such requirements and base reconsideration only on your organization's needs and their own specific areas of interest.

Assuming that you can reapply to a particular funder, you should begin to informally explore other funding possibilities and areas of mutual interest with each of your current funders as you approach the end of the current grant period. The *least* desirable approach, although it has been done, is to send in your organization's new proposal along with its final narrative and fiscal reports to each funder. The best approach is to have informally explored possibilities with the foundation or corporation prior to submitting these reports. After the reports have been submitted, and after a period of time sufficient for review of these documents has passed, the staff member or other contact at the funder should be called for his or her reactions to the reports and to see if any additional information is needed to complete the grant file. At this point, unless there are problems with the grant or the report materials, it is usually appropriate to meet in person or by phone to discuss future funding from this source. Your organization should be prepared to present some specific options for consideration by the foundation or corporation when this call is made. The person making the call should try to determine, if it is not already known, the schedule for applying and dates when proposals will next be considered. As always, get suggestions and advice on other possible funding sources for the particular projects or programs under development by your organization.

If you have been developing and maintaining a true negotiated partnership with each funder, and if the funder's recent grant experience with your organization has been successful from its perspective, this will be an easy call to make. Your follow-up meeting or call should proceed well as you now should have a strong relationship with the funder and see your contact as a source of help and advice.

Chapter 15

Fund Raising and Nonprofit Management Consulting

Helmer Ekstrom

Organizations seeking to develop a corporate and/or foundation fund-raising strategy, or expand an existing one, often engage consulting firms. Generally, they want such outside expertise to do one or more of the following:

- Assess their situation and potential for success.

- Be the architect of the strategy.

- Assist with its implementation.

Each of these is a key step in any project and cannot be left to chance. Many organizations do not usually have sufficient expertise or time available in-house. Often, they turn to outsourcing. Because of such needs, the selection and use of consultants is often a valuable skill for nonprofit executives to have.

Whereas few of us have not heard at least one horror story of a consultation that turned out badly, these are rare. A more common occurrence is underachievement. Too often an organization will be left only somewhat better off than it was, but woefully short of its potential. Why do some consultancies fail or produce mediocre results? Why are some extraordinarily successful? Is it good luck or good planning?

Luck may help, but good planning is everything. There are three key elements essential to success:

1. Knowing why, for what purpose, and when you need a consultant.

2. Choosing the best firm for your situation.

3. Effectively managing the consultant/client relationship to yield maximum benefit.

Knowing Why, for What, and When

Knowing why, for what purpose, and when a consultant is needed is not an exact science. It is subjective and far from easy. Deliberating over it wears at one's confidence. So it should be no surprise that generally organizations tend to copy the patterns of others. Further, since the funds to hire consultants often must come from sources outside the budget, thereby requiring special justification, "It's what everybody else does" is a popular and effective rationale.

However, to be effective, the timing and target of a consulting engagement must reflect the circumstances peculiar to that organization. Whereas there are many similarities among nonprofit organizations and institutions, it is, after all, the *differences* that draw the philanthropic investment of donors, foundations, and corporations. Carbon copies simply will not do. Some common failed approaches include:

- Too much too soon, or too little too late, or any combination and variation thereof, are common outcomes of the "copy cat" approach.

- Missed opportunities abound while waiting to do what everyone else does.

There is no formula for determining the answers to the why, what, and when questions when hiring a consultant. Hiring is a judgment call best made by someone in tune with his or her organization. This argues persuasively for periodic organizational self-assessment, conducted with or without outside expertise.

It is especially useful to have an understanding of the consulting profession: its history, core dimensions, theory, practice, and standards. Having a sense of what is within the art of the possible is an enormous advantage.

What Is a Consultant?

What is a consultant, anyway? an expert pair of hands? a fountain of expertise? an advisor? a teacher? a coach? the purveyor of a special method that is guaranteed to work for you? Is a consultant a diagnostician who will pinpoint your flaws? a prescriber of solutions to problems? a mapmaker who charts a course to your success? someone who does what you do not want to do, cannot do, or

dare not do? Of course a consultant can be all of the above—sometimes. In the course of the history of the field of nonprofit consulting, consultants have played each of those roles and a few more.

A Brief History of Consulting

The history buffs of the field generally concede that modern nonprofit consulting is rooted in the turn-of-the-century YMCA movement. Two or three creative and energetic YMCA secretaries (this is what "professional" staff were called in those days) developed the "campaign" model for raising funds. It worked so well (some suggest *they* made it work so well), that under the auspices of the YMCA, they took it on the road. Traveling to YMCAs in need in various locales to conduct the program, these itinerant staff, with their model method in hand and the know-how to use it, helped "client" Ys achieve their dreams. In each case, local staff, trustees, and volunteers were indoctrinated. The method and some of the know-how was transmitted. The residual effect was an increased capacity of the local people to pursue other fund-raising goals. Methods were refined and altered to suit particular circumstances. Some local staff, once students of the pioneering fund raisers, became experts themselves.

In time these individuals formed independent consulting firms that would serve a wide variety of charitable, social, educational, cultural, and religious organizations. These were the forerunners of the modern consultants to nonprofits.

Core Dimensions and a Theory of Consulting

While much has changed since those early consulting firms were formed, certain core dimensions of the field remain. Just as back then, today the approach or style of a consulting practice can be described in terms of points along two continuums (see Figure 15–1).

Those who teach and write about the field of management consulting will refer to a particular firm as either "method-based" or "expertise-based." The same could be said about fund raising and other consulting to nonprofits. In the extreme, the ex-

1. expertise based ←——→ method based

2. capacity builder ←——→ surrogate

Figure 15–1 Styles of Consulting Practice

pertise-based firm assesses a client's unique situation and then crafts a custom method. The method-based firm has the "perfect solution," which can be applied in nearly every circumstance.

The other continuum offers a sort of teach-a-person-to-fish versus give-a-person-the-fish choice. The capacity builder, in the extreme, puts all energy into the long-term capacity of the client to self-sustain and grow. The surrogate, again in the extreme, solely interested in the here and now, acts for the client.

The mention of these core dimensions in any gathering of consultants to nonprofits is sure to spark lively, if not passionate, debate. There seems to be no shortage of arguments in support of any point on either continuum, even the extremes. Most consulting firms have a style that falls within a wide bell-shaped curve straddling the midpoint and covering two-thirds of the spectrum.

There is rarely one and only "best" style for a particular situation. What is important is how well the general orientation of a firm's style along the continuum fits with an organization's short- and long-term goals. When the consultation is completed, what will be left? What goals will have been advanced and by how much?

The Practice Today

The practice of consulting to nonprofits has evolved just as the complexity of their challenges has. Special expertise is required more frequently for more purposes. Yet the need is not always obvious. Nonprofits can, and do, muddle along just as in the for-profit sector. Those that excel, however, tend to be very good at the timing, placement, and focus of special expertise. Whether it be in the form of volunteers, in-house staff, or outside consultants, or better, a blend of all three, mastering that skill is the key to quantum leaps toward an organization's full potential.

Disciplines and Areas

Special expertise in consulting can be said to come in two categories, "discipline" and "area." Whereas there may be a certain fuzziness between the two categories, they do provide a useful way of thinking about making the right match between needs and expertise.

A consulting discipline is a certain set of fundamental skills applied in particular combinations to yield a specific result. The field of consulting today reflects a wide range of disciplines. Some practices are multidisciplinary, while others focus on one or two specialties. Among the most common disciplines in practice today are:

- fund-raising counsel

- campaign management

- telemarketing/telecommunications counsel

- training

- planned giving

- executive search

- organizational development

- strategic planning

- management

- marketing

- public relations/communications

- prospect research

- information technology

- direct mail

The area of a firm's practice is most often related to its experience, mission, and values. The most common areas in practice today fall in the following categories:

- education

- arts and culture

- social services

- health care and hospitals

- environment

- religion

Today there are firms that focus only on sub-areas of these categories, such as museums or independent schools. Others specialize in zoos, or community colleges, or a particular religious denomination, or community development projects, and many more. Many firms have extensive experience in several areas.

Over time a firm builds a reputation in certain areas. This is due primarily to referrals. Executives within an area have collegial relationships within that area. They naturally seek advice from one another, including recommendations of good consultants. The best firms receive over 80 percent of their new client engagements as a result of recommendations of previous clients. Be cautious, however, about putting firms in pigeonholes. Expertise can be transferred in many cases. It may be a source of much-needed fresh ideas and approaches.

Ethical Standards and Professional Practices

Today, there are many more nonprofit organizations, more individuals entering the profession of fund raising and advancement, more consulting firms serving the needs of nonprofits, and more demands on institutions. But there is also a growing lack of public confidence in many of these institutions and people.

Scandal and reports of questionable practices persist. Although representing less than 1 percent of charitable solicitation and activity, scandals receive over 90 percent of the media attention. This is further exaggerated by a lack of public confidence in all institutions, generally. Nonprofit organizations and those that serve them, in the future, will have to distinguish themselves from the blurry mass of the tainted.

Professional service firms dedicated to the well-being of institutions whose purposes and practices are in the public interest must be committed to striving for the highest quality practices. Extraordinary steps must be taken to provide the public, volunteers, donors, and trustees assurance of that quality. The American Association of Fund-Raising Counsel (AAFRC), for example, has long been known for its rigorous requirements for induction into membership—including obtaining references from all the clients of prospective members for the previous five years. In 1996 AAFRC added a periodic credentials review for its members. Every three years an independent review, including a confidential survey of current and recent clients, is conducted. AAFRC uses this process both to renew its seal of approval and to inform its professional development program for members.

Anyone considering the use of consultants should be thoroughly familiar with the standards of the profession. It is essential for distinguishing the best firms. AAFRC publishes its standards and makes them available free upon request. Among the key provisions are:

- Fees should be mutually agreed upon in advance.

- Fees must be based upon the level and extent of professional services provided, not on the amount raised.

- Fund-raising expenditures should remain within the authority and control of the client.

- All funds contributed are always in the custody and control of the client.

- A firm should not profit directly or indirectly from materials or services provided by others.

- All potential conflicts of interest should be fully disclosed.

Contracts providing for contingency fees, commissions, or percentage of funds raised are suggested by some as the only answer for struggling nonprofits who cannot afford fees based on work done. They are wrong.

There are, of course, other answers. More importantly, while on the surface percentage-based compensation and the like looks like an easy answer, it is no answer at all. Such contracts are harmful to the relationship between the donor and the nonprofit. They abound with potential conflicts of interest and are detrimental to the financial health of the organization. The incentives they provide are simply not in the best interests of the organization or the donor.

But then what is a struggling nonprofit to do? To start with, it is never a bad idea to take a fresh look at the organization's current budget. A reevaluation of priorities often yields dollars to do what really needs to be done. Also, it may be useful to think about the consultancy in stages. Some firms will work with clients on a sequential contract basis. In this way the client receives services as it is able to afford them.

Another approach is seeking outside funding. Foundations, corporations, and even individuals provide "technical assistance" support to hire outside expertise, especially when it solves fundamental problems and/or builds an organization's capacity.

Ethical standards and professional practice is no place to cut corners. In this era, demanding the highest ethical standards and professional practices is not only the right thing to do, it is the smart thing to do.

Choosing the Best Firm

Choosing the right firm that best fits a particular organization and its circumstance is essential. A good process for selecting counsel has two primary purposes:

1. Eliminate down-side risk by ensuring that the wrong firm is not selected, and disaster, therefore, is avoided.

2. Maximize up-side potential by ensuring that the best firm is selected, and full potential can be attained.

The American Association of Fund-Raising Counsel, Inc., publishes a complete guide to "How To Choose Counsel." It is available at no cost.*

STEP A: IDENTIFYING PROSPECTIVE CONSULTANTS

Once the desire to seek outside counsel is affirmed, the first task is to identify a pool of candidate firms. The three most common sources for prospective consulting firms are:

1. **Referrals**—Colleagues who have recently used outside counsel are an excellent source. Firms accredited by membership in the American Association of Fund-Raising Counsel report that over 80 percent of their projects are the result of client referrals.

2. **Resource guides and directories**—In addition to the guides periodically published as advertising supplements in various nonprofit trade journals, the membership directory of a consultants' association is commonly referred to.

3. **Advertising**—Consulting firms often advertise in trade publications, conference programs, and the yellow pages, as well as exhibit at conferences.

STEP B: PRE-SCREEN TO NARROW THE FIELD

Sending out a request for proposal (RFP) to a long list of consulting firms is a waste of time and money. It is far better to obtain basic information on each firm—what services they provide, types of projects they have handled, and their approach to their work—by telephone. Then narrow the field down to three or four firms.

The steps are:

1. **Telephone inquiry**—Gather basic information.

2. **Narrow the field to three or four**—Select the firms that best seem to understand your needs,

---

*Source: Reprinted with permission from *How to Choose a Fund-Raising Counsel,* © 1996, AAFRC Trust for Philanthropy.

have the right type of experiences, receive the most positive referral references, and demonstrate the highest standards of ethical practice and professional conduct.

3. **Face-to-face briefings**—Arrange to meet with each firm on the shortened list to obtain more detailed information. Describe the goals or objectives for each of the services you seek. Remember, their answers to your questions *as well as* the questions they ask you provide substantial insight into a firm's capabilities.

4. **Request proposals**—After the briefings, request written proposals from each firm. Proposals should clearly state the services to be provided, schedule, costs, fees, and provide at least four references, including a client who may have been less than satisfied. While the proposal should address the specific services you have delineated, be open to alternate approaches the consultant may suggest.

STEP C: PROPOSAL REVIEW AND PRESENTATION

1. **Check references**—Thoroughly check each reference. Does the information provided by the former client suggest any particular questions you should ask a candidate firm?

2. **Determine proposal specifics**—Create a chart which shows, side by side, the facts of each firm's response to your requirements. Note the "intangibles," as well.

3. **Presentation of proposals**—Provide an opportunity for each firm to make a presentation of their proposal. These are best done involving the key people, staff and volunteers, who will be closest to the project. Usually all presentations are held on the same day.

STEP D: MAKING THE DECISION
With the views of key staff and volunteers in mind and presentations still fresh in memory, it is time for the final decision.

1. **Compare the facts**—Review in detail what each firm said it will do.

2. **Compare the people**—What is your impression of the key staff people in the firm?

3. **Compare the credentials**—What assurance of quality is there in the accreditation held by the firms and their key personnel?

4. **Double check references**—It is likely there are now additional questions upon which references can assist.

5. **Consider the cost and fees**—Expect that responsible bids for services tailored to meet your specific needs, rather than cookie-cutter approaches, will vary. There is no simple way to compare these. The highest or lowest bid is often meaningless. What is most important is the *expected short- and long-term return from what you invest.* Proposals assessed in that context can then be compared on a cost/value received basis.

6. **Chemistry**—The consultant/client relationship is professional. The selection process should be driven by the head, not the heart. Yet, it is a coaching and advising relationship. Chemistry does count.

7. **Notify candidates**—Notification to candidates of your decision in a timely manner is essential. Waiting for word of your decision could delay the scheduling of services to other clients. As a professional courtesy, explain briefly the reasons for your choice to those not selected.

STEP E: CONTRACT AND IMPLEMENTATION

1. **The contract**—This is a key document because it specifies the expectations the client and consultant have of each other. It should at least address the following points:

- Services to be provided

- Schedule

- Fees, expenses, payment arrangements

- Communication channel between client and consultant

- Provision to handling changes and difficulties

- Personnel

2. **Regulations**—Compliance with regulatory requirements is essential. Since each state sets its own regulations for charities and fund-raising professionals, the requirements vary widely. Contact the regulatory authority in the state(s) where your project will be conducted for the specific requirements.

A summary of state laws, including addresses and telephone numbers of the regulatory entities, is available from the AAFRC Trust for Philanthropy. In some locales there are county or municipal requirements. As well, under a few circumstances, federal regulations may apply. This would likely have to do with postal or interstate trade matters.

Managing the Consultancy

The best consulting firm has been engaged and your work is done . . . wrong! Clients can miss out on twice the value from a consultancy if they do not effectively manage their relationship with the consultant. An effectively managed consulting relationship begins with clear expectations. This means that work plans, schedules, and who is responsible for what should be agreed upon in advance and in writing. Nothing is left to question or misunderstanding. Certainly these can be amended as circumstances develop and the project evolves, but not retroactively. Rather they should be done proactively based upon progress monitoring.

An effectively managed consulting engagement continues that way when communication is both frequent and clear. It is essential that primary contacts for the client and the consulting firm be identified at the beginning and known by all involved. Confused communication channels have ruined a fair number of consultancies.

> **Confused communication channels have ruined a fair number of consultancies.**

Time must be set aside for scheduled periodic communication between the client and the consulting firm. In most cases, weekly is not too often. These can be brief and accomplished simply by telephone. If other key persons need to be involved at some point, they can join the calls as required. Face-to-face meetings should be scheduled, as well. These are best arranged when the consultant can meet with others or conduct planned activities or provide specific services on the same trip. This is an efficient way to use valuable time and save money.

If the chemistry between the client and firm contacts is not good, a change is in order. Their relationship must foster open communication. Hesitation in raising issues in a timely manner can undermine a project. Often early warning signals go unseen, unheard, and unheeded, simply because of a strained relationship.

Finally, clients who refuse to accept, or worse, do not even listen to a consultant's diagnosis that differs from their own are asking for trouble. One of the substantial benefits of securing outside expertise is the objectivity and perspective that the consultant brings. Of course, healthy skepticism is entirely appropriate . . . turning a deaf ear is not. Ultimately, it is the client who must make the decision on whether or not to take a consultant's advice.

Tips on Using a Consultant

- **Local vs. out-of-town?** Don't be misled by the myths. There very well may be the perfect consulting firm for your project right in your own backyard. On the other hand, the cost of a few airline tickets is a small price to pay to get the right match with your needs. Keep an open mind.

- **Large firm vs. small firm?** There is no rule of thumb; only a few myths. The facts are that quality comes in all sizes. So, too, does mediocrity. That is why it is so important to check references thoroughly.

- **Hire a firm or a specific person?** Certainly the person(s) with whom you will work closest must be "the right" person(s). However, take into account the full resources and expertise of the firm you are hiring. There are sure to be unanticipated problems that will require swift, appropriate, and effective response. Having the right resources available for an emergency is excellent insurance.

- **Cost of fund raising?** When is it a cost and when is it an investment? It should always be thought of as an investment. What are the results that you seek over time—dollars, a broader constituency, new donor relationships, increased donor giving? Often, the costs of planning and developing a fund-raising program are more appropriately amortized over several years.

- **Feasibility studies—are they all the same?** No! The methods used in such planning studies may be similar, but an important difference is how effectively the persons conducting the study draw out information and interpret it. Beware, there are no short cuts and there is no such thing as a good "cheap" study.

- **Big firms—big overhead?** Not always! Many larger firms have streamlined substantially. In some, "overhead" has been stripped away by the use of technology and smart management. What is left is reserve expertise and capacity that these firms are ready to provide your project when necessary.

- **How do I know these people are good?** Check references thoroughly. It is very serious business and well worth the time and effort required. Two key questions: 1) Would you hire this firm again? 2) What do you now know as a result of their consultation that you did not know when they started?

- **Credentials!** Check a firm's credentials thoroughly. Not all "memberships" are credentials. Many indicate simply the ability to fill out the form and send in a check. Know what it takes to become a "member."

- **Why hire a consultant to do what I am already paid to do?** Don't! except when you need additional expertise, perspective, or objectivity—or when you simply do not have time available to do everything that needs doing!

Chapter 16

A Look Inside: The Funders Speak

Much of this book represents personal opinions based on experience as both a foundation officer and as a fund raiser/consultant. From its inception, this book was also intended to include other voices and opinions. Some of these have been incorporated throughout the text but it is now time for some of the funders to have their voices and views heard.

During the early stages of the development of this book a brief survey was sent to several current and former senior staff of foundations and corporate giving programs. The survey was generally designed to seek information on the same areas covered by the book and, in part, sought opinions that extended beyond the particulars of each foundation or corporation. Below is a sampling of the responses; these were selected because the respondents have broad experience in the field of philanthropy, their foundations represent a mix of types, and the responses themselves give diverse views on the foundation and corporate grant-seeking process.

In reviewing these responses, you will notice some differences of opinion from what has been presented earlier as well some new thoughts and views. This is simply a reflection of the diversity of corporate and foundation grant makers. As should be obvious by now, there may be many paths to success in seeking grants and building relationships with funders. It all depends on your point of view.

The following responses to the survey are arranged by the individuals who provided them. In one case, the individual wished to remain anonymous. Each question on the survey is numbered, followed by the responses. All responses are quoted as they were provided and are published with the permission of each respondent.

Source: Dr. John E. Hopkins
                President/CEO
                Kalamazoo Foundation (MI)
Type of Foundation: Community Foundation

1) What characterizes a good relationship between a funder and a potential grantee?

- Honesty, trust, openness, no surprises, and if funded—keep in touch.

- Ask for input before asking for support.

- Identify where in priority of grant-seeking organizations the request falls.

2) How should this relationship be established?

- By directly communicating with the program officer or staff person who works with project development in the appropriate area. It is beneficial to speak personally with the program officer over the phone or in a meeting, to clarify your needs and build rapport, before sending in a full proposal.

3) What are four or five common mistakes made by those seeking funds from organized philanthropy?

- Grant applicant has not done their "homework" in learning about the foundation.

- Sending in a full proposal without talking with the foundation staff.

- Applicant wants to do something "to" a target population rather than working "with" the people they are trying to help.

- Applicant doesn't want to invest their agency's dollars in the project, but will only undertake the project if a foundation grants the entire budget.

- Applicant is more interested in finding a project to match the foundation's priorities than in seeking support for their organization's top priority needs.

4) What are four or five common reasons proposals are denied?

- No plan for sustaining the project after foundation funding is scheduled to cease—makes little sense to invest in a project that will end after foundation funding ends.

- Applicants do not have the board or staff resources to carry out the project.

- Applicant doesn't want to invest their agency's dollars in the project, but will only undertake the project if a foundation grants the entire budget.

- Agency comes back to the same foundation over and over again.

- Grantee comes to the foundation for lower priority needs of the organization—only come to the foundation with top priority needs.

5) How and why are exceptions made to usual grant guidelines and restrictions?

- In emergency cases.

6) What are the respective roles of staff, board, and/or any committees in your proposal review and grant-making process?

- Staff roles include: meeting with prospective grantees to better learn of the organization, presenting problem, the organization's solution, and the project budget.

- Staff also review the written proposal once it is submitted and summarize for their board the proposals—who, what, where, when, how, and why, as well as the strengths and weaknesses of the proposal.

- Staff evaluates proposal in terms of foundation's priorities and offers recommendation.

- Board role is to review the proposal and rate it on a scale of 0–3. They subsequently determine whether to fund it and for how much.

7) What is the return your foundation is seeking from its "investment" in an organization?

- The foundation is looking for innovative and comprehensive approaches to problem situations that involve the people that the grantee is trying to help.

8) What are the five to six basic questions always covered in your grant review process?

- Does the proposal fit the foundation's focus area and goals?

- Is the project sustainable after foundation funding ceases?

- Does the proposer work collaboratively with other groups and organizations within the community?

- Does the organization have the board, staff, and other resources to carry out the project?

9) Besides dollars, are there other ways organized philanthropy can assist organizations?

- Foundations can be excellent sources in terms of critiquing the proposal and suggesting other potential donors or foundations that might invest in the project.

10) What characterized the best proposal you ever received and reviewed?

- The project was the agency's top priority. The proposal was creative and practical, showed that the agency was well-managed, had fiscal integrity, commitment, the potential to make a real difference in the lives and well-being of the people of the county, and the project was sustainable.

11) What do you think are the two or three major issues that will affect foundation and corporate giving over the next 3–5 years?

- Measuring the impact of foundation funded projects.

- Challenges of devolution [of federal spending to states].

- Investment performance.

Source: Rayna Aylward
            Executive Director
            Mitsubishi Electric America
            Foundation

Type of Foundation: Corporate Foundation

1) What characterizes a good relationship between a funder and a potential grantee?

- Basically, the relationship would be characterized by a sense of partnership, with each side open to the learnings and benefits offered by the other.

2) How should this relationship be established?

- From the very beginning, identify common goals, agree on processes for achieving them, and respect the underlying values of each partner.

3) What are four or five common mistakes made by those seeking funds from organized philanthropy?

- First and foremost, not reading guidelines carefully

- Submitting proposals that are obviously "boilerplates"

- Providing either too little or too much information on the organization/project

- Not taking "no" for an answer if a proposal is declined

4) What are four or five common reasons proposals are denied?

- Scarcity of funds

- Not directly related to mission

- Outcomes not clearly defined

- Project duplicates others

- Poor quality of proposal

5) How and why are exceptions made to usual grant guidelines and restrictions?

- Project has support of one of our companies or board members.

- Project is so unusual, innovative, and time-sensitive that we process proposal outside of regular timetable.

6) What are the respective roles of staff, board, and/or any committees in your proposal review and grant-making process?

- Staff: initial screening

- Advisory Committee: review

- Executive Committee: final cut

- Board: grant approval

7) What is the return your foundation is seeking from its "investment" in an organization?

- At the most immediate level, we want to see that the goals proposed have been met and the target audience benefited.

- Longer range, the results should be made known and, when appropriate, applied to a wider constituency.

- Concomitantly, the role of the foundation in bringing about these results should be properly recognized.

8) What are the five to six basic questions always covered in your grant review process?

- Why is this project/organization needed?

- Who will benefit as a result?

- Are there sufficient capacity, experience, and planning to carry it out?

- Can it eventually be self-sufficient?

- Does it offer opportunity for employee involvement/is it a good "business fit"?

9) Besides dollars, are there other ways organized philanthropy can assist organizations?

- product donations

- volunteers

- in-kind services

- referrals to other resources

- constructive feedback on proposals, public relations materials and funder outreach

10) What characterized the best proposal you ever received and reviewed?

- Well-written and engaging narrative; clear, concise budget; concrete examples of results to be sought; and clear delineation of potential benefits to company

11) What do you think are the two or three major issues that will affect foundation and corporate giving over the next three to five years?

- Strategic alignment of philanthropy and corporate goals

- Reduction of government spending/devolution to states

- Need for partnerships among both nonprofits and funders

Source: Bill Somnerville
           President
           Philanthropic Ventures
           Foundation

(former executive director of the Peninsula Community Foundation, consultant to over 112 foundations)

Type of foundation: Public Foundation

1) What characterizes a good relationship between a funder and a potential grantee?

- Candor, honesty, openness—no hidden agendas, no secrets

2) How should this relationship be established?

- Give and take between the two parties

- On the funder's side, a desire to see the applicant succeed in his work

3) What are four or five common mistakes made by those seeking funds from organized philanthropy?

- Making assumptions, i.e., using acronyms, for example

- Not giving detailed budgets

- Not giving an abstract paragraph at the start of a proposal

- Not giving the names of professionals familiar with the project or who could be reference persons

- Exaggerating, e.g., "This is a unique effort."

4) What are four or five common reasons proposals are denied?

- [They are] not in our area of interest.

- We do not accept applications.

- [They are] not a vital request.

- We don't fund continuing support.

5) How and why are exceptions made to usual grant guidelines and restrictions?

- Someone knows the donor or a board member.

6) What are the respective roles of staff, board, and/or any committees in your proposal review and grant-making process?

- I make the funding decisions in accord with the wishes of donors.

- The Board approves these.

7) What is the return your foundation is seeking from its "investment" in an organization?

- Positive impact in the community.

8) What are the five to six basic questions always covered in your grant review process?

- [Refer to foundation guidelines.]

9) Besides dollars, are there other ways organized philanthropy can assist organizations?

- Funding Resource Library—*every* community foundation should have one.

- Management seminars for nonprofit personnel

10) What characterized the best proposal you ever received and reviewed?

- I can't answer this—there are no "bests" in my work.

11) What do you think are the two or three major issues that will affect foundation and corporate giving over the next 3–5 years?

- Corporate giving is disappearing!

- Community foundation giving is increasing very much but *not* having much impact.

- Foundations will initiate funding ideas more vs. waiting for the mail.

Mr. Somerville also added the following, based on his 36 years of experience in nonprofit and philanthropic work:

12) What are four to five common mistakes made by members of organized philanthropy?

- Much too wordy in application literature.

- Telling, or implying, to the applicant what you want to hear—e.g. "we only fund first-of-kind programs."

- Using application blank and expecting applicant to "fit in."

- Meeting only once or twice a year and expecting applicant to just wait.

- Not answering the mail—even with a turn-down.

- Being haughty—this has *got* to stop.

Source: Anonymous

Type of foundation: Community Foundation

1) What characterizes a good relationship between a funder and a potential grantee?

- Mutual respect.

- A good match of goals and style.

2) How should this relationship be established?

- It's a two-way street. Funders have a responsibility to get to know key organizational leaders in their issue area.

3) What are four or five common mistakes made by those seeking funds from organized philanthropy?

- Not understanding that many funders have a strategy or specific focus or interest.

- Not reading guidelines carefully.

- Not understanding the particulars of the type of donor they are approaching—corporate, family, community foundation, etc.

4) What are four or five common reasons proposals are denied?
(not responded to)

5) How and why are exceptions made to usual grant guidelines and restrictions?
(not responded to)

6) What are the respective roles of staff, board, and/or any committees in your proposal review and grant-making process?
(not responded to)

7) What is the return your foundation is seeking from its "investment" in an organization?
(not responded to)

8) What are the five to six basic questions always covered in your grant review process?

- What is the capacity (board, staff) of this organization?

- Why is this proposal more compelling than others?

- What track record does the organization have?

9) Besides dollars, are there other ways organized philanthropy can assist organizations?

- Yes, relationships with community leaders are key for funders to be successful—so funders can offer ideas, meeting space, work collaboratively to issue RFPs, etc.

10) What characterized the best proposal you ever received and reviewed?

- Enthusiasm

- Vision

- A solid work plan

- Achievable goals

- Strong board leadership and management

11) What do you think are the two or three major issues that will affect foundation and corporate giving over the next 3–5 years?

- Devolution of federal spending to the states will mean that many service delivery systems will change, affecting foundation grantees.

Conclusions

Underlying this entire book is a point of view: foundations and corporations, and those that are associated with them as staff and board, can be valuable resources to your organization even beyond the funds they may make available to support your needs. If your point of view is that a potential funder is only a source for a check and you can measure success by the size of the check from each source, you are ready to join Mr. Custer (i.e., doomed!). But if your point of view is that your real goal with each potential funder is the creation of an ongoing negotiated partnership based upon mutual interests, needs, and understanding of the key roles each of you play in the funding process, your efforts at seeking support will be rewarded in many ways beyond the funds raised for your organization.

Proposals, reports, meetings, correspondence, research, understanding the variety of funders, and knowing your organization are only parts of the grant-seeking process. The real heart of the process, as with all effective fund raising, is people. Foundations and corporations are not closed, monolithic structures. They involve people who reflect all of the diversity and variety elsewhere in life. Some you will not enjoy working with; these individuals may see themselves as more important than others because they are associated with a foundation or corporation. But the majority of foundation and corporate staff, in my 20 years of experience in this field, will respond to being treated as helpers and advisors—and may become true partners with your organization.

Fund raising involves much hard work. Your point of view can help guide you and your organi-

---

The real heart of the process, as with all effective fund raising, is people.

---

zation's preparation and planning. But also keep an eye out for the fun part of fund raising—the things that can and often do happen by chance or serendipity that result in meeting your organization's needs while surprising and amazing you. A potential funder of scholarships may look up and see some cracks in the ceiling, and the result may be a grant twice as large as was being sought. That cold, calculating foundation staff member may suddenly want to share her vacation experience with you and get your ideas for her next vacation; now you are a resource to her. Or a call to explain a major problem to a potential funder may get turned into a long-term relationship and several grants.

Overall, to return to our very first example, the basic secret to success is your point of view, a lot of hard work, and even some fun. And remember, thousands survived Custer's Last Stand. You, too, will survive and prosper in your grant seeking with the right point of view.

Glossary

A Fool and his words are soon parted; a man of genius and his money.

William Shenstone

Did you ever get a new computer and start to read the manual that came with it? At least in the early days those writing these manuals assumed you were part of their arcane brotherhood or sisterhood, and already knew what they were talking about when they said the computer had "16 megabytes of RAM and a cache of 256K." In most cases, attempts have been made to define the words and phrases used in this book.

Foundations and other funders have their own sometimes unique vocabulary. While there is not really total agreement on how words and phrases related to philanthropy should be used, there have been some attempts within the field to standardize the vocabulary. It is important to understand how foundations use and define certain key words so that you can better navigate through the proposal and grant process. For example, if you are notified that the foundation has approved a three-year declining grant, what does that mean? Here, in mini dictionary form, are some of the key words and phrases you should know.

administrative costs: (also called **general expenses**) Expenses incurred to administer or manage an organization.

Source: Reprinted with permission from E.A. Scanlan and J.B. Scanlan, eds., *A Lexicon for Community Foundations*, © 1988, Council on Foundations.

assets: The properties owned by an individual, business enterprise, or nonprofit organization.

awards: (also called **grants, prizes, recognition awards**) Grants to individuals or organizations, usually on a competitive basis, to encourage activities in which the foundation is interested.

building fund campaign: (also called **building fund program, bricks and mortar campaign**) A capital campaign, mounted specifically to raise funds for construction and/or renovation of buildings.

campaign: (also called **fund-raising campaign**) An organized effort to solicit funds for an organization or institution.

capital campaign: An organization's efforts to raise funds for building construction and/or renovation, major property acquisition or improvement, major equipment purchase, or similar items.

capital grant: (also called **building grant, bricks and mortar grant, equipment grant**) A gift to be used for the purchase, construction, or improvement of property including land, buildings, or equipment.

challenge grant: (also called **challenge gift**) A grant that carries a stipulation that the recipient raise a specified amount of funds (cash and/or pledges) from other sources, usually within a specified period of time before payment of all or a portion of the grant. Alternately, the grant may specify other requirements be met before payment of the grant.

collaborative funding: (also called **cooperative funding, joint funding**) Grants made by a foundation and one or more other sources to an organization.

committed funds: That portion of a [foundation's] philanthropic budget that has already been allocated or pledged to organizations, groups, or specific programs.

contingent grant: (also called **contingency grant**) A grant to an agency that requires the agency to meet certain specific conditions before the grant or a portion of it will be paid.

contribution: (also called **donation, gift**) Assets given by a donor (an individual, a group, an organization, or through a trust, estate, or other vehicle) to a charitable organization. The assets may be cash, securities, property, equipment, time and skills, services, or other forms.

corporate donor: A for-profit corporation that gives cash gifts, supplies, equipment, services, volunteer assistance, or other contributions to a charitable organization.

corporate foundation: (also called **company foundation, company-sponsored foundation**) A private philanthropic organization set up and funded by a corporation. A corporate foundation is governed by a board that may include members of the corporation board and contributions committee, or other staff members, and representatives of the community.

corporate giving program: (also called **corporate contributions program**) A philanthropic program operated within a corporation. The program may be managed through a department of its own or through a community affairs (or similar) department. Grant-making policy is usually determined by a contributions committee.

decline: (also called **turn down, reject**) The decision by the distribution committee of a foundation not to fund an organization that has requested support.

declining grant: (also called **decreasing grant**) A multiyear grant that decreases in amount each year and usually has a termination date.

defer: (also called **postpone**) The decision by the distribution committee of a foundation, after a review of a proposal, to act on a grant request at a later time.

deficit financing grants: (also called **debt financing grants**) Grants to help an agency repay outstanding liabilities.

designated fund: (also called **designated endowment, agency endowment fund**) A component fund [of the foundation] whose beneficiaries have been specified by a donor or the governing board.

distribution committee: The formal organization within a foundation that is responsible for overseeing the foundation's philanthropic activities, which may include determining the contributions policy and budget; defining priority funding areas, guidelines for grant applications, and criteria for applicant eligibility; doing a final review of grant requests; and making decisions as to whether or not to approve grants. The committee may set amounts for grants, special conditions, and requirements, and may review final and fiscal reports from grantees.

donee: (also called **recipient, beneficiary**) The individual, organization, or institution that receives a gift.

donor: (also called **contributor, benefactor**) The individual, foundation, or corporation that makes a gift.

donor-advised fund: (also called **consult and advise fund, donor-advisor fund**) A fund that is formally structured to enable the donor to suggest specific grants from the fund; such recommendations are not binding upon the foundation but are taken into consideration when grants are decided upon.

earmarked: A gift restriction.

endowment campaign: A campaign to obtain funds specifically to create or supplement an organization's endowment fund.

endowment grants: Gifts to an organization that carry the stipulation that the principal is to be maintained inviolate and in perpetuity; the gift may allow income earned on the principal to be expended.

estate: The legal status or position of an owner with respect to property and other assets; total assets of a deceased person.

executive committee: A formal group to which responsibility has been delegated by the governing board [of a foundation] for direct operation and management of an organization between full board meetings.

expendable funds: Funds in which both principal and income can be used for operations, construction, renovation, or other approved purposes.

family foundation: A foundation whose funds are derived from members of a single family. Generally, family members serve as officers or board members of the foundation and play an influential role in grant-making decisions.

field of interest fund: A component fund [of a community foundation] established to support a class of charitable beneficiaries, institutions, organizations, associations, or a specific geographic area's charitable agencies. Donors do not name the specific agencies to receive assistance. The governing board may have full discretion in using the funds.

final report: The report detailing the use and results of grant funds and submitted by a grantee to a foundation at the end of a grant period.

form 990: (also called **990**) A report (information return) annually submitted by nearly all tax-exempt organizations and institutions (except religious) to the Internal Revenue Service; the report includes financial information on income sources, expenditures, and activities.

form 990-PF: Annual tax return form that private foundations must file with the Internal Revenue Service. A similar form is filed with the appropriate state offices. Includes information about the foundation's assets, income, operating expenses, contributions, paid staff and salaries, name and address of a person or persons to contact, program funding areas, grant-making guidelines and restrictions, and grant application procedures.

fund: An entity established for the purpose of accounting for resources used for specific activities or objectives in accordance with special regulations, restrictions, or limitations. Also, a self-balancing group of assets, liabilities, fund balance, and changes in fund balance.

general purpose foundation: An independent private foundation that awards grants in many different fields of interest.

general purpose grant: (also called **operating grant**, **operating support**) A grant to an organization to further its basic mission or overall work rather than assist a specific purpose, project, or program.

grant agreement: (also called **grant contract**, **grant acceptance document**) A formal statement of the responsibilities of the foundation and the grantee in executing the grant project and in accounting for the use of and reporting on money received by an agency.

grant application: (also called **proposal**, **grant request**) The document(s) submitted to the foundation or other potential funding source in which the organization presents its request for support.

grant categories: (also called **grant subject categories**, **grant areas**, **giving categories**) The grouping of grants by subject areas or types of recipients.

grant commitment: (also called **unpaid grant**) Grant authorized or approved but not yet paid.

grant conditions: (also called **grant requirements**) The foundation's expectations of the grantee organization, usually stated in the grant agreement.

grant limitation: (also called **grant restriction**) Limitation of the purposes for which grants will be awarded by a foundation or conditions or restrictions placed on a grant so that it will be used solely for specific purposes.

grant-making policy/priorities: (also called **grant policy**, **grant guidelines**, **contributions policy**, **funding guidelines**) The formal statement of the foundation's primary areas of interests and concentration of grants; the statement may also include areas, organizations, programs, or services which the foundation will not fund.

grant monitoring: (also called **grantee monitoring**) Ongoing assessment of the progress of activities funded by the foundation, with the objective of determining if the terms and conditions of the grant are being met and if the goal of the grant is likely to be achieved.

grant payment: Payment made to a designated recipient by a foundation in accordance with the terms and conditions established by the foundation.

grant period: (also called **grant duration**) The defined length of time that the grant covers.

in-kind contribution: (also called **noncash contribution**) A contribution of equipment, supplies, personnel, space, services, or things of value other than money, securities, or appreciated property.

interest: (also called **earnings on investment**) Income earned by savings accounts, interest-bearing checking accounts, or financial instruments or securities such as certificates of deposit, U.S. Treasury obligations, or corporate bonds. Income payments from mutual funds invested in such vehicles, such as money market funds, are usually referred to as "dividends."

leverage: (also called **leveraging grant**) Funding a program so as to enhance or encourage financial participation by other private, public, or individual sources.

loaned executive: A management-level employee who is granted temporary, full-time or part-time paid leave from his or her duties to serve in some capacity (usually related to his or her job skills) with a nonprofit, charitable or educational organization.

matching grant: (also called **matching gift**) A grant that matches an amount contributed [from another source].

multiyear grant: (also called **multiple-year grant**) A grant made by a foundation and set up to be paid out over a period of more than one year from the date of the grant.

narrative report: (also called **project report**) A descriptive report on a project or program, usually detailing progress to date, results of any evaluation carried out, and plans as well as any changes in the program, adjustments in the schedule, major problems, or other pertinent information.

noncash gifts: Gifts other than cash or easily negotiable securities.

operating costs: (also called **operating expenses**) Expenses incurred in conducting the ordinary activities of an organization, including running its programs, raising funds, and administering the organization.

payout requirement: The Internal Revenue Code requirement that all private foundations, including corporate foundations, pay out annually (usually in the form of grants and contributions) the equivalent of five percent of the value of their investment assets. This is not required of community foundations.

philanthropic dollar: Generally, that portion of the Gross National Product allocated to support philanthropic causes.

philanthropy: The philosophy and practice of giving to nonprofit organizations through financial and other contributions; all voluntary giving, voluntary service, and voluntary association and initiative.

pilot/demonstration project grant: (also called **demonstration grant**) A grant to assist a new program or project that is specifically designed to be carried out as a test, usually on a smaller scale, of the feasibility and effectiveness of the program or project before it is fully implemented.

planning grant: A grant to fund the planning process of an organization, program, or project.

pledge: (also called **commitment**) A commitment to make a gift over a specified period, payable according to terms set by the donor; the total value of such a commitment. Some forms of pledges may be legally enforceable.

post-grant evaluation: (also called **grant evaluation, grant effectiveness evaluation**) A review of the results of a grant with the emphasis upon whether or not the grant achieved its desired objective.

pre-grant evaluation: (also called **proposal review, proposal evaluation**) Study of the grant proposal prior to making funding decisions.

principal: All investment assets.

private foundation: A 501(c)(3) organization that is originally funded from one source, that derives revenue from its earnings on investments, and that makes grants to other charitable organizations as opposed to administering its own programs.

private operating foundation: (also called **operating foundation**) A foundation that devotes most of its earnings and assets directly to the conduct of its tax-exempt purposes, rather than making grants to other organizations for these purposes.

program officer: (also called **grants officer**) Staff member in a foundation or corporate contributions office who is responsible for screening grant applications, researching the organization or program seeking funds, reviewing proposals, and making recommendations about grants, often in a particular area, to the distribution committee or board.

program-related investment: A loan made by a private foundation to a profit-making or nonprofit organization for a project related to the foundation's stated purposes and interests. Program-related investments are often made from a revolving fund; the foundation generally expects to receive its money back (with a return at or below current interest rates).

project support grant: (also called **program grant**) A grant used to fund the expenses associated with a specified activity of an organization, usually a part of its ongoing operations.

public charity: Any charitable organization classified under Section 501(c)(3) of the Internal Revenue Service Code and defined under Section 509(a)(1), (2), (3), or (4). In order to qualify for classification under these sections, the organization must meet one or more of several tests or definitions whereby the organization demonstrates that 1) a minimum specified percentage of its total support comes from the public, or 2) it meets certain organizational definitions.

public-private partnership: (also called **public-private venture, cooperative venture**) A cooperative venture between the public sector, such as a government agency or agencies, and the private sector, such as a corporation or a nonprofit organization.

query letter: (also called **letter of inquiry**) A brief letter outlining an organization's activities and its need for funding; an inquiry sent to a foundation to determine the appropriateness of submitting a formal grant proposal.

regional association: (also called **regional association of grant makers, RAGS**) Membership organization of grant-making groups, such as foundations and corporate contribution programs, based in a specific area; may be citywide, statewide, or regional in scope. Associations provide a variety of member services (workshops, conferences, monitoring of relevant legislative activity, publications) according to members' needs. Association budgets are supported by member dues.

request for proposal: (also called **RFP**) A formal announcement by an organization that it is seeking written offers of assistance for services it desires, or it is seeking requests for funding support for a specified area of interest.

rescind: (also called **revoke**) To cancel a grant that has previously been approved.

restricted fund: Funds that have limitations on the types of grants that may be made from the funds; the types of agencies, programs, services, or served groups that may receive grants from the funds; and/or the procedures for making grants from the funds. The limitations may be specified by the donor or the governing body.

return: In terms of the grant-making process, the decision, usually by the foundation staff, to return a request for a grant to the applicant organization without formal review by the distribution committee.

seed grant: (also called **start-up grant**) A grant, frequently representing only a portion of the total expenses, which is intended to help initiate a new project or program.

site visit: Fact-finding visit by a grant maker to an organization that has applied for or received funding. A visit to the area(s) and institutions that are affected by the grant request.

special projects campaign: A fund-raising effort for one or more specific objectives, such as programs or projects that do not comprise an organization's total fund raising.

special purpose foundation: A public foundation that focuses its grant-making activities on one or a few special areas of interest, e.g., a foundation that makes grants only in the area of cancer research or child development.

technical assistance: The providing of specific skills, advice, or training by one agency or individual to an agency.

technical assistance grant: (also called **TA grant**) Funds provided by a foundation or other funding source to an agency so that it can obtain needed technical skills and expertise from an outside source.

terminal grant: (also called **tie-off grant**) A final grant to an organization, usually a previous recipient of grants from the foundation. "Final" is usually taken to mean that the organization cannot reapply for a grant from the foundation for a specific period of time.

unrestricted fund: (also called **general fund, general purpose fund, discretionary fund**) A component fund [of a community foundation] that has no external restriction on its use or purposes and can be used for any purpose designated by the governing board.

unrestricted grant: (also called **outright grant/gift**) A grant that may be used for any purpose of the organization, including operating costs, debt retirement, endowment building, capital needs, or any other purposes of the organization.

year-end financial report: (also called **un-audited financial report/statement**) A comprehensive fiscal report prepared internally (usually) by an organization after the close of its fiscal year to show income, expenditures, change in fund balances, and other financial transactions of the organization.

Bibliography

AAFRC Trust for Philanthropy. 1995. *New Times, Tight Money: How Corporate Leaders Respond: Giving USA Special Report: Trends in Corporate Philanthropy.* New York: AAFRC Trust for Philanthropy.

AAFRC Trust for Philanthropy. 1995. *Giving USA Special Report: Trends in Corporate Philanthropy.* New York: AAFRC Trust for Philanthropy.

AAFRC Trust for Philanthropy. 1996. *How To Choose a Fund-Raising Council.* New York: AAFRC Trust for Philanthropy.

The Foundation Center. 1995. *Highlights of the Foundation Center's Foundation Giving, 1995 Edition.* New York: The Foundation Center.

"Foundation Leaders Urge Grant Seekers To Do More Homework." *The Chronicle of Philanthropy,* 4 April 1996.

Independent Sector. 1994. *Giving and Volunteering in the United States: Findings from a National Survey.* Washington, DC: Independent Sector.

Kaplan, A., ed. 1995. *Giving USA 1995.* New York: AAFRC Trust for Philanthropy.

Kaplan, A., ed. 1996. *Giving USA 1996.* New York: AAFRC Trust for Philanthropy.

Nielsen, W. 1985. *The Golden Donors.* New York: Truman Books.

The 1996 World Almanac and Book of Facts. F. Famighetti, ed. 1995. Mahwah, NJ: World Almanac Books.

Plinio, A. and J. Scanlan. 1986. *Resource Raising: The Role of Non-Cash Assistance in Corporate Philanthropy.* Washington, DC: Independent Sector.

Scanlan, E., ed. 1989. *Community Foundations at 75: A Report on the Status of Community Foundations.* Washington, DC: Council on Foundations.

Scanlan, E. and J. Scanlan, eds. 1988. *A Lexicon for Community Foundations.* Washington, DC: Council on Foundations.

Tanner, R. 1996. *Stonewall in the Valley.* Mechanicsburg, PA: Stackpole Books.

Thompson, T. "The Changing Face of Philanthropy." *The Washington Post,* 31 March 1996, sec. A–1, A–17.

Welch, J. with P. Stekler. 1994. *Killing Custer.* New York: W.W. Norton & Company.

Wolpert, J. 1996. "What Charity Can and Cannot Do." New York: The Twentieth Century Fund.

Suggested Readings

Chapter 1: Overview

Anderson, A. 1996. *Ethics for Fundraisers.* Bloomington, IN: Indiana University Press.

>   Applied ethics and ethical decision making in fund raising and how to keep on track ethically in your work, despite outside pressures.

Driscoll, D. et al. 1995. *The Ethical Edge: Tales of Organizations That Have Faced Moral Crises.* New York: MasterMedia Limited.

>   Case studies of businesses and nonprofits that have encountered or created moral crises and have passed the test—or failed it.

Glaser, J. 1994. *The United Way Scandal: An Insider's Account of What Went Wrong and Why.* New York: John Wiley & Sons, Inc.

>   A classic but modern story of what can happen—and what it means for the nonprofit sector.

Greenfield, J. 1991. *Fund Raising: Evaluating and Managing the Fund Development Process.* New York: John Wiley & Sons, Inc.

>   An excellent resource on how to plan and evaluate the fund-raising function in an organization, including sections on annual campaigns, capital campaigns, foundations and corporations, and management.

Hall, P.D. 1992. *Inventing the Nonprofit Sector and Other Essays on Philanthropy, Voluntarism and Nonprofit Organizations.* Baltimore: The Johns Hopkins University Press.

>   Historical perspective on the growth of the sector, current issues and trends, public policy, and what the near future may hold.

Joseph, J. 1995. *Remaking America: How the Benevolent Traditions of Many Cultures Are Transforming Our National Life.* San Francisco: Jossey-Bass Publishers.

>   A cross-cultural look at the impact of other philanthropic traditions and heritage on the American vision of community and the charitable practices.

Josephson, M. 1992. *Ethics in Grantmaking and Grantseeking: Making Philanthropy Better.* Marina Del Rey, CA: Joseph & Edna Josephson Institute of Ethics.

>   Probably the only resource to address ethical issues on "both sides of the table," this book includes many practical items such as sample conflict of interest documents and the Council on Foundation's Principles and Practices statement.

Lauffer, A. 1984. *Strategic Marketing for Not-for-Profit Organizations: Program and Resource Development.* New York: The Free Press.

How to apply the business strategic marketing approach to the nonprofit sector, including specific steps to take, integrating marketing into the total organization, and fund raising.

O'Connell, B. 1987. *Philanthropy in Action*. New York: The Foundation Center.

A compilation of stories of how religious, corporate, foundation, and individual gifts have helped transform society, and of the relationships between donors and recipients.

Van Til, J., ed. 1990. *Critical Issues in American Philanthropy*. A Publication of the AAFRC Trust for Philanthropy. San Francisco: Jossey-Bass Publishers.

Includes sections and essays on understanding philanthropy (history and definitions, conditions), philanthropy and society, and strengthening philanthropic practice, including legal aspects, teaching philanthropy, research, board roles, ethics, and the future.

Chapter 2: Foundations, Corporate Foundations, Corporate Giving Programs

Hodgkinson, V. et al. *Nonprofit Almanac 1992–1993: Dimensions of the Independent Sector*. San Francisco: Jossey-Bass Publishers.

A periodic statistical compilation and analysis of the nonprofit sector including data classified by various types of nonprofit organizations such as sources and uses of funds, numbers of new nonprofits and closed nonprofits, demographics, donors, etc.

Hodgkinson, V. et al. 1996. *The Impact of Federal Budget Proposals upon the Activities of Charitable Organizations and the People They Serve, 1996–2002*. Washington, DC: Independent Sector.

The source of the data and analysis of the impact of federal budgetary proposals and changes on the nonprofit sector and the basis for the 20th Century Fund Report.

Internal Revenue Service. *Statistics of Income Bulletin*. Washington, DC: Internal Revenue Service.

A quarterly journal of data based on tax returns and other reports, including information on foundations and corporations.

Chapter 3: Corporate Foundations and Corporate Giving Programs

Bennett, J. 1989. *Patterns of Corporate Philanthropy*. Washington, DC: Capital Research Center.

A book that is addressed to corporate philanthropic decision makers and that provides an examination, including data, of why and how companies make their grant decisions.

Koch, F. 1979. *The New Corporate Philanthropy*. New York: Plenum Press.

Although an older resource, still a practical guide on how to develop an effective corporate giving strategy—and a valuable look at "the other side of the table."

Logan, D. 1989. *U.S. Corporate Grantmaking in a Global Age*. Washington, DC: Council on Foundations.

An interesting look at corporate giving overseas, giving for international purposes in the U.S., and trends and issues in corporate grant making for international purposes.

Nelson, D. and P. Schneiter. 1991. *Gifts-in-Kind: The Fundraiser's Guide to Acquiring, Managing & Selling Charitable Contributions Other Than Cash and Securities*. Rockville, MD: Fund Raising Institute.

A step-by-step approach to gifts-in-kind, including acquiring, valuing, and selling them.

Chapter 4: Private Foundations

Odendahl, T., ed. 1987. *America's Wealthy and the Future of Foundations*. New York: The Foundation Center.

A series of essays and research, including interviews, on the future of organized philanthropy.

Chapter 5: Community Foundations

Magat, R. 1989. *An Agile Servant: Community Leadership by Community Foundations*. Washington, DC: Council on Foundations.

A comprehensive look at the purposes, growth, resources, grant-making initiatives, and other roles of community foundations, including case studies.

Chapter 6: Foundation Boards and Staffs

Council on Foundations. 1993. *Evaluation for Foundations: Concepts, Cases, Guidelines, and Resources*. San Francisco: Jossey-Bass Publishers.

A detailed and systematic approach to how foundations can evaluate the impact of their funding and an inside look at some of the key areas you might need to consider when preparing a proposal.

Council on Foundations. 1993. *Foundation Management Report: Seventh Edition*. Washington, DC: Council on Foundations.

A periodic detailed statistical analysis of patterns of foundation management and staffing, including finances, investments, governing boards, staffing, and personnel administration.

National Society of Fund Raising Executives Institute. 1996. *The NSFRE Fund-Raising Dictionary*. Alexandria, VA: National Society of Fund Raising Executives.

A newly published dictionary of terms used in fund raising.

Young, D. and W. Moore. 1969. *Trusteeship and the Management of Foundations*. New York: Russell Sage Foundation.

Two essays that focus on the roles and responsibilities of foundation trustees, providing insights into the principles, legal aspects, and ethical responsibilities of the trustees.

Chapter 7: Where to Start: Know Your Organization

Anthony, R. and R. Herzlinger. 1980. *Management Control in Nonprofit Organizations*. Homewood, IL: Richard D. Irwin, Inc.

A comprehensive classic textbook of nonprofit management, including controls, financial reporting, evaluation, programming, and other aspects.

Bryson, J. 1990. *Strategic Planning for Public and Nonprofit Organizations: A Guide to Strengthening and Sustaining Organizational Achievement*. San Francisco: Jossey-Bass Publishers.

A guide to developing strategic thinking in an organization, including a resource section with specific steps for getting the strategic planning process started.

Connors, T., ed. 1988. *The Nonprofit Organization Handbook: Second Edition*. New York: McGraw-Hill Book Company.

Another comprehensive look at nonprofit management covering almost all aspects of the nonprofit organization.

Drucker, P. 1990. *Managing the Nonprofit Organization: Principles and Practices*. New York: Harper-Collins Publishers.

The famous author applies his principles to the nonprofit sector by providing a guide to leadership and management in the nonprofit sector, with a focus on the individual's role in the organization.

Herman, R. & Associates, eds. 1994. *The Jossey-Bass Handbook of Nonprofit Leadership Management*. San Francisco: Jossey-Bass Publishers.

A series of essays on nonprofit management and issues, including the areas of leadership, operations, financial resources, and people.

Chapter 8: Researching Funders: Reading between the Lines

Hickey, J. and E. Koochoo. 1984. *Prospecting Out the Philanthropic Dollar.* Washington, DC: The Taft Group.

A re-issue and updating of an older text, but still a good resource on both getting information on foundation, corporate, and individual prospects, and keeping track of it, including sample tracking forms.

Jenkins, J. and M. Lucas. 1986. *How to Find Philanthropic Prospects.* Ambler, PA: Fund-Raising Institute.

Although somewhat dated, Volume I is still an excellent systematic approach to prospect research on individuals, foundations, and corporations, plus other sources.

See also the extensive materials developed by The Fund Raising School at the Indiana University Center on Philanthropy.

Chapter 12: Proposals: One Means of Approach

Barber, D. 1994. *Finding Funding: The Comprehensive Guide to Grant Writing.* Long Beach, CA: Bond Street Publishers.

Primarily discusses writing the proposal, but some strategy and research information and suggestions; includes a computer diskette of funding sources, sample letters, and other materials.

Miner, L. and J. Griffith. 1993. *Proposal Planning and Writing.* Phoenix, AZ: Oryx Press.

A comprehensive "how to" book on writing proposals for public, corporate, and private funding with some information on finding funding sources and getting information.

Ruskin, K. and C. Achilles. 1995. *Grantwriting, Fundraising, and Partnerships: Strategies That Work!* Thousand Oaks, CA: Corwin Press, Inc.

Primarily focused on the process of writing proposals, but with some strategy tips (mainly discusses educational grants, but still useful).

Index

About the Author

Eugene A. Scanlan, PhD, CFRE, has been involved with not-for-profits for over 30 years. His experience includes serving as a professional staff member of one of the largest foundations in the country; he has also held management, consulting, development, and teaching positions with several organizations, including national, regional, and local groups, colleges, and universities.

From 1976 to 1980 he was a staff member of The Chicago Community Trust, a grant-making foundation with over $400 million in assets. While there, he also worked closely with grantees and monitored grants ranging in size from $700 to $300,000, and also managed the internal fiscal operations.

In 1980 he joined Alford & Associates, Inc. Notable client activities included carrying out assessments/feasibility studies and directing or assisting in implementation of recommendations and campaign management for major fund-raising efforts by Providence-St. Mel High School (over $4.7 million raised), the DuPage Easter Seal Center (original capital campaign goal exceeded by 50 percent), North Park College, the Copernicus Cultural and Civic Center, and strategy development for the corporate component of Wheaton College's successful $36 million campaign.

During the period 1984–1987, he served as Development Officer of The Brookings Institution in Washington, D.C., where he was responsible for annual foundation grants of over $2 million, and as Director of Development for Defenders of Wildlife. He returned to full-time consulting in 1987 and, as Vice President of his own firm, Nonprofit Group Services, Inc. (incorporated in 1985), has provided consulting services (including organizational assessments/feasibility studies, campaign design and management, and project management) to clients including the Council on Foundations, Defenders of Wildlife, the Women Judges' Fund for Justice, the National Wildlife Refuge Association, and Independent Sector. He subsequently was selected by The Alford Group Inc. to develop their East Coast operations. His recent clients have included the United States Olympic Committee, the American Society for Parenteral and Enteral Nutrition, the American Podiatric Medical Association, The Credit Research Foundation, The Dole Foundation, The YMCA of Metropolitan Chicago, Volunteers in Overseas Cooperative Assistance, the Brightside for Families and Children, Roland Park Place Senior Center, the Chicago Academy of Sciences, Boys Town, the Carnegie Institution, the Personal Communications Industry Association, and the Franklin Delano Roosevelt Memorial Commission.

Gene is an active member of the National Society of Fund Raising Executives (NSFRE) where he served on the Greater Washington, D.C., Area Chapter Board of Directors for six years and was the Chapter's 1994 President. He has served as Vice-President for Communications, Editor of the Chapter's Newsletter, and a member of several local and national committees of NSFRE. He has been Adjunct Professor for George Washington University's Fund Raising Management Certificate

Program and frequently teaches a monthly seminar at The Foundation Center of Washington, D.C. He was recently appointed to the Board of the AAFRC Trust for Philanthropy, the publishers of *Giving USA*. He is also a member of Washington Independent Writers. He coordinated and authored a major two-year national study of community foundations for the Council on Foundations. He has a Ph.D. in higher education administration from Loyola University of Chicago (1972) and an M.Ed. in counseling from the University of New Hampshire (1966). He has been a Certified Fund Raising Executive since 1982. He is married to Joanne Belenchia Scanlan, Ph.D., Vice-President for Research and Professional Services at the Council on Foundations in Washington, D.C.